NEXTGEN INDIE BOOK AWARDS

INDEPENDENT PUBLISHER BOOK AWARDS

PRAISE FOR FLAK PAK

Expertly presented and notated, informed and informative, this book is an invaluable addition to the growing library of World War II memoirs and histories.

— *Midwest Book Review*

Armed with a splendid array of graphics, *Flak Pak* paints a larger picture of the struggle in the Pacific theater and of a bygone era. Providing engaging prose coupled with images of hundreds of artifacts, Kemp brings WWII vividly to life in this well-crafted labor of love and appreciation.

— *Booklist*

FLYING WITH THE FLAK PAK

A PACIFIC WAR SCRAPBOOK

KENNY KEMP

Alta Films
PRESS

FLYING WITH THE FLAK PAK

Graphic design and maps by Bonnie Sheets.

Library of Congress Cataloging-in-Publication Data

Kemp, Kenny.
Flying with the Flak Pak : a Pacific war scrapbook / by Kenny Kemp.
pages cm
Includes bibliographical references.
ISBN 978-1-892442-70-3 (pbk. : alk. paper)
1. Kemp, O. C., 1924-1990.
2. United States. Army Air Forces. Bombardment Group (H), 494th--Biography.
3. World War, 1939-1945--Aerial operations, American.
4. World War, 1939-1945--Campaigns--Pacific Area.
5. Bomber pilots--United States--Biography.
I. Title.
D790.253494th .K46 2013
940.54'4973092--dc23
[B]
2013019629

03 04 05

www.kennykemp.com
www.flyingwiththeflakpak.com

FOREWORD

My father died in 1990. When my mother died twenty years later and the children met to settle her affairs, I ignored furniture and paintings and dishware and asked only to be entrusted with Dad's World War II memorabilia. I knew there was a black wooden footlocker in the mezzanine, a bunch of medals in a dresser drawer, and his officer's cap on the closet shelf in the master bedroom. But by the time I got everything in the back of my pickup, I had discovered much more: period magazines, photo albums, orders on coarse brown paper, dusty training manuals, dozens of books about the War, and an eighteen inch stack of letters.

At home, I spread everything out in the library. The room, now smelling of fountain pen ink, musty paper, and ancient rubber and mothballs, transported me to the 1940s. Service patches, flight gear, Japanese money, and even a plastic container of pilot's wings testified that I had a long cataloging process before me.

I knew little about my father's War experience. I knew he had been initially drafted into the Army and transferred to the Army Air Force. I knew he had served on a tiny island (or two) in the Pacific. I knew (from the number of bombs stenciled on an old suitcase he had) that he'd flown 15 missions. I knew he loved the officers on his crew: Oly Olson, Jack Berger, and Fred Sperling. And I knew he made it back alive. I knew little more than that. But the items stacked high on the table promised they'd tell his story if I had the patience to sort it out.

Soon the project became more than choosing the contents of a shadow box display. It occurred to me that his adventure was common to tens of thousands of young men of his time. I knew there were few of his contemporaries left; they were dying at an astonishing rate. Within a few short years there would be none who could use the pronoun "I" when talking about the War.

I also knew people of my generation knew little about the Pacific War between the landmark events of Pearl Harbor and Hiroshima. Our fathers may have talked about the War—most didn't—but we half-listened with one ear. The TV was on and Dad was droning on again about the Japs.

My father has been dead for almost a quarter century. As I began sorting his belongings, how I wished I could have one more hour with him: What was life like on Angaur Island? What was your C.O. like? How did it feel to lift a bomb-laden B-24 Liberator bomber off the runway? To be responsible for the lives of nine other young men? To be shot at? To kill another human being?

He could not answer, but the things he saved spoke eloquently of a time when the world was tipping from its axis and young men like him stepped forward and righted it.

Maybe they knew the risk they were taking, maybe not. But the War taught them. They saw friends die in battles or from a sniper's bullet; saw a plane lose control on landing and collide with a fuel truck and explode into a fireball; saw a nearby plane hit by flak spiraling earthward with no blossoming parachutes issuing from it.

Yes, they knew. In a small way, in putting this book together, I have come to know as well. And in reading it, I hope you will too.

But this I *do* know: they were heroes and we were lucky to know them.

— Kenny Kemp

DEDICATED TO

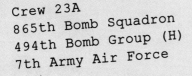

Crew 23A
865th Bomb Squadron
494th Bomb Group (H)
7th Army Air Force

Omer Carroll Kemp was born on 29 February 1924—a leap year baby—the oldest son of Omer Kemp and Abbie Kimball Kemp. From the first he was known as "O.C."—his middle name an homage to his father's younger brother Carroll. Mavis followed O.C. in 1927 and Gloria came five years later. Dean arrived in 1937.

O.C.'s father was a warehouse manager and his mother Abbie a housewife. They were members of the Church of Jesus Christ of Latter-day Saints (Mormons) and attended church with their congregation at the Independent Order of Odd Fellows hall in La Mesa, a suburb east of San Diego.

They were a close family who loved rock-hunting in the deserts of southern California and shell-collecting on the beaches of Mexico. They had a little tear-drop trailer Omer would park on the beach in Ensenada, Mexico. Abbie and the kids would stay down there during the summer and Omer would drive down on weekends to join them.

While the kids played in the breakers or built sand castles, Abbie sat under an umbrella with a great floppy hat and painted oil landscapes. Though her love of art far outstretched her talent, Omer lovingly framed each painting as if it were going to be displayed at the Louvre. As a final touch, he would meticulously glue hundreds of tiny shells they'd scavenged off the beach in orderly rows on the frame surrounding a red rock desert vista or a pastel ocean scene.

Once, Abbie painted—on her garage door no less—two almost life-sized black bears battling over a salmon on an exposed rock in the midst of a rushing mountain stream. As her grandchildren came of age, she took orders for landscapes or Indian portraits. Each of her nearly thirty grandchildren possess one of her signed originals.

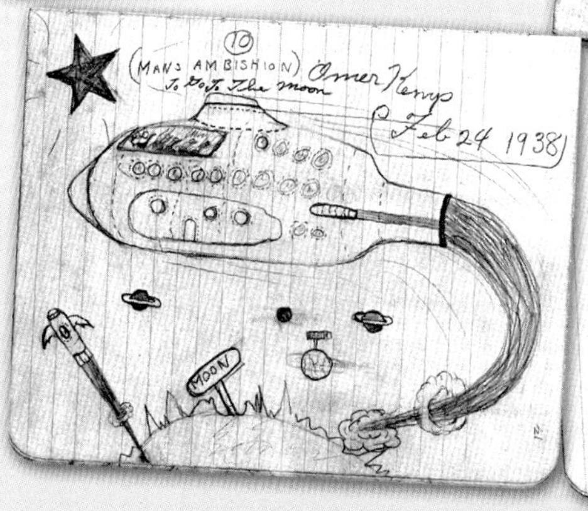

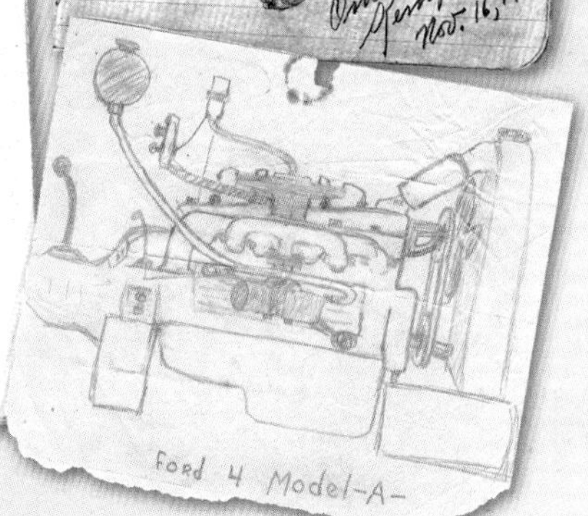

FLIGHTS OF FANCY

Consider the drawings above. They were made when O.C. was in elementary and junior high school. They reveal not only an artist's eye but an engineer's attention to detail. His grasp of perspective grows over the years, as does his perception of light, shadow, and shading. His grades during those years were generally *S* (for satisfactory) or *R* (for commendable). He wrote evocative poetry and sensitive, colorful English essays.

Now look at the high school report cards below. Algebra, English and History: *Cs* and *Ds*. An *F* in Geometry. He even nearly fails a class he enjoys and is inarguably good at: Mechanical Drawing. And his behavior is little better than his academic grades.

O.C. is a good boy. He doesn't get in trouble. He is a kind brother, a faithful friend, and an obedient son, but he simply does not care about school. His is the first generation to graduate from high school in great numbers—their parents, as a rule, did not. College, taken for granted nowadays, was little more than a daydream of the working class back then. Sports, cars, and girls are all that matter to the boys in O.C.'s circle.

He does, however, manage an *A* in gym.

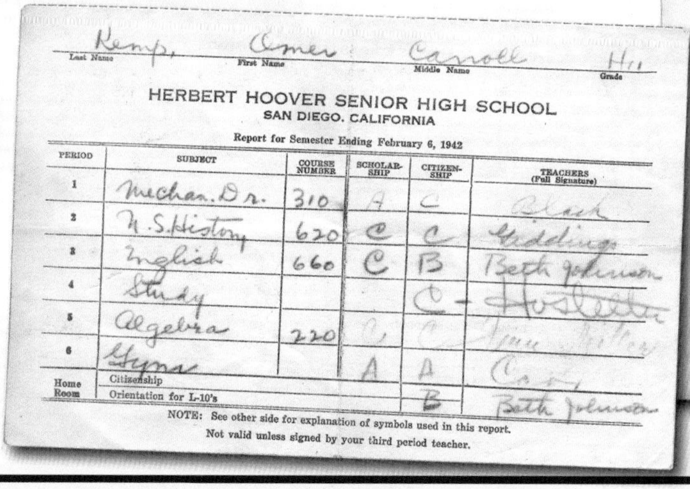

Kemp, (Last Name) Omer (First Name) Carroll (Middle Name) H11 (Grade)

HERBERT HOOVER SENIOR HIGH SCHOOL
SAN DIEGO, CALIFORNIA

Report for Semester Ending February 6, 1942

PERIOD	SUBJECT	COURSE NUMBER	SCHOLARSHIP	CITIZENSHIP	TEACHERS (Full Signature)
1	Mechan. Dr.	310	A	C	Black
2	U.S. History	620	C	C	Giddings
3	English	660	C	B	Beth Johnson
4	Study			C-	Hostetter
5	Algebra	220	C	C	[illegible]
6	Gym		A	A	[illegible]
Home Room	Citizenship				
	Orientation for L-10's			B	Beth Johnson

NOTE: See other side for explanation of symbols used in this report.
Not valid unless signed by your third period teacher.

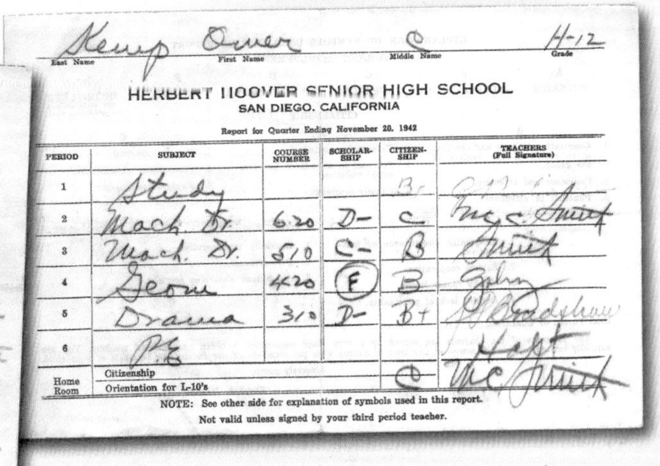

Kemp (Last Name) Omer (First Name) C (Middle Name) H-12 (Grade)

HERBERT HOOVER SENIOR HIGH SCHOOL
SAN DIEGO, CALIFORNIA

Report for Quarter Ending November 20, 1942

PERIOD	SUBJECT	COURSE NUMBER	SCHOLARSHIP	CITIZENSHIP	TEACHERS (Full Signature)
1	Study			B	[illegible]
2	Mach. Dr.	620	D-	C	McSmith
3	Mach. Dr.	510	C-	B	Smith
4	Geom	420	F	B	[illegible]
5	Drama	310	D-	B+	G Bradshaw
6	P.E.				[illegible]
Home Room	Citizenship			C	McSmith
	Orientation for L-10's				

NOTE: See other side for explanation of symbols used in this report.
Not valid unless signed by your third period teacher.

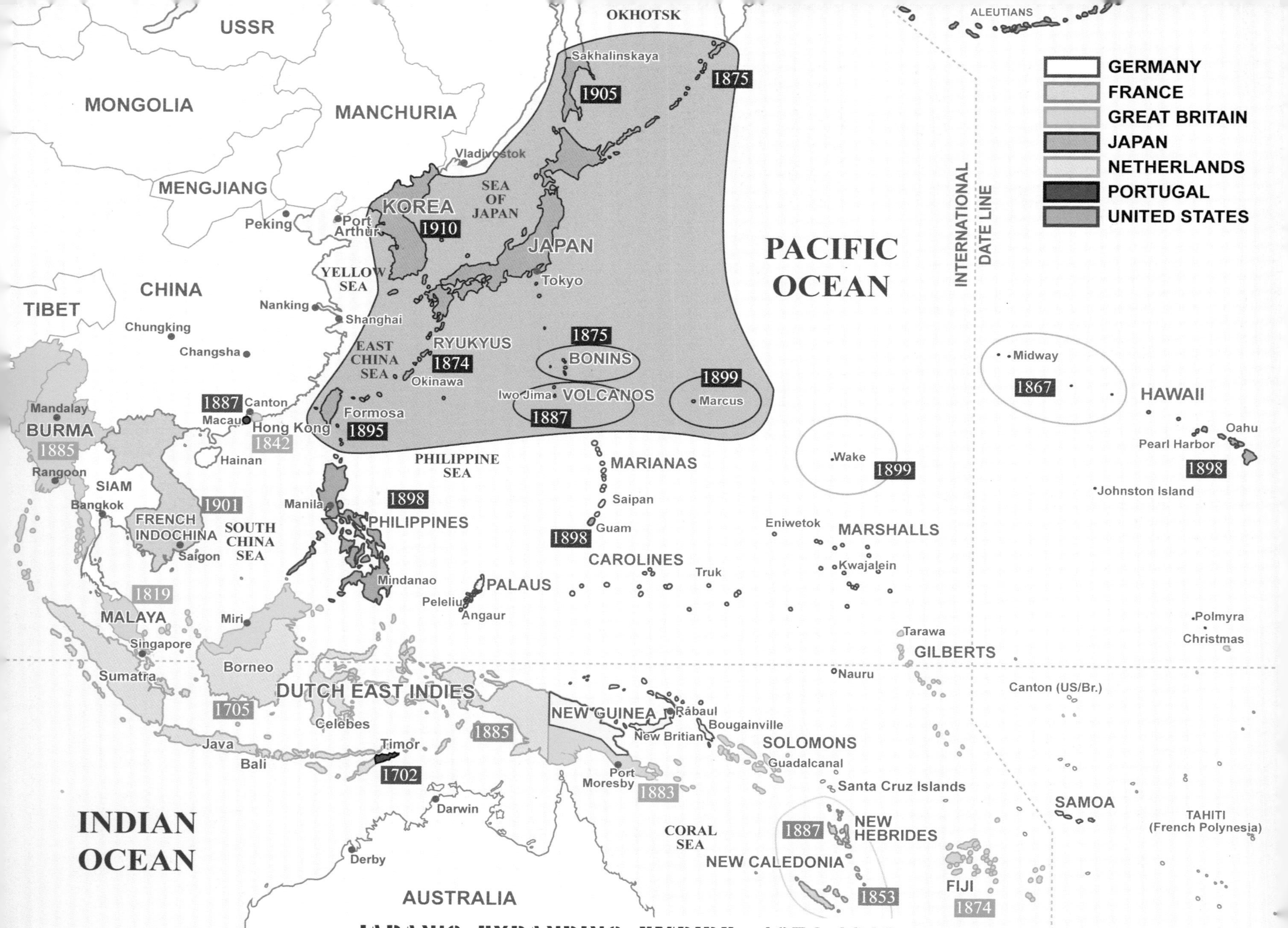

JAPAN'S EXPANDING EMPIRE: 1874-1910

TRAGIC THEOCRACY

The roots of modern Japanese aggression grew over decades, with unintended aid from the Western powers. In 1902, Britain, unable to protect its Pacific colonies, signed a treaty with Japan in which it would modernize the Japanese fleet in return for Japan's oversight of Crown possessions. Thus, during World War I, the new Japanese navy escorted Australian and New Zealand forces to war zones.

Japan always had expansionist desires, fueled by poverty, an inability to feed its growing population, and its own lack of natural resources. In addition, nearby China and Korea, backwards, poor, and disorganized, were a great temptation. Between 1874 and 1910, Japan steadily encroached on its neighbors, taking the Bonin and Volcano Islands, Marcus Island, Formosa, the Ryukyus, and Korea.

Japan entered World War I on the Allied side, ostensibly to deny Germany its ports and property in China. But its true goal was to increase its mainland holdings. After the War, when the Treaty of Versailles was signed, Japan was granted the Shantung Peninsula in China (across the Yellow Sea from Korea) and a whole string of Pacific islands. These "mandates" included the Marshalls, Carolines, Marianas, and Palau island chains.

What made Japan a questionable ally and a dangerous enemy was its culture. The Tenno (Emperor) traced his legacy and power back 1400 years. After rejecting Christianity in the 16th century, Japan sealed itself off from the European world, which was developing notions of individual moral responsibility, concepts that never quite pierced Japanese culture. This would prove catastrophic both for Japan and the world.

Fearing colonization by Europe, in the mid-1800s Japan began modernizing, abolishing *shogun* (military) rule and making the Emperor the actual sovereign. But the Tenno ruled a country without a formal written legal code; courts operated willy nilly. So in the early 1900s, the aristocracy determined that a belief framework was necessary to support modernization. Shinto ("spirit path"), the worship of ancestors and the idea of the Tenno as a god-mortal, was promoted by the state.

In addition, the philosophy of *bushidō* ("way of the warrior")—an acceptance of one's lot in life, loyalty to family, the study of military arts, and discipline of mind and body—resulted in the growing power of the military, which soon operated independently of the Tenno's court and the aristocracy.

Political parties devolved into legal mafias. The outlawed Samurai made a resurgence, forming gangs of hired thugs and assassins. Every civil servant—and indeed even the Emperor—feared for his life should he run afoul of the clans.

In the early 1920s, while Leninism was growing in Russia, its "will to power" and violent methodology also found a sympathetic culture in Japan.

In 1922, the two-decades old British-Japanese treaty was scrapped under pressure from the U.S., which had limited Japanese emigration, furthering the pressure on Japan's burgeoning population. In return, America promised to not build bases west of Hawaii or north of Singapore. At the same time, the U.K. unilaterally disarmed, weary of war and unable to afford to care for its far-reaching colonies otherwise.

By 1927, the Japanese civilian government had all but collapsed and the military ruled the country. The timing was right for the 1931 invasion of China, which had ended its monarchy, creating a vacuum of power. It had no money and hence no army. A select few warlords ruled the vast nation and Japan's invasion of Manchuria, Menjiang, Shanghai, and numerous ports thus went virtually unopposed. Japan called its mainland spoils "protectorates," quickly taking control of manufacturing, food production, and brutalizing the population.

Thus the table was set for a newly resource- and manpower-rich Japan to continue in its violent voracity. Next on the menu: the valuable oil fields of Java and Sumatra.

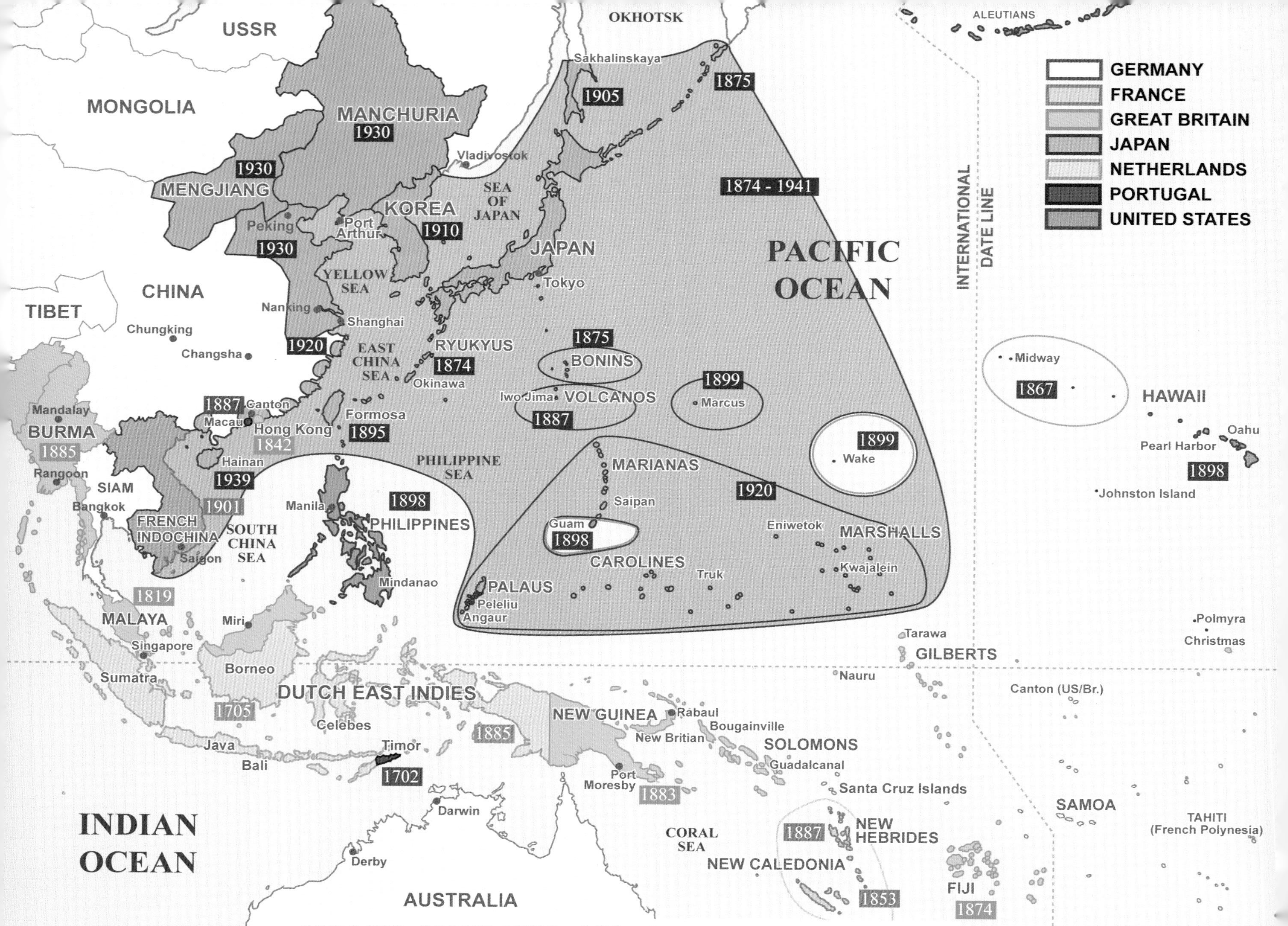

JAPAN'S MANDATES AND CONQUESTS: 1920-1941

BRUTAL BEDFELLOWS

When Japan invaded Manchuria in 1931, it held its breath, waiting for Western retaliation that never came. Lulled into self-disarmament and obsessed with its own economic woes, the West was unwilling to help China. Besides, an aggressive Japan on Russia's border would occupy the Great Bear in the east, minimizing its infiltration of the West.

In the 1930s, the U.S. economy was in a shambles, and its tariff and emigration policies enraged Japan. While Japan militarized its factories, the U.S. Army shrunk to just 132,000 men, sixteenth in the world.

In 1933 Japan left the League of Nations. Two years later, the U.S. passed the Neutrality Act. Isolationism was the siren song of the day, allowing the predator states of Russia, Germany, Italy, and Japan free reign.

Japan's food worries encouraged expansion. Yet even after its Chinese conquests, half its budget still went to the military.

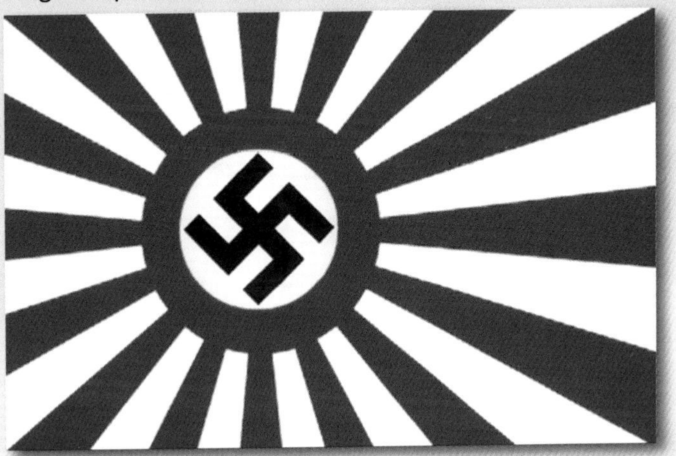

By 1935 constitutional law in Japan had ended and the collective (with its lack of personal conscience and accountability) created an anarchy of terror at home and aggression abroad.

In the early 1930s Japan watched as Hitler rearmed Germany in violation of the Treaty of Versailles and no one stopped him. When Germany assimilated Austria without a shot, then weeks later took over Czechoslovakia with no reprisals from France or Britain, Japan knew her proposed forays into Southeast Asia, so far from America and Europe, would likely be ignored.

For years, Japan asserted that its China policy was intended to "pacify a brother," but in 1937 full-scale war broke out between Japan and a weak alliance of Chinese communists and nationalists. America was pro-Chinese and Roosevelt violently anti-Japanese, but still the U.S. did nothing. Even when Japan attacked the capital Nanking, murdering 300,000 people and causing the Nazi ambassador to exclaim it "the work of bestial machinery," the U.S. merely condemned the butchery, nothing more.

In 1936, Japan and Germany, each country seeing a devilish use for the other, signed the "Anti-Com-Intern Pact," aimed at Russia, which would now be faced with enemies on both the west and the east. Together they would destroy Russia, then each would push south, Germany through the Middle East and Japan through Southeast Asia after drawing America into war in the Pacific. They would meet at India and thus destroy the British empire's largest outpost.

What the Japanese did not know was that Hitler was even then planning an alliance with Stalin, which was signed in 1939 and which reduced the Anti-Com-Intern Pact pledges to rubble. Then Hitler again changed course and invited Japan into the Axis a year later, though he never gave Japan any real help until Japan attacked the U.S. on 7 December 1941, after which Germany also declared war, the only benefit of which to Germany was its now unrestrained ability to attack American ships supplying Britain across the Atlantic.

As early as 1940, Japan should have known better than to attack America, but it was enveloped in what can only be termed rational hysteria, a psychology of desperation that had devolved into a determination to risk everything. Though it had occupied all of China's great cities, seized her economy, controlled her communications arteries, a stalemate with China persisted and Japan's economic troubles remained and grew.

The temptation to look to the relatively undefended French, British and Dutch empires of Southeast Asia and the Philippines for conquest was foolhardy. They were no different than China: Japan had not the manpower nor the resources to defend them once acquired through a tactic learned from her ally Germany: the *blitzkrieg*, or "lightning war."

It was this lightning that would start a great fire that would destroy not its enemies but Japan itself.

YOUTH

1939 - 1943
Hoover High School
4474 El Cajon Blvd.
San Diego, California

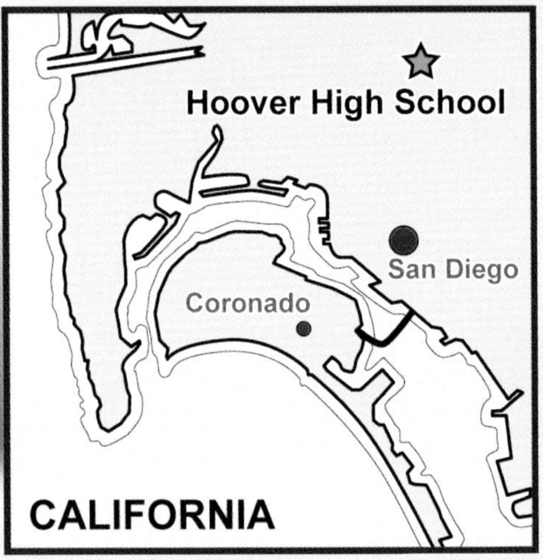

ALL-AMERICAN BOY

O.C. had a stocky, athletic build, a natural for football. He played tackle on the Hoover High "Cardinals" football team. Though the pads and the helmet were leather (and there was no face mask), he survived the games with minor bruises and cuts. Unfortunately, front-yard football was responsible for the worst injury of his life. He was throwing a football with a friend, went back to catch a pass, and plunged into a hedge. A sharp twig punctured his eardrum and he lost forever the hearing in his left ear, suffering from tinnitus (ringing in the ear) for the rest of his life. For the most part a mere aggravation, his hearing loss almost kept him out of the service.

AUDIO TRANSCRIPT 01:01:00

When I first heard about the war, it was of course in 1941, and I was still in high school. I remember when the war started, we said, "Well, we'll clean up those Japs in about two weeks and the war will be right over."

A lot of kids my age were running down and joining the Army and Dad said, "Wait. Hold your horses. You'll get in it soon enough. You finish high school," which was really good advice.

So I waited.

I SHALL RUN WILD...

The heroic anarchy of Japanese culture was never more clearly evident than in the bizarre "liaison conferences" conducted in front of the Japanese emperor, Toshiro Hirohito. The Emperor-God sat between two incense burners on a dais in front of a gold screen, with his generals at tables at right angles to him. Special archaic court language was used. The Tenno signified approval by banging his gold seal, but otherwise he did not deign to speak to the mortals arrayed before him. He did not ask questions or express opinions. That was done by the President of the Counsel, who responded according to what he *thought* the Tenno intended to say. Decisions were mostly made out of the Emperor's presence in private conversations, or everyone simply went ahead and did what he believed was best.

As a result, Hideki Tojo, though he had been War Minister for over a year, was informed of the intended bombing of Pearl Harbor just eight days before it happened. He called it "entirely impermissible and hurtful to the national honor."

The plan went ahead anyway.

When asked how Japan could possibly accomplish a ninety day Pacific war (as had been promised by the Army) when they had been in China for three years with no end in sight, Admiral Nagano said, "If I am told to fight regardless of the consequences, I shall run wild for six months or a year. But I have utterly no confidence in the second and third years."

Admiral Yamamoto, architect of the Pearl Harbor attack, went even further: "We cannot hope to win a war against Britain and America, however spectacular our initial victories."

Finally, logistics expert Colonel Iwakuro spoke: "The differentials in American and Japanese production are: steel twenty to one, oil one hundred to one, coal ten to one, aircraft five to one, shipping two to one, labor force five to one. Over all ten to one."

In expressing these opinions, each man risked assassination or removal; these views were contrary to popular bushidō thought. After Yamamoto expressed his opinion, he had to be given a sea command to keep him out of the reach of his would-be killers.

But Japan had to move forward, not only for food and honor, but because the spoils of war (if Germany won) promised to be substantial. Germany had already knocked France out of the War, and its airfields in Indo-China were thus given to Japan, which sparked American economic sanctions, including a total oil embargo. Now, not only were Japan's people starving, so were its industries and military.

Roosevelt imposed the embargo to incite Japan; he wanted to get into the War, but the American public did not. Hitler was perhaps mad but not so mad as to attack America. The President hoped Japan was as insane as it seemed and would do something foolish. He did not, however, expect Pearl Harbor. Rather, he (like Britain) supposed Japan would attack British holdings in Southeast Asia.

In keeping with the Japanese leadership's inability to confront facts or plan the War more than six months out, realities such as the long-term availability of oil and steel seemed to escape the generals' considerations. Theoretically, they could add to their stores by attacking Australia or India but initially they had no plan to attack America, to knock her out of the War, or destroy her capacity to wage it.

All they had to go on was an arrogant belief in the superiority of the Japanese soldier and the cowardice of his American counterpart, based on what evidence is not clear. But the belief persisted throughout the War, right up until the atomic bombs were dropped. Japan never believed America would stand for the casualties it would inevitably inflict on the U.S.

Japan was wrong.

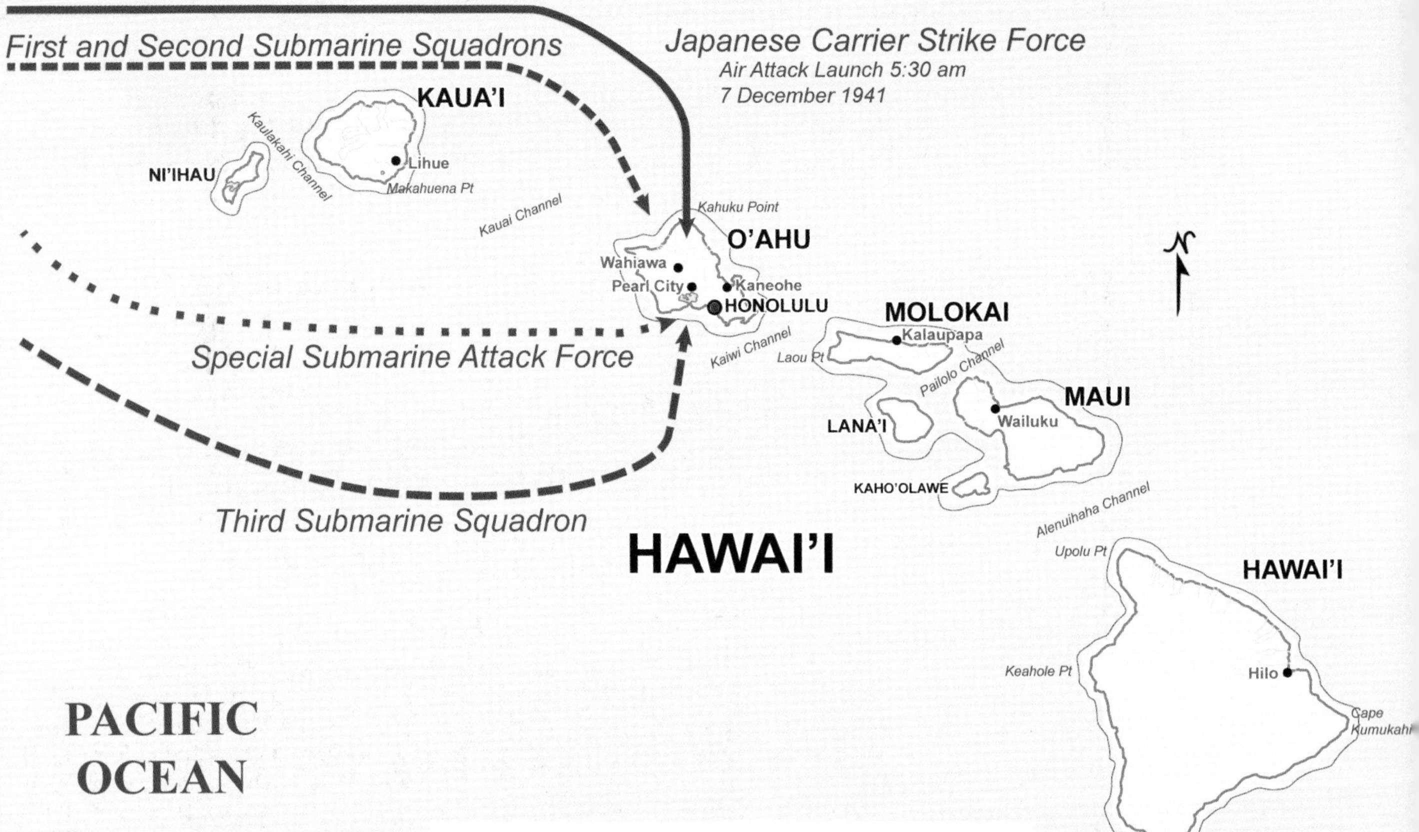
First and Second Submarine Squadrons
Japanese Carrier Strike Force
Air Attack Launch 5:30 am
7 December 1941
KAUA'I
Kaulakahi Channel
NI'IHAU
Lihue
Makahuena Pt
Kauai Channel
Kahuku Point
O'AHU
Wahiawa
Pearl City
Kaneohe
HONOLULU
MOLOKAI
Kalaupapa
Special Submarine Attack Force
Kaiwi Channel
Laou Pt
Pailolo Channel
MAUI
Wailuku
LANA'I
KAHO'OLAWE
Third Submarine Squadron
Alenuihaha Channel
HAWAI'I
Upolu Pt
HAWAI'I
Keahole Pt
Hilo
Cape Kumukahi
PACIFIC OCEAN
South Cape

JAPANESE FLEET MOVEMENTS

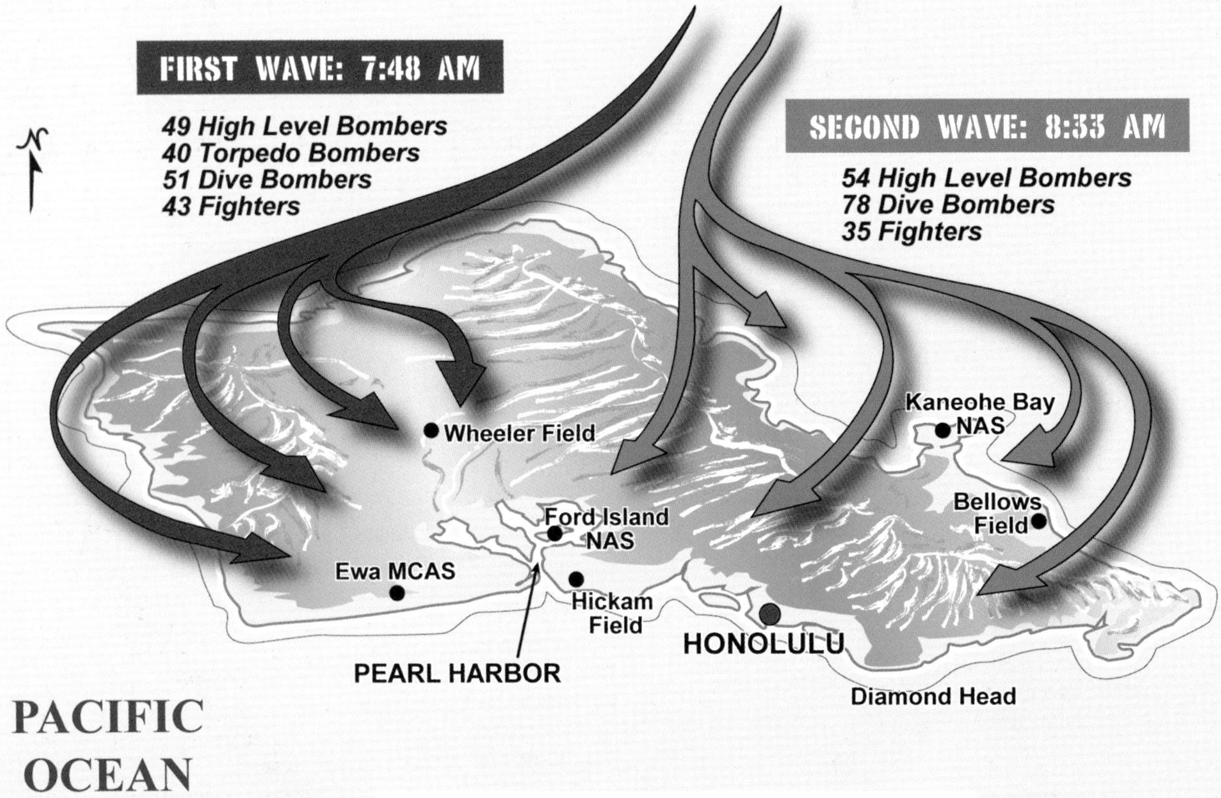
FIRST WAVE: 7:48 AM
49 High Level Bombers
40 Torpedo Bombers
51 Dive Bombers
43 Fighters
SECOND WAVE: 8:33 AM
54 High Level Bombers
78 Dive Bombers
35 Fighters
Wheeler Field
Kaneohe Bay NAS
Bellows Field
Ford Island NAS
Ewa MCAS
Hickam Field
HONOLULU
PEARL HARBOR
Diamond Head
PACIFIC OCEAN

O'AHU ATTACK WAVES

EXTRA! **Pacific Post** EXTRA!

Section One | SUNDAY, DECEMBER 7, 1941 | Ten Cents

JAP SNEAK ATTACK!

PRESIDENT ROOSEVELT CALLS IT A "DAY OF INFAMY"

HONOLULU, O'AHU, TERRITORY OF HAWAII, Dec. 7 – Though the sky was clear on this warm tropical morning, it soon clouded into a perfect storm of devious preparation and astonishing luck on Japan's part and equal parts carelessness and bad luck on America's.

The new radar on Opana hill was working well: it revealed the cluster of aircraft approaching northeast O'ahu—but Lt. Kermit Tyler thought these were the 12 B-17 bombers due from Hamilton Field, Cal., on their way to Manila.

The Japanese had taken a northerly route through the Pacific in complete radio silence, relying only upon light signals to communicate between ships of the fleet.

Admiral Yamamoto never thought Japan could defeat the U.S.—the industrial might of America was greater than any nation on earth—but he believed in Japan's rightful domination of Asia and America stood in the way. In order for Japan to prevail, America's presence in the Pacific must be destroyed—or at least crippled for a time.

By 1941, Japan had invaded Korea, Manchuria, French Indochina, Burma, and China proper. America believed Japan would eventually attack British possessions in Southeast Asia, likely Singapore, Hong Kong, or Malaya.

Smoke billows from the U.S.S. Arizona

Though the U.S. had broken the Japanese radio code (one communique actually contained a general attack plan for Pearl Harbor), the silence of the missing Japanese fleet gave Admiral Kimmel pause. 25% of his force had been transferred to the Atlantic; he was left with just 3 aircraft carriers, 21 light and heavy cruisers, 53 destroyers, and 23 submarines with which to defend America in the largest ocean on earth.

Fortunately, two aircraft carrier task forces were at sea on December 7 and Yamamoto's knock-out blow missed them. This would prove to be a decisive mistake.

The ocean north of O'ahu had been unpatrolled since December 4, when the PBY scout planes were grounded for routine maintenance.

At pre-dawn, 183 aircraft took off from Yamamoto's task force, and submarines south of O'ahu released their two-man mini-subs, which would quietly enter Pearl Harbor and torpedo ships docked side by side at Ford Island.

In the darkness, the Japanese pilots tuned their radios to KGMB in Honolulu, using the station playing Hawaiian music as a homing beacon, where they heard the weather report: visibility good, with wind out of the north at ten knots.

When the Zeros swooped over the Koolau Ridge at 7:50 A.M. on Sunday morning, Honolulu was literally asleep. In preparation for the next inspection, live ammo had been locked away. Holiday routine was in force; men were on liberty. Fighters at Hickam and Wheeler fields sat defenseless, their guns removed and gas tanks empty. Watertight ship compartments were left unsealed to air out for the Admiral's visit.

Squadron commander Mitsui Fuchida was the first to see Pearl Harbor. No alarm had been sounded; not a plane was in the air. Keying his radio mike, he confirmed to his fellow pilots that their attack was a complete surprise, shouting, "Tora! Tora! Tora!" and banking his plane sharply, diving toward Battleship Row as he thumbed the bomb release catch aside.

At Kaneohe Bay, 30 new PBY scout planes were destroyed. At Wheeler Field, 140 fighters were riddled with bullets and destroyed with bombs.

The War in the Pacific had begun.

Latest War Bulletins

MANILA, PHILIPPINES – U.S. Aircraft carrier *Langley* was reported to be damaged in an action with Japanese forces.

NEW YORK - British radio quoted Tokyo broadcasts as saying Germany will probably declare war on the U.S. within 24 hours.

TIENTSIN, CHINA – 63 American soldiers guarding the American Consulate were captured and disarmed.

WASHINGTON, D.C. – During President Roosevelt's meeting with legislative leaders and his Cabinet, word was received from General MacArthur that "enemy planes were over central Luzon in the Philippines."

MANAGUA, NICARAGUA – Nicaragua tonight declared war on Japan.

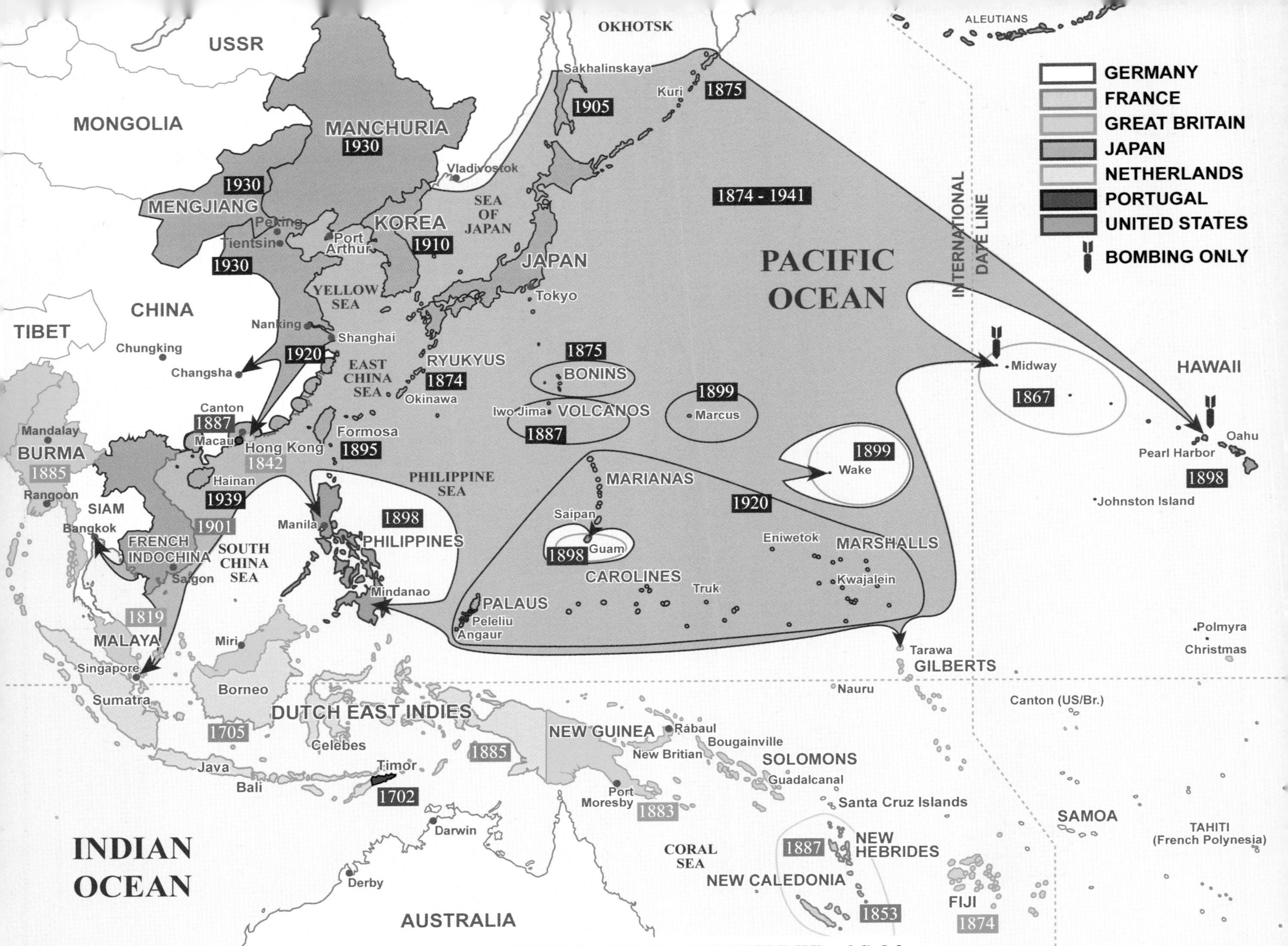

JAPAN'S LIGHTING WAR: DECEMBER 1941

EXTRA! **Pacific Post** EXTRA!

Section One — THURSDAY, DECEMBER 11, 1941 — Ten Cents

JAPANESE JUGGERNAUT

PACIFIC PLUNDERED AS JAPAN BEGINS OFFENSIVE

Wake Island

Wake Awakened

WAKE ISLAND, Dec. 11 – The invasion of Wake Island actually took place before the Pearl Harbor attack, due to the fact that the coral atoll composed of three tiny islands encircling a turquoise lagoon 2,300 miles west of Hawaii sits on the far side of the International Date Line.

27 Japanese Mitsubishi Nell bombers based in the Marshall Islands attacked, destroying 12 U.S. F4F Wildcat fighters on the ground. The Japanese obviously meant to keep the airstrip intact for use as a stepping stone eastward, perhaps once again toward Hawaii.

The 500 Marines on Wake drove off the first landing wave three days later, after which Commander Winfield Cunningham answered the Navy's question as to what he needed, saying, "Send us more Japs!" a taunt that became the by-word of determined GIs from then on.

But the Navy was unable to resupply Wake and it fell to the second assault fifteen days later. The Marines were taken prisoner along with some 1,200 civilian contractors working on the island.

Luzon Attacked

LUZON, PHILIPPINES, Dec. 8 – Just ten hours after Pearl Harbor, Japanese paratroopers touched down, surrounding Clark Air Field in Luzon, the largest of the Philippine Islands, as Japanese aircraft strafed and destroyed American fighters on the ground.

Now lacking air support, the American Asiatic Fleet has withdrawn to Java.

Hong Kong Assaulted

HONG KONG, Dec. 8 – Continuing their "Blitzkrieg in Asia," Japanese air and land forces simultaneously invaded Hong Kong on mainland China, Siam, and cities on the Malay Peninsula. This attack too, was begun precisely as Japanese warplanes were bombing Pearl Harbor.

It is clear now that Japan's ostensibly peaceful "Greater East Asian Co-prosperity Sphere" is a thinly-veiled gambit to militarily expand its empire in southeast Asia.

Japan, a nation almost entirely without natural resources, has already taken control of China and Manchuria. Hong Kong, a British protectorate, is the lone western hold-out on mainland China.

British Warships Sunk

SINGAPORE, MALAYA, Dec. 10 – British Royal Navy battleship *HMS Prince of Wales* and battle cruiser *HMS Repulse* were sunk today by land-based bombers and torpedo bombers of the Imperial Japanese Navy. Four destroyers of Force Z, which had been ordered to intercept the Japanese fleet near Malaya, escaped.

Air support was declined by Admiral Sir Tom Phillips because he wished to maintain radio silence.

It now appears that even our most heavily armored ships, if not protected by air cover, are susceptible to Japanese air assaults.

Revenge of the Tiger

RANGOON, BURMA, Dec. 19 – Claire Chennault, architect of the air resistance to the conquest of China, has brought his famous "Flying Tiger" Squadron south to join the fray at Rangoon, engaging a formation of 10 Mitsubishi Sally bombers. 12 P-40 Warhawk fighters pounced on the bombers, downing 6 and losing one of their own which went down in the jungle but whose pilot later appeared with only minor injuries.

Though the origin of the "tiger" appellation is unknown, Fuchida's shouts over Pearl Harbor, "Tora! Tora! Tora!" mean "Tiger! Tiger! Tiger!"

Latest War Bulletins

TOKYO, JAPAN – A Japanese army communique declared that Japanese landing forces occupied the capital of Guam today, capturing 350 Americans, including Capt. George G. McMullin, Governor, and other officers. These, the communique said, included the Vice-Governor and the commandant of the naval station. They said 25 Japanese found interned on the island were released.

BERLIN, GERMANY (Official radio received by AP) – The German high command said today the Russians had suffered heavy losses in Eastern front fighting, but remain entrenched.

LOS ANGELES, CALIFORNIA – Another black-out is set for tonight in the Los Angeles area, Army and city officials announced.

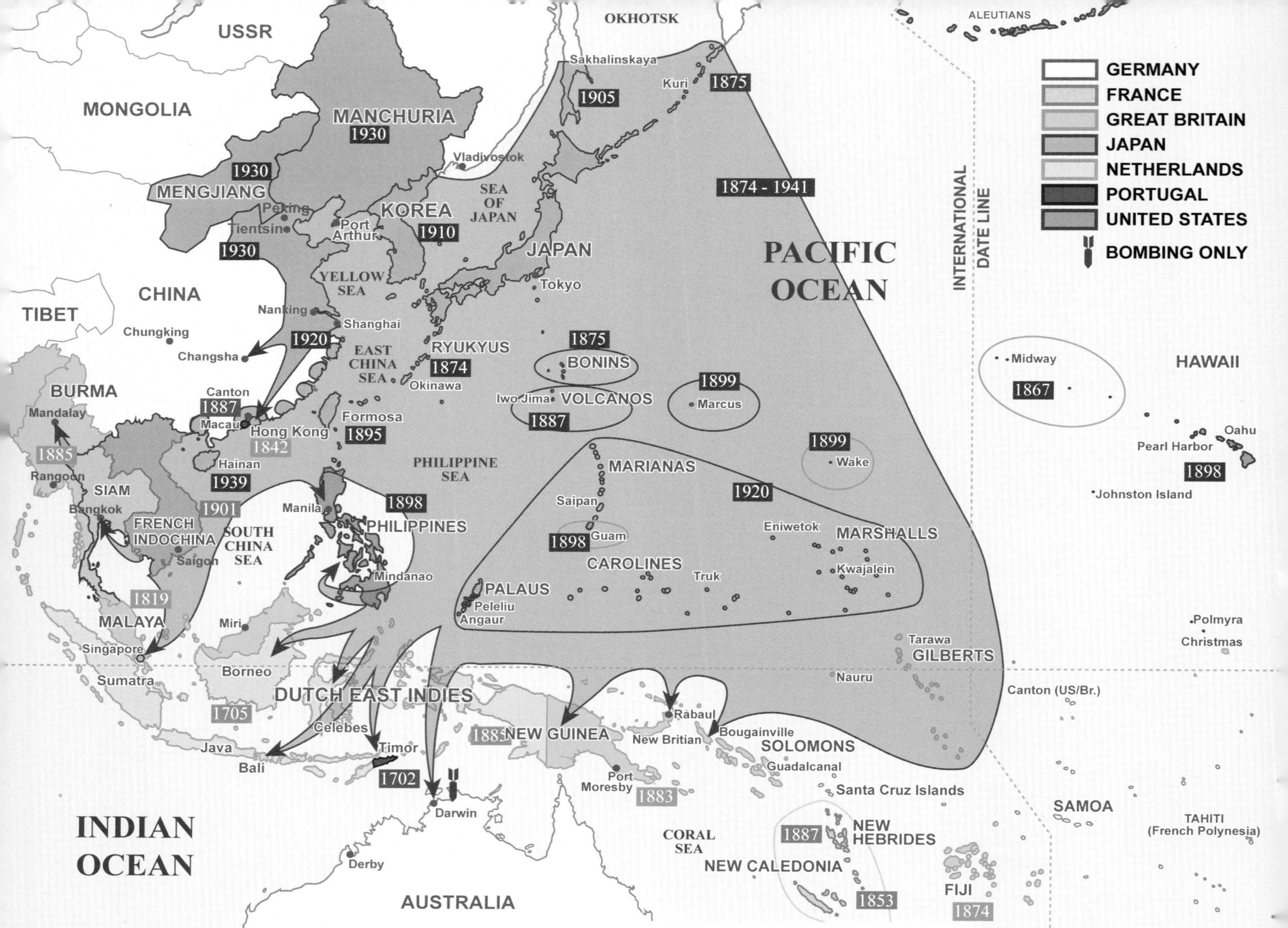

JAPAN'S LIGHTNING WAR: JANUARY–APRIL 1942

EXTRA! **Pacific Post** EXTRA!

Section One | DECEMBER 1941 — APRIL 1942 | Ten Cents

AN ENDLESS EMPIRE?

JAPANESE FORCES MARCH ACROSS SOUTH PACIFIC

DECEMBER 1941

BRITISH EAST INDIES, Dec. 15 – Japanese forces began their attack with landings on Borneo, swarming over the archipelago, targeting air fields and oil installations, and moving forward to capture the British Solomon Islands.

LUZON, PHILIPPINES, Dec. 23 – Yesterday's Japanese landings on Luzon Island were resisted heavily, but to no avail.

Though defending forces outnumbered the invaders by a 3 to 2 margin, the Japanese 14th Army swiftly overran most of Luzon from the north and are headed southward toward Manila and General Douglas MacArthur's Far East Forces based there.

MacArthur, recently serving as Field Marshall of the Philippine Army, was recalled to U.S. service by President Roosevelt last July and made commander of U.S. forces in the Far East in preparation for inevitable Japanese aggression.

WAKE ISLAND, Dec. 23 – After holding out for 15 long days, American forces at Wake Island surrendered to the Imperial Japanese Navy.

BRITISH HONG KONG, CHINA, Dec. 25 – British forces in Hong Kong surrendered today to Japanese forces.

PERAK RIVER, BRITISH MALAYA, Dec. 26 – Pressured by Japanese infantry and air assaults, British forces have retreated to the Perak River, the last Malay stronghold north of Kuala Lumpur.

Darwin, Australia attacked

JANUARY 1942

DUTCH EAST INDIES, Jan. 10 – Japanese began landing today in Northern Dutch Indonesia.

KUALA LUMPUR, MALAYA, Jan. 11 – Japanese forces captured Kuala Lumpur, routing the British defenders.

MANILA, PHILIPPINES, Jan. 15 – Japanese forces captured Manila, New Guinea, and Rabaul.

FEBRUARY 1942

PALEMBANG, SUMATRA, Feb. 15 – The Royal Dutch Shell oil refineries in Sumatra are a prize longed for by Japan, which launched an attack on the 13th. Allied forces initially repulsed the invasion force, but were required to withdraw when it was learned that Japanese forces were about to attack Java, a more strategically important island.

SINGAPORE, Feb. 15 – After being driven out of Malaya, Allied forces first resisted in Singapore but surrendered today. About 130,000 Indian, British, Australian and Dutch personnel were taken prisoner. Also fallen are the islands of Bali and Timor.

DARWIN, AUSTRALIA, Feb. 19 – Japanese aircraft attacked Darwin today, killing at least 243 people, mostly civilians, in a daring, unexpected raid.

JAVA, Feb. 27 – The Imperial Japanese Navy (IJN) inflicted a resounding defeat on the American-British-Dutch-Australian naval force in a battle in the Java Sea.

BATAAN, PHILIPPINES, Feb. 29 – Japanese forces continue their stranglehold attack, cutting off Allied forces on the Bataan Peninsula.

MARCH 1942

JAVA & SUMATRA, Mar. 12 – Allied forces on Java and Sumatra capitulate.

BURMA, Mar. 21 – The Japanese military advances into central Burma.

Latest War Bulletins

SANTA BARBARA, CALIFORNIA, Feb. 24 – A Japanese submarine made a direct hit on an oil field north of Santa Barbara, but no lives were lost. The 16 shots fired from the sub were seen by several witnesses.

OWEN'S VALLEY, CALIFORNIA, Mar. 22. – Upon order of the President, nearly 35,000 Nipponese living in the Southland began their removal to the Owens Valley Concentration Center today.

CORREGIDOR, PHILIPPINES, Mar. 22 – General MacArthur warned about false hopes, even as Japanese forces opened a new Bataan offensive. The long-expected attack on Luzon has been launched by Admiral Yamashita with sea blockade and bombardment.

WASHINGTON, D.C., Mar. 22 – A German U-boat was sunk off the eastern seaboard today by depth charges and machine gun fire from an American bomber. The destruction of the sub was affirmed when massive amounts of oil and debris floated to the surface.

EASTERN FRONT, EUROPE – Hardened Russian Siberian divisions are now poised to attack Nazi positions on the Eastern front.

AMERICA SCRAMBLES

Though the Pearl Harbor attack achieved tactical surprise, the results were meager. The eighteen warships sunk in shallow water were soon raised and repaired and nearly all returned to active service.

Fortunately, the American carrier fleet was absent on maneuvers when Pearl was attacked. Admiral Nagumo had neither the time nor the fuel to pursue and destroy them. Nor did his fighters eliminate the most valuable assets: oil storage tanks and drydocks.

What Japan had accomplished was to awaken a sleeping giant. America, hitherto rendered ineffectual by its remoteness, its racial diversity, and its pusillanimous leadership, found itself instantly united, angry, and committed to wage total war with all its outraged strength.

DECEMBER 7th
Remember Pearl Harbor
WORK-FIGHT-SACRIFICE
The National Cash Register Company

But Japan *had* succeeded in shocking the world with its boldness. Only three days later, England was stunned with the sinking of two battleships off the Malayan coast. Churchill realized there were now no British or American capital ships in the Indian Ocean or the Pacific except the survivors of Pearl Harbor, who were hastening back to California. Over this vast expanse of water, Japan now reigned supreme.

Within hours of the attack, Hawaiian Japanese-American leaders were rounded up and placed in high-security camps. In the ensuing months, over 100,000 Nisei on the mainland found themselves interned in camps from California to Arkansas. Eventually, however, the government offered to release detainees if they agreed to serve in the Army. Only 1,200 did so.

Immediately following the Pearl Harbor attack, tens of thousands of men joined the military, though the draft had been instituted the year before. There was very little draft evasion and many 4-F men, termed physically unfit for service, cheated to get in the military. In fact, so many men joined up that there was soon a surplus and many men already in the service were placed in the Enlisted Reserve Corps to work in essential industries, to be called back to active duty only if the Army needed them.

Men who were fathers were not usually drafted, and drafting 18 year-olds was vetoed by public opinion. Minorities were drafted at the same rate as whites, but blacks served in all-black units.

Japan, like Germany, never hoped to defeat the U.S., only to press her to a stalemate and a negotiated peace. Both Axis powers ran shortage economies. Japan, at least, had no alternative. Despite heroic efforts, by 1943 they were able to increase total production from 1940 levels by only 2%. During the same time period, U.S. production rose a staggering 36%.

Stalin knew that "war is won in the factories." So did Roosevelt, and he had been pressing for a re-arming of America since the mid-1930s, at least as a way to generate much-needed employment during the Depression.

Within a single year the number of tanks built by America grew to 24,000 and planes to 48,000. By the end of the first year of the War, America had raised its army production to the total of all three Axis powers combined, and by 1944 had doubled it yet again, while at the same time creating a citizen army which passed the 7 million mark in 1943.

The totalitarian states that opposed the Allies had resources to match America's, but their command and control economies stifled creativity and did not reward innovators. Much has been made of the so-called Military-Industrial Complex (which is mostly a myth) and its free-wheeling capitalist war profiteers, but these men, to the extent that they profited, also actually provided the goods that would eventually win the War: from bullets to bombers, no nation on earth could compete with America once she put on her work gloves.

EXTRA! **Pacific Post** EXTRA!

Section One SUNDAY, APRIL 19, 1942 Ten Cents

TAKE THAT, TOJO!

JIMMY DOOLITTLE'S "RAIDERS" STRIKE AT THE EMPIRE'S HEART

TOKYO, JAPAN, Apr. 19 – Reeling from the catastrophic losses of Wake, Guam, and Luzon, America was desperate for good news. They got it from a man who delivered what he promised, even though he almost lost almost everything in the doing.

For months after Pearl, talk never strayed from vengeance for Japan's outrage. But how could it be accomplished? There were no airports within striking distance of Japan and no ships dared approach the home islands because the Japanese now had the most powerful navy on earth.

But Capt. Francis Low, the operations officer under Admiral Ernest King, had an idea: what if they could find a bomber pilot crazy enough and skilled enough to take off from an aircraft carrier?

Not land again, mind you; no bomber could possibly land on an aircraft carrier. Once off the ship, he would have to fend for himself.

Lt. Col. James Doolittle was already famous: following service in WWI, he flew a de Havilland DH-4 cross-country in just 21 hours. He received the nation's first PhD in aviation from MIT. He had won air speed races and was the first person to perform an outside loop, previously thought to be fatal. He invented instrument flight. And he was the only man smart enough *and* crazy enough to take Low's idea and make it a reality.

B-25 Mitchell takes off from the U.S.S. Hornet

The B-25 Mitchell, a twin-engine medium range bomber, was chosen as the aircraft and Doolittle picked two dozen crews to train in total secrecy for a mission dubbed "The First Special Aviation Project."

A giant rubber gas tank was loaded midships, and heavy radio equipment, unnecessary on a secret mission, was removed. The tail guns were also removed, replaced by broomsticks painted black to ward off attacking fighters.

The famous Norden bombsight, devastating at 20,000 feet, was useless at the target altitude of 1,500 feet and so the gunnery officer devised a simple, inexpensive bombsight, which cost about twenty cents and was still deadly accurate.

Most of all, it was a daunting task to lift a bomber off in 500 feet, one-tenth the distance normally required by a B-25 take-off roll.

Doolittle himself was afraid he would not be permitted to join in the attack. He was 45, twice the age of the other flight crews. But his legendary determination secured him a place in the lead plane . . . and in history.

Accounting for unexpected problems and crew sickness, 16 Mitchells were loaded onto the deck of the *USS Hornet* in Alameda, California. Soon they were heading out to sea, waving at spectators on the Golden Gate Bridge, and hoping there were no Japanese spies snapping pictures of the strangely-laden carrier deck.

Unknown to Doolittle, landing on Chinese airfields would prove impossible. The Chinese military was notoriously untrustworthy, and information about the raid would be known by the Japanese within days if it were shared with the Chinese. Doolittle and his men did not know this, but it wouldn't have mattered anyway; they knew they stood little chance of even reaching Japan undetected, much less surviving the bombing run over Tokyo and making it safely to landing strips in China.

Task Force 16 was still 200 miles from their preferred launch point when a Japanese patrol boat was spotted. Though it was quickly dispatched, it was able to get off a radio warning.

Doolittle and his crews had no choice: they took to the air immediately.

The planes, timed to take off as the carrier crested a wave in the rough seas, would disappear below the deck and then emerge in near stall attitude, grimly struggling to gain altitude.

Yet they all got off without incident and the *Hornet* turned homeward.

At 12:30 P.M. on Sunday, 19 April, Doolittle's Raiders delivered a pointed, devastating message to Hideki Tojo, Japan's Prime Minister. Admiral Nagano had been right: after Pearl Harbor, the Japanese Navy would run wild for six months, and then, he said, "I have no confidence in our ultimate victory."

Poor weather, darkness, and an inability to raise their Chinese hosts on the radio required Doolittle and his crew to bail out.

Of the 84 men who started the mission, 71 made it back safely. Three men were caught, tried, and executed.

In vengeance for the attack, Tojo angrily ordered the assault on Midway Island.

EXTRA! **Pacific Post** EXTRA!

Section One SATURDAY, MAY 9, 1942 Ten Cents

STALEMATE IN THE CORAL SEA

JAPS LOSE PORT MORESBY, U.S. LOSES THE *LEXINGTON*

CORAL SEA, May 9 — The first naval battle in history in which the shipbound antagonists never even glimpsed their foe ended today in the idyllically-named Coral Sea, northeast of Australia.

Since Pearl Harbor, Japan has swept southward, consolidating land-grabs in China, French Indo-China, Siam, Malaya, and Borneo. Formosa fell, as did the Philippines, the British and Dutch East Indies, and northern New Guinea.

The Empire's encircling gambit apparently seeks outposts in the New Hebrides, Gilberts, Fiji, and Samoa, with an ultimate northern turn to the Line Islands, just 1,000 miles south of Hawaii.

May 3: "Operation MO" began when a Japanese amphibious operation struck Port Moresby on New Guinea's southeastern coast.

At the same time, they struck Tulagi in the Solomon Islands, which ring the Coral Sea at the two o'clock position.

The attacks were supported by land-based airpower and naval forces led by the carrier *Shoho*. Distant air cover was to be provided by the carriers *Shokaku* and *Zuikaku* and their task forces.

Fortunately, on April 5th, the British intercepted and deciphered the radio message sending the *Shokaku* and *Zuikaku* to the Coral Sea. The carrier *Lexington* was dispatched from Hawaii to meet the carrier *Yorktown*, recently in Tonga.

U.S.S. Lexington afire after attack by Japanese.

The two remaining carriers in the U.S. fleet, the *USS Hornet* and *USS Enterprise,* had just returned from the Doolittle Raid and were unable to join the battle.

The Japanese sent four subs to scout a line southwest of Guadalcanal (3 o'clock position) to give advance warning of U.S. warships, but the *Yorktown* task force had already slipped into the Coral Sea and escaped detection.

May 4: Informed of the landing at tiny, undefended Tulagi Island, northwest of Guadalcanal, the *Yorktown* sent aircraft to harass the Japanese, sinking several ships. Japanese engineers, undeterred, continued their work on Tulagi's airstrip.

May 5: The *Shokaku* and *Zuikaku* carriers arrived at Tulagi, searched the Solomons for the attackers, found nothing, and headed southward.

May 6: Advised that two Japanese carriers intended to support the Port Moresby invasion, the *Yorktown* headed north toward New Guinea (10 o'clock position).

By mid-morning, the Japanese received warning of the location of the U.S. carrier force, but were too far away to engage. At the same time, B-17s out of Australia attacked the Japanese at Port Moresby but without success.

By late night, the opposing carrier forces still had not seen each other, though at one point only seventy miles of ocean separated them.

May 7: Scout aircraft from the *Shokaku* located the American ships and so launched 78 planes, sinking the destroyer *Sims* and the oiler *Neosho*. At the same time, *Lexington's* F4F Wildcat fighters and SDB Dauntless dive bombers attacked the *Shoho*, sinking her.

The Japanese carrier invasion convoy at Port Moresby then turned south to engage the American carrier fleet.

May 8: Heavy clouds obscured the sky, but scout planes from both sides located the task forces, 200 miles apart. *Yorktown* and *Lexington* dive bombers damaged the *Shokaku*, causing her to retire from the battle.

The Japanese struck back, torpedoing and sinking the *Lexington* and damaging the *Yorktown*. Initially, the damage to the *Lexington* was manageable, but sparks ignited gas fumes below decks and the resulting fire soon got out of control. By 5 o'clock, the crew began abandoning ship.

May 9: The *Yorktown*, badly damaged, limped south past New Caledonia (4 o'clock), with Japanese forces in hot pursuit. Unable to find the escaping carrier, the Japanese turned back toward Rabaul, New Britain (12 o'clock).

Japanese losses in the Coral Sea battle resulted in the cancellation of the Port Moresby invasion.

Though a tactical victory for the Japanese, the battle was a strategic victory for the Allies because for the first time in six months Japanese expansion was turned back.

More importantly, two Japanese carriers were made unavailable for the coming Battle of Midway, which was just four weeks away.

And the loss of Port Moresby resulted in Japanese vulnerability in the South Pacific, allowing the Allies to launch the Guadalcanal and New Guinea campaigns.

The tide had already begun to turn.

EXTRA! **Pacific Post** EXTRA!

Section One SUNDAY, JUNE 7, 1942 Ten Cents

AMBUSH AT MIDWAY

SURPRISE ENSURES DECISIVE VICTORY FOR U.S. CARRIER FLEET

Midway atoll
Sand Island (top), Eastern Island (bottom)

MIDWAY ISLANDS, Jun. 7 — It was the most decisive blow in the history of naval warfare, and it proved Admiral Osami Nagano, chief of staff of the Imperial Navy, a true prophet: "For six months I will run wild in the Pacific . . . after that, I make no guarantees."

The man who designed the Pearl Harbor attack, Admiral Isoroku Yamamoto, knew that the absence of America's four carriers from Pearl Harbor that Sunday morning six months before might yet prove Japan's downfall. He had hoped that the sinking of the *Lexington* and crippling of the *Yorktown* in the Coral Sea would push America out of the South Pacific. When that did not happen, he determined to finish off the remaining carriers and also avoid another embarrassment like the Doolittle Raid in a carefully-set trap at Midway atoll, 1,200 miles northwest of Kauai.

What he did not know was that America had broken the Japanese naval code even before the Battle of Coral Sea, and so he was unaware that America knew all about his carefully-laid plans.

Knowing the date and location of the impending attack, Admiral Chester Nimitz, Commander of the U.S. Pacific Fleet, planned an ambush of his own: he ordered the *USS Enterprise* and *USS Hornet*, recently returned from Doolittle's daring raid, to join the *Yorktown* (repaired after Coral Sea in an astonishing 72 hours at Pearl Harbor) northeast of Midway, to lay in wait until the Japanese carrier fleet took the bait of the apparently unguarded atoll.

Yamamoto ordered a feint to the Aleutian Islands to draw off any American ships that might be in the North Pacific. Meanwhile, the battleship *Yamato* was to land 500 troops at Midway, while the four Japanese carriers, *Akagi, Kaga, Soryu, and Hiryu*, provided invasion support.

Jun. 3: Before sunrise, a PBY Catalina flying boat spotted the Japanese force, and fighters lifted off from Sand Island at Midway to harass the strike force. They did little damage.

Later that morning, 100 Japanese planes attacked Midway's airstrips. Another 150 aircraft were held in reserve, armed with torpedoes to attack American carriers, if and when they took the bait Yamamoto had offered.

With only land-based F4F Wildcat fighters attacking him, Yamamoto believed the American fleet was nowhere in the vicinity and decided to finish off Midway. He thus ordered the torpedo-laden aircraft refitted with bombs.

And yet, in mid-exchange, a Japanese reconnaissance aircraft reported sighting ten American ships, including a carrier, 200 miles to the northeast.

Yamamoto knew his trap had been sprung, so that night all aircraft were outfitted with torpedoes to attack the American task force at dawn the following morning. Midway could wait another day to be invaded.

Jun. 4: While it was still dark, an American scout aircraft located the Japanese fleet. Though the ships were at the limit of TBF Avenger torpedo bomber range, Nimitz launched 150 planes at dawn anyway.

The first wave of Avengers were decimated by Japanese anti-aircraft fire and Zero fighters, but as the Japanese began putting their own torpedo bombers into the air, fifty American SDB Dauntless dive bombers, unmolested by any Zeros (which were chasing the last of the Avengers), swooped in and within five minutes the *Akagi, Kaga,* and *Soryu* were engulfed in flames.

The remaining Japanese carrier, the *Hiryu*, some miles away and engulfed in a storm squall, emerged from the heavy weather and engaged the *Yorktown*, seriously damaging the veteran carrier, which sank two days later.

The *Hiryu* was not destined to survive, however: On the afternoon of June 4, U.S. dive bombers turned the carrier into a blazing hulk.

The Battle of Midway turned the tide of WWII in the Pacific. The Japanese lost four aircraft carriers, a cruiser, over 300 aircraft, and more than 2,000 men. In contrast, the U.S. lost one carrier, a destroyer, 137 planes, and 300 men.

Even after these terrible losses, Admiral Yamamoto considered engaging the Americans in a surface battle, but the Americans, aware that they had seriously crippled the Imperial Japanese Navy, destroying four of her ten carriers, quickly withdrew and claimed victory.

Admiral Yamamoto then called off the Midway invasion and for the remainder of the War, the Japanese were obliged to fight defensively.

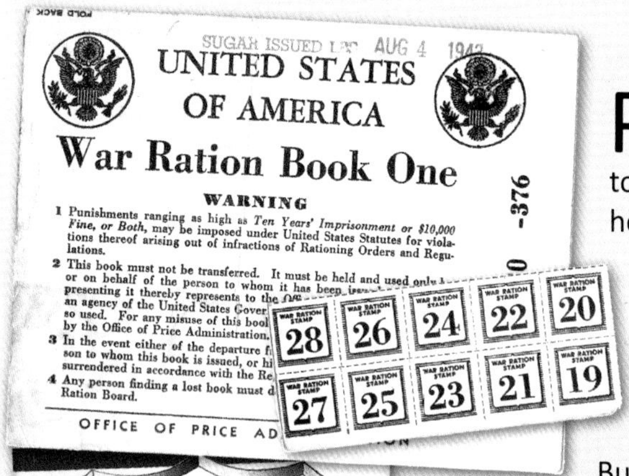

THE BEST DEFENSE

Prior to the attack on Pearl Harbor, the U.S. aided Britain under the Lend-Lease Act. Once at war, the economy quickly shifted to a military footing. The Depression, a wound that would not heal, was finally salved by the poultice of wartime production and near 100% employment. Consumer consumption rose even as 40% of the GDP was earmarked for military use. Tens of millions of workers, including students and housewives, moved into high-tech jobs. Union membership grew dramatically and most unions signed no-strike agreements.

But though incomes were increasing, there was little leisure time and little to buy. Durable goods were simply unavailable. Meat, clothing, sugar, and gasoline were tightly rationed. And though prices and wages were controlled, American savings accounts swelled.

Housing supplies dwindled and households doubled up to save money. Blackout curtains hung over windows and streetlights went dark as communities, fearful of German U-boat shelling on the East Coast and Japanese incendiary balloons on the West (which actually started several forest fires) threatened the mainland.

Taxes were raised to historic levels with top rates of up to 94%. Bond sales also financed the War effort. Roosevelt even attempted to tax 100% of incomes above $25,000 but was flanked by Congress. Dozens of new government agencies were created, including the Office of Price Administration, the Office of War Information, and the War Production Board, to name just three.

With most men in the service, civilians joined the Civil Air Patrol and acted as neighborhood wardens, ensuring compliance with government regulations. Civilians manned searchlights and used their own boats to patrol the coasts.

The United Service Organization (USO), formed jointly by the Salvation Army, the YMCA and YWCA, and other religious groups, boosted morale of servicemen at home and abroad. Women volunteered with the Red Cross and wore out their shoes at dime-a-dance servicemen socials.

Ninety million people went to the movies every week and Hollywood made hundreds of patriotic films to keep them entertained. The Office of War Information worked closely with producers, directors, and writers before filming started to make sure the themes reflected patriotic values.

The Office of Censorship published a code of conduct for print and broadcast media, though it did not require government pre-approval of content. Of course, subjects such as troop movements, weather forecasts, and the President's travel schedule were forbidden topics. And, unlike World War I, journalists were not required to publish positive propaganda.

Families planted victory gardens, recycled rubber, tin, and newspaper, saved fat drippings for making soap, and collected scrap copper and brass for use in artillery shells. Children harvested milkweed for use in life jackets. Virtually everyone in the country sacrificed for the War effort.

And it paid off.

EXTRA! **Pacific Post** EXTRA!

Section One | FRIDAY, AUGUST 7, 1942 | Ten Cents

GUTS & GLORY ON GUADALCANAL

AMERICAN LAND FORCES FINALLY ENGAGE JAPANESE

SOLOMON ISLANDS, Aug. 7 – Their return to Hawaii stymied at Midway, Japan turned once again to the Coral Sea to solidify their holdings in the Solomons, which were conquered in May 1942.

To that end, engineers were in the process of building an air field at Point Lunga on the northern shore of Guadalcanal, the largest island in the island chain.

The Allies had to stop them in their first offensive attack, which would sorely test Allied mettle in a battle for an insect-infested, jungle-covered island just 90 miles long. It would also be the first engagement of 11,000 untested Marines.

Point Lunga was eerily silent on 7 August when the Marines waded ashore. Aside from sporadic sniper fire, there was no resistance as they moved inland toward the airbase. There they found construction equipment but no Japanese, who had fled into the jungle. It seems it was America's turn to surprise the enemy.

By the end of 9 August, the airfield was secure and renamed Henderson Field.

Across the eastern channel, Tulagi and Florida islands had also been taken in spite of fanatical resistance, which required the killing of almost every Japanese soldier.

Then Japanese planes struck from New Britain, 650 miles to the north. A day-long battle was bitter and hard-fought. Joined by a cruiser force, the two navies engaged in the sea north of Point Lunga in a fierce battle which the land-bound Marines watched with mounting horror. In the end, the Allied task force withdrew for lack of fuel, leaving the Marines on the island to fend for themselves, short of supplies and ammunition.

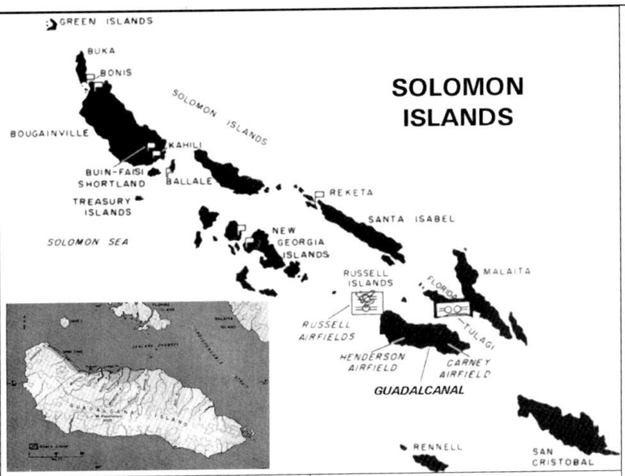

To make matters worse, Japanese were constantly landing fresh soldiers on the island, and soon they outnumbered the Americans. The Marines dug in while more soldiers and dive bombers landed under constant shelling from the Japanese fleet offshore.

At the same time, the Japanese 17th Army began an amphibious landing while other units made a suicidal attack on Henderson Field, suffering 90% casualties.

Over the next few weeks, both Allied and Japanese forces rallied to the island, until each side boasted about 24,000 men. The Americans braced for the inevitable attack on Henderson Field.

While preparing, the Marines suffered dysentery to the extent that at times up to 25% of all men were incapacitated.

On 7 September, the Japanese began their all-out assault on Henderson Field, attacking at night at what came to be called the Battle of Edson's Ridge. Many lives were lost on both sides.

Out at sea, the navies engaged as well and the carrier *USS Wasp* was lost.

Over the next few weeks, several land battles took place with astonishing casualties: the Battle of Tenaru River, the Matanikau actions, and the Battle for Henderson Field on 24 October, where 1,500 Japanese soldiers were killed while the Allies lost just 60 men.

After this rout, the Allies went on the offensive on 1 November and engaged the enemy at Point Cruz, Koli Point, and Bloody Ridge, but in the end, tropical disease and lack of food killed more Japanese on Guadalcanal than did bullets and bombs. By 4 December the Japanese realized they had lost and began evacuating.

Now the Allies had a stronghold in the Solomons and began their move northward, their destination: Tokyo.

Latest War Bulletins

NEW YORK, NY, Jun. 11 – German submarines have begun a mine-laying program in U.S. coastal waters off the eastern seaboard.

CAIRO, EGYPT, June 30 – After a decisive victory at Tubruk, Libya, General Erwin Rommel swept eastward toward the Suez Canal, engaging Allied forces at El Alamein, near Cairo.

MOSCOW, USSR, Aug. 12 – Winston Churchill met with Soviet dictator Josef Stalin to discuss German bombardment of Stalingrad and the possible Allied response.

STALINGRAD, USSR, Sep. 13 – Germany shifted its attention way from Moscow and toward Stalingrad in a massive offensive through Ukraine into Crimea and toward the Caucusus in order to capture Soviet oil fields.

ALGIERS, ALGERIA, Nov. 8 – Allied forces began their African campaign with Operation Torch landings in Casablanca, Oran, and Algiers.

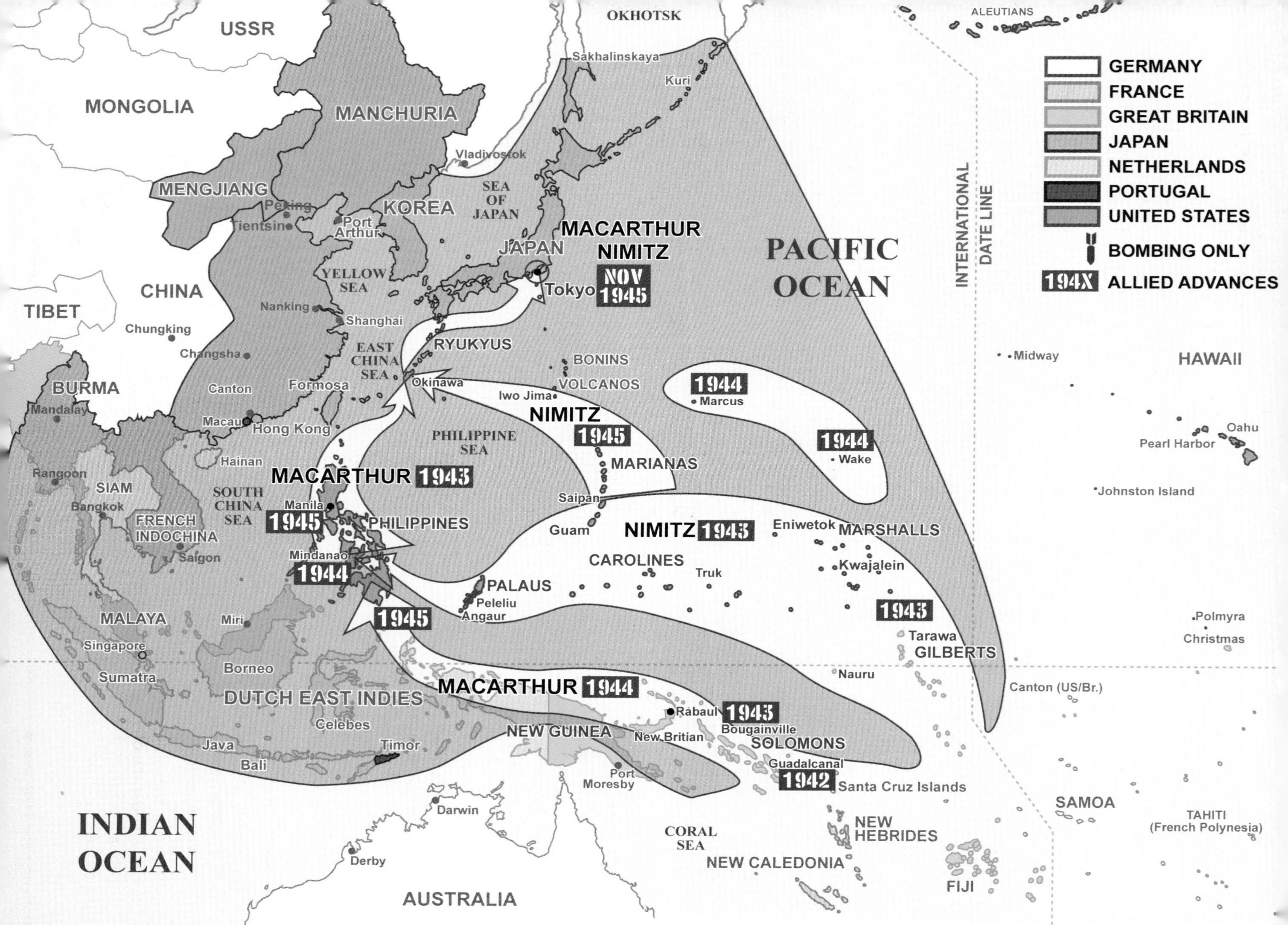

ALLIED ADVANCES: 1942-1945

THE GENERAL AND THE ADMIRAL

In military circles, "unity of command"—with one commander per theater—is an ideal honored more in the breach than in the keeping. Eisenhower never had total control in Europe; he had no say about the Mediterranean or the Eastern fronts. Similarly, Supreme Allied Commander General Douglas MacArthur presided only over the Southwest Pacific. Admiral Chester Nimitz controlled the Central Pacific Ocean Area. Given that both the Navy and the Army thought the Pacific War should be their domain and each had powerful supporters in Washington, unity of command was not an option and tremendous inefficiency, waste, and a piecemeal strategy resulted.

Both MacArthur and Nimitz proposed "leapfrogging" strategies to Roosevelt. The idea was to bypass heavily fortified Japanese positions and concentrate limited resources on strategically important islands that were not well defended but capable of supporting the drive to the islands of Japan.

General MacArthur wanted to consolidate the Solomons, push north and isolate Rabaul on New Britain (Japanese headquarters in the Southwest Pacific), then move west through New Guinea and retake the Philippines. From there he predicted he could attack the Japanese homeland.

Nimitz's proposal was to strike Japanese mandates and conquests in the Central Pacific, destroying them when necessary, isolating them when possible, and moving generally north toward the Bonins and west toward Formosa. He saw no reason to invade the heavily-defended Philippines when the freeing of Formosa would likely open the Chinese coast for use as bases from which to attack Japan.

For his part, MacArthur thought leaving 300,000 Japanese soldiers to their rear in the Philippines while the Allies attacked Japan was a recipe for disaster.

Roosevelt knew neither man would be effective serving under the other; each must be given his own command, notwithstanding the inevitable inefficiency. He thus approved both plans, and each commander set to work according to his personality: MacArthur, fiery and effusive, seemingly unfazed by tremendous battles and losses, worked his way through the Bismarck Sea and along New Guinea's northern coast. Nimitz, soft-spoken and relaxed, reinforced by his study of Japanese tactics at the Naval War College, sent Naval fighter planes and Army Air Force bombers to pound objectives and allowed the Marines ashore only when he felt the enemy had been neutralized.

In this he underestimated the Japanese, who proved time after time that only ground combat would succeed. But with each island battle, Nimitz escalated the pre-invasion bombardment and by the time he reached Iwo Jima, the engagements were the bloodiest on record. But he made progress and saved lives bypassing chains like the Carolines.

Meanwhile, General Henry "Hap" Arnold, head of Army Air Forces, reasoned that all air power in the Pacific should be under *his* command because of the difficulty of coordinating air campaigns between the services. Though he "loaned" Army Air Force groups to MacArthur or Nimitz as needed, he nevertheless retained overall control. So it was that Arnold secured a separation from both the Navy and the Army, preparing for his service's full independence as the Air Force in 1947.

Progress on both fronts was painstaking, but by mid-1944 Nimitz had invaded the Marianas Islands and MacArthur was securing New Guinea. Both men began to press the President for a decision for the moment the tips of their spears met in the Far East: Would the Philippines or Formosa be the jumping-off point for the Japanese invasion?

1944 was an election year, and Roosevelt feared upsetting MacArthur and his vast number of conservative supporters, so he gave the General the go ahead: the Philippines it was. Nimitz, disappointed but a team player, supported the conquest while simultaneously pressing toward Okinawa, where, in early 1945, the General and the Admiral met to plan the November invasion of the Japanese homeland.

THE NEED FOR SPEED

As a young man, O.C. loved sports and cars and excelled at both. Rumor has it that when he was still too young to drive, he found a dilapidated Ford Model A rusting away in a neighbor's yard. After getting permission, he hauled it home and worked on it for months, rebuilding the engine. It was ready to go when he got his driver's license.

And go it did. His sister Mavis reports that he once roared down a two-lane highway in Mission Valley at over 100 miles an hour, howling with laughter as she huddled fearfully on the floorboards of that same Model A.

Later, when he was stationed at Muroc Army Air Force Base in California's Mojave Desert, he drove that car to San Diego on weekends.

He had a life-long love of speed and typically drove a car well past its useful life. Before junking a vehicle, he would pry off the metal name plate and post it on a wall in the garage. At his death, he had more than a dozen proudly displayed.

THE KEMP HOME

Omer and Abbie were from working class families and raised their children according to those traditional values. The Depression, while present in California, was less destructive in the south because San Diego had always been a military town, with the Navy stationed on North Island in San Diego Bay and the Marines at Camp Pendleton up the coast.

Omer, a warehouse foreman for McKesson, worked long hours, saving money by riding the bus to and from work. Abbie, when her children were old enough, worked at Consolidated Aircraft and Rohr Aircraft doing office work.

Behind their little frame house on Winona Street they built a small rental which supplemented their income. When O.C. went to war, they even considered renting out his bedroom for a little additional cash.

ENLISTMENT

February 1943
North Island Naval Base
Coronado Island
San Diego, California
U.S. Navy

NAVY TOWN, NAVY BOY

Like all young men, the War was of paramount concern to O.C. He would have to choose, and choose soon, whether he was going to enter the armed forces of his own accord—choosing his preferred branch: Army, Navy, or Marines—or be drafted. So, like most of his friends, O.C. joined the Navy. Born and raised in San Diego, he knew many men who served in this branch of the military.

CONSOLIDATED AIRCRAFT

While he waited to be inducted, O.C. went to work at Consolidated Aircraft Corporation, the builders of the B-24 Liberator long-range heavy bomber, where he drove a parts cart around the factory. He tells of crashing the cart several times because the turning controls were non-intuitive. Embarrassed, he was glad to get out of the factory after just two weeks when Uncle Sam sent him a letter that would change his life.

AUDIO TRANSCRIPT 01:00:25

I went to work at Consolidated. Because the war was on, anyone out of high school could get a job. I was carrying parts on this little flat bed truck. It was electric and you stood up on it and pushed on a lever to give it the gas and steered with another lever. I only worked there for two weeks before they called me up.

INDUCTION

23 February 1943
U.S. Army Depot
San Pedro, California
U.S. Army Service Forces

OUR WAY AND THE HIGHWAY

Within days of joining the Navy, O.C. got a letter from the government saying all men of draft age would no longer be permitted to join their preferred branch of the military, but would have to wait to be drafted, though they would be permitted at that time to choose the branch in which they wished to serve. Within two weeks O.C. *was* drafted. Angry at the Navy for not taking him weeks before, he went down to the draft board and chose the Army.

ARMY SERVICE FORCES

O.C. then said goodbye to his family and caught a bus up to San Pedro, where he was sworn into the Army Service Forces, one of three elements of the United States Army: Ground, Services, and Air.

The patch on the right was worn on the upper left sleeve of his uniform. All armies, groups, and divisions were subordinate to the ASF.

AUDIO TRANSCRIPT 02:00:00

In the spring of 1943, I had the honor (or misfortune) of being one of the chosen many to be drafted into the Army of the United States. Having a fair background in mechanics, I applied for Machinist in the Air Corps. Just when I felt sure of my appointment, I found I was needed in the Infantry.

BASIC TRAINING

3 March - 26 April 1943
Camp Swift Army Base
Camp Swift, Texas
Company D
97th Infantry Division
12th Army Group / 15th Army

A LOT OF GOOD

Camp Swift is 28 miles east of Austin and was built in 1942, designed to accommodate 44,000 troops. The camp was named after Eben Swift, a World War I commander and author.

As the War progressed, it also gained the notoriety of housing almost 4,000 German war prisoners who were put to work on local farms while our boys were fighting their brothers in Europe.

By the early 2000s, Camp Swift continued to provide training for the Texas Army National Guard.

O.C.'s letters home said he was up at 6:00 a.m., reveille at 6:30, chow at 6:45, exercises at 7:30, class from 8:00 to noon. "Then we eat and fall out after mail call. At 1:00 p.m. we run three miles out in the woods. Back by 5:00 with a little time before dinner at 6:00. If we don't have KP or detail we're free until 7:00, when we have Manual of Arms until 8:00. You also have your rifle to clean and some studying to do, which I haven't got around to doing much of yet." After asking about his mother's job at Consolidated Aircraft, he says, "I got a GI haircut: 1/2 inch long. Really short." He concludes with, "And don't worry about me in the Army. It's doing me a lot of good."

Like all servicemen, in each letter he begs for letters from home and promises to write as often as he can. He kept his word pretty well; we have an eighteen inch stack of letters from his time in the service. At this point, he was writing several girls from school and so his studies went like they did in high school: poorly.

He'd have to change that soon.

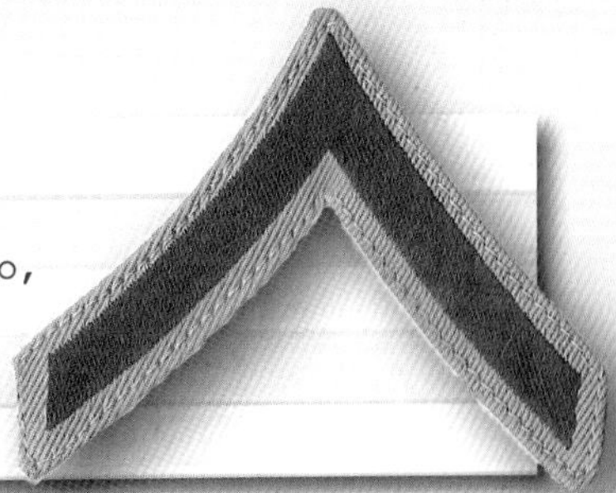

AUDIO TRANSCRIPT 01:04:30

All the San Diego boys were inducted in San Pedro, near Los Angeles. They sent me straight off to the infantry, to carry a gun, a knapsack, and a rifle with a bayonet. I was transferred to Camp Swift, Texas.

12th ARMY GROUP

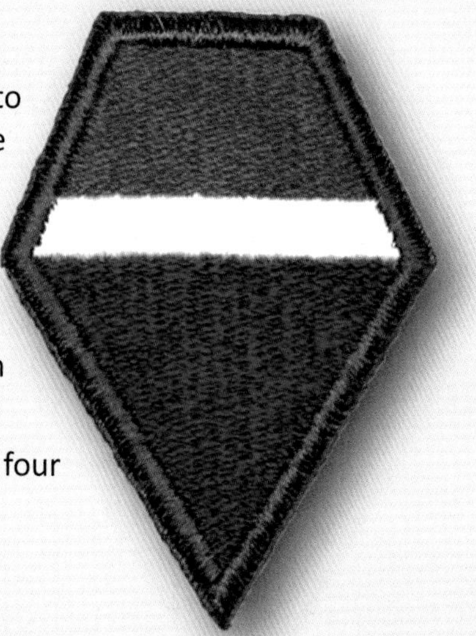

The 12th United States Army Group was the largest U.S. Army formation to ever take the field. It controlled the majority of American forces on the Western Front in Europe in 1944 and 1945 and was commanded by General Omar Bradley from his London headquarters.

The units forming the 12th Army Group occupied the right flank of the Allied lines during the Battle of Normandy and then moved to the center of the Western Front, sandwiched between the British-led 21st Army to the north and the U.S.-led 6th Army Group to the south.

As the 12th Army Group advanced through Germany in 1945, it controlled four field armies: the 1st, 3rd, 9th, and the 15th.

By V-E Day, the 12th Army Group numbered over 1.3 million men.

15th ARMY

One of the four subdivisions of the 12th Army Group, the 15th Army was the last field army to see service in northwest Europe during World War II. It was also the final command of General George S. Patton.

Activated in 1943, it engaged in Operation Husky, the July invasion of Sicily and thereafter Italy. The Axis forces in Italy were finally defeated in the Group's spring 1945 offensive in Italy, their surrender taking place in May.

The 15th Army served two separate missions: First, it trained and rehabilitated units and acted as a defensive line against counterattacks. Second, after the War, its mission was to carry out occupation duties and gather historical information related to the European Theater of Operations (ETO).

The 15th Army was deactivated in 1946 and has not been activated since.

97th INFANTRY DIVISION

The 97th Infantry served briefly in the World War I. In January 1945 the 97th Infantry was assigned to the 15th Army in preparation for the invasion of Europe. It started out as an Air Corps training division and was noted for having the highest average IQ of any American army division. It did not, however, remain long under the Air Corps (later the Army Air Force) but was made a part of the "regular" Army when the terrible casualties of Normandy took place and more regular infantrymen were needed on the European front.

By the time O.C. was drafted, it was a foregone conclusion that the 97th Infantry Division would go to Europe to support the push toward Germany. After completing basic training at Camp Swift, the Division participated in the Louisiana Maneuvers during the fall and winter of 1943-1944. The grueling training in the bayous, swamplands, and burned-out stump forests of Louisiana increased the stamina of the soldiers and strengthened their military skills. When they met battle in Europe, they would be well-prepared fighters, but no one could foresee the horrors they would witness there.

PROPHYLAXIS? 'NUFF SAID

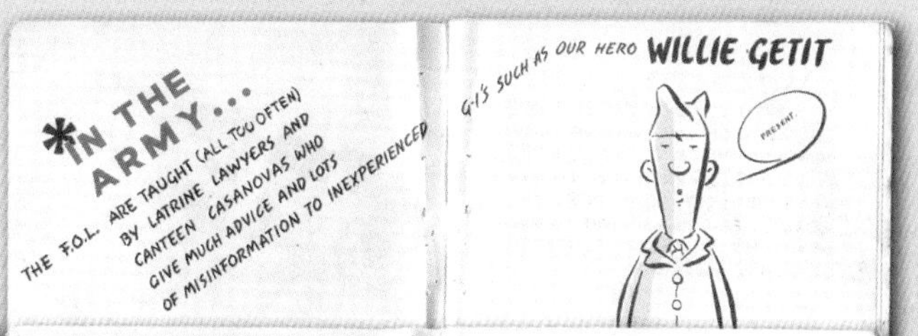

DON'T LEAVE HOME WITHOUT IT

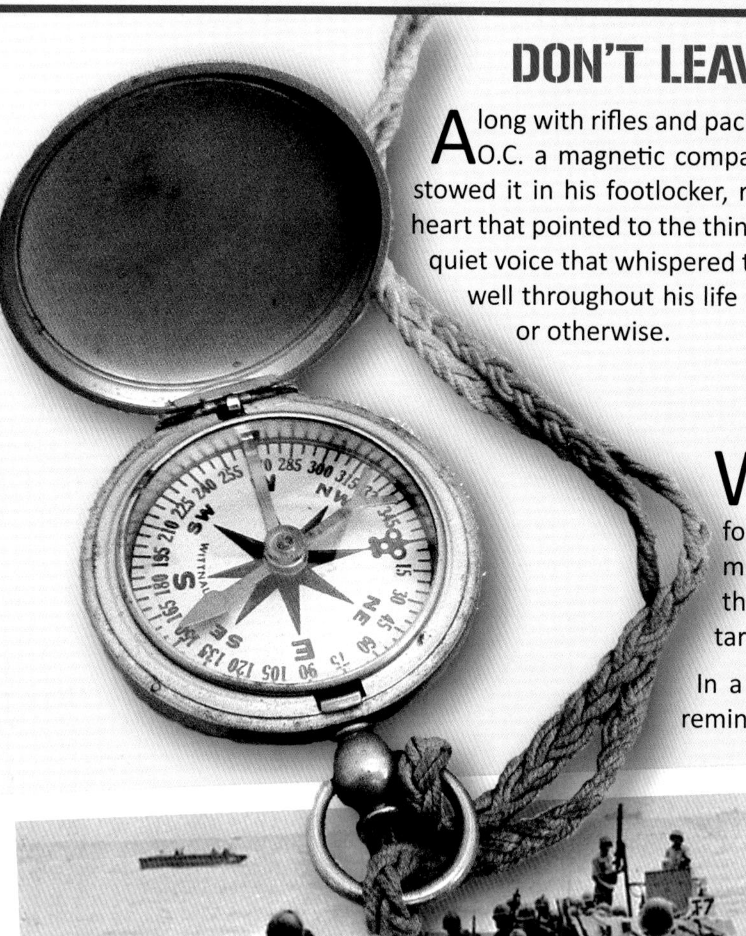

Along with rifles and packs and wills and field manuals, the Army gave O.C. a magnetic compass. He kept this compass his whole life but stowed it in his footlocker, rarely consulting it. His daily compass was a heart that pointed to the things he had been taught by his parents and the quiet voice that whispered to him from within. That compass served him well throughout his life and never indicated any deviation, magnetic or otherwise.

REALITY CHECK

While at Camp Swift, O.C. relished the rifle range, where his marks were quite good for a kid who'd never been around firearms much. He was disappointed, however, that on the prone firing test, he mistakenly shot at the target next to his, ruining his perfect score.

In a letter from his father in late April, he was reminded of the nearness of the War. His dad wrote, "Jim Gay (the Marine that used to rent our house in the rear) just got home from Guadalcanal in the Solomon Islands. He has been over there through all the battles with the Japs.

"He had malaria fever and is jarred up quite a bit. He is in the naval hospital here. Olive [Jim's mother] came out from Oklahoma to be with him a while. She is staying with us. Jim sure told us a lot about fighting the Japs. He said they were sure dirty fighters and loved to torture more than kill."

DOG TAGS

They're called "dog tags" because they resemble the tags used to identify dogs. O.C.'s are below. The top one is his Army tag, imprinted with his serial number 39285108 and noting his blood type (A), his religion (protestant), and his parents' street address. When he transferred to the Aviation Cadets, he was discharged and re-inducted, receiving the bottom tag and a new serial number: 0-710957.

Note the notches on the edge of the tags. A common belief among servicemen is that when a man dies, his dog tag is placed on edge between his upper and lower teeth to keep the mouth open and prevent bloating of the corpse. The notch keeps the tag in place. The truth is somewhat less gruesome: the notch aligns a blank aluminum tag with the stamping die.

AUDIO TRANSCRIPT 02:00:00

I ended up in Texas. I was very discouraged and blue about it because I realized I had probably done something that I didn't really want to do. I certainly didn't want to be a foot soldier. I really wanted to get into the Air Force, but I didn't quite know how.

Some of the guys who did pick the Army got into the Air Force at that time. All you were able to choose was one of the three services; you couldn't pick the branch of the service, although I had tried. Looking back on it now, it's a good thing I did because if I had gone a different route I probably would have never been able to do what I did.

And so one night, I went out on the parade ground. There were some small trees that were far enough away from the barracks that nobody could see you. I knelt down there and began to pray about my problem. I made a promise to the Lord that if I could get transferred out of the infantry and to get into the Air Force, I wouldn't forget Him.

You gotta watch it when you make a bargain with the Lord, 'cause sometimes He just goes ahead and fixes it up.

Looking back on this now, I realize how overwhelming the odds were. I didn't know how to go about getting what I wanted. All I knew is I wanted to be in the Air Force and I wanted to work on airplanes.

I never dreamed I would fly one.

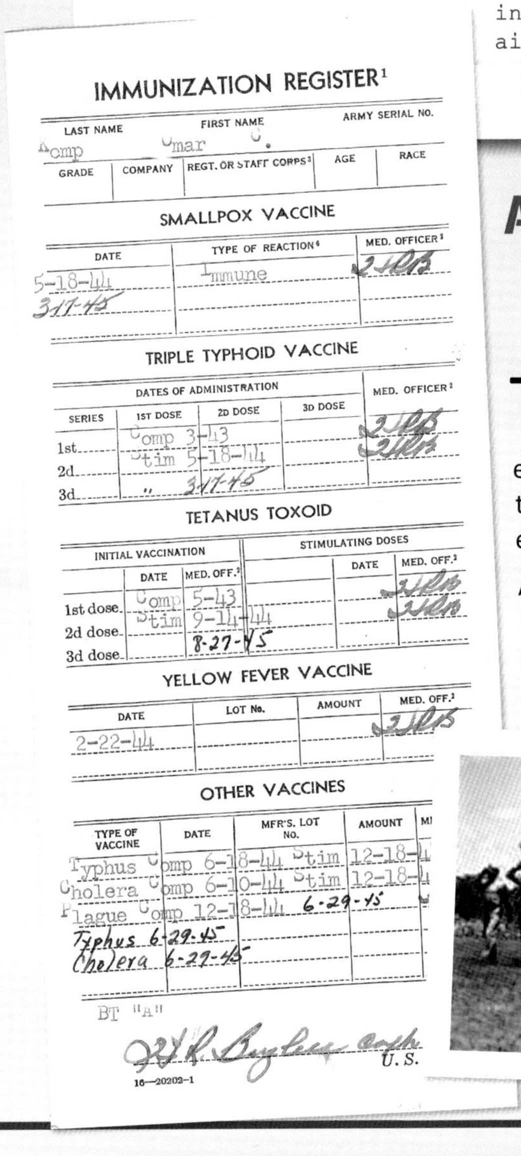
IMMUNIZATION REGISTER[1]

LAST NAME	FIRST NAME	ARMY SERIAL NO.
Komp	Omar C.	

GRADE	COMPANY	REGT. OR STAFF CORPS[3]	AGE	RACE

SMALLPOX VACCINE

DATE	TYPE OF REACTION[6]	MED. OFFICER[2]
5-18-44	Immune	[signature]
3-17-45		

TRIPLE TYPHOID VACCINE

SERIES	DATES OF ADMINISTRATION 1ST DOSE	2D DOSE	3D DOSE	MED. OFFICER[2]
1st	Comp 3-43			[signature]
2d	Stim 5-18-44			[signature]
3d	" 3-17-45			

TETANUS TOXOID

	INITIAL VACCINATION DATE	MED. OFF.[2]	STIMULATING DOSES DATE	MED. OFF.[2]
1st dose	Comp	5-43		[signature]
2d dose	Stim	9-14-44		[signature]
3d dose		8-27-45		

YELLOW FEVER VACCINE

DATE	LOT No.	AMOUNT	MED. OFF.[2]
2-22-44			[signature]

OTHER VACCINES

TYPE OF VACCINE	DATE	MFR'S. LOT No.	AMOUNT	M
Typhus	Comp 6-18-44	Stim	12-18-4	
Cholera	Comp 6-10-44	Stim	12-18-4	
Plague	Comp 12-18-44	6-29-45		
Typhus	6-29-45			
Cholera	6-29-45			

BT "A"

[signature] U.S.

16—20202-1

AS IF BULLETS WEREN'T ENOUGH

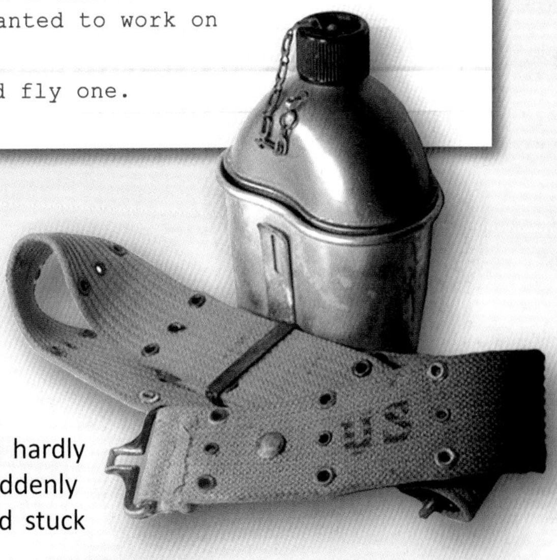

These poor guys!

Most of them grew up hardly ever seeing a doctor and suddenly they were being poked and stuck every which way.

And the diseases they were inoculated against send shivers up our modern spines: smallpox, typhoid, yellow fever, even cholera and plague. Seems like getting shot might have been one of the lesser dangers of military service.

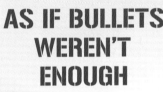

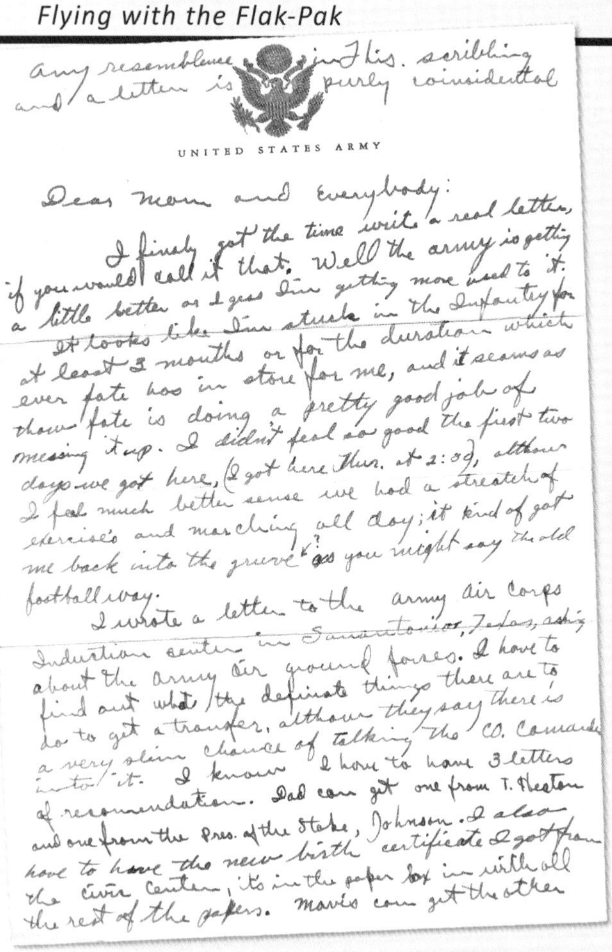
any resemblence in this. scribling
and a letter is purly coinsidental

UNITED STATES ARMY

Dear mom and Everybody:

I finaly got the time write a real letter,
if you would call it that. Well the army is getting
a little better or I gess Im getting more used to it.
It looks like Im stuck in the Infantry for
at least 3 months or for the duration which
ever fate has in store for me, and it seams as
thow fate is doing a pretty good job of
messing it up. I didn't feal so good the first two
days we got here, (I got here Thur. at 2:00), althow
I feel much better sense we had a streatch of
exercise's and marching all day; it kind of got
me back into the gruve ? as you might say the old
football way.

I wrote a letter to the army air Corps
Induction center in San antonio, Texas, asking
about the army air ground forces. I have to
find out what the definate things there are to
do to get a transfer, althow they say there is
a very slim chance of talking the C.O. Comander
into it. I know I have to have 3 letters
of recomendation. Dad can get one from T. Heaton
and one from the Pres. of the Stake, Johnson. I also
have to have the new birth certificate I got from
the Civic Center, it's in the paper box in with all
the rest of the papers. Mavis can get the other

"DEAR MOM AND EVERYBODY...

"I finally got the time to write a real letter, if you would call it that. Well, the army is getting a little better or I guess I'm getting more used to it. It looks like I'm stuck in the Infantry for at least 3 months or for the duration which ever fate has in store for me, and it seems that fate is doing a pretty good job of messing it up.

"I didn't feel so good the first two days we got here, although I feel much better since we had a stretch of exercises and marching all day. It kind of got me back into the groove, you might say, the old football way.

"I wrote a letter to the Army Air Corps Induction Center in San Antonio, asking about the Army Air ground forces. I have to find out what to do to get a transfer, although they say there is a very slim chance of talking the C.O. into it.

"There are about [CENSORED] men here so I guess Camp Swift is about the biggest Army camp there is in the country.

"Well, I'm waiting to hear from you. Love, O.C."

TESTING METTLE

He needed three letters of recommendation and a lot of luck. The letters arrived in late March and O.C. submitted them with his formal transfer request. Not long after, he received a notice that he was to go to San Antonio to take a series of tests to decide whether he would be allowed to transfer to the Army Air Force. He was excited because he loved airplanes and engines and knew he'd be a good mechanic.

AUDIO TRANSCRIPT 02:02:48

When I went to take the test, I got there about 7:00 A.M. I went in the door and realized for the first time that I was applying for the Aviation Cadets. And it wasn't just to be an aircraft mechanic. They would not have accepted anyone anyway in that situation and if I'd known that, I never would have gone; I never made very good grades in school because of my eyes and my hearing too, but I thought, "Well, I'm here anyway, I might as well take the test."

And I got a 78. The minimum was a 75.

One thing I'd learned from the Navy was how to cheat. I knew if I ever let them know I couldn't hear in my left ear, I wouldn't have gotten in the Navy or the Air Force, either one. And so I was torn with the thought: Should I should or should I shouldn't cheat?

But I thought, well, maybe this is the only way I can get into the Air Force and then I'll wash out, and then I'll be in the Army Air Force and I can go to ground school and learn how to be an airplane fixer.

And so I put my finger in my ear and they gave me whisper tests, but I never plugged my right ear when they were testing my left, so I could still hear a little. It worked in the Navy (that's where I learned to do it), and so I tried it in the Air Force, and it worked there too.

"YOU LUCKY DOG!"

After taking the tests in San Antonio, O.C. went back to Camp Swift and got on with his basic training. His transfer request, accompanied by the letters of recommendation he got from his football coach and the vice-principal of Hoover High, had managed at least to get him a chance to fail yet another test. He felt bad about cheating on the hearing part, but he was genuinely worried about the aptitude tests. There were IQ tests, motor-skills tests, and hand-eye coordination tests and he felt he'd done poorly on all of them, especially the IQ tests.

All the time he'd spent goofing off in high school suddenly came back and cuffed him on the back of the head. "Idiot!"

"I know," he said inwardly. "Serves me right if I get shot in Germany for being lazy in Geometry."

But soon he forgot about the test. His platoon had graduated from organizing footlockers, marching for hours on the parade ground, standing at attention, and ten mile hikes. They were now spending most days on the gunnery range learning to fire the powerful M-1 Garand rifle, and for the first time O.C. was enjoying being in the Army.

Then one day Sergeant Mancuso strode onto the range with a piece of paper in his hand, looked around, spotted O.C., and shouted, "Kemp! You lucky dog! You got orders to transfer in the morning to the Aviation Cadets!"

O.C. stood up in shock and everyone stared at him in disbelief. He'd won the lottery! But it was a bittersweet victory: he would be leaving the Infantry at the precise moment he was finally starting to have some fun.

He found out later that out of a battalion of 500 men, just two men had even applied for transfers.

But the timing!

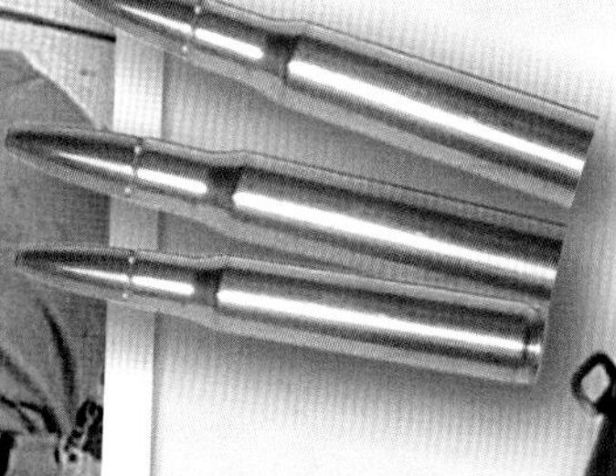

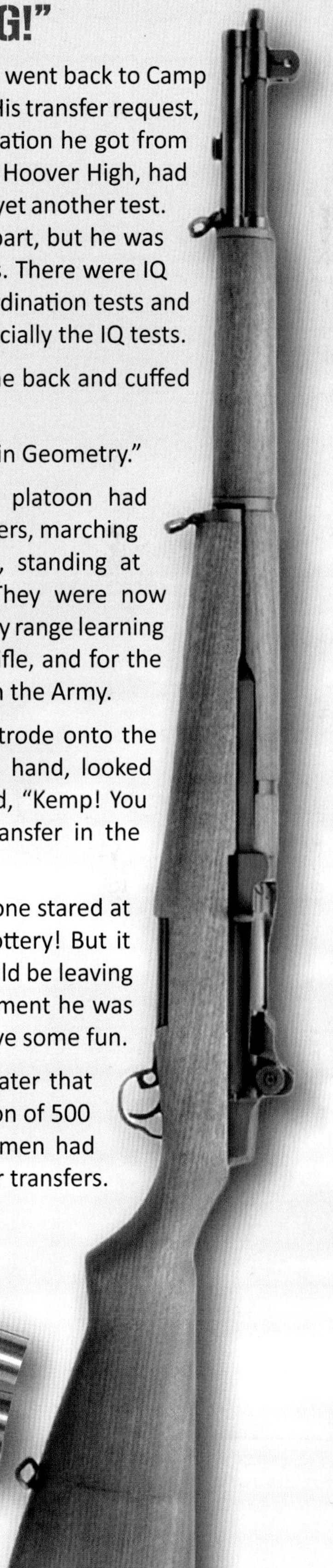

THE ARMY HAS AN AIR FORCE?

The Army Air Force insignia was designed by James Rawls, a member of commander of the AAF General Harold "Hap" Arnold's staff. Arnold wanted a new insignia for the new Air Force and Rawls submitted many designs, most incorporating wings, but Arnold rejected them all.

Dejected by his lack of success, Rawls remembered a picture of Winston Churchill giving his well-known "V for Victory" sign. He made a quick sketch bending the wings up, and Arnold said, "That's just what I wanted." The winged star was thereafter known as the "Hap Arnold" emblem.

The blue disk represents the air. The white star with red disk had been the symbol of U.S. military airplanes since 1921. (The red disk was removed from aircraft markings in 1942 to prevent confusion with Japanese insignia.) The golden wings, of course, symbolize victory.

ARMY AIR FORCES TRAINING COMMAND

The U.S. Army Air Forces Training Command was the short-lived (1943-1946) branch in charge of training new pilots by the tens of thousands, and doing it quickly. The national headquarters was at Randolph Field in San Antonio, Texas. Over its three-year term, the AAFTC trained over 75,000 pilots. It had three sections, the Southeast, Gulf Coast, and West Coast branches. Training took place in five phases:

- **Classification**: 2 weeks: cadets were separated into navigators, bombardiers, or pilots.
- **Pre-Flight:** 9 weeks: mechanics and physics of flight. Cadets must pass courses in mathematics, hard sciences, aeronautics, deflection shooting, and three-dimensional thinking.
- **Primary Pilot Training:** 9 weeks: at civilian-operated flight schools, cadets began their actual flight training in the Stearman PT-13, the PT-17 Kaydet, the Fairchild PT-19 Cornell, and the Ryan PT-20 Recruit.
- **Basic Pilot Training:** 9 weeks: formation and instrument flying, aerial navigation, night flying, and cross-country training took place in the Vultee BT-13 Valiant. Cadets were evaluated to determine aptitude for single-engine or multi-engine training and after this phase were sent to different schools depending upon that determination.
- **Advanced Pilot Training:** 9 weeks: single-engine (fighters) and multi-engine (transports and bombers) training. Single-engine students flew the AT-6 Texan and multi-engine students flew the Curtis AT-9 Jeep, the Beechcraft AT-10 Wichita, or the Cessna AT-17 Bobcat.

PHASE 1: CLASSIFICATION

1 - 10 May 1943
Aviation Cadet Center
San Antonio, Texas
116th Squadron
78th Flying Training Wing
Army Air Forces Central
Training Command

By the time of the attack on Pearl Harbor, the Air Corps had 21,000 recruits at three basic training centers. The subsequent phenomenal growth of enlistments made these three centers inadequate, so the number of basic training centers expanded to twelve by the spring of 1943.

Shortly thereafter, the basic training mission declined in size because requirements for training were being met. Consequently, some of the thirteen centers were inactivated, while others were moved to technical training centers such as Amarillo Field, Texas, that had previously not had basic training centers.

The number of trainees at basic training centers increased to its peak of 135,795 in February 1943, when O.C. was drafted in San Diego. In July 1943 this command merged with the AAF Flying Training Command to form the Army Air Forces Training Command.

At the Center, O.C. was put—as he had feared—through a battery of IQ tests, the failure in which would render him "GDO": fit for ground duty only.

There were motor coordination tests where the cadet had to put a needle in a hole without touching the sides while listening to the tester tell a story with numbers between sentences. When it was over he had to recount the story accurately, as well as the numbers.

One nice thing, instead of being addressed derisively as "Private," he was now called "Mister," albeit just as derisively. He looked longingly across the road to Kelly Field, where cadets were shooting landings. His teeth ached to fly.

But a gnawing fear remained in the back of his mind: that they would give him a test that was impossible to pass: a hearing test of his left ear.

After voicing his doubts to his mother, Abbie wrote back: "Don't be too disappointed if you don't get to be a pilot. Stop being afraid and show 'em your stuff. Quit worrying. Period."

EXTRA! **Pacific Post** EXTRA!

Section One TUESDAY, JUNE 30, 1943 Ten Cents

CARTWHEEL ROLLS OVER JAPS

THE ARCHITECT OF THE PEARL HARBOR OUTRAGE IS KILLED

THE BISMARCK ARCHIPELAGO, Jun. 30 – Nestled east of New Guinea and northwest of the Solomon Islands is the Bismarck Archipelago, named after German Chancellor Otto von Bismarck. Captured by Australia in WWI and after the war ceded to the Aussies, the island chain was a crucial Japanese land-grab shortly after Pearl Harbor, with the attack on Port Moresby in southern New Guinea in December 1941 and the invasion of Rabaul on New Britain on January 1942 in a gambit designed to cut off American supply convoys to Australia.

General MacArthur, ejected from the Philippines in February 1942, promised to return, and Guadalcanal was his first step back. Now, he's moving northward, and liberating the Bismarcks is a crucial part of his plan. His Operation Cartwheel attacked throughout the archipelago, seizing strategic objectives utilizing surprise and air power instead of the traditional "island-hopping," a pushing back of the enemy by direct frontal pressure, which historically resulted in heavy casualties.

For this reason, the Japanese stronghold of Rabaul was skirted and attacks on June 30 targeted Woodlark Island (off eastern New Guinea) and New Georgia Island (northwest of Guadalcanal in the Solomons) were initiated.

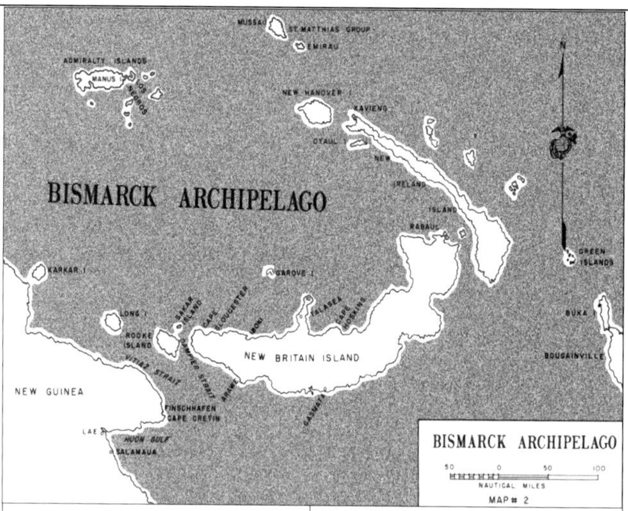

Over the remainder of 1943, Allied forces closed the gap in the Archipelago, invading Treasury Islands (north of New Georgia), and Bougainville (map, above), culminating in December 1943 with the bloody invasion of western New Britain at Cape Gloucester. Rabaul was not invaded, but major Japanese lines of communication were severed, along with a virtual blockade of the Japanese outpost.

Yamamoto Killed

RABAUL, NEW BRITAIN, Apr. 18 – Admiral Isoroku Yamamoto, architect of the Pearl Harbor and Midway campaigns, was killed today when his plane was shot down by American aircraft.

A career naval officer who was educated at Harvard and spoke perfect English, Yamamoto opposed the 1931 Japanese invasion of Manchuria and the subsequent land war with China, as well as the 1940 Tripartite Pact with Nazi Germany and Fascist Italy. But his fealty to the Emperor was total and though he advised against attacking the U.S., saying, "It is not enough that we take Guam and the Philippines, nor even Hawaii and San Francisco. To make victory certain, we must march into Washington and dictate the terms of peace in the White House," it was his ingenious plan that nearly destroyed America's Pacific naval power on 7 December 1941.

But after losing face after the Midway rout, Yamamoto was forced to pursue the defensive strategy in the Solomons he had earlier opposed. But the Army failed to hold up its end of the battles, and the Navy, unable to draw the Allies into a decisive sea battle, could not advance. The loss of numerous destroyers during the Solomon engagements severely weakened Yamamoto's naval forces, forcing retreat.

To lift morale, Yamamoto planned a tour of outposts in the Archipelago, but the Allies, having long ago broken Japanese secret radio codes, learned his itinerary and were ready for him when he flew with several aircraft from Rabaul to a tiny island near Bougainville.

16 P-38 Lightnings engaged the convoy and Yamamoto's plane was last seen on fire, crashing into the jungle.

Latest War Bulletins

NORTH ATLANTIC, Apr. 26 – German submarines sank the carrier *USS Ranger* in the Atlantic.

TUNISIA, AFRICA, Apr. 26 – Lt. Gen. McNair, chief of U.S. ground forces in Africa, is wounded on the Tunisian front.

BLACK SEA, USSR, Apr. 26 – Berlin admits that Reds have seized mountains rimming the Black Sea port of Novorossiysk.

RANGOON, BURMA, May 31 – In an effort to cut of Allied aid to China using the India-Burma-Chinese Road, Japan captured Burma in March 1942. Thereafter, China could be supplied only by flying over the Himalayas ("The Hump") from India, or capturing territory in Burma and building a new road—the Ledo Road. By early December 1942, British troops re-entered Burma and began engaging the Japanese.

PHASE 2: PRE-FLIGHT

10 May - 17 July 1943
Aviation Cadet Center
Randolph Army Air Field
San Antonio, Texas
Group 13, Squadron 1
78th Flying Training Wing
Army Air Forces Central
Training Command

After waiting weeks doing practically nothing, things finally got underway at the Aviation Cadet Center and O.C. entered the two-week classification phase. He was asked to rate on a scale of 1 to 9 whether he'd like to be a pilot, a navigator, or a bombardier. O.C. put a "9" for pilot and a "1" for the other positions. He was starting to believe he might actually learn to fly. At the very least, he was now guaranteed to be on an airplane. He was, however, a *little* worried: one of the ways they decided what you would be was to give you an IQ test. In a letter home, he reasoned that, "I'm pretty sure they won't let me be a navigator, because a person has to have quite a few brains on math to do that and I haven't got any. That leaves it between bombardier and pilot. Quite a few of the boys got classified today so maybe I'll get it tomorrow."

The next day, on 14 May, O.C. was classified "pilot" and would start pre-flight training in ten days. In the meantime, one of the best things about being a cadet was no more KP or clean-up details. All they were expected to do besides study was walk guard duty on occasion.

But as a reminder that there was a war on, they had a "gas" drill during a hike. An A-20 attack bomber dove down on them and gassed the recruits. But because the pilot was late and they knew he was coming, they had already put on their masks. O.C. said he was more concerned about sunstroke than the gas.

ABOVE The cadet patch was worn on the right upper sleeve. Cadets who graduated at the top of their class were usually graded Flight Officers (Warrant Officers) and were then given extra responsibilities. All the graduates became second lieutenants. Those who washed out of pilot training were sent to navigator or bombardier school.

LEFT The iconic administration building of Randolph Army Air Field, location of the San Antonio Aviation Cadet Center.

RIGHT O.C. had to stand in line for hours to get his cadet photo taken. The girls he was writing in San Diego all wanted a picture of the dashing young cadet.

AVIATION CADETS MARCHING TO CLASS – S.A.A.C.C.

TAKING THE HEAT

During Pre-flight Training, SAACC upperclassmen were merciless hazers, "racking back" underclassmen by shouting at them, making them eat a "square meal" by forcing them to raise their food to their mouths using only right angles, and entering the barracks one at a time, requiring everyone in the room, no matter what he was doing, to snap to attention.

In a letter home, O.C. wrote: "We have to come to attention every time an upper classman comes in the barracks. They make us do all the things an officer could make us do." As proof, his letter-writing was interrupted a half dozen times when an upper classman came into the room and he had to jump to attention.

After a couple of weeks of this—which made studying almost impossible—a federal law was passed outlawing the most egregious hazing, due to the fact that by this time in the War, many experienced, combat-savvy soldiers had entered flight training and when an upperclassman (whom they called "four week wonders") started hazing them, they'd knock the man down. When a critical number of men were washed out for striking a superior, the practice received its deserved scrutiny and was abolished.

O.C. was grateful because he probably would not have done as well in pre-flight if he'd had to endure more abuse than he did.

Cadets were in the sack by 10:00 p.m. and up at 4:30 a.m. Days were spent at lectures, physical training, and drill, as well as "rock detail," policing the grounds. What was "chow" in the regular Army was now called "mess." Everywhere they went, they had to run in cadence and sing their marching songs at the top of their lungs.

CLASSROOM INSTRUCTION

In his spare time, O.C. wrote a couple of articles for the "Talespinner" camp newspaper.

O.C.'s father regretted to have to tell him that a friend, Ross Tenney, was reported lost on a bombing raid over Germany. Ross had already been shot down twice and got back across enemy lines both times. O.C. told his father he hoped Ross was as lucky this third time. (He was.)

A PICTURE AND A THOUSAND WORDS

We have a stack of manuals that O.C. studied at SAACC. Ground school continued right through his primary, advanced, multiple-engine, and bomber training. Although never a stand-out student prior to enlistment, he became adept at the complex physics of flight, due primarily to the fact that he simply *loved* the idea of flying.

Most of the basic flight manuals are fully illustrated for two reasons: a picture truly *is* worth a thousand words and many of the young men entering the service at that time had little formal education.

Below we see that an early form of helicopter—the autogyro—was a functioning reality even before the War broke out.

Coincidentally, these drawings are only a little more advanced than the ones O.C. drew through his primary education.

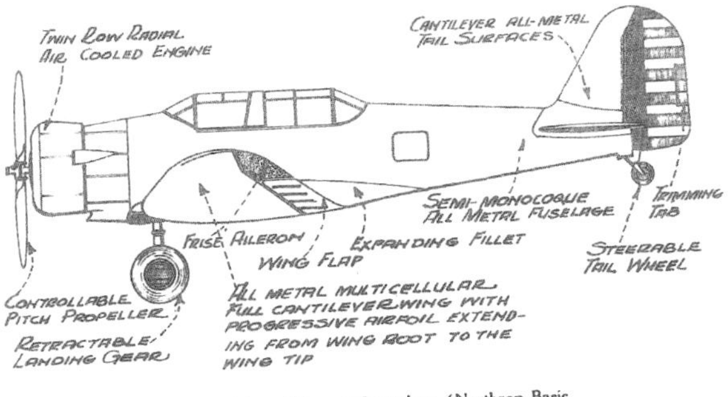

A Typical Low Winged Monoplane (Northrop Basic Trainer).

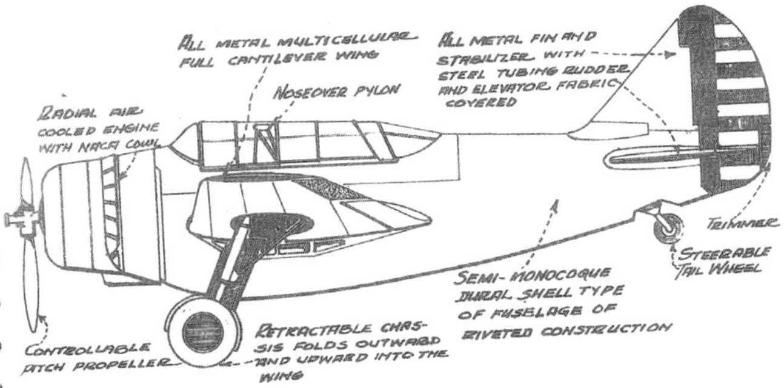

A Typical Mid-wing Monoplane (North American O-47 U.S. Air Corps).

Classes at the Center focused on Morse Code, aircraft and ship identification, physics, math, and map and chart reading.

Physics in particular was gruelling: “Physics is just a bunch of measurements and forces of gravity, wind and weather. It deals with grams, centimeters, and kilograms and all kinds of new measurements that sound like Greek to me.”

There was no leave for the first month, so the cadets had nothing to do *but* study.

O.C.’s mom Abbie wrote saying, “There is someone in the Kemp family who thinks it’s impossible for you to get where you are and we are getting quite a kick out of it because we know you can make it.”

It wasn’t all work. The cadets had a dance in early June. O.C. went but didn’t dance because, he said, “I didn’t have any shoes. All I have is the rubber-soled GI shoes. You can’t buy any shoes, either, unless you have a stamp or special commander’s permission,” a reminder that everyone was using ration stamps for buying everything from gas to sugar to shoes.

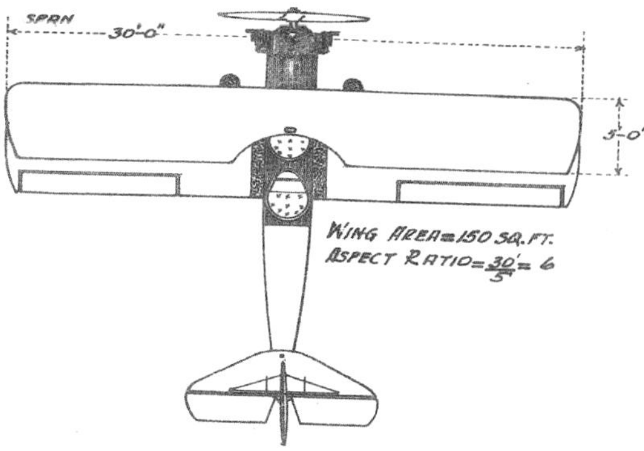

The Aspect Ratio Determination for a Modern Airplane (Fleet Trainer).

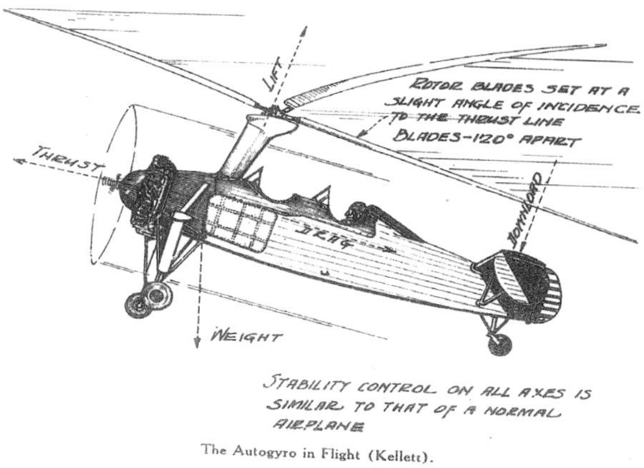

The Autogyro in Flight (Kellett).

SOMETHING ELSE TO WORRY ABOUT

Shortly after beginning pre-flight training, cadets were tested for altitude sensitivity. O.C. wrote this essay in a college freshman English class after the War. It received a C+ from an instructor who was obviously suffering from anoxia.

SIX MILES UP

Two weeks before graduation, an Army Air Force cadet of a twin-engine flying school must undergo an altitude test. This is necessary because of the high altitudes bombing planes must fly. Experience has taught Army officials that an air cadet is not fully trained until he knows the dangers of the lack of oxygen in high-altitude flight. The term for oxygen starvation is anoxia.

To more clearly show the effects of anoxia, we must follow a group of cadets through a test in the altitude chamber.

This chamber looks like a giant boiler lying on its side. Usually painted gray, it stands about six feet high, six feet across, and approximately eighteen feet in length. The interior walls are lined with benches with sets of masks, gauges, and regulators hung above the benches. The wall at the far end of the chamber features an altimeter and a clock. The walls are of heavy iron plating and the windows are an inch thick.

After a brief lecture, a group of twenty men and two instructors file into the chamber. The instructors take their places at either end of the chamber and the heavy iron door is bolted shut. The air is then slowly sucked out by a pump. A telephone connects the instructors with the men who are outside controlling the air pressure. The ascent to altitude is simulated and the only difference between this and actual flight is the fact that the temperature remains the same. At actual altitude, the temperature changes at the rate of two degrees per thousand feet.

At 10,000 feet the cadets put on their masks because the air has become too thin for a crew member to responsibly fulfill his duties. The rate of ascent is five hundred feet per minute, making it possible for every man to clear his ears. For some this is easy, while for others it may be quite painful. The common head cold may clog up the eustachian tube, making it difficult to clear the trapped air. Descent is much more apt to cause trouble than ascent. Air must be forced into the inner ear artificially if the eustachian tube does not release the pressure building up behind the ear drums. Closing the mouth and holding the nose, combined with building up of pressure inside the mouth, will force the air through the eustachian tube into the inner ear. This action must take place every few minutes during the ascent or descent.

At the altitude of 38,000 feet, the instructor asks a volunteer to remove his mask. As he does, the instructor will tell the remaining men what to look for in oxygen starvation. The man's fingernails start to turn blue. To him, the lights in the chamber seem to turn a light purple or bluish color. A few more seconds pass and the man without the mask starts acting playful or carefree. He might become violent and need two or three men to hold him down. He is suffering from anoxia and if oxygen is not immediately administered, unconsciousness and death will occur within 90 seconds after he loses consciousness.

The descent is then started by slowly forcing the air back into the chamber. The group reaches ground level and files out through the heavy iron door. If there were no severe pains above the eyes (indicating sinus trouble) or failure to clear the ears of pressure, the group passes the test.

This altitude test has proved to be of great value and help to crews in their later training and combat flights.

WAR GOES BETTER WITH... COKE?

Aviation cadets received this pamphlet, which had dozens of pages of aircraft silhouettes, published to aid "1,000,000 civilians who man observation posts on the home front." It was published by Coca-Cola, and contained several ads promoting the soft drink with pictures of our allies, such as the Chinese soldier.

THE HOME FRONT

He was knocking himself out studying and physics was doing the punching, but O.C. got a 94 on his final exam. He scored 100% on his aircraft identification test and passed his Morse Code class, transcribing the minimum required eight words a minute. "I passed Pre-Flight by the skin of my teeth," is what he told his mom. She said she wasn't surprised that he'd made it; she knew his poor grades in school were a result of lack of interest, not ability. As she would say, "Period."

RIGHT O.C. wrote everyone in his family a letter a week, and they reciprocated in kind. His sixteen year-old sister Mavis kept him up on doings at Hoover High and gave him solid advice about girls, some of which he may have needed. He was pining for one that signed her letters, "Sincerely," not exactly what he was hoping for. Mavis also let him know how much his letters home meant to their mother Abbie:

"This morning when your letter arrived, Mother dropped everything to read it. She left some bacon burning up in the frying pan and left the ice-box door open and the cat got in it. So the house was in kind of an uproar."

But in a good way.

YOU JUST THINK THEY LOOK BORING

Just one 3" stack of manuals O.C. had to devour during his short, busy time at SAACC. A perusal reveals two important things: First, aviation instruction back then was even more demanding than it is now. O.C. must have gulped when he first opened these books. Second, note the headings. These are not military manuals but were produced by the Civil Aeronautics Administration. The military, long in stand-down from WWI, had almost no training facilities or instructional materials during the first months of the War and so relied heavily upon civilian contractors to get aviation cadets through the first three phases of their flight training.

July 27, 194

San Antonio Aviation Cadet Center
San Antonio, Texas

Dear Mavis,

I sure am glad you wrote me cause I was just about to think you had forgotten me.

See that little plane at the top of this picture. Well I went over to Brooks and asked the operations office if they had any seats empty for me. He said, "Shure, get a chute and wait for 043 to come in and he will take you up". It came in and the officer said for me to ride with one of his cadets. He cadet had about 2 more days before graduation. We tookoff at 4:00 and

The sleek AT-6 Training ships used in training our future flyers are something the Cadet at S. A. A. C. C. looks forward to getting his hands on. Their trim silver bodies make a beautiful sight etched against the brilliant blue of a Texas sky. They are both a reminder and a promise, to the civilian who watches them skimming the clouds, of his future protectors. To the future pilot they are a step to being a protector of our way of life!

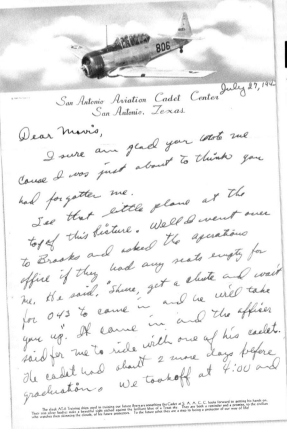

A FIRST TIME FOR EVERYTHING

He had never been up in an airplane, but they had filled his imagination (along with rocket ships and cars) since he was a boy. But now he was training to be a pilot and it might be a good idea to see if he also had the *stomach* for flying. So he took some steps and later wrote home to his sister Mavis:

"See that little plane* at the top of this picture? Well I went over to Brooks Field and asked the operations office if they had any empty seats for me. He said, 'Sure, get a chute and wait for 043 to come in and he will take you up.'

"It came in and the officer said for me to ride with one of his cadets who had about 2 more days before graduation. We took off at 4:00 and flew formation with about 6 planes. We were third in line. We had what they call a 'rat race' where we follow the leader. We sure did put that plane through the paces. I don't think I have ever had so much fun in my life.

"I know now that I won't worry about being air sick as much as I thought I would. I stayed up for an hour. Makes me want to fly all the time.

"They just can't keep me out of the air now."

---

*The AT-6 "Texan" has a 600 hp radial engine and can reach up to 200 mph.

. . . AND LIBERTY FOR ALL!

But at a price. While O.C. is training (and doing a little sightseeing as well) in San Antonio, back home even high school students were doing their part. *The Cardinal* was Hoover High's student newspaper, but it reads like any other daily of the time: a rallying cry for sacrifice of time and money for the War. Even O.C., who wanted to buy a pair of dress shoes to wear to a dance, had to get a stamp from his seven year-old brother's ration booklet to be allowed to buy the shoes. One of the apparent lessons of the War is that shared sacrifice brings a war to a quicker conclusion.

Coleman, auto shop instructor. during the week-end.

FROM WILLIE TO ADOLPH

SAVE...SERVE
CONSERVE
A BOMB FOR ADOLF FROM WILLIE JONES

Let's Tell The World!

"Let's tell the world" when we win a football game. Let's have a red flag for the Red team and a white one for the White team to be flown on our flag pole when victory is won.

What do you say, Cards and Coeds? "Let's tell the world."

VICTORY SPECIAL

THE CARDINAL

THE OFFICIAL PUBLICATION OF HERBERT HOOVER SENIOR HIGH SCHOOL

VOLUMN XIII — SAN DIEGO, CALIFORNIA, OCTOBER 28, 1942 — NUMBER 5

Preference Shown For Formal Dress

Student Ticket Sales Increase From 8 To 10

At a meeting held Friday in the auditorium, 201 Senior A students decided what they wanted to wear for graduation and the prom. They chose formal dress for both affairs. Seniors also had their choice between formal dress or cap and gown for commencement, and formal or sport dress for the Ball. Results in the Commencement voting were: 107 in favor of formal dress, 50 for cap and gown. For the Senior Ball or Dinner, 108 chose to wear formal attire while 43 voted for sports dress.

Other Business Settled

Dues were set at $3.50 and will include all class activities, flowers for graduation, Vespers, the Prom and Dinner, the Annual, and Ditch Day. The required number of tickets to be sold by each Senior A was increased from eight to ten.

For the first time in Hoover's history, Commencement will be held in the auditorium on Wednesday, February 5 at seven in the evening, the time voted upon by the class.

One Alone!

Seniors Publish February Annual

"For the first time since 1935, the February graduating class will have an "Annual" of its own," Janet Bowman, Senior A Annual editor announced today.

Staff Chosen

Those chosen to edit the yearbook are: art editor, Betty Balkner, assistant art editor, Charles Morse and business manager, Winifred Newell. Only Senior A activities will be included in the 48 page edition. "Pictures of seniors, administration, senior activities and novel features will be used to make the senior's publication attractive," declared Janet.

"The reason for a separate Annual at this time is to enable students to have their yearbook now, instead of waiting until June and returning for it," stated Miss Delight Smith, Senior A adviser.

Production, Community, Air, Land, Sea Divisions Comprise Victory Corps

Leading Hoover's Victory Corps is Mr. Myron Green, with a faculty committee consisting of Miss Agnes Work, history teacher; Mrs. Ora Wilson of the mathematics department; Mr. C. Gerald Hasty, English instructor and Mr. Malcom Smith, mechanical drawing teacher.

Hoover Organizes

Hoover, along with other high schools throughout the country, is organizing classroom offerings, extra-class activities and personal programs to aid the war effort. The training of students for war service which will come after they leave school, and their active participation in the community's war effort while they are yet in school, are two of the objectives of this organization.

Program Objectives

Whether curricular or extra-curricular in character, the objectives of the high schools' wartime program which the Victory Corps will foster and promote are: Guidance into critical services and occupations, wartime citizenship, physical fitness, military drill, competence in science and mathematics, preflight training in aeronautics, preinduction training for critical occupations and community services.

Proposed As Nationwide

Democratic and voluntary in character, the Victory Corps is proposed as a nation-wide wartime student organization for secondary schools. Youth are invited to participate as equal partners in the war effort. They are asked to select ttheir areas of special service and to help plan their programs of study and extra-class activitty. High schools are given opportunity to affiliate their present student organizations in one pattern of organization which will serve to stimulate and channel youth's enthusiasm, by giving recognition for appropriate war preparation and services.

Requirements Listed

Any student who meets the following requirements may be enrolled as a general member of the Victory Corps. He must be participating in a school physical fitness program appropriate to his abilities; be studying or have studied school courses appropriate to his age, grade, ability, and probable immediate and future usefulness to the nation's war effort;

Quake Cracks

Heard during and after last Wednesday's 'little shake-up' were such remarks as:

Dot Summers: "Was there an earthquake? I didn't feel it. Where was I?" (You're asking us!)

La Verne Hicks: "It wasn't a bad quake at all. It only knocked me across the room."

Jane Ellis: (addressing a student in back of her) "Stop jerking my desk!"

Don Smedley: (during the Commissioners' meeting) "We eagerly clustered around the radio in Mr. Johnson's office when we were told that a very important announcement would be made. A voice solicitously inquired, "Do you have

Old Autos To Salt Shakers Contributed; Red Cross Salvage Drive Closes Today

Most energetic scrap metal col- Various Contributions Made

PHASE 3: PRIMARY TRAINING

17 July - 3 October 1943
Chickasha Air Field
Class 44-B, Barracks B-5
Chickasha, Oklahoma
316th Contract Flying School
Army Air Forces Central
Training Command

In 1939, the Civil Aeronautics Authority (CAA) launched the Civilian Pilot Training Program (CPTP), which by 1940 had over 13 colleges and 300 schools across the country. While both the Army and Navy had their own schools, the CAA program was deemed superior, so the military used these existing programs for pilot training.

When O.C. finished his preflight training at SAACC, it was now time to move on to Primary Training. The Army thus engaged private contractor W&B Flying School of Chickasha, a central Oklahoma town of just 5,000 people, to train him and 200 of his fellow cadets to fly. All over America, the Army Air Force (AAF) had constructed scores of airfields and had contracted with local flying schools to teach the young cadets.

CLASS 44-B

That was the name of O.C.'s flight class, a designation it would retain throughout the last three phases of training at three different training facilities. He and his fellow cadets at W&B were taught to fly by 20 instructors—that's one instructor per ten cadets and thus a lot of pressure on everyone.

This nine week phase was designed to acclimate the cadet to flight and if O.C. didn't wash out, he would graduate in late October 1943.

In a letter home, O.C. gushes over the school, if not the town: "Chickasha sure hasn't got hardly a thing. It's just a country town. But W&B Flying School is one of the two best flight schools in the whole bunch. The other is in St. Louis, Missouri.

"They issued us a helmet and goggles. Boy, you ought to see me in them. We will probably go out on the line Monday afternoon. They are really surprisingly strict here, more than we expected.

"And I must tell you about the wonderful meals. They are served cafeteria style, and I guess they have about the best meals I've ever tasted in the Army. W&B is run mostly by civilians.

"I guess this is about the best place for a flying school but it sure is a hell hole for a town."

LEFT O.C. visits the Hades that is Chickasha, a town that ended up exceeding his initial perceptions.

FAIRCHILD PT-19 "CORNELL"

The Fairchild PT-19 (PT stands for Primary Trainer) was used by the Army Air Forces as the pre-solo phase trainer. It first flew in May 1939 and won a fly-off competition later that year against seventeen other designs for the new Army training airplane. Fairchild was awarded its first Army contract for an initial order on 22 September 1939. Over 6,000 were built during the War.

The tail-dragging, low-wing monoplane with fixed landing gear had tandem seating and an open cockpit. The student sat in the front seat, the instructor behind him. The simple but rugged construction included a fabric-covered welded steel tube fuselage. The remainder of the aircraft used plywood construction, with a plywood-sheathed center section, outer wing panels and tail assembly. The use of an inline engine allowed for a narrow frontal area which was ideal for visibility while the widely set-apart, fixed landing gear allowed for solid and stable ground handling. It also could be equipped for instrument flight training by attaching a collapsible hood to the front cockpit.

Unfortunately, in 1943, there were durability issues with the plywood wings of the PT-19. The high temperatures and wilting humidity in Texas, Oklahoma, and Florida meant that wooden wing sections had to be replaced after only two to three months' active service because of rot and ply separation issues.

Subsequent to this, the USAAF required all-metal wing sections on all future fixed-wing training aircraft, which is the reason O.C. is wearing a parachute.

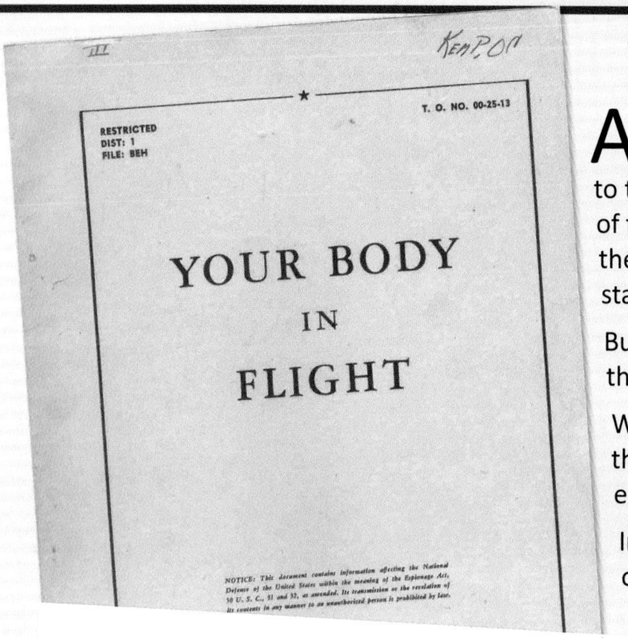
RESTRICTED
DIST: 1
FILE: BEH

T. O. NO. 00-25-13

YOUR BODY
IN
FLIGHT

NOTICE: This document contains information affecting the National Defense of the United States within the meaning of the Espionage Act, 50 U. S. C., 31 and 32, as amended. Its transmission or the revelation of its contents in any manner to an unauthorized person is prohibited by law.

RESTRICTED
T. O. No. 00-25-13

YOU'RE COMING ALONG, TOO

After the War, O.C. kept a stack of his flight instruction manuals in his footlocker, which contain concepts familiar to those who learned to fly decades after he did. They're full of the same sort of illustrations and thought-problems about the nature of flight, the characteristics of the airfoil, avoiding stalls and spins, and proper landing attitude.

But there was one volume I found marvelously quirky and, at the same time, tremendously important: *Your Body in Flight.*

Written just weeks before O.C. got his copy, it incorporates the newly-discovered notion that, even in technical education, a picture is worth a thousand words.

In fact, it is quite direct with this concept, starting on page one. And though the drawings—appearing on every page of this 84 page booklet—are comic-like, they deal with matters of serious concern to a pilot, whether he knows it or not at this stage of his training.

Though the same method is used in this book, the Army came up with the name: "Thought-Pictures."

BOTTOM LEFT Of course O.C. already knew a lot about thought-pictures. Here's an idea of what was on his mind.

"THE BEST THERE EVER WAS"

On 3 August, O.C. made his first official training flight. Thereafter, after morning ground school classes, they would fly for an hour or two in the afternoon.

Two other young men went up first with the instructor and they both got sick. O.C. was the last, and he didn't, saying later that "I felt better in the air than I did on the ground."

After a time the instructor reached over O.C.'s shoulder and grabbed the windshield, indicating that O.C. was to fly the aircraft. The cadet said, "I made some very sloppy turns which were still very much a thrill to me."

"All I can say is this flying is the best there ever was," he continued. "I just have to make it go and graduate."

"Funny thing," he said. "The PT-19 is a very stable plane and is a better flyer by itself than when you have control of it.

"It won't be long before I solo, I guess. They solo here at ten hours, which should be Tuesday after next or sooner if my instructor thinks I can do it."

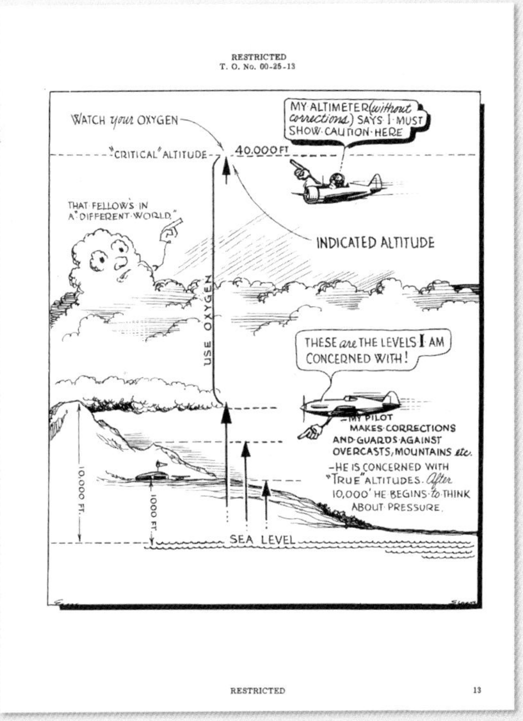

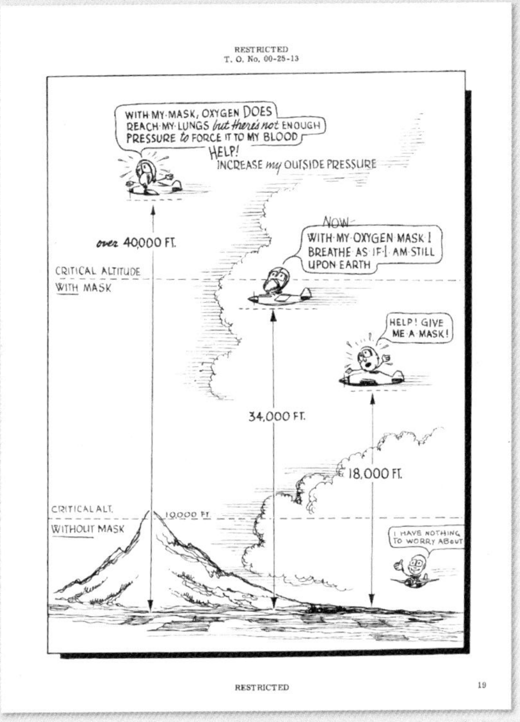

ABOVE Imagine for a moment all the airplanes that crashed, killing valuable souls, before these facts about the dangers of altitude flying became accepted wisdom. The greatest danger is overconfidence and the manual hammers that salient point home.

BELOW When you're approaching 10,000 feet, a lack of oxygen (hypoxia) results in euphoria. For non-drinkers, flying at altitude without oxygen is as close as they'll ever come to the sensation of being tipsy.

During the day, the color-perceiving "cones" in our eyes help determine what an object is, but at night we use only the "rods," which are a thousand times more sensitive. When we look directly at an object at night, we use the cones at the rear of our eye surrounding the optic nerve—not a rod in sight. So when you want to see something clearly at night, peer at it out of the corner of your eye and let the rods do the work.

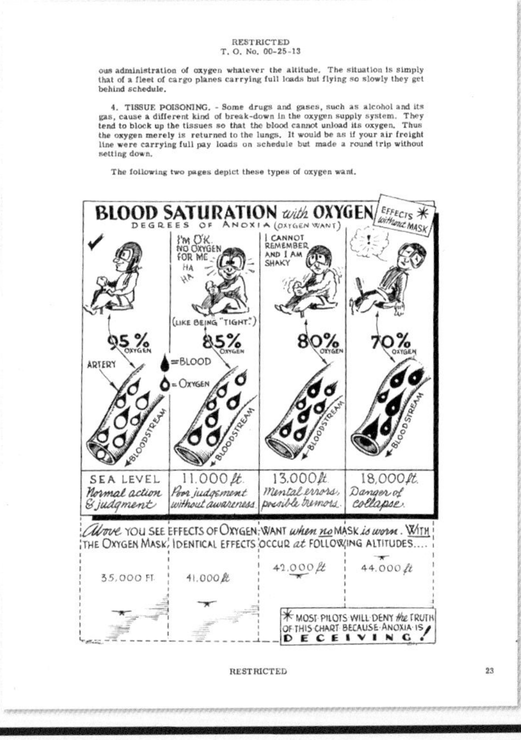
RESTRICTED
T. O. No. 00-25-13

ous administration of oxygen whatever the altitude. The situation is simply that of a fleet of cargo planes carrying full loads but flying so slowly they get behind schedule.

4. TISSUE POISONING. - Some drugs and gases, such as alcohol and its gas, cause a different kind of break-down in the oxygen supply system. They tend to block up the tissues so that the blood cannot unload its oxygen. Thus the oxygen merely is returned to the lungs. It would be as if your air freight line were carrying full pay loads on schedule but made a round trip without setting down.

The following two pages depict these types of oxygen want.

RESTRICTED
23

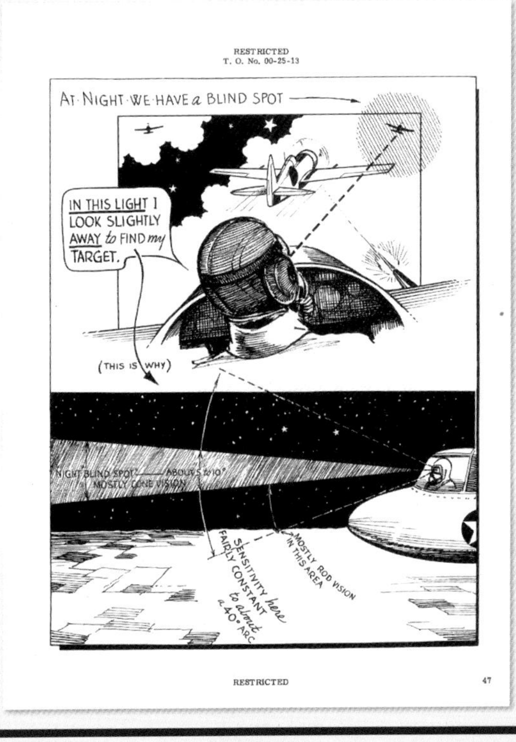

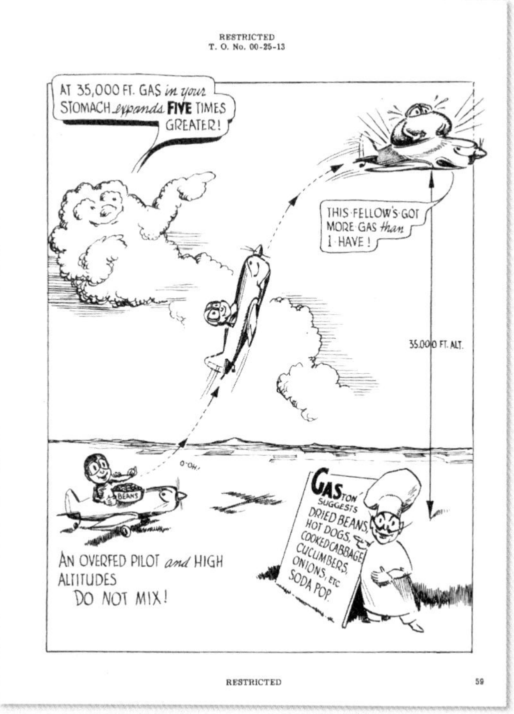

ABOVE LEFT Unfortunately for spicy food lovers, some cuisine is just out when it comes to pre-flight mess.

ABOVE RIGHT Learning to trust the dials more than your inner ear and your eyes is difficult but essential when you find yourself in instrument meteorological conditions (IMC).

BOTTOM LEFT It's hard to believe that a man in combat could let his personal life interfere with the mission at hand, but of course the answer is a universal *what-makes-him-different-than-you?* He's not, of course.

BOTTOM RIGHT The most serious page in the book. A salute to the brave men who did their job and trusted their fellow crew members to keep them alive if their job bit them back.

RESTRICTED
T. O. No. 00-25-13

There are two don'ts for wounds involving the stomach, liver, kidneys, and intestines: Don't permit the patient to move. Don't give him coffee or any other liquids to swallow. The abdomen should be tightly wrapped with overlaying pressure bandages to reduce internal bleeding. If the intestines spill through an open wound, don't push them back in unless it is certain that they are not punctured. If they are, they should be covered with gauze compresses which must be kept moist with a reasonably sterile, preferably warm, liquid. The compresses should be held in place with a fairly snug bandage. If the exposed intestine is not punctured, it should be sprinkled with sulfanilamide powder and gently pressed back into place in the abdomen with compresses. Then bandage the wound.

EXTRA! **Pacific Post** EXTRA!

Section One | SATURDAY, JULY 31, 1943 | Ten Cents

THIS IS *HOW* WE FIGHT!

A COURAGEOUS G.I. SHOWS THE WORLD AMERICAN RESOLVE

NEW GEORGIA, SOLOMON ISLANDS, Jul. 31 — Northeast of Guadalcanal lies a cluster of about a dozen large islands and hundreds of tiny ones which present a problem for an invasion force: the largest, New Georgia, home to 10,000 dug-in Japanese, is partially surrounded by a coral barrier, inside of which are large, shallow lagoons with dangerous coral outcrops.

Munda Point on New Georgia Island, the largest of the group, is inaccessible to large vessels, but to the south, across Blanche Channel, lies Rendova and a sheltered harbor, where American soldiers made their first landfall on 30 June.

At the same time, GIs landed on north New Georgia and fought their way inland, heading toward the Japanese stronghold at Munda Point.

The plan was to take New Georgia, then the next island north, Kolombangara, then to Bougainville Island.

Having learned the lessons of Guadalcanal, the brass spared no effort to ensure that the soldiers had everything they needed, including vast stores of supplies, food, armaments, and ammo, cases of which littered Guadalcanal beaches, ready for delivery to New Georgia at a moment's notice.

And also like Guadalcanal, the Japanese were surprised at the northern landing points, and even Rendova was a cinch,

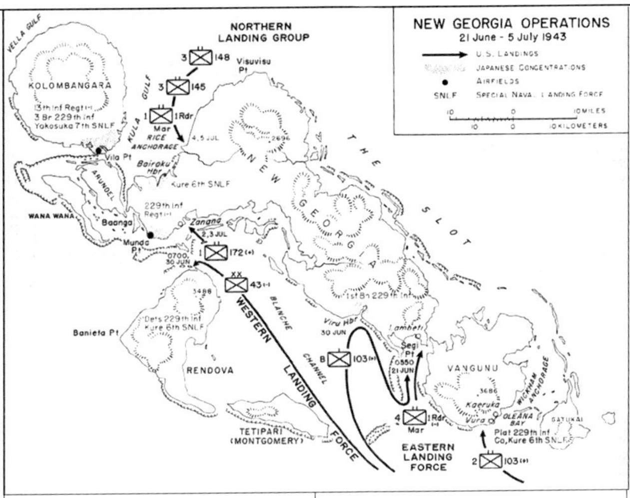

though the Japanese recovered quickly and shelled the Americans as they disembarked from their landing crafts.

And finally, like Guadalcanal, the defenders escaped into the jungle, offering stiff resistance, causing the offensive to grind to a halt on 7 July.

The Munda Airfield was our main objective. It was still in Japanese hands, but neither they nor we knew about the Company B's secret weapon: Rodger Wilton Young, a 5'2", bespectacled, almost deaf private who, on 31 July showed the world how big the American soldier really is.

Late that afternoon, Young's 20 platoon was scouting Japanese positions near Munda airfield. As they were returning to U.S. lines, they were ambushed and pinned down by machine gun fire from an elevated position 75 yards away that killed two soldiers in its first burst of fire. Two more men were killed when a flanking maneuver was ordered and after that the platoon commander realized they were whipped and ordered the troops to withdraw.

But Young knew they were sitting ducks and would never make it back to the protection of the jungle. Pretending not to hear his commander's retreat order, he began crawling toward the machine gun nest and was soon shot.

He did not stop. Continuing forward, he was hit a second time but kept advancing, attracting enemy fire and answering with shots of his own. When he was close enough to the gun emplacement, he let loose several hand grenades. As the last one left his hand, he was shot a third time and killed, but his grenade destroyed the machine gun nest.

Meanwhile, his astonished comrades used the cover Young provided to retreat to safety without further loss of life.

This was a soldier who, when his eyesight and hearing began failing him, requested a demotion in rank from sergeant to private so as not to endanger his subordinates.

This was a soldier who, when told his ailments would keep him from joining the New Georgia invasion, begged his superiors to be allowed to take part with his comrades in the attack.

This was a soldier who posthumously received the Medal of Honor from a grateful nation on 6 January 1944.

This was a soldier.

CAN WORK BE FUN?

If the work is learning to fly, yes.

O.C. wrote home, dismayed at the amount of work flying had turned out to be: "We sure are getting the works now. I've just completed four hours and the instructor is really cracking down. I'm doing my turns and coordination exercises all right but I sure miss a lot of other things. We are working on stalls and spins. I tried one today and did all right, I guess. I messed up again on flying a rectangle. Boy, the instructor sure does eat on you all the time you are up there. I guess it does some good 'cause I don't do the same thing twice after he hollers at me.

"We're supposed to use flaps to come in for a landing and if you forget to use them or come across the taxi line with them still down, you have to buy the whole line Cokes. It's rather expensive but you don't do it again after that."

Then, voicing his real concerns, he said, "I hope you don't worry about me flying a bomber or a fighter because there is an awful big chance that I won't make it at all. At least they won't keep me wondering. I should know in a couple of weeks if I wash out or not."

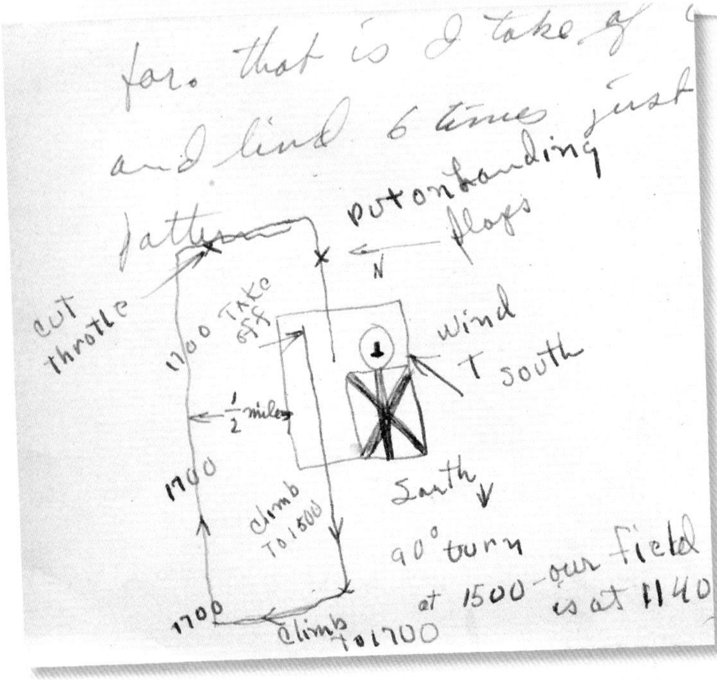

...NOT IF YOU WASH OUT

O.C. wrote home, worried. He wasn't doing so well. Instead of trying to explain what he meant by "soloing," he drew a picture of the traffic pattern of an airport. Thus far, he had landed six times with the instructor on board. To solo, he had to fly the rectangle, make smooth turns, control engine power, keep the aircraft straight and level, raise and lower the flaps as required, and hit the tarmac smoothly, then give it the gas and do it twice more—all by himself.

"Looks complicated, doesn't it?" he wrote. "It is when the wind changes.

"But if I wash out I will try for bombardier if my grades are good enough. If not, I will try for radio/gunner."

On another note, he obliquely reminds his parents that he's still a 19 year-old kid: "I guess I won't go to town next week 'cause I got off the ball and I have to do some ramp walking. Six hours worth."

FIRST SOLO

It's 20 August 1943. Elimination Day.

By this time in the War, the AAF had a surplus of student pilots and were going to wash them out in any way possible to release more men to the infantry for the coming European land invasion.

After dozens of take-offs and landings accompanied by an instructor, a cadet must prove he can fly the aircraft by himself. The instructor stays on the ground and the cadet flies three circuits of the "pattern" (a rectangle) around the field, taking off and landing three times. If he doesn't do so smoothly and safely, he washes out, and O.C. almost did.

Best of Luck Kemp
& hurry back to see
us in a P-40
Lt Bill Cosby

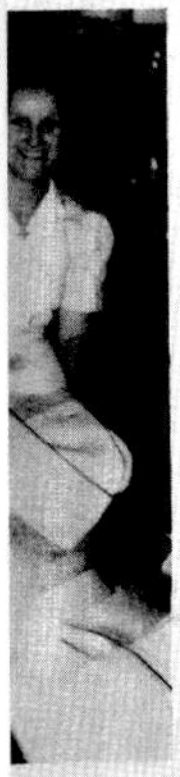

Lt. Cosby in his favorite type of transportation

my Solo - Elimination Lieutenant

After a previous day in which he flew two flawless pattern circuits, he botched the third (his go-cart opposite foot steering as a kid confused him).

CENTER LEFT When they went to a nearby auxiliary field for his solo test, Lt. Bill Cosby, his "elimination" lieutenant, said, "I'm giving you one more chance. Either you land it right this next time or you're through."

". . . And I greased it in," said O.C.

Cosby was pleased. "You're the first one I've passed this year. I've washed everybody else out."

BELOW O.C.'s log book marks the notable event.

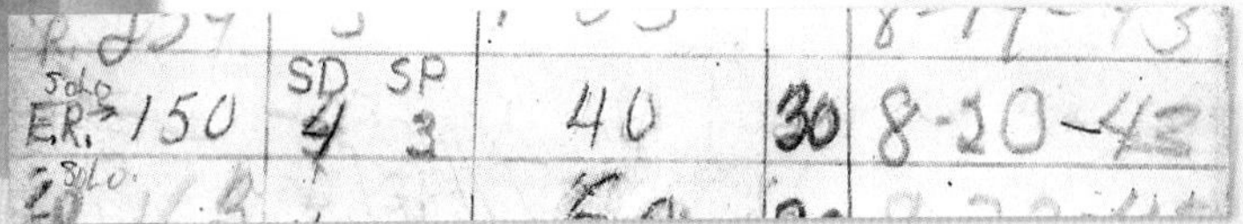
Solo
E.R. 150
SD SP
4 3
40
30
8-20-43

Within days O.C. was soaring around the sky on his own, zipping in and out of clouds. "I did spins until I was blue in the face," he told his dad in a letter. "Also some elementary acrobatics."

FYI: Inadvertent spins are responsible for more aircraft crashes than any other flight maneuver. When a pilot tries too hard to gain altitude by raising the nose, beyond a certain point the air no longer moves smoothly across the wings and the plane literally quits flying. The left wing drops suddenly and the nose follows and the aircraft plunges downward in a spin. Recovery is not difficult, but many a pilot has died due to disorientation and panic. Nowadays flight schools do not train for spins, and more's the pity. Every time a plane takes off, there is a danger of a spin.

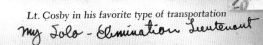

HEY, SIGN MY ANNUAL, WILL YA?

W&B Flying School published a yearbook for each cadet class. Here we see the cover and a couple of typical pages. If you look closely, you'll see O.C. in the top right photo sitting in the rear instructor's seat.

In his graduation photo, notice the metal tubes descending from the ears of his flight helmet. Cockpit communications in the PT-19 were not electronic but rather used hollow rubber tubes, which meant a great deal of shouting to be heard over the roar of the engine and the wind in the open cockpit. This was actually quite fortunate for O.C. as the shouting helped him hear—he had only one good ear, after all.

BELOW LEFT The original photo used for the *Warrior* yearbook, which was posed to replicate the familiar "V" for victory sign popularized by Winston Churchill above the Morse Code for "V," three dots and a dash. O.C. is prone in the right wing of the "V."

BELOW RIGHT The photo as it appeared in the *Warrior*.

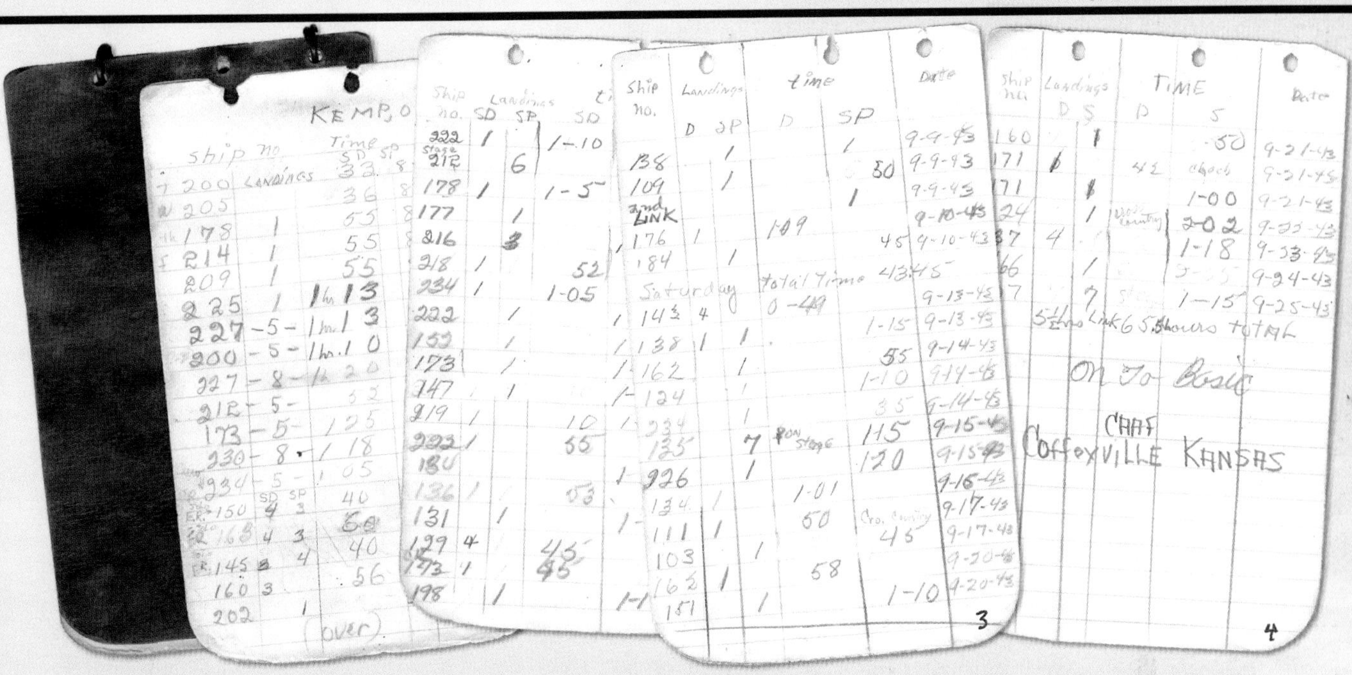

LOG BOOK

Once overseas, O.C. was not allowed to keep a log book for security reasons. But during training, he kept this hand-written pad in his pocket, recording every flight, starting with his first on 3 August 1943 in "ship" number 200 (likely a PT-19 Cornell trainer).

He logged just 33 minutes on that first flight and made his first instructor-assisted landing two days later. Each day he flew a different aircraft, sometimes logging 8 take-offs and landings in just over an hour—a busy day.

These four pages record all his flights at Chickasha Army Air Field. On the last page he notes: "On to Basic (CAAF) Coffeyville, Kansas."

BELOW The Army keeps meticulous records and O.C.'s flight training is no exception. Every minute in the air, each landing, and all instrument training sessions are carefully logged. The purpose: train our boys to go against the finest pilots in the world: the Japanese and the Germans.

STUDENT FLIGHT RECORD	O.C. KEMP
STATION	Chickasha, Oklahoma
ORGANIZATION ASSIGNED	316th A.A.F.C.F.S. (P)
FLYING CLASSIFICATION	Student Pilot
MONTH	**August - September**
AIRCRAFT TYPE	PT-19A
LANDINGS	152
STUDENT DUAL TIME (DAY)	32:17
STUDENT FIRST PILOT TIME (SOLO) (DAY)	32:48
INSTRUMENT TRAINER	5:30
TOTAL STUDENT FIRST PILOT TIME	32:48
TOTAL STUDENT PILOT TIME	65:05

PHASE 3: BASIC PILOT TRAINING

3 October - 2 December 1943
Coffeyville Army Air Field, Flt D
Coffeyville, Kansas
824th Bomber/Fighter Training Sq.
32nd Flying Training Wing
Army Air Forces Central
Training Command

Coffeyville Army Air Field (CAAF) in southeastern Kansas was the first of eleven Kansas training installations built during the War. It graduated the state's first class of cadets in early 1943. The site was located seven miles northeast of Coffeyville on a 1,456-acre tract of land. In addition to the main base and airfield, there were four auxiliary fields used for pattern work and takeoff and landing practice.

On 3 October, O.C. was transferred to Coffeyville for Phase Four of his training: ten weeks consisting of 70 hours of flying in advanced, single engine trainers, 94 hours of ground school, and 47 hours of military training. A cadet's typical day would start with reveille at 6:15, followed by breakfast at 6:30. Flying began at 7:45. If a cadet was not scheduled to fly he would be in ground school, drill, or involved in required athletics.

O.C.'s first letter home mentioned living in tar-paper barracks, which were ugly but well-built. It was much colder than it had been in Oklahoma.

Flying gear was issued, termed "swell" by the cadet. "They have about a half dozen zippers and pockets on the legs just above shoe tops."

"Our food isn't as good as it was at W&B," he continued. "But that can't be helped as we are now on field rations like the rest of the Service. But there is a movie house, bowling alley, gymnasium, and quite a few other things for the cadets on the post."

Coffeyville trained about 800 cadets, making it about twice as large as Chickasha. Mornings were spent in ground instruction, afternoons flying and "PT" (physical training). That kept them warm as winter set in.

BELOW LEFT CAAF in a period photo.

BELOW RIGHT O.C.'s rendition of the air field in his log book.

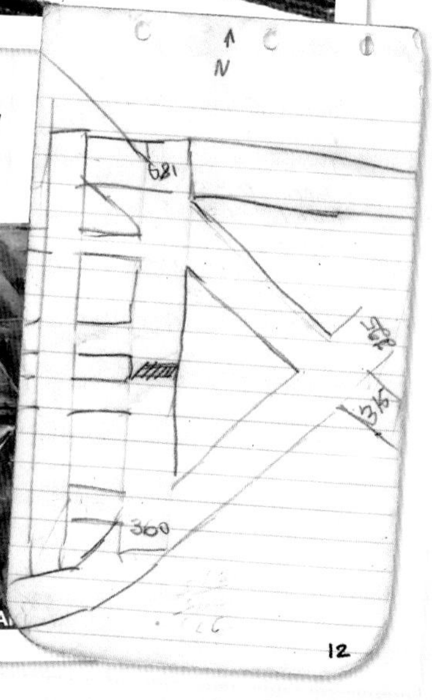

VULTEE BT-13A "VALIANT"

The Vultee BT-13 Valiant had a 450 hp radial engine and was faster and heavier than the AT-19. The flaps were operated by a crank-and-cable system. It was a good transition aircraft between primary and advanced trainers, but was not without its faults. The tail was secured by only three bolts and after several in-flight failures, the Navy prohibited aerobatic maneuvers in it. Before the end of the war, the Army replaced the BT-13 with the AT-6, which it closely resembles, though the BT-13 has fixed gear and those on the AT-6 retract.

It was nicknamed the "Vultee Vibrator" because (1) it had a tendency to shake violently as it approached stall speed, (2) during more adventurous maneuvers, the canopy also vibrated, (3) on takeoff, the aircraft caused windows on the ground to vibrate, and (4) the two-stage propeller had an irritating vibration at high pitch.

But it was heaven for O.C. "Our first time on the ramp today," he wrote, "and we learned the starting procedure. It sure is a swell ship. There are about a hundred things to remember but I think I know most of them already. The best thing is the starter: it's electric, so we don't have to crank it. Tomorrow we will go up for a ride and look over our area." Within a week he was doing stalls and spins with an instructor in the back seat. After ten hours he would solo. The Vibrator had twice as many controls as the PT-19: a variable-pitch prop, three flap positions, and a radio, "VD-59, this is 234. Radio check. Over."

Unfortunately, due to the time of year, cadets were often grounded because of bad weather and had to work hard to get the flight hours they needed.

After the War, virtually all Valiants were sold as surplus for a few hundred dollars each. Many were purchased for their engines, which were mounted on surplus biplanes such as Stearmans for use as crop dusters. The BT-13 airframes were then scrapped.

BOTTOM LEFT O.C. in his Valiant.

450hp. BASIC TRAN. 13-A

LOG BOOK & CHECKLIST

These log pages show progress amidst bad weather, numerous check rides, acrobatics training, and even some "bad flying" that O.C. notes himself on 16 October. But he loves flying so much he sometimes overstays and when he comes down, he gets a "star," which costs him 25¢ and an hour walking the ramp on guard duty. So far he's racked up 6 stars. Cross-country flights (more than 100 miles) have now been added. On 3 November he flies to Ft. Scott, northeast of Coffeyville, and the next day he flies to Nevada, Kansas.

The Checklist (below) contains flight instructions. O.C. mentions in letters home that they constantly practice "stages" (landings). Each airplane type has unique landing characteristics and lack of preparation for landing or care when you touch down can result in tearing off the landing gear, killing the pilot.

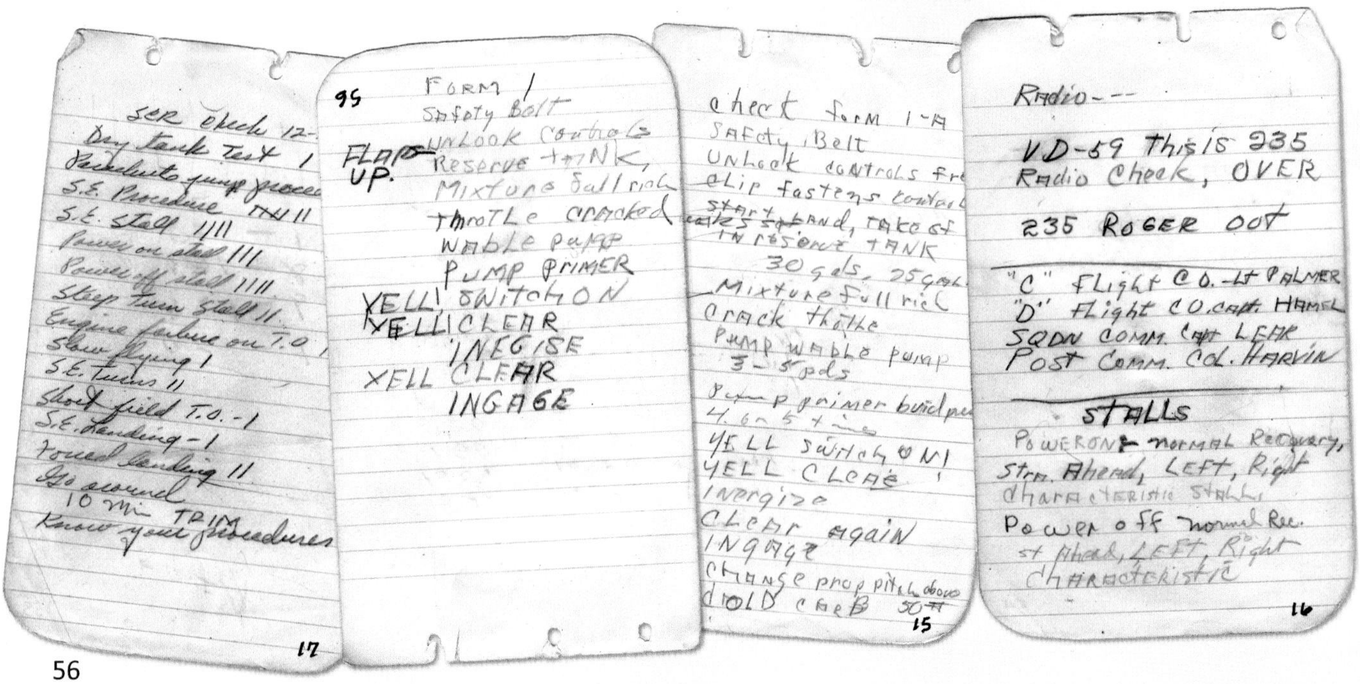
Radio---
VD-59 This is 235
Radio Check, OVER
235 ROGER OUT
"C" Flight C.O. Lt PALMER
"D" Flight C.O. Capt. HAMEL
SQDN COMM. Capt LEAR
Post Comm. Col. HARVIN
STALLS

EXTRA! **Pacific Post** EXTRA!

Section One | MONDAY, NOVEMBER 1, 1943 | Ten Cents

BLISTERING BOUGAINVILLE

"CARTWHEEL" OPERATION ROLLS ON WITH "CHERRY BLOSSOM"

BOUGAINVILLE, SOLOMON ISLANDS, Nov. 1 – In early 1942, Japan took the Solomon Islands to act as a choke-point that would interrupt American shipping to Australia.

At that time, Bougainville, named after the French explorer who identified the island in 1768, was lightly defended by about 20 Australian soldiers, who were evacuated when the Japanese came ashore in March 1942.

Alone with their prize, the Japanese built airfields in the north, east, and south, but none in the west of the 120 mile long island. They also dredged an anchorage at Tonolei Harbor near Buin and shipped in 65,000 defenders to hold the island.

On the nearby Treasury and Shortland Islands they built airfields, naval bases and anchorages. All these bases helped protect Rabaul, the major Japanese garrison and naval base near New Guinea, while allowing continued expansion to the southeast down the Solomon Islands chain to Guadalcanal.

After Guadalcanal was secured in February 1943, Bougainville was the next roadblock to be cleared. On 1 November, the 3rd Marines established a beachhead at Cape Tokorina.

At this time the Allies planned only to secure an area big enough to build an airfield

within range of Rabaul, 400 miles to the northwest.

The next day the Japanese fleet attacked the invasion force but lost the Battle of Empress Augusta Bay, just off Cape Tokorina.

A subsequent attempt by Japanese land forces to push the Allies into the sea was defeated in the Battle of Koromokina Lagoon.

To secure the airfield, the Marines struck inland, battling the enemy in fierce fighting including the Koiari Raid, Piva Trail, Coconut Grove, and Piva Forks engagements.

During November and December, Japanese artillery shelled the airfield at Tokorina, culminating in the battle for "Hellzapoppin' Ridge," a natural fortress overlooking the beachhead, which finally fell to the Marines on Christmas day.

For the next six months, the 3rd Marines concentrated on securing the airfield at Tokorina and encircling the Japanese land forces holding up in the interior of the island.

Endless jungle skirmishes, malaria, snipers, and incessant rain (regularly over 100 inches a year) took their toll on both sides. The Army relieved the Marines in December and defended against a major Japanese counterattack in March 1944 at Hill 700 and Cannon Hill, after which the Japanese withdrew to the deep interior of the island where they concentrated on survival.

Aiding the fight was the first black American combat unit, the 93rd Infantry Division. It was assisted by the Fiji Infantry Regiment.

In October 1944, a full year after the invasion, America handed Bougainville off to the Australian II Corps, who were tasked with defeating the Japanese holdouts.

The Aussies went to work, attempting to drive the Japanese—still numbering over 40,000 men—to a central point but did not obtain their ultimate surrender until 21 August 1945 following the nuclear bombing at Hiroshima and Nagasaki.

All in all, 516 Australians were killed and another 1,572 were wounded in the battle for Bougainville Island. 700 Americans were killed. 8,500 Japanese were killed while disease and malnutrition took another 9,800. 23,500 Japanese troops and slave laborers surrendered at the end of the War.

Three Victoria Crosses were awarded to two Aussies and a Fijian for outstanding bravery at Bougainville.

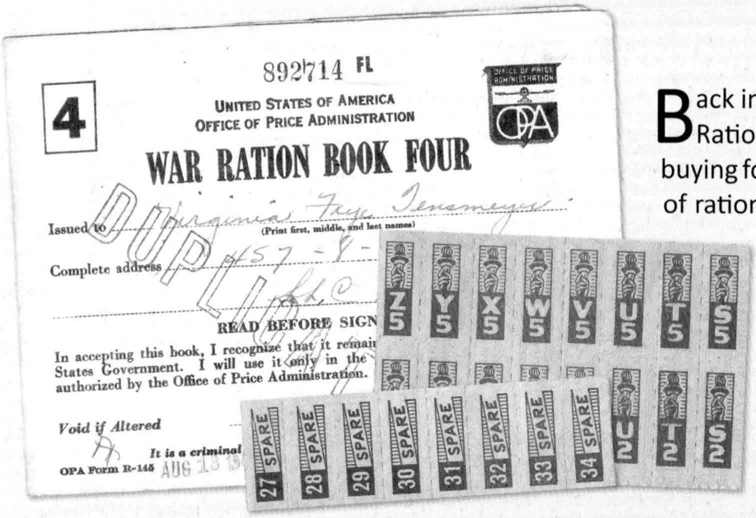

THE HOME FRONT

Back in San Diego, the War was on everyone's mind. Rationing made travel, entertainment, and even buying food difficult. In October 1943, the fourth series of ration books was issued, with stamps used to buy necessities as basic as sugar and gasoline. The book notes in bold type that defrauding a customer or a retailer was a criminal offense. Inside, the user was reminded that, "If prices go up your dollars buy less," and "Never pay more than OPA [Office of Price Administration] ceiling prices."

Like most people, the Kemps planted a "Victory Garden." Abbie reported growing chard, tomatoes, cucumbers, lettuce, and carrots, and canning fruit, vegetables, and jams. She also found time to work at Convair, which built the B-24 bomber, as a parts sorter.

O.C.'s friends still in high school tried to forget the War. The Hoover High football rivalry with powerhouse San Diego High looked like it might turn out different for once. With so many boys joining the service before finishing high school, Hoover had a diminished roster, but they still won their first game with La Jolla, 13-0.

O.C. wrote letters to friends, including several girls, three of whom wrote him regularly, often sending him copies of Hoover's *Cardinal* school newspaper in their letters, which mostly concerned who was "pinned" to whom, who had broken off their relationship, sports, mean teachers, the worthlessness of Latin, and movies.

LEFT One girl in particular, Marian Ingham, was dear to O.C., but since she was president of the Deb-Ettes girls club and quite popular, he figured she was just writing him as a friend. After receiving a picture of her, he wrote his mother, "I guess she is just about the most beautiful girl in the world to me just now. There I go again. What's the use?"

His buddies were all either in the service or eagerly awaiting being called up. Most San Diego boys joined the Navy or Marines, which both had their West Coast headquarters in San Diego County.

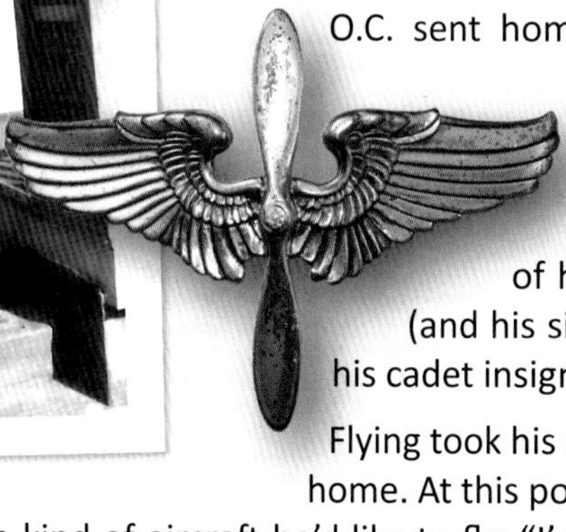

O.C. sent home photos of him proudly standing outside his tar-paper barracks. He also sent each of his female friends (and his sister) a replica of his cadet insignia (left).

Flying took his mind off girls and home. At this point, he was asked to start thinking about the kind of aircraft he'd like to fly. "I'm really debating whether I should ask for Twin Motor Advanced where I would fly a bomber or Single Engine Advanced where I would fly a fighter or pursuit P-38, P-40 or P-47. The more I think about it the more I think I would like to fly a fighter or P-38. I guess I still have that old speed bug in me left from my car driving."

EXTRA! **Pacific Post** EXTRA!

Section One | WEDNESDAY, NOVEMBER 24, 1943 | Ten Cents

GALVANIC: TERRIBLE TARAWA

MARINES BATTLE NATURE HERSELF TO WIN DECISIVE BATTLE

BETIO, TARAWA ATOLL, GILBERT ISLANDS, Nov. 24 – Though hard to believe, the tiny island at the left was the first massive stepping-stone toward Japan. But it came at a terrible cost.

After securing the Solomons, MacArthur and Nimitz both set out toward Japan: MacArthur's land troops heading up the north coast of New Guinea toward the Philippines and Nimitz island hopping to the east. The Gilbert Islands, 2,400 miles southwest of Hawaii, were Nimitz's first step. Then came the Marshalls, and finally the Marianas, from which long-range bombers could attack Japan and return safely.

But the Gilberts were first and the Tarawa atoll, located about halfway up the north-south island chain, was a tough nut to crack. After allowing Marines to storm ashore Guadalcanal without resistance, the Japanese determined to meet them on the beach next time, and so tiny, flat Betio island, less than two miles long and only 800 yards wide at its widest point, was, over the course of 1943, fortified with 500 cement pillboxes, four mighty 8" cannons, and 2,600 crack Imperial troops hunkered down in bunkers with 2 foot thick walls

After reconnaissance photos revealed this island fortress, Nimitz ordered up a force of 17 carriers, 90 ships, and 34 transports bearing 35,000 Marines of the 2nd Division.

For four hours before dawn on 20 November, the Navy began bombing the island. Dive bombers came next, followed by another shelling, and then at dawn the Marines entered the lagoon on Betio's north shore. Spirits were high: how could *anyone* survive a bombardment like that?

But Nature was on Japan's side. Though the attack had been scheduled for high tide, the planners did not reckon on the twice-monthly neap tide when the sun and moon stand at right angles to each other, cancelling out high tide and resulting in four foot shallows above the coral reef encircling the lagoon. Hung up on the reef, the Higgins landing boats stranded Marines hundreds of yards offshore, forcing them to slog to the beach in chest-deep water, easy pickings for the machine gun batteries on the shore.

If not for the "Alligator" tracked LTVs, which were able to climb over the reef, every one of the Marines in the lagoon would have been killed. As it was, we took 1,500 casualties the first day, most before our boys reached the narrow beach and took cover behind a palm log and cement seawall, where they still came under fire from a machine gun emplacement at the end of a long pier jutting out into the lagoon.

Fortunately, Japanese communication lines had been destroyed in the shelling and they were unable to mount a counter-attack that first day, which would have wiped out the 1,000 Marines clinging to life behind the seawall.

Day 2 saw the Marines push inward under heavy fire, dividing the defenders into two groups. One group attempted to escape to the islet to the east, but were beaten back in close fighting. By nightfall, the entire west end of Betio island was in American hands, but the fight was not yet over.

On Day 3 the 6th Marines landed on the west end of Betio to reinforce the 2nd. They skirted a pocket of defenders near the middle of the airport and pushed across the island, which by now was torn to pieces, nearly every tree shattered and torn bodies everywhere, floating in the lagoon and buried in beach sand. Burning tanks, acrid smoke rising from pillboxes cleaned out with flamethrowers, and constant explosions caused more than one Marine to think he'd landed not on an island paradise, but in hell itself.

Before dawn on Day 4, the Japanese made a desperate banzai charge. 300 perished in the ensuing artillery fusillade.

At the end of the day, only 3 Japanese surrendered—nearly 2,600 had fought to the death.

A movie crew accompanied the Marines ashore at Betio and the resulting short film *With the Marines at Tarawa* was so horrifying it took the President himself to okay its release. When Americans saw Marine bodies floating in the lagoon and torn apart on the beach, the perception of the Japanese soldier as an ignorant, myopic, buck-toothed midget was finally put to rest. And when the death toll of 3,300 Marine casualties was revealed shortly thereafter, many wondered why so many had died to take such a tiny piece of sand.

America finally realized that this enemy, driven by a fanatic belief that their emperor was God himself, would be incredibly difficult to defeat. And the Marshalls and Mariana Islands still lay ahead.

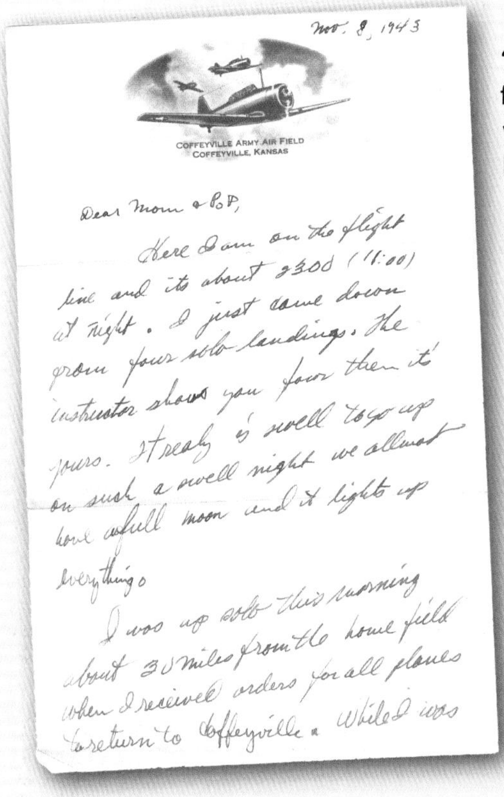
Nov. 8, 1943

COFFEYVILLE ARMY AIR FIELD
COFFEYVILLE, KANSAS

Dear Mom & Pop,

Here I am on the flight line and its about 2300 (11:00) at night. I just came down from four solo landings. The instructor shows you four then it's yours. It realy is swell to go up on such a swell night we allmost have a full moon and it lights up everything.

I was up solo this morning about 30 miles from the home field when I recieved orders for all planes to return to Coffeyville. While I was

NOW IT'S GETTING INTERESTING

"Here I am on the flight line and it's about 2300. I just came down from four solo landings. The instructor shows you four and then it's yours. It really is swell to go up on such a night with a full moon. It lights up everything.

"I was up soloing this morning about thirty miles from the home field when I received orders to return to Coffeyville. While I was out there a snow shower had moved in very fast on CAAF. I started back and fell in with a lot of other ships. The snow forced us down to about 100 feet, where we finally saw the field. The snow was thin and didn't hurt much except visibility.

"The weather cleared up so we are flying again tonight. I have to spend an hour or so in that freezing wind. It's cold with the canopy open while I'm in the traffic pattern and during landings and take-offs. I guess I won't get to bed till 1:00 and I have to get up at 8:00."

ABBIE THE RIVETER

There was plenty of stateside work for those who did not fight overseas. It seemed everyone was either in the service or making weapons for those who were.

When O.C. was still in high school, his mother Abbie got a job working for Consolidated Aircraft, building the B-24 Liberator bomber. She sorted parts and later worked as a filing clerk, which was easier on her back and legs than working the line had been.

In 1943, Abbie quit to be home for the summer with the younger kids, Gloria and Dean. When everyone went back to school in the fall, she got a job working for Ryan Aircraft, makers of the engine of the very plane O.C. was flying at Coffeyville. Though they initially promised her secretarial/guard duty, she got assigned another job she rather enjoyed.

"I am still plugging along in the tool crib," she wrote O.C. "I make band saws and extension drills. The drills are welded on a rod, then I sand them and anneal (temper) them. They will teach me how to sharpen drills before long. They're paying me 75¢ a hour, which comes in handy because the water heater at home just popped a leak."

MARCHING ORDERS

Ground school was finished. O.C. got his 65 hours of flying in. Instrument flying was getting less terrifying and more fun. And finally the orders came in: Twin engine school in Pampa, Texas.

"Dear Mom & Pop,

"We left CAAF at 1:30 and got as far as Wellington, Kansas. We got off the train for supper and marched through town to a church where the Red Cross women had the most wonderful dinner you could imagine. I guess the people here don't have many soldiers around because they all came out to see us marching down the street. We sang our songs like we always do when we march.

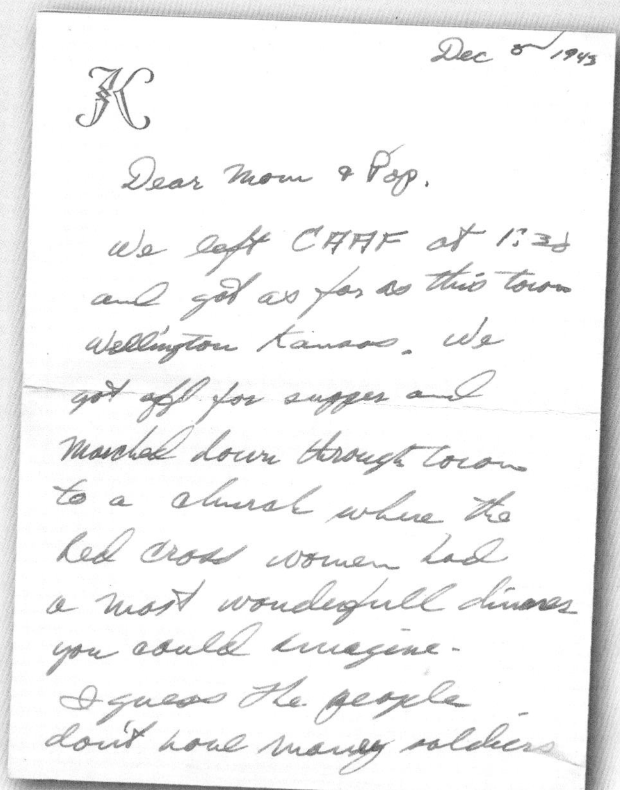
Dec 5/1943

K

Dear mom & Pop.

We left CAAF at 1:30 and got as far as this town Wellington Kansas. We got off for supper and marched down through town to a church where the Red Cross women had a most wonderfull dinner you could imagine. I guess the people don't have many soldiers

"After dinner, we had from 6:30 till 8:00 to walk around town and look in the store windows. This sure seems like a pleasure vacation 'cause we have never gotten off the train before. They gave us coffee and cookies. They really were good, too.

"We have Pullmans. Three of us to four seats. We flipped coins to see who would get the upper berth. I won, so here I am. We are still sitting on the siding so I don't know when we will start. I wish you would look up my leather rabbit fur gloves 'cause I'll really need them before long.

"The train just started so I guess we'll really have a nice cozy ride all night. All I can say is this is the best we have traveled as yet. They seem to treat us better as we get along in our training. The boys say we will order our uniforms a couple of weeks after we get to Advanced Training. Well, I guess that's all I can write because this train is jumping all over the place. Love, O.C."

THE HOME FRONT

Hoover High won its homecoming game against San Diego High, 7-3, even though a San Diego player caught a pass in the end zone at the last moment. The referees called it back—he was out of bounds when he caught the ball. Both sets of fans stormed onto the field. There was almost a fight but a dozen policemen came out onto the field and calmed things down.

O.C.'s dad took 6 year-old Dean to the game. Dean was astonished at how much toilet paper the older kids wasted throwing rolls onto the field. When he climbed over the low chain link fence to pick up a roll, a policeman told him to climb back and stay there. "Mama needed it," he said sadly, handing the roll to the cop.

O.C.'s 16 year-old sister Mavis had fun at the homecoming dance, though Chauncey Rogers, a young Marine she had met at a church dance a few months before and was informally engaged to, had shipped out a couple of weeks ago for parts unknown.

RIGHT Eddie Crain, (right) a teammate of O.C.'s, was the star running back on the 1943 Cardinal football team.

PHASE 4: ADVANCED TRAINING

4 December 1943 - 7 February 1944
Pampa Army Air Field
Pampa, Texas
1102nd Twin Engine Training Squadron
32nd Flying Training Wing
Army Air Forces Central
Training Command

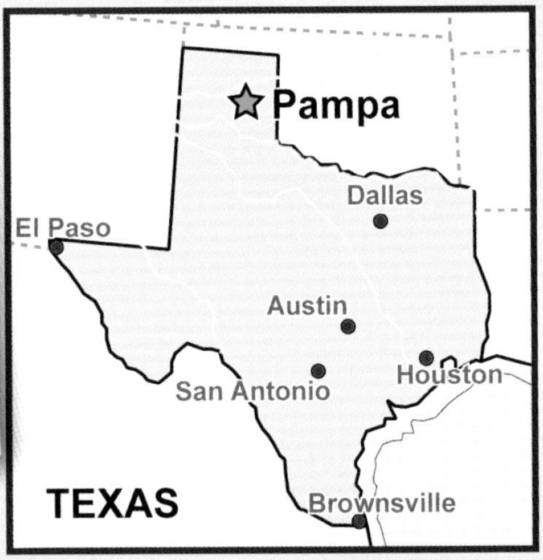

When it came right down to a choice, O.C. opted for multi-engine bombers because he felt that the lack of hearing in his left ear would be less of a deficit in an aircraft with a co-pilot. Up to this point he had told no one about his deafness, afraid if he did he would be washed out. He was determined to be a pilot.

The Army commenced construction on Pampa Army Airfield in June of 1942, building three concrete runways, several taxiways, a large parking apron, four large hangars, and a control tower. Most of the buildings sat on concrete foundations and had frame construction clad in little more than plywood and tar-paper. It was intended as a temporary installation, designed to last only for the duration of the War. The base opened for business just two months later on 3 August 1942.

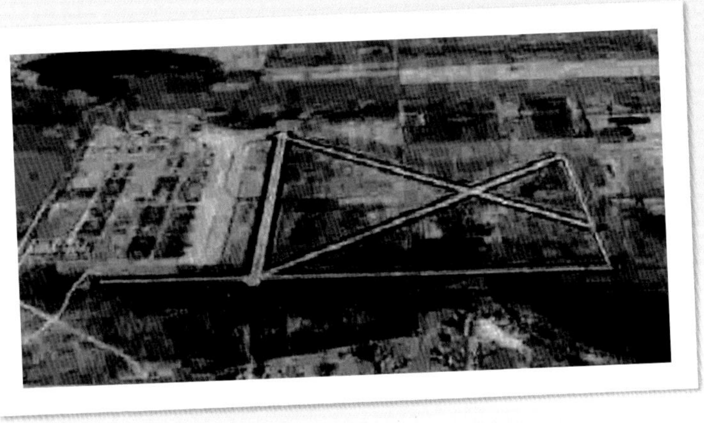

Known as the "Eagles' Nest of the High Plains," PAAF did twin-engine training in AT-10s, AT-9s, B-25s, and AT-17s.

WHO WANTS A WHITE CHRISTMAS?

In his first letter home after arriving, O.C. says, "We were issued those sheepskin flying suits with a hat and big shoes that fit right over GI shoes. We really do need them too because it really does blow around here.

"The officers are really strict but the mess is tops, all the milk you can drink and a very good menu. Our ground school sounds rather interesting: we are supposed to do all kinds of cross-country flights while we are here. I'll have an Army Air Force instrument rating when I graduate also, which would be really hard and expensive to get as a civilian. I figure the AAF has so far spent about $8,000.00 on making me a pilot.

"We have to watch when we land now 'cause we have to remember to put the wheels down. This plane [UC-78] is just like a real tactical combat bomber. When we graduate we will be able to start right in on B-24s or twin engine ships."

CESSNA AT-17 / UC-78 "BOBCAT"

The Cessna AT-17 Bobcat was used during WWII to bridge the gap between single-engine trainers and twin-engine combat aircraft and was a military version of the commercial Cessna T-50 light transport, a wood and tubular steel, fabric-covered, consumer aircraft. A low-wing cantilever monoplane, it featured retractable main landing gear and wing trailing-edge flaps, both electrically actuated. Because the wing structure was of laminated spruce spar beams with spruce and plywood ribs, it was dubbed the "Bamboo Bomber" by those who flew it.

In 1940, the Army Air Corps ordered 33 Bobcats under the designation AT-8 as multi-engine advanced trainers. The designation changed to the AT-17 with the change of engines. Finally, the Bobcats delivered after 1 January 1943 were designated UC-78s.

By the end of the War, Cessna had produced more than 4,600 Bobcats, but the aircraft did not last long after the War and few Bobcats were in service when the U.S. Air Force was formed in September 1947.

After the War, surplus UC-78s were used by small airlines, charter companies, bush operators, and private pilots, but by the 1970s they were obsolete because of the maintenance their aging wood wing structures and fabric covering required. FAA records show 378 T-50s, 10 AT-17s and 30 UC-78s still registered today—but that does not mean they are airworthy or even existent.

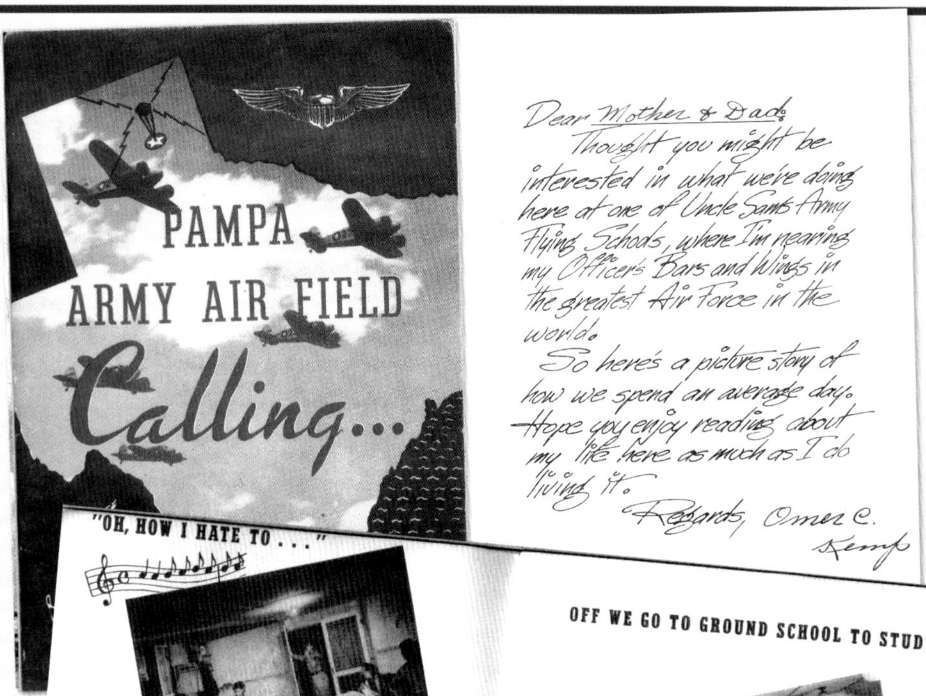

PAMPA
ARMY AIR FIELD
Calling...
Dear Mother & Dad,
Thought you might be interested in what we're doing here at one of Uncle Sam's Army Flying Schools, where I'm nearing my Officer's Bars and Wings in the greatest Air Force in the world.
So here's a picture story of how we spend an average day. Hope you enjoy reading about my life here as much as I do living it.
Regards, Omer C. Kemp

"OH, HOW I HATE TO . . ."
. . . AT 5:30 A. M.
We whack the whiskers every morning . . . inspection's tough!
But this morning chow is great!
OFF WE GO TO GROUND SCHOOL TO STUDY
AIRCRAFT IDENTIFICATION

TWO BIRDS . . .

Upon arrival at Pampa Army Air Field, each cadet received an orientation pamphlet that, once he had read it, he was supposed to sign and send home to his folks.

The pamphlet lays out a typical day of a student pilot, beginning at 5:30 a.m: shaving—whether they need it or not—then mess, then classes in flight theory and lessons in identifying enemy aircraft.

But along with all the hard work, both mental and physical, the cadets were occasionally granted "time for a Coke and a smoke" during breaks.

All across the country, thousands of young men are training at similar installations. The cadets in these pictures will go on to fly the bombers: B-17s, B-24s, and B-25s.

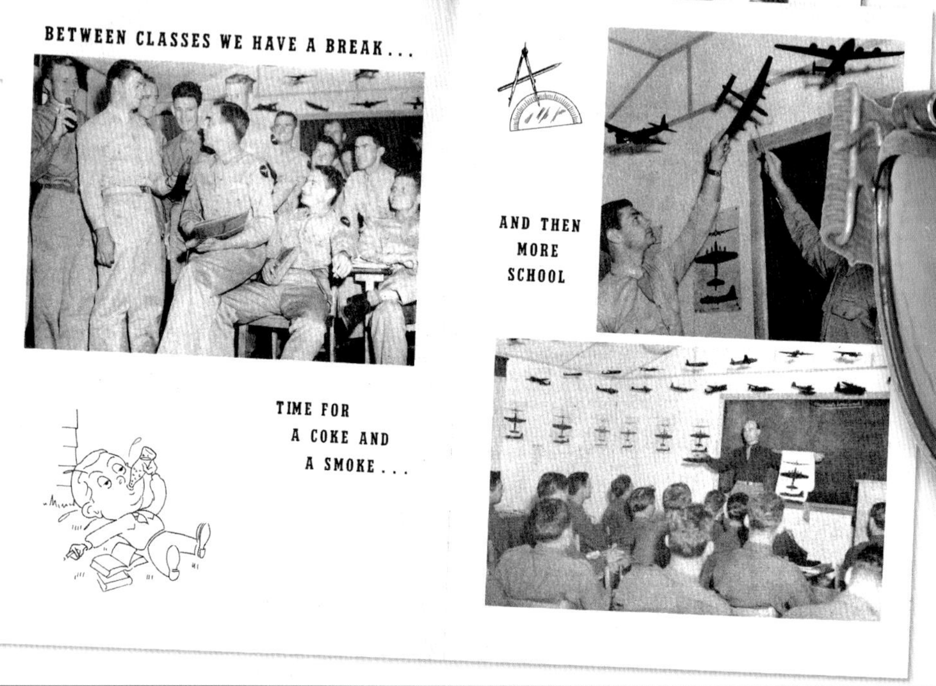

. . . WITH ONE STONE

Sports and drilling in the Texas sun burned the men brown and toughened their resolve.

When they weren't tempting fate in the sky, they were on the ground hardening their bodies and minds for combat.

As noted, the purpose of this phase of training was to transition the student from single-engine aircraft to multi-engine in preparation for bomber training.

These new high-performance dual-engine airplanes were quite a handful and it was easy, if the pilot wasn't careful, for these fast planes to "get ahead" of him, a real problem on landing approaches.

THIS PART OF THE DAY IS *Fun!*

The Air Forces require healthy, hardened pilots . . . our "P. T." instructors, plus the Texas sun, have us in tip-top shape.

. . . AFTER A MORNING LIKE THAT, WE'RE READY TO EAT AGAIN!

We may be student pilots, but this is still the Army! Drill and parades are an important part of our day!

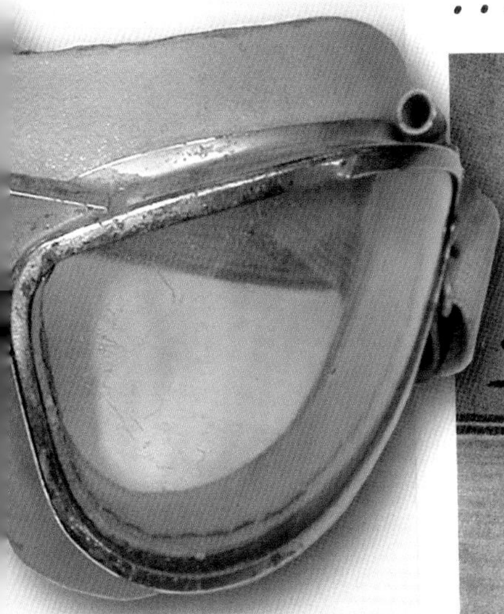

. . . And Off We Go!

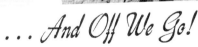

THIS FORMATION FLYING IS THE STUFF . . .

. . . And we get it night and day!

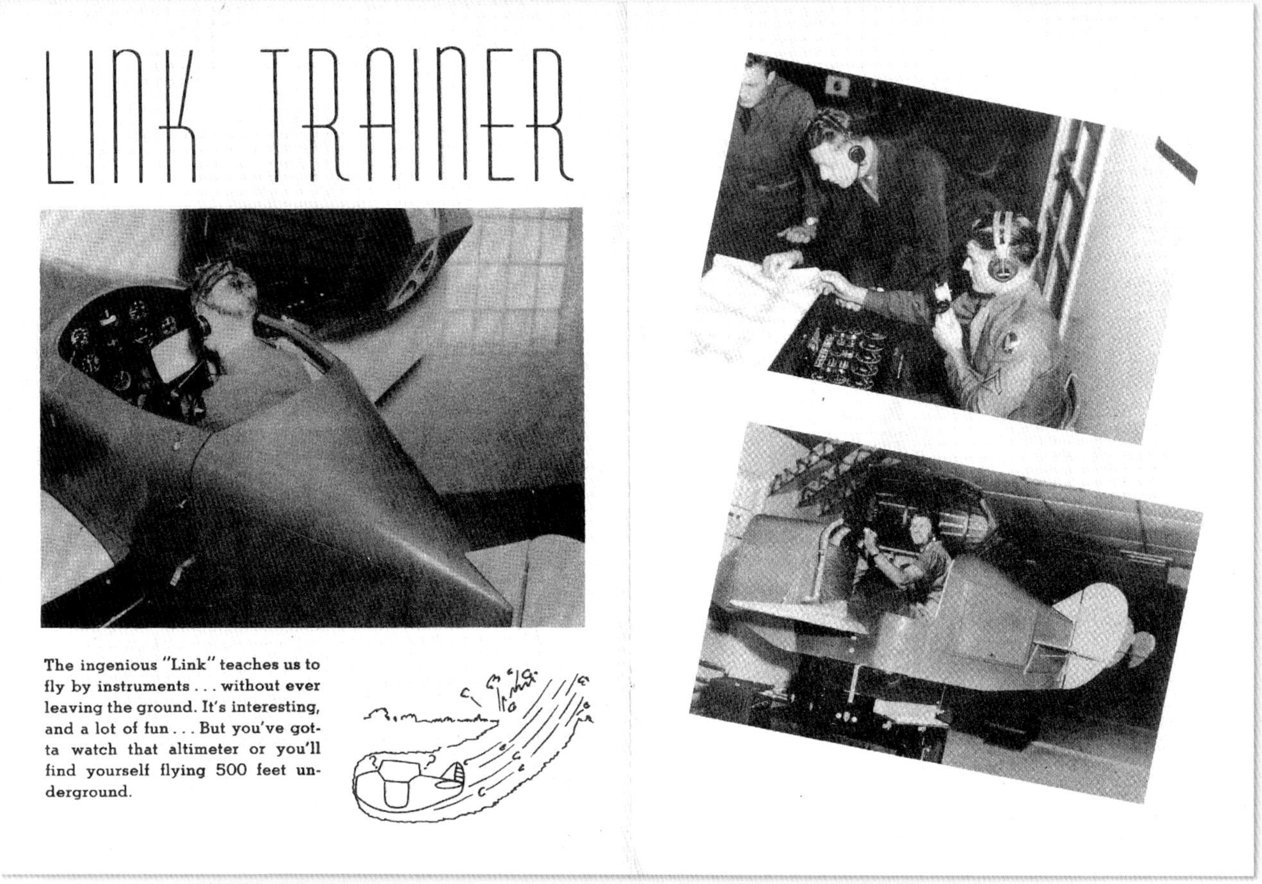

LINK TRAINER

The ingenious "Link" teaches us to fly by instruments . . . without ever leaving the ground. It's interesting, and a lot of fun . . . But you've got-ta watch that altimeter or you'll find yourself flying 500 feet un-derground.

THE WORLD'S FIRST FLIGHT SIMULATOR

The Link Trainer was invented by Ed Link in 1929, based on technology his family used in their organ and nickelodeon manufacturing business. The flight simulator consisted of a wooden cockpit box connected to a base with a universal joint. The cockpit contained a pilot's seat, aircraft controls, and a full suite of flight instruments. Three sets of bellows controlled the pitch, yaw, and roll planes. An electrical slip ring on the universal joint allowed the simulator to turn in a continuous 360 degree circle, modeling common flight conditions such as pre-stall buffeting and spins. It also had an opaque canopy, which when lowered simulated blind flying and was particularly useful for instrument and navigation training.

A nearby instructor's station had a large map table, a repeated instrument display, and a moving marker known as a "crab." The crab moved across the glass surface of the map table, plotting the pilot's track. The pilot and instructor communicated via headphones.

Link's first military sales came as a result of a tragedy when twelve U.S. Air Mail pilots were killed in a 78 day period due to their unfamiliarity with instrument flying conditions. The Air Corps looked at a number of solutions, including Link's trainer. Link himself gave them a convincing demonstration of instrument flight when, in 1934, he flew to a meeting in foggy conditions that the Air Corps evaluation team regarded as unflyable. As a result, the Air Corps ordered six Link Trainers at the then astronomical cost of $3,500 each.

More than half a million Allied pilots were trained on Link simulators. Unfortunately, Japan and Germany also had Link trainers which they had obtained before the War.

The Link Company, now the Link Simulation & Training division of L-3 Communications, continues to make aerospace simulators.

CURTIS-WRIGHT AT-9 "JEEP"

The AT-9 was a low-wing cantilever monoplane with retractable landing gear powered by two Lycoming R-680-9 radial engines. It had a maximum speed of 200 knots and was termed a "hot" trainer, because, as a trainee quipped, "It took off at 120 mph, flew at 120 mph and landed at 120 mph!"

The first prototype flew in 1941 and the production version entered service in 1942. The prototype had a fabric-covered steel tube fuselage, wings, and tail, but production models were of stressed metal skin construction. The AT-9 was purposely designed to be difficult to fly, which made it particularly useful for teaching new pilots to cope with the demanding flight characteristics of high-performance multi-engine aircraft such as the B-26 Marauder and the P-38 Lightning.

AT-9 production lasted just two years. A total of almost 800 were built before fabrication ended. Because of its difficult flying characteristics, the AT-9 was not offered for sale to civilians after the war, although many non-flying examples were given to ground schools for training purposes.

Only two AT-9s survive today.

IT'S COLD ON THE GROUND, TOO

By now O.C.'s getting the feel of bigger aircraft with multiple engines (and individual controls and gauges for each one) and having his instructor sit at his side but still figuratively looking over his shoulder.

CENTER RIGHT Winter is here and O.C. is outfitted in his sheepskin-lined hat, jacket, and boots, posing with his flight plan before his UC-78 in this poorly-focused photo.

LEFT O.C.'s bomber jacket. You'll note it's not the one in the picture below; the jackets they wore in Pampa stayed behind for the next class of cadets to use. O.C.'s cold weather flight suit is in remarkable condition, considering the wear and tear it got in the War, as well as the 70 years since. He often wore it while working on his family's cars.

BELOW CENTER Detail of the insignia on the left thigh pant leg. Note also the detail of the trousers: a myriad of pockets and clasps against the cold.

BELOW RIGHT His boots were also wool-lined with leather uppers, which did not fare well over the ensuing years.

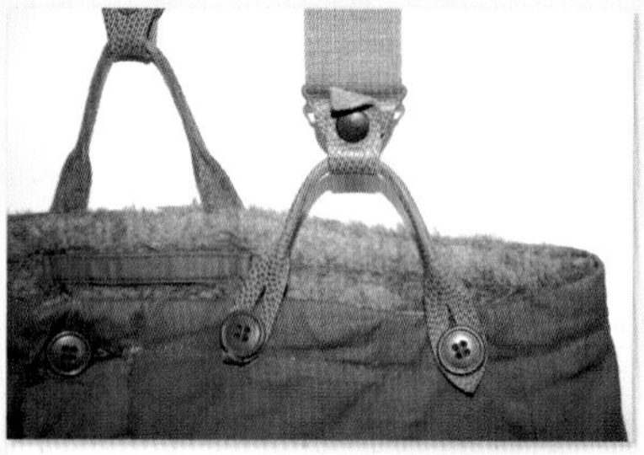

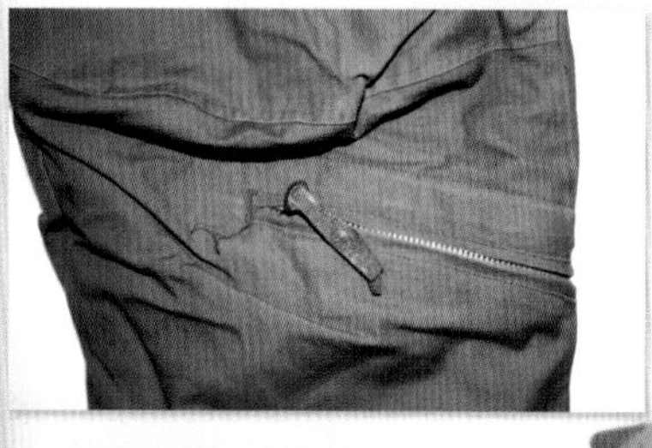

(ALMOST) LIKE HOME

All through November, everyone at home was asking if O.C. would be home for Christmas. He knew better. The Army had him till early February and they weren't going to give him up for any old holiday.

He was studying hard and flying in between Texan panhandle snowstorms, which he called "real blowers."

He got a dozen or so cards from family and the girls he was writing, even from his crush, the inscrutable Marian Ingham. His cousin Jack Kemp, in San Antonio at the SAACC, wrote that he had just finished classification and had been rated a pilot as O.C. had been a few months earlier. "I was lucky," said Jack. "Over 40% of the guys in my group got GDOs." ("Ground Duty Only")

But Christmas in Texas wasn't so bad. The base had a dance, complete with a formal invite (right), and O.C. wrote home:

THE WILCO CLUB

Cordially invites you to attend a dance
in honor of Class 44-B

Saturday, December 18, 1943
9:00 p. m.

Recreation Building
Pampa Army Air Field

Pampa, Texas

"I went to Amarillo on Christmas afternoon and stayed at the USO. While I was hanging around, a lady asked me if I wanted to go to dinner. So I took off for that. It really was swell and I don't mean maybe.

"I got up Sunday and went over to the LDS church. There were about ten members there and of course someone asked me over for dinner afterwards. On top of all that I had a wonderful dinner on Christmas day at the field. All in all, I had a pretty nice Christmas."

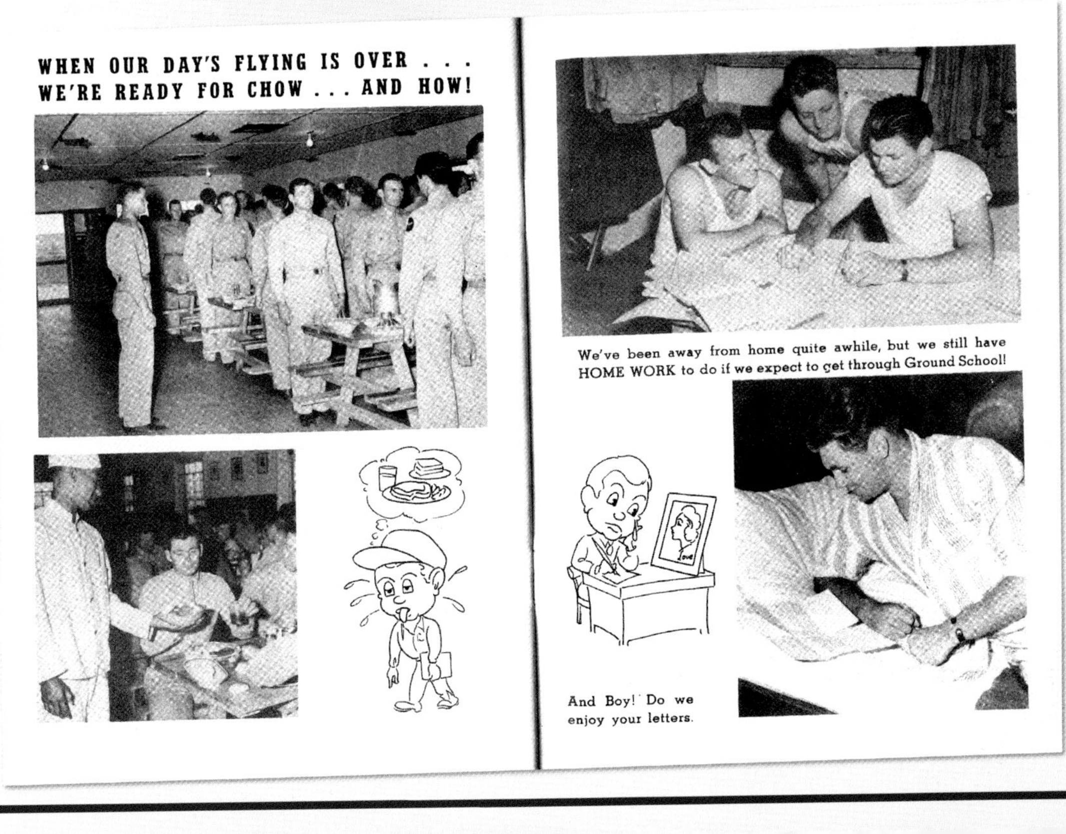

WHEN OUR DAY'S FLYING IS OVER . . .
WE'RE READY FOR CHOW . . . AND HOW!
We've been away from home quite awhile, but we still have HOME WORK to do if we expect to get through Ground School!
And Boy! Do we enjoy your letters.

LEFT Imagine: flight training four hours a day, drilling on the ground in January, gorging on the carb-rich Army chow, ground school, homework, and finally, at the end of a day, mail call and a letter or two to be written.

EXTRA! **Pacific Post** EXTRA!

Section One TUESDAY, FEBRUARY 1, 1944 Ten Cents

HELLFIRE AND HAILSTONE

THIS WAR IS JUST ONE DAMN ISLAND AFTER ANOTHER

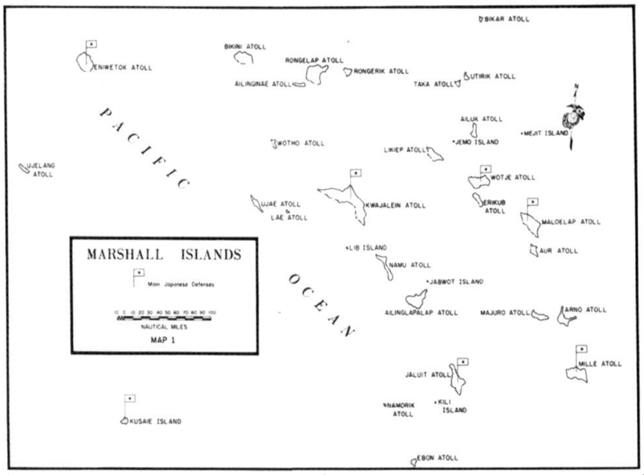

KWAJALEIN ATOLL

MARSHALL ISLANDS, Feb. 1 – The Marshalls, located halfway between Hawaii and Japan, were our next Pacific goal. They had been mandated to Japan after WWI, but had been illegally fortified and were being used as forward bases for attacks on American vessels and holdings.

Admiral Masashi Kobayashi had 28,000 men to defend the chain, but he was still undermanned. Less than half the 8,000 defenders on the Kwajalein atoll were combat-trained soldiers, and many were reluctant Korean forced laborers.

The lessons of Tarawa—that the Japs needed a pounding before ground forces went ashore—meant that the 7th Air Force's B-24 Liberator bombers would be called on to do the pounding.

Because until Tarawa the Japs did not know our amphibious vehicles could cross coral reefs and land on the lagoon side of an atoll, their strongest defenses faced the open ocean.

And because Kwajalein is so small—just 2.5 miles long and 880 yards wide—they had to meet their attackers on the beach.

On 31 January, neighboring islands around Kwajalein were captured to be used as artillery bases for the next day's assault. Then the bombardment by battleships, B-24 bombers from Apamama in the Gilberts, and artillery began devastating the island. "It looked as if it had been picked up 20,000 feet and then dropped," said one soldier.

By the time the 7th Division went ashore there was little resistance. By nightfall it was estimated that only 1,500 of the defenders were still alive.

The victory at Kwajalein was significant: for the first time, we had fought the Japs on their own soil.

TRUK ATOLL

TRUK ATOLL, Feb. 16 – Known as the "Gibraltar of the Pacific," the 30 by 40 mile Truk lagoon lies north of New Guinea and is Japan's main base in the South Pacific. It boasts five airstrips, seaplane bases, a torpedo boat station, submarine repair docks, and a radar station. In short, Truk atoll is the Japanese equivalent of Pearl Harbor and the attack thereon was our chance to repay Admiral Yamamoto's kindness.

Because the atoll is the only major Japanese airbase within range of the Marshall Islands and is a significant source of support for Japanese garrisons located on islands and atolls throughout the Central and South Pacific, it is the focus of Operation Hailstone.

Before dawn on 15 February, nine carriers launching more than 500 aircraft, as well as seven battleships and numerous cruisers, destroyers, submarines, and other support ships attacked islands inside Truk atoll, sinking 60 ships and destroying 250 aircraft, most on the ground.

However, like the Americans at Pearl Harbor, luck favored the Japanese: fearing the base was becoming too vulnerable, the Japs had already relocated their carriers, battleships, and heavy cruisers to the Palau Islands a week earlier.

Nevertheless, the three days of bombardment resulted in the wholesale destruction of Japan's most important South Pacific base and made Truk lagoon the biggest ship graveyard in the world.

ENIWETOK ATOLL

MARSHALL ISLANDS, Feb. 17 – The heart-shaped atoll of Eniwetok, northeast of Kwajalein, was being used by the Japs as a refueling station for air sorties launched from Truk. It was also their regional command post and thus it had to go.

After the fall of the Gilberts, the Japs reinforced the atoll with 2,500 soldiers, most billeted on the northern Engebi islet, near the airstrip.

As a part of Operation Hailstone, all supplies and reinforcements to the atoll were cut off. The 22nd Marine regiment landed on Engebi the next day. Resistance was light, and the island was secured within six hours.

But because captured documents indicated that defenses on Eniwetok island would be light, pre-landing bombardment of only a limited nature took place and when the 106th Infantry Regiment went ashore, they were met with withering automatic fire.

The island was not secured until 21 February at the cost of 37 Americans lives. 800 Japanese defenders died.

NOT WHETHER, BUT WEATHER

January on the Great Plains is, well, just as you'd imagine it: horizontal freezing rain or snow. Endless gray skies and socked-in, foggy airports. January 1944 was the worst winter they'd had in fifty years, and O.C. and the other cadets didn't get much flying in.

"We've had quite a bit of lousy weather," he wrote home. "And we are quite a bit behind on our flying. We have a lot of cross-country flying to do and the weather changes so fast that we've arrived at way points only to find we can't even find them for the clouds. But we're getting a lot of practice flying on instruments."

EENIE, MEENIE . . .

You'll recall that O.C. was in a quandary about what kind of aircraft he wanted to fly: single or multiple engines. His arrival at Pampa seemingly put that question to rest, but he still muses about the options in a letter home: "I want to fly B-24s to experience four engines, but I sure would like to fly a P-38!

"In a couple of days we're flying down to San Antonio to take our altitude test. They take us up to 30,000 feet for three hours and if we don't get sick, we're cleared for the big bombers like the 24 or the 17. We wear oxygen masks, of course, but some men still get sick. If I don't do well (who knows?), then I'd like to fly the B-26."

NO GOLD FEVER HERE

As he neared the end of his training, O.C. had to fork out $150.00 for his dress uniform, including $65.00 for a trench coat and $45.00 for his "blouse," or dress coat. His hat was only $6.00.

In addition, there was some discussion among the cadets about who would be chosen as flight officers. Eighteen men in the previous class received the honor. "The only difference is the bars they wear," wrote O.C. "The flight officer has a blue stone bordered by a gold band. I sure hope I don't get flight officer after all this time wanting to be a lieutenant. The pay is the same but it's more work and I don't know if I can *do* any more work than I'm already doing."

O.C. was training to be a pilot and would be one even if he wasn't chosen as a flight officer, who were airmen who often served as a squadron leader or assistant squadron leader or in some other detail.

FROM ONE OFFICER TO ANOTHER . . .

Oscar Lewis, a high school buddy, was a plane captain on a ground crew at an advanced flying naval base in Florida. His job was shepherding the Navy's carrier-based Wildcat fighters to and from their parking areas and overseeing maintenance and gassing up.

"If I go out for it," Oscar wrote, "I can get a Third Class rating. You'll come out a 2nd Louie, isn't that right? You' be sitting on top of the world then. You'll feel just like President Roosevelt.

"But I'll be damned if I salute you! Ha Ha!"

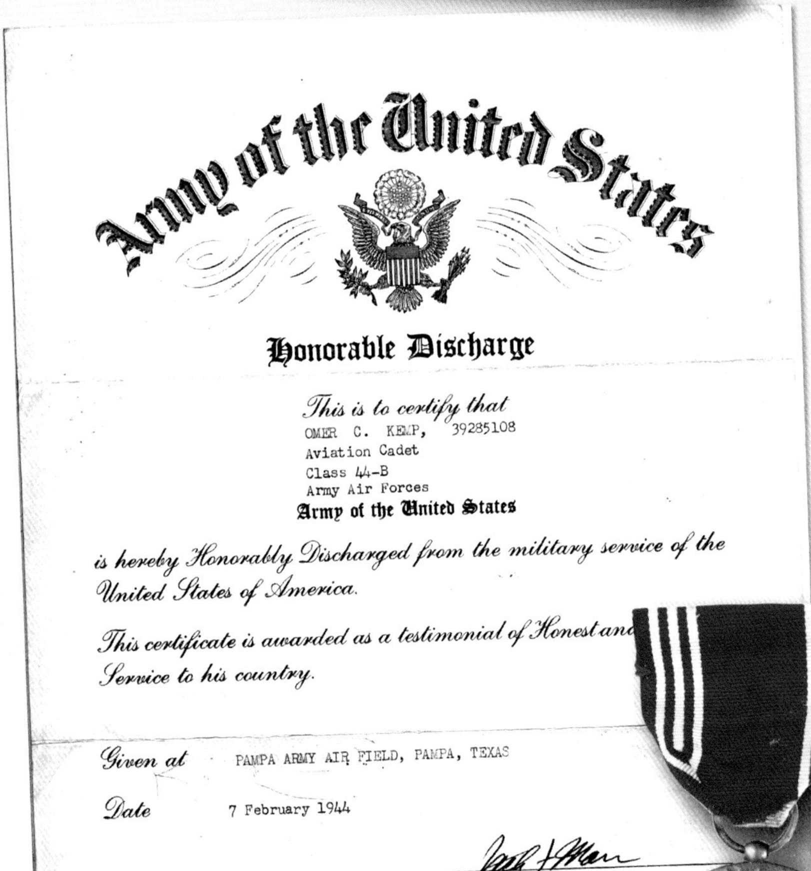

Army of the United States

Honorable Discharge

This is to certify that
OMER C. KEMP, 39285108
Aviation Cadet
Class 44-B
Army Air Forces
Army of the United States

is hereby Honorably Discharged from the military service of the United States of America.

This certificate is awarded as a testimonial of Honest anc
Service to his country.

Given at PAMPA ARMY AIR FIELD, PAMPA, TEXAS

Date 7 February 1944

JACK F. MARR,
Major, Air Corps,
Director of Training.

W. D., A. G. O. Form No. 55
January 22, 1943

ANOTHER ANNUAL

Just like Chickasha, Pampa Army Air Field published a yearbook,which it dubbed *The Gig Sheet*. A "gig" is a demerit, something you get when you fail to perform an aeronautical maneuver to the instructor's satisfaction.

WELCOME BACK, SIR

No, he didn't wash out. This Honorable Discharge is merely the way the Army celebrated O.C.'s graduation from aviation cadet to commissioned officer.

On 7 February 1944, O.C. was discharged from the Army and then immediately commissioned as a second lieutenant in the Army Air Force. And, much to his relief, he was *not* chosen as a flight officer.

LEFT By order of the President, every man in the Army who had served one year after Pearl Harbor with a good record received the Good Conduct Medal. O.C.'s one year anniversary coincided with his receiving his wings and accepting an officer's commission in the Army Air Force.

A PRAYER GOT HIM WINGS

We still have O.C.'s dress officer's uniform and cap as well as several of his wings, most of which were in poor condition prior to cleaning but which when restored to their original luster are as impressive now as they were the day he donned them. The cap is in remarkable condition—not a scratch on it.

The uniform is made of 100% wool and a testament to the longevity of this heavy woolen fabric. It was exceptionally well made, and new officers understandably took great pride in wearing it.

As well they should. It cost, as they said back then, "a pretty penny."

A second lieutenant in the Army Air Corps was usually a flight commander or assistant flight commander.

Because of the inexperience of the newly-commissioned officers, called "second Louies," enlisted men often called them "butterbars," for obvious reasons.

R E S T R I C T E D

SPECIAL ORDERS)
:
NO. 34)

HEADQUARTERS PAMPA ARMY AIR FIELD

Pampa, Texas, 8 February 1944

E X T R A C T

3. DP each of the following named Offs (Race: White), having this date been aptd 2D LTS, AUS, and having graduated from Two Engine Advanced Flying (Pilot) Course, this sta, and rated Pilot, is ordered to EAD at this sta, effective 8 Feb 45, and is atchd unasgd to 1102nd TE Flying Tng Sq. Each Off will rank from 8 Feb 44 and is asgd to dy with the AC:

KEMP, OMER C. 0710957

9. The following named Offs and Flt Offs, AC (Type Tng Recd TE) are reld from attachment unasgd to 1102 TE Flying Tng Sq and are asgd to Liberal AA Fld, Liberal, Kansas, and will depart so as to arrive not later than 20 Feb 44, for B-24 Transition Tng Course, Cl 44-4-B, of 9 weeks duration, beginning 21 Feb 44:

KEMP, OMER C. 0710957

Above named Offs are atzd a 11 day delay enroute. TDN TPA 1-5250 P 431-01, 02, 03, 08, A 0425-24. (Auth: Tg, P-1516B, AAFCFTC, RF, Tex, 6 Feb 44.)

By order of Col CAMPBELL:

RICHARD A. FAUST
1st Lt., AGT
Asst Adjutant

TRANSFER ORDERS

O.C. has now graduated from Two Engine Advanced Flying at Pampa and has been assigned to Liberal Army Air Field in Kansas, ordered to arrive no later than 20 February 1944 for B-24 Transition training. During its three years of operation, Pampa Army Airfield graduated 6,292 cadets, trained 3,500 aircraft mechanics, and had one of the best safety records in the United States Training Command. Flight training ended at Pampa on 28 December 1944. The installation remained on inactive status until 1948 and was declared "excess" in 1955 and scheduled for divestment by the Army. In 1957 the last tract of land was sold to agricultural interests. As of 2012, the site is a dairy.

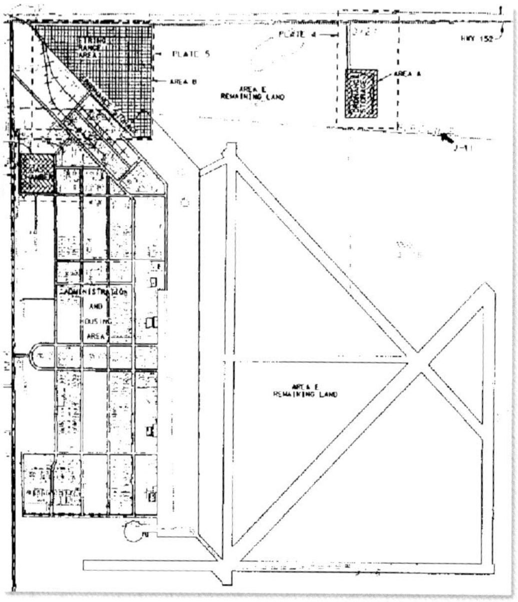

BOTTOM RIGHT
In this 1996 photo, the ramp and housing areas at Pampa are still clearly seen on the left, but if you look carefully, you can see the outlines of the old runways out in the fields.

DUTY ON THE HOME FRONT

He intended to waste no time getting home. The TWA $65.00 air fare was a lot of money—two weeks' pay, but as opposed to several days on a bus each way, it was worth it. O.C. had been good about his money thus far; his father had commended him for it, using a good portion of the money the young trainee sent home to buy War Bonds.

Just before graduation, O.C. went down to the Army clothier and got fitted for his officer's uniform, including the coveted "pinks," dress shirts that only officers were allowed to wear. The Army allotted them $100.00 for the uniform, but it wasn't enough; he had to buy the extras (hats, bars, wings) himself. But it was no imposition.

Before leaving, the Army issued him a B-4 soft luggage bag, winter flying gloves, goggles, summer and winter flying helmets, a 24-foot seat-type parachute, winter flying shoes, and a summer flying suit. He was reminded that he was responsible for these items "for the Duration." The parachute came with Form 46, a Historical Record Card, which traced the life, use, and ongoing condition of the chute.

He graduated 8 February 1944. Due to the poor weather of the previous months he was still making up flying hours two days before the ceremony.

ABOVE LEFT This brochure mailed to O.C. from Amarillo contains every one of TWA's daily national flights in 1945. There were so few that in addition to numbers, flights had names like "Sky Chief," "Night Hawk," and "Sun Pacer." Passengers were asked not to "take two when one would do," referring to luggage, freeing precious space for wartime cargo.

BELOW O.C.'s pay stub covering 2.5 months, with $300.00 mustering out pay, which, if not counted, means his pay as an Army Air Force pilot is about $100.00 per month. Notice where he sends the payment.

WAR DEPARTMENT

PAY AND ALLOWANCE ACCOUNT

(Commissioned Officers, Army Nurses, Warrant Officers, Contract Surgeons)

	Amount
CREDITS:	
(16) Base and longevity pay from 1 Oct, 19 43, to 12 Dec, 19 43	$ 360.00
(18) Flying, aeronautical, rating from 27 Nov, 19 43	67.50
(21) Mustering out from 12 Dec, 19 43, to 12 Feb, 19 44	300.00
(24) Subsistence from 1 Oct, 19 43, to 12 Dec, 19 43	51.10
(25) Rental from 29 Oct, 19 43, to 12 Dec, 19 43	66.00
(26) Travel, mileage status from 24 Oct, 19 43, to 28 Oct, 19 43	40.28
TOTAL CREDITS	$ 884.88
DEBITS:	
(32) Class "E" Allotment from 1 Oct, 19 43, to 31 Oct, 19 43	$ 150.00
(33) Class "N" Nat'l serv. life insurance from 1 Oct, 19 43, to 12 Dec, 19 43	19.50
(23) Partial Payment 10/28	80.00
TOTAL DEBITS	$ 249.50
NET BALANCE	$ 635.38

(44) Mail check(s) to me at the following address: 4766 Winona, San Diego, Calif.

R & R

9 - 19 February 1944
Omer & Abbie Kemp home
4766 Winona Street
San Diego, California

He's been gone almost a year and great changes have occurred in his life: he went from the Army at Camp Swift, Texas to the Aviation Cadets at San Antonio, on to Chickasha, Oklahoma, then to Coffeyville, Kansas, then back to Texas at Pampa, where he got the wings he proudly displays in this series of photos.

BELOW O.C. poses with his parents, Omer and Abbie Kemp, and his siblings Gloria (13), Dean (7), and Mavis (16) in front of their home. Mavis is tickled to see her brother in his uniform but is also sad. Her beloved Chauncey was fighting somewhere in the Pacific with the 1st Marine Division. She wrote him every day and gushed about him in her letters to O.C. "I know we're young, but I also know I could never love anyone as much as I love him. I miss him terribly." (PFC Rogers was prohibited from telling Mavis his location, but during this time he was fighting in the Battle of Cape Gloucester on New Britain Island in the Solomon chain.)

AUDIO TRANSCRIPT 06:00:00

I got to San Diego and the neighborhood just couldn't believe it was me, because I had been gone since March of '43, not even a year, and here I was walking in the house with lieutenant's bars and wings and a pilot! And the neighborhood and even the church people knew me and they just couldn't believe it. My folks were really busting their vests, they were so puffed up over it.

LET THE WOLVES HOWL!

ABOVE Well, this wolf is really a wolf-cub: a young man who was too shy to ask Marian Ingham if she had time to see him when he got home. And yet Marian wondered aloud to O.C.'s sister Mavis if he was going to look her up when he got to San Diego. Of course, O.C. was hopelessly enamored of Marian, but she was a bright star at Hoover High and far too popular to go steady, especially with an absent serviceman.

BELOW LEFT AND CENTER O.C. was also close friends with Verna Taylor, who wrote him regularly, gradually warming from signing off "Sincerely" to "Love, Verna." That's O.C.'s letterman sweater she's wearing.

BELOW RIGHT But in the end, O.C. was still a lone wolf, as seen in the photo at bottom right, on the sidewalks of downtown San Diego.

TRANSITION SCHOOL: 4-ENGINE

20 February - 18 May 1944
Liberal Army Air Field
Liberal, Kansas
527th Bomber HQ
32nd Flying Training Wing
II Bomber Command - 2nd Army Air Force

Liberal Army Air Field (LAAF) was a 2,000 acre development one mile west of Liberal, Kansas. It was completed by the 2nd Air Force just eight months before O.C. and his fellow Class 44-B pilots arrived. Its mission was to turn newly-commissioned officers into B-24 Liberator heavy bomber pilots. The training cycle was nine weeks, with a new class entering as its predecessor was halfway through training. LAAF trained about one-quarter of all U.S. B-24 pilots.

In his first letter home after arriving at LAAF, O.C. said, "I came out onto the field, which was quite a disappointment. There is such a hold-up that the previous class is just getting started on their flying.

"They send up seven planes at a time here. In other words, if I get any time in the pilot's seat during the first month it will be a wonder. The good part is we've been all over one of these bombers and it really is a lot of airplane."

After victory in Europe in May 1945, the training program at LAAF became erratic because of the frequent changes in Training Command policies. However, with the surrender of the Japanese in August 1945, the mission of the school was over. LAAF went on stand-by status because the B-24 was obsolete, eclipsed by the B-29 Superfortress long-range strategic bomber.

ABOVE LEFT Emblem of the 2nd Air Force.

BELOW LEFT LAAF during the War. Variable winds made three runways necessary.

BELOW RIGHT 1996 photo of Liberal Municipal Airport,location of the Mid-America Air Museum.

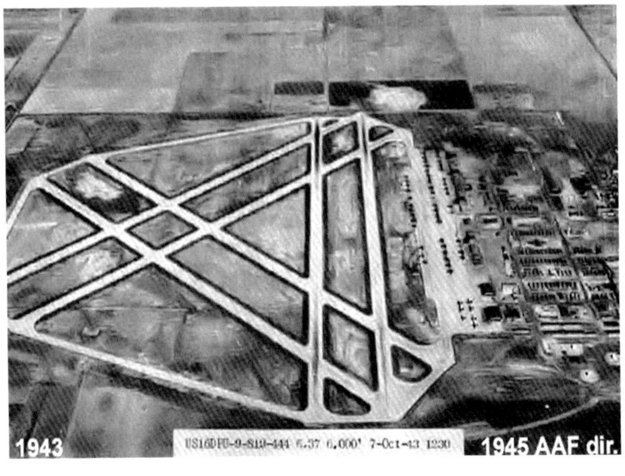

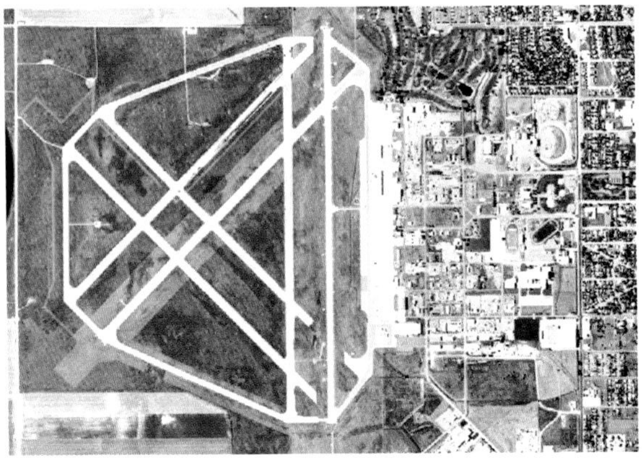

CONSOLIDATED B-24 "LIBERATOR"

First flown in December 1939, Consolidated's XB24 prototype bettered the famous Boeing B-17 Flying Fortress with improved range and payload capabilities, though it was harder to fly and less survivable in ocean ditching scenarios. Each copy cost almost $300,000 to build, but almost 19,000 B-24s (including the Navy's version styled the PB4Y-1) were built during the War, more than any other American aircraft in history.

The first Liberators were produced in San Diego, where 45,000 people built 6,724 planes. But even that impressive capacity was inadequate, so in 1941, Consolidated merged with Vultee Aircraft, setting up a second factory in Fort Worth, TX. (Eventually the union was renamed "Convair.")

Other manufacturers also built the B-24, including Douglas Aircraft in Tulsa, OK and North American in Dallas, TX. Eventually the largest factory became Ford's Willow Run, MI facility, which turned out 6,792 completed aircraft and 1,893 disassembled airframes for final assembly elsewhere. In 1944 alone, Willow Run equaled the production of the entire Japanese aircraft industry and half the German output.

The B-24's design formed the platform for more than sixty variations including bomber, patrol bomber, reconnaissance, cargo, tanker, trainer, experimental, civil, and other variants. On the following pages we'll consider several versions O.C. flew. The differences between them are subtle, but were crucial to the crews, because the changes made to each succeeding variant were almost always in safety, combat ability, and performance.

Pilots, preferring sleek aircraft, called the slab-sided plane the "flying boxcar," but like all workhorses, it delivered with ten .50 caliber machine guns, able to fly 24-hour missions with more than a 3,000 mile range.

In Europe it supplied Patton's tanks, countered the German U-Boat offensive, and made the spectacular and tragic oil field raid at Ploesti, Romania. In the Pacific, it eventually broke Japan's back, pummeling each stepping-stone island in turn and eventually the Japanese homeland itself. Today, only eight Liberators still exist, six in museums and two flying, including *Diamond Lil*, above, a B-24A.

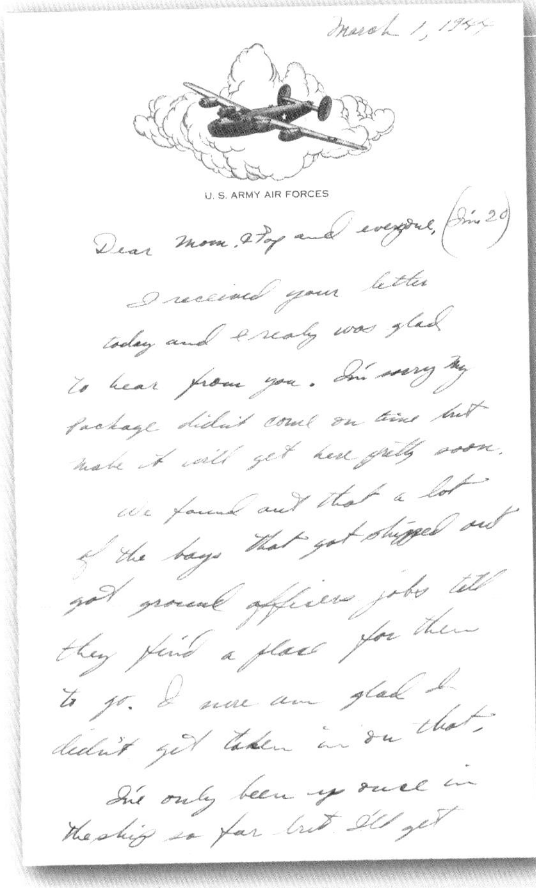
March 1, 1944

U. S. ARMY AIR FORCES

Dear Mom, Pop and everyone,

I received your letter today and I really was glad to hear from you. I'm sorry my package didn't come on time but maybe it will get here pretty soon.

We found out that a lot of the boys that got shipped out got ground officer jobs till they find a place for them to go. I sure am glad I didn't get taken in on that.

I've only been up once in the ship so far but I'll get

HERE'S THE SCUTTLEBUTT . . .

Liberal was Rumor Central. A harsh winter was delaying flight training. Initially shuttled into mass barracks until their two-men-to-a-room quarters were complete, the new pilots were anxious to get started. The overcrowding spawned a rumor that Class 44-B would be shipping out. One possible destination was Salt Lake City, Utah, which meant OTU, the Overseas Training Unit, and almost immediate overseas duty.

The rumor was partly true. O.C. was one of sixteen men in his group who would remain at Liberal; the rest would be shipped to other training centers. "I don't know why I was chosen out of 90 men," he wrote home, "but maybe it's for the best. We'll graduate as scheduled in 9 weeks."

Fearing he had been left behind because the Army believed he wasn't up to the OTU, a few days later O.C. discovered that most of the 74 who shipped out had been assigned ground officer training until they found a place to train them in B-24s. O.C. was actually considered one of the *best* pilots in his class, which was why he was kept on schedule at LAAF.

"I worked out on the ship myself today during my flying period. I have to get acquainted with all the crew jobs on a B-24, so I'm learning how to work the bombsight. It's really interesting. We also have a radio class which has no end of things to learn."

Unfortunately, in the first two weeks in Liberal, O.C. got to fly just twice due to poor weather. "It rains one day and it's now blowing dust all over the place. I guess I know why they call it the dust bowl.

"I finally got to go up again the other day, that makes twice I've actually been in the B-24. I'm a passenger, of course, because they haven't gotten around to letting me fly as yet. We have an awful lot to learn about this job. I guess we'll never know about all the equipment on the plane, but I can sure see why it costs $300,000.00."

"We're scheduled to graduate in nine weeks if we get the 105 hours flying and pass all the required checks."

YOU can't afford
to miss EITHER!
BUY BONDS EVERY PAYDAY

DOING HIS PART . . . AND THEN SOME

Each and every month, in addition to the money he sent home to his folks and his tithe to his church, O.C. bought a War Bond for about 75% of its ten-year redemption value. There wasn't much money left over for poker.

B-24A

While the most visually distinctive aspect of the Liberator is its twin tail, the most *invisibly* distinctive aspect is the Davis Wing, which when first wind-tunneled at CalTech beat contemporary wing efficiency by a whopping 20 percent. No one could believe it—except its inventor David Davis, who had predicted the result all along.

Though the wing, stabilizers, and fins were all metal, the ailerons, elevators, and rudders were fabric-covered. The semi-monocoque fuselage (the skin being an integral part of the plane's strength) had a boxy cross section. Bomb bay doors rolled up the sides to reveal two racks in each of the two bays. A narrow, nine-inch wide catwalk between the racks allowed brave crewmen to transit between the forward and aft fuselage sections.

For the layman, the way to differentiate the various B-24 versions is to pay attention to the nose. The A variant had a "greenhouse" nose, where the bombardier sat with a full view of coming attractions. He had a single machine gun for forward defense, which proved inadequate when the planes started seeing combat.

Only nine B-24As were built. These views are of *Diamond Lil,* which is still flying.

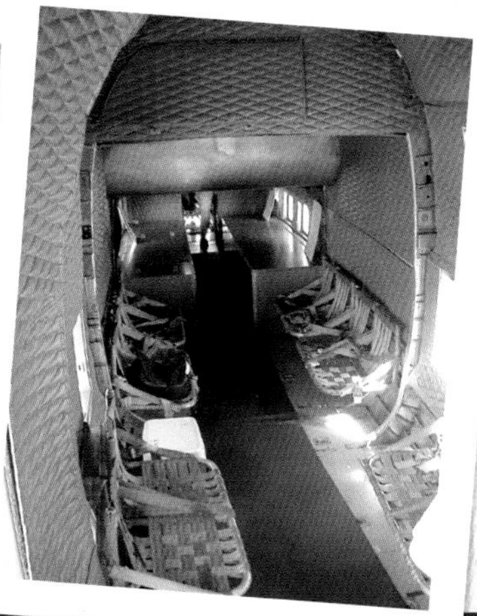

B-24D

The B-24D was the first major production variant, of which 2,738 were built by 1942. It was 110 feet wide and 64 feet long, had a 32,000 foot ceiling and a range of 3,500 miles. Powered by four Pratt & Whitney 1,200 hp engines, it had a maximum speed of 300 mph. It had ten .50 caliber machine guns, including a retractable Sperry ball belly turret instead of a single ventral gun. It could carry up to 8,000 pounds of bombs inboard and another 4,000 pounds under the wings.

The most obvious change were two large *pitot* (pee-toe) tube arms rising on either side of the fuselage forward of the cockpit, as seen in these photos. The pitot tube captures ram air, yielding airspeed, and in prior models tended to ice up and become useless.

Two of the photos on this page are of *Strawberry Bitch,* which is on display at the Air Force Museum in Dayton, Ohio. At bottom right, a D variant engages in a test flight over Coronado Island in San Diego. In the background, beyond Lindbergh Field, the white buildings of Consolidated Aircraft glisten. They still stand today.

The first Liberators O.C. flew were the B-24E at Liberal, Kansas, almost identical to the B-24Ds.

B-24E

Most of the B-24Es that O.C. flew at Liberal were produced at the Ford factory at Willow Run, Michigan, or in San Diego, California.

The E series retained the ventral machine guns instead of the Bendix/Sperry belly turret that was being fitted onto newer models. For this reason, most of the Es served domestically and were used for crew training. The greenhouse nose was replaced with a rotating turret containing two .50 caliber machine guns, and the bombardier was given his own compartment underneath the nose gunner's position.

By the first week of March, O.C. finally got to sit in the co-pilot's seat. "I sure was a busy beaver up there," he wrote his mother. "It is a good-sized job to fly one of these things. We also have ground school which covers the B-24 from nose to tail. We're required to know every part by the time we get out of here. It really is interesting. We have mock-ups which are cut-away pieces of engines or airplane sections so we can see how everything works. A lot of the ships we fly were made in San Diego in 1943, when you were working there, Mom! It really does give me a thrill to ride in a ship made in good old San Diego."

"IF I WAS A LITTLE MORE NORMAL"

In a letter home in mid-March, O.C. voices his greatest fear. He's been granted his fondest wish—to fly airplanes—but now he's afraid he might not be up to it:

"I've been in the co-pilot's seat a couple of times and I really have a tough time of it. This is the first time I've had to learn from the left side and I can't hardly hear what's going on at all. I don't know what I'm going to do.

"It makes me feel like quitting sometimes, but I don't think I'll give in till I have to. It sure is hard to get along with one ear when I could do so much better if I was a little more normal.

"If I can only get to combat before they know what's going on, I think I'll be all right. On the other hand, I'm doing all right in ground school. I have passed twelve words per minute in Morse Code and I got the third highest in Aircraft Equipment class."

LEFT Kansas in March averages about 40° F., so O.C. appears in this photo in his sheepskin bomber jacket.

B-24G / B-24H

By 1943, B-24 production was in full swing. The latest G and H models were almost a foot longer, had a powered gun turret in the nose to reduce vulnerability to head-on attack, and were fitted with an improved bombsight, autopilot, and fuel transfer system. Consolidated, Douglas, and Ford all manufactured the H, while North American made the G. All five plants switched over to the almost identical B-24J in August 1943.

The ventral (belly) Sperry ball turret, experimental on the D model, has now become standard equipment. With the new forward Emerson turret containing two .50 caliber machine guns, the B-24 is now less susceptible to forward and lower attacks. The nose turret addition alone required more than 50 airframe changes, including a new bombardier compartment.

Other improvements incorporated to improve the defensive strength of the aircraft include a new tail turret design with larger Plexiglas windows, a higher top turret bubble for increased visibility, and offset waist gunner positions to prevent the waist gunners from interfering with each other in battle.

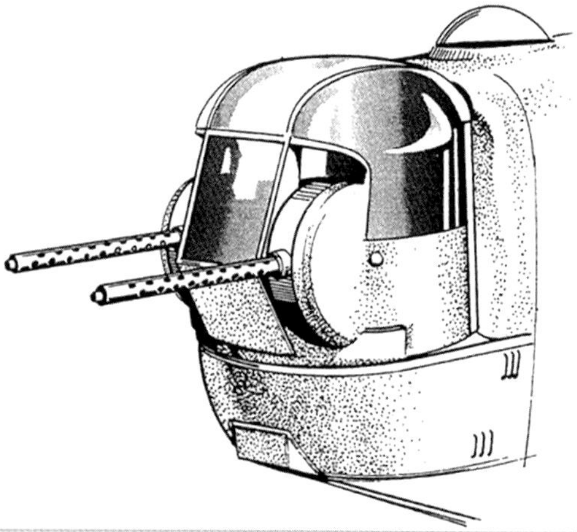

AUDIO TRANSCRIPT 06:03:20

We flew these old B-24s that looked like they had been through the war. The first time I saw all the instruments for the four engines I thought, "My word, I'll never learn anything about this thing; I'll never make it."

And yet it was just such a sweet airplane. You start down the runway and all four of those engines are singing along together and it was such a marvelous feeling.

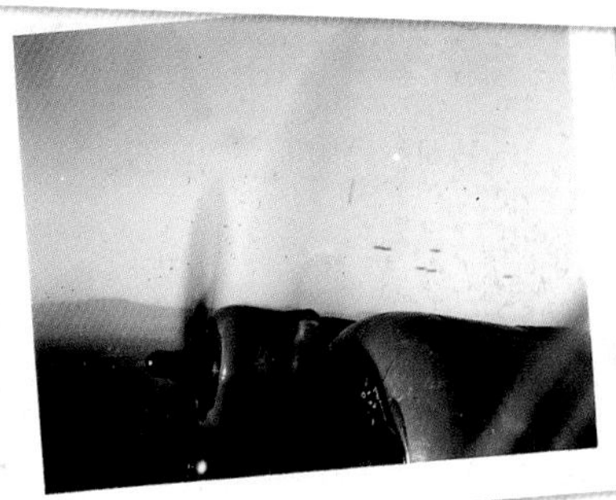

They stuck me in the left seat because I was becoming an airplane commander. And if you weren't in the left seat, you were standing between them, learning, with another student in the left seat.

Soon as we'd take off, the instructor would start hollering -- and of course by then we had emergency procedures drilled into us -- and he'd pull a throttle back and the airplane would yaw around and then he say, "Well, what are you going to do? You lost number three!"

And of course, because when the propeller is throttled back, it's like a big disk, pushing into the air, and it just pulls the airplane to the right and the plane wants to flop over on its back and you gotta get right on the rudder real quick or it will do just that. And you've got all the other engines on maximum trying to climb and you holler, "Check the mags! Check the fuel! Check the RPMs! Check the manifold pressure!"

And we'd go through a checklist and the instructor would say, "OK," and he'd give you back your engine or maybe he'd pull another one back and now it's all you can do to hold it. In fact, one pilot can't do it with two engines out, so you'd hold it as long as you could and then you'd yell, "Feather!" and he'd say, "No!" and you'd then have trouble on another engine 'cause he's putting them through quite a strain.

And if you couldn't hold them, you'd say, "Get on that rudder and help!" And he'd say, "OK, whatever you say," and he'd get on it.

But you had to prove you were in charge of that airplane. There was no time to be milquetoast or anything, you know.

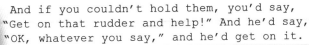

LEFT When he wasn't in the left seat getting yelled at by his instructor, O.C. snapped photos with his Eastman Kodak 116 "Premo" camera, including those on the right.

OFF WE GO . . .

"I landed and took off today for the first time," writes O.C. on the last day of March 1944. "It really is an easy airplane to land but it will take a lot of work to get those take-offs down to where they should be. That should make 20 hours in a whole month, which sure is slow progress.

"I'm going out at 11:00 A.M. tomorrow to drop bombs down in Texas somewhere. Practice bombs, of course.

"I finished my engineering class and got a pretty fair grade of 83%. The class average was 81%. We are sweating out Navigation, which will wind up our ground school here at Liberal.

"Now that I'm in the left seat, my ear doesn't seem to bother me as much. You see, we have to talk to each other and we don't use earphones or the radio much. It isn't as noisy as you would think. All the noise is on the outside and behind the pilot's compartment.

"Sometime when I can afford for them to know about my ear, I'll see what I can do about it. I'm not going to let it get me down as long as I can get along."

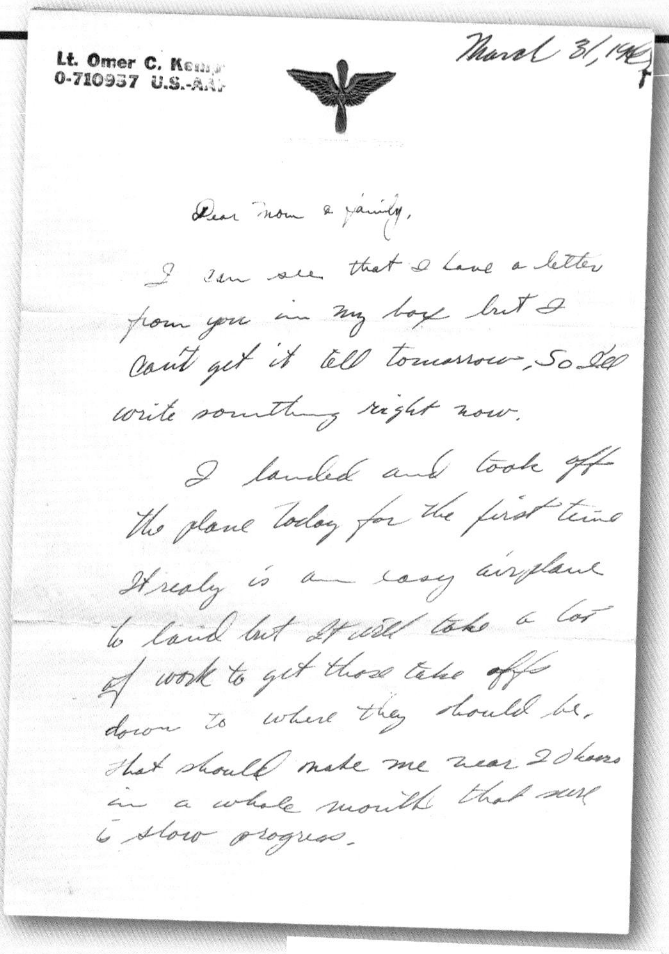
Lt. Omer C. Kem
0-710937 U.S.-A.

March 31, 194

Dear Mom & family,

I can see that I have a letter from you in my box but I can't get it till tomorrow, So I'll write something right now.

I landed and took off the plane today for the first time It realy is an easy airplane to land but It will take a lot of work to get those take offs down to where they should be. That should make me near 20 hours in a whole month that sure is slow progress.

. . . ON THE OTHER HAND

Ground school is almost over and now all that is left is flying. "I'm building a P-47 model airplane in my spare time," he wrote. "That really *is* getting bad, isn't it?"

Outside of class and flying, life at Liberal Air Field was boring. O.C. went to Wichita one weekend to attend church and to see the Boeing factory where they were building B-29s. "That sure is a big bomber," he wrote home. "Almost twice the size of our B-24."

Beyond that, there was the bowling alley, skeet shooting, and the movie house. War pictures were common, and he saw T*he Fighting Seabees* and everything else that came along. "Outside of that," he continued, "there isn't much to do in Liberal except get drunk." He was surprised that men would pay $12.00 for a bottle of whisky and then grouse they didn't have enough money for poker.

"Buy me another War Bond," he told his dad.

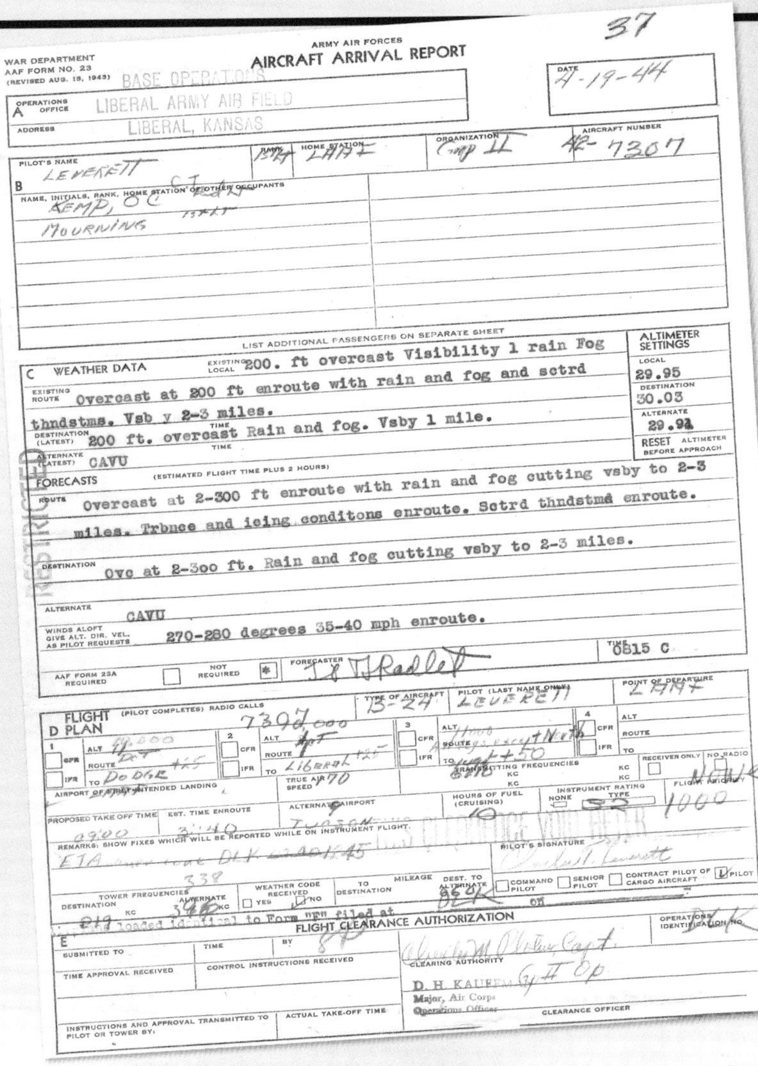
37

WAR DEPARTMENT
AAF FORM NO. 23
(REVISED AUG. 15, 1943)

ARMY AIR FORCES
AIRCRAFT ARRIVAL REPORT

DATE 4-19-44

A OPERATIONS OFFICE BASE OPERATIONS LIBERAL ARMY AIR FIELD
ADDRESS LIBERAL, KANSAS

B PILOT'S NAME LEVERETT RANK 1st Lt HOME STATION LAAF ORGANIZATION Grp II AIRCRAFT NUMBER 42-7307

NAME, INITIALS, RANK, HOME STATION OF OTHER OCCUPANTS
KEMP, O C
MOURNING 1st Lt

LIST ADDITIONAL PASSENGERS ON SEPARATE SHEET

C WEATHER DATA
EXISTING LOCAL 200. ft overcast Visibility 1 rain Fog
EXISTING ROUTE Overcast at 200 ft enroute with rain and fog and sctrd thndstms. Vsb y 2-3 miles.
DESTINATION (LATEST) 200 ft. overcast Rain and fog. Vsby 1 mile.
ALTERNATE (LATEST) CAVU

ALTIMETER SETTINGS
LOCAL 29.95
DESTINATION 30.03
ALTERNATE 29.92
RESET ALTIMETER BEFORE APPROACH

FORECASTS (ESTIMATED FLIGHT TIME PLUS 2 HOURS)
ROUTE Overcast at 2-300 ft enroute with rain and fog cutting vsby to 2-3 miles. Trbnce and icing conditons enroute. Sctrd thndstms enroute.
DESTINATION Ovc at 2-300 ft. Rain and fog cutting vsby to 2-3 miles.
ALTERNATE CAVU
WINDS ALOFT GIVE ALT. DIR. VEL. AS PILOT REQUESTS 270-280 degrees 35-40 mph enroute.

TIME 0815 C

AAF FORM 23A REQUIRED ☐ NOT REQUIRED ☒ FORECASTER

D FLIGHT PLAN (PILOT COMPLETES) RADIO CALLS 7307
TYPE OF AIRCRAFT B-24 PILOT (LAST NAME ONLY) LEVERETT POINT OF DEPARTURE LAAF
ALT 11,000 ROUTE TO DODGE
ALT ROUTE TO LIBERAL
TRUE AIR SPEED 170
AIRPORT OF FIRST INTENDED LANDING
PROPOSED TAKE OFF TIME 0900 EST. TIME ENROUTE 3:40 ALTERNATE AIRPORT
HOURS OF FUEL (CRUISING) 10
INSTRUMENT RATING NONE TYPE
FLIGHT PRIORITY NONE
REMARKS: SHOW FIXES WHICH WILL BE REPORTED WHILE ON INSTRUMENT FLIGHT. ETA
PILOT'S SIGNATURE
DESTINATION TOWER FREQUENCIES ALTERNATE WEATHER CODE RECEIVED YES ☐ NO ☐ TO DESTINATION MILEAGE DEST. TO ALTERNATE COMMAND PILOT ☐ SENIOR PILOT ☐ CONTRACT PILOT OF CARGO AIRCRAFT ☐ PILOT ☒
OPERATIONS IDENTIFICATION

E FLIGHT CLEARANCE AUTHORIZATION
SUBMITTED TO TIME BY
TIME APPROVAL RECEIVED
CONTROL INSTRUCTIONS RECEIVED
CLEARING AUTHORITY
D. H. KAUFFMAN
Major, Air Corps
Operations Officer
INSTRUCTIONS AND APPROVAL TRANSMITTED TO PILOT OR TOWER BY:
ACTUAL TAKE-OFF TIME
CLEARANCE OFFICER

RESTRICTED

THE FLIGHT PLAN

LEFT Previous to every flight, a pilot gets a weather report and files a Flight Plan like this one, which is the only surviving Flight Plan we have from O.C.'s military service—quite a valuable find.

Modern Flight Plans have not changed much, even in their layout.

On this flight, the pilot/instructor was 1st Lt. Leverett, with O.C. and 1st Lt. Mourning on board. The flight is from Dodge City, Kansas on 19 April 1944 and was scheduled to begin at 9:00 a.m. for a return to Liberal Army Air Field. The flight was estimated to take three hours and forty minutes.

The sky that day was overcast at 200 feet with rain and fog en route, though it was likely clear at 11,000 feet, their planned altitude. Up there, it was beautiful, no doubt.

BELOW The Flight Record for April. Note that O.C. has now more than tripled the amount of time he spends in the left seat as a Qualified Pilot, although he's still watched over by his instructor, hence the "Dual" qualification.

INDIVIDUAL FLIGHT RECORD	O.C. KEMP
STATION	LAAF, Liberal, Kansas
FLYING CLASSIFICATION	Plt. 2-8-44
ORGANIZATION ASSIGNED	AAFCFTC AAFTC 34th FTW AAFPS4E 527th B.H. & A.B. Sq. S.O.D.
MONTH	**April 1944**
AIRCRAFT TYPE	B-24E
LANDINGS	83
COMMAND PILOT	
CO-PILOT	17:20
QUALIFIED PILOT (DUAL)	25:15
FIRST PILOT (DAY)	
FIRST PILOT (NIGHT)	
NON-PILOT DUTY (PASSENGER)	21:35
INSTRUMENT (DAY)	14:30
INSTRUMENT (NIGHT)	4:30
INSTRUMENT TRAINER	
TOTAL TIME THIS MONTH	42:35
TOTAL PILOT TIME TO DATE	279:50

PROFICIENCY CHECK

RIGHT Of course it wasn't all flying. There was ground school and that means tests. Here's a very practical one: an Airplane Commander's Proficiency Check, which means O.C. is being groomed for the left seat.

BOTTOM LEFT And so O.C. looks "commanding" in the pilot's seat in his B-24E, lovingly named *Hunk O Junk*, most likely by those who knew her best: the mechanics.

BOTTOM RIGHT O.C. in the hatch aft of the dorsal "high hat" turret. Plexiglas was a boon to wartime aircraft because of its strength, light weight, and flexible characteristics.

MIDDLE LEFT No. 46 may very well be a *Hunk O Junk,* or it may just be undergoing routine maintenance as seen by the canvas shroud enveloping the number three engine.

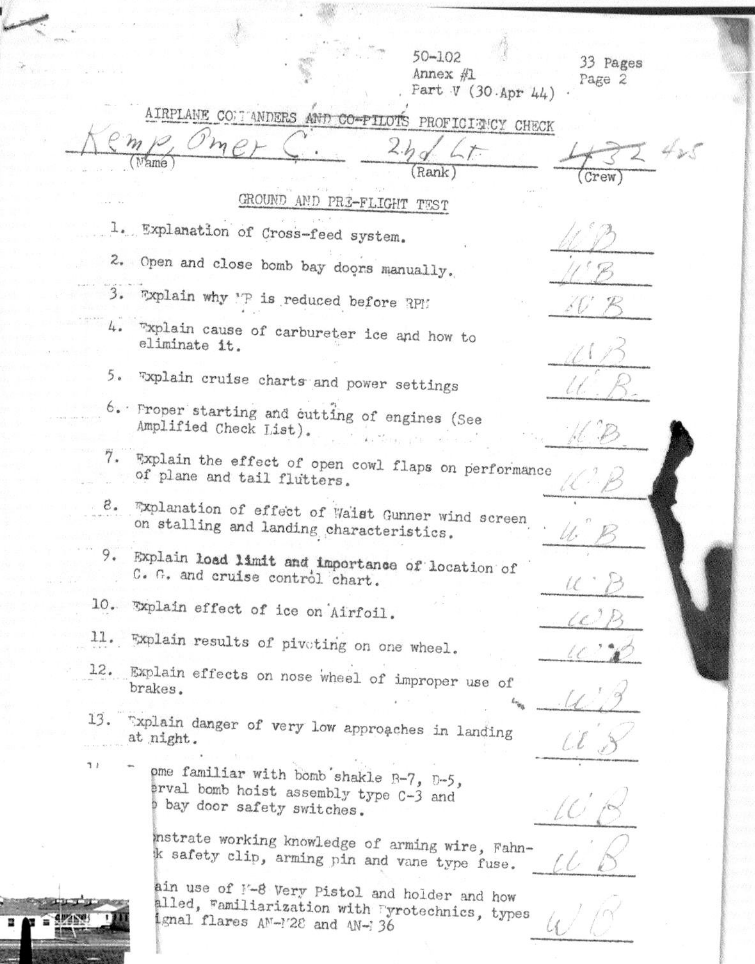
50-102
Annex #1
Part V (30 Apr 44)

33 Pages
Page 2

AIRPLANE COMMANDERS AND CO-PILOTS PROFICIENCY CHECK

Kemp, Omer C. (Name) 2nd Lt. (Rank) ~~432~~ 425 (Crew)

GROUND AND PRE-FLIGHT TEST

1. Explanation of Cross-feed system.
2. Open and close bomb bay doors manually.
3. Explain why MP is reduced before RPM
4. Explain cause of carbureter ice and how to eliminate it.
5. Explain cruise charts and power settings
6. Proper starting and cutting of engines (See Amplified Check List).
7. Explain the effect of open cowl flaps on performance of plane and tail flutters.
8. Explanation of effect of Waist Gunner wind screen on stalling and landing characteristics.
9. Explain load limit and importance of location of C. G. and cruise control chart.
10. Explain effect of ice on Airfoil.
11. Explain results of pivoting on one wheel.
12. Explain effects on nose wheel of improper use of brakes.
13. Explain danger of very low approaches in landing at night.

...ome familiar with bomb shakle B-7, D-5, ...erval bomb hoist assembly type C-3 and ... bay door safety switches.

...nstrate working knowledge of arming wire, Fahn-...k safety clip, arming pin and vane type fuse.

...ain use of M-8 Very Pistol and holder and how ...alled, Familiarization with Pyrotechnics, types ...ignal flares AN-M28 and AN-M36

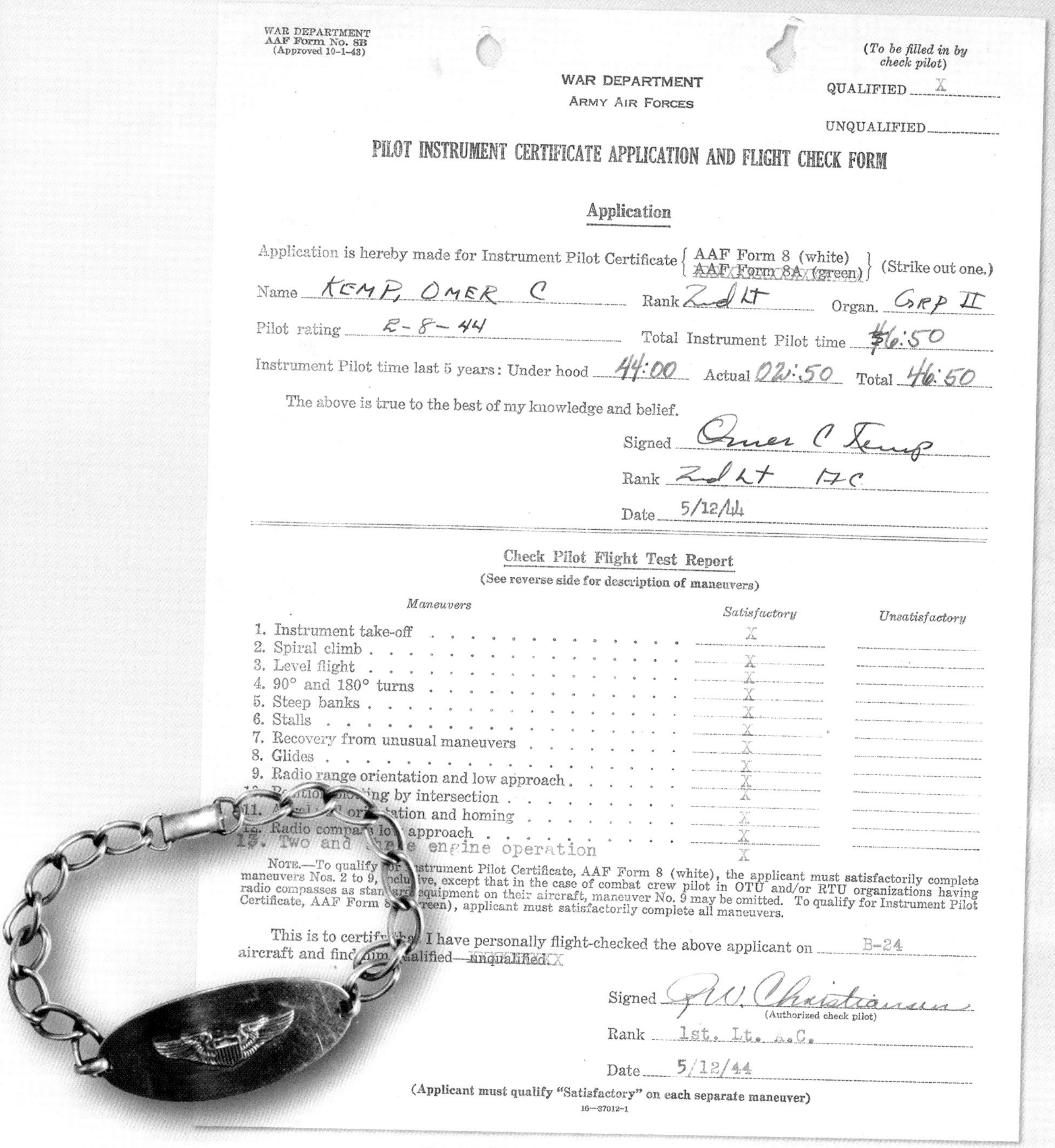

WAR DEPARTMENT
AAF Form No. 8B
(Approved 10-1-43)

(To be filled in by check pilot)

WAR DEPARTMENT
ARMY AIR FORCES

QUALIFIED X

UNQUALIFIED

PILOT INSTRUMENT CERTIFICATE APPLICATION AND FLIGHT CHECK FORM

Application

Application is hereby made for Instrument Pilot Certificate { AAF Form 8 (white) / ~~AAF Form 8A (green)~~ } (Strike out one.)

Name KEMP, OMER C Rank 2nd Lt Organ. GRP II

Pilot rating 2-8-44 Total Instrument Pilot time 46:50

Instrument Pilot time last 5 years: Under hood 44:00 Actual 02:50 Total 46:50

The above is true to the best of my knowledge and belief.

Signed Omer C Kemp

Rank 2nd Lt AC

Date 5/12/44

Check Pilot Flight Test Report

(See reverse side for description of maneuvers)

Maneuvers	*Satisfactory*	*Unsatisfactory*
1. Instrument take-off	X	
2. Spiral climb	X	
3. Level flight	X	
4. 90° and 180° turns	X	
5. Steep banks	X	
6. Stalls	X	
7. Recovery from unusual maneuvers	X	
8. Glides	X	
9. Radio range orientation and low approach	X	
10. [illegible]ing by intersection	X	
11. [illegible] orientation and homing	X	
12. Radio compass low approach	X	
13. Two and [illegible] engine operation	X	

NOTE.—To qualify for Instrument Pilot Certificate, AAF Form 8 (white), the applicant must satisfactorily complete maneuvers Nos. 2 to 9, inclusive, except that in the case of combat crew pilot in OTU and/or RTU organizations having radio compasses as standard equipment on their aircraft, maneuver No. 9 may be omitted. To qualify for Instrument Pilot Certificate, AAF Form 8A (green), applicant must satisfactorily complete all maneuvers.

This is to certify that I have personally flight-checked the above applicant on B-24 aircraft and find him qualified—~~unqualified~~.

Signed R.W. Christiansen
(Authorized check pilot)

Rank 1st. Lt. A.C.

Date 5/12/44

(Applicant must qualify "Satisfactory" on each separate maneuver)

16—37012-1

BIG DAY: MAY 12, 1944

Fly. Study. Test. These are the three events that seem to mark each day of a student pilot's life in this hothouse environment, where the Army Air Force intends to turn cadets into pilots capable of handling a $300,000.00 aircraft—that's over $4 million in today's dollars.

In this form, O.C. is making formal application for Instrument Certification, a huge step on this path. So far he's got 44 hours "under the hood" but less than three hours actual instrument time. No matter, he's tested well in everything, as indicated by the column of "X"s in the lower half of the form. R.W. Christiansen certified that O.C. is instrument qualified on a B-24 on 12 May 1944.

ABOVE LEFT It was the custom, in addition to dog tags, for Army Air Force officers to wear a brass bracelet inscribed on the back with their name and serial number. This is O.C.'s bracelet.

RESTRICTED

Here's where they separate the men from the boys. You can be one of the best B-24 pilots ever trained and still fail as an airplane commander. In addition to qualifying yourself as a top-flight pilot, you have the job of building a fighting team that you can rely on in any emergency. Failure of any member of the crew to do the right thing at the right time may mean failure of your mission, unnecessary loss of life and possible loss of your airplane.

6

You Can't Pass the Buck

Your authority as airplane commander carries with it responsibility that you can not shirk. Your engineer is a trained specialist, but his training is incomplete. He knows how to transfer fuel, but does he know how to transfer it in the particular airplane you are flying? It isn't enough that he **thinks** so. You must **know** what he knows. It is up to you to perfect the basic training he has been given. An oversight

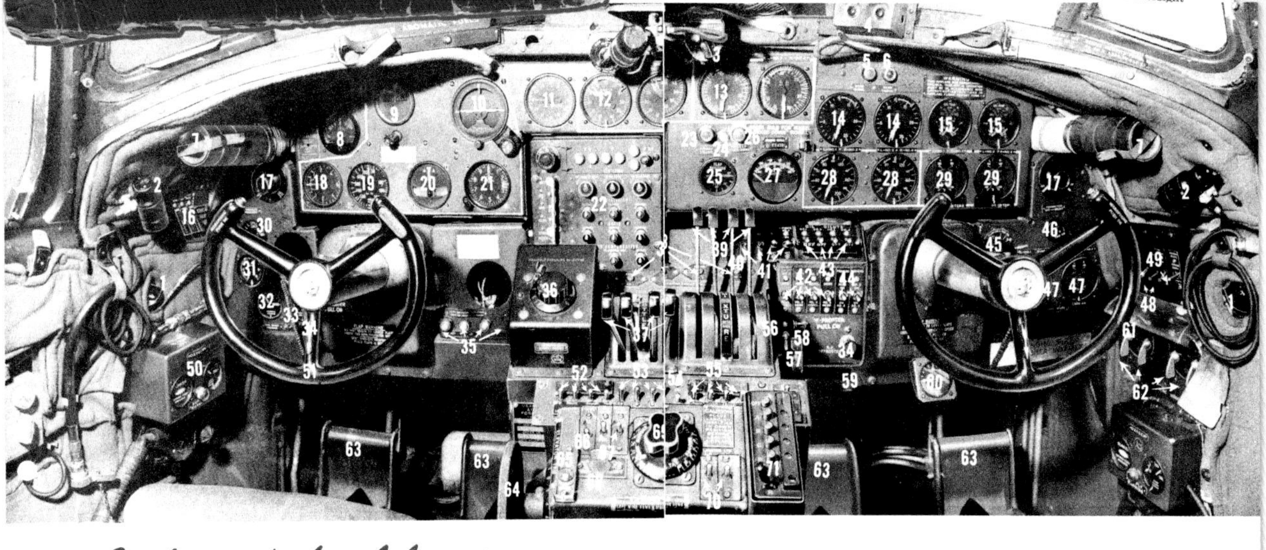

Cockpit of the Liberator... **B-24 PILOT'S INSTRUMENTS AND CONTROLS**

1. Fluorescent Light Switches
2. 24 Volt DC Fluorescent Light
3. Magnetic Compass Light Rheostat
4. IFF Radio Destroyer Switch
5. Bomb Doors Indicator
6. Bomb Release Indicator
7. Defroster Ducts
8. Pilot Director Indicator
9. Directional Gyro
10. Gyro Horizon
11. Radio Compass Indicator
12. Manifold Pressure Gages
13. Tachometers
14. Fuel Pressure Gages
15. Cylinder Temperature Gages
16. Chemical Release Switches
17. Ventilators
18. Rate-of-climb Indicator
19. Airspeed Indicator
20. Turn and Bank Indicator
21. Altimeter
22. C-1 Automatic Pilot
23. Marker Beacon Indicator
24. Landing Gear Indicator Test Button
25. Flap Position Indicator
26. Landing Gear Indicator
27. Free Air Temperature Gage
28. Oil Pressure Gages
29. Oil Temperature Gages
30. Hydraulic Pressure Gages
31. Suction Gage
32. Inboard Brake Pressure Gage
33. Outboard Brake Pressure Gage
34. Defroster Controls
35. Propeller Governor Limit Lights
36. Turbo Boost Selector
37. Throttles
38. Propeller Feathering Circuit Breakers
39. Mixture Controls
40. Bomb Bay Fuel Transfer Switch
41. Booster Pump Switches
42. Engine Starter Switches
43. Oil Dilution Switches
44. Primer Switches
45. Anti-icer Control
46. Formation Lights Rheostat
47. Carburetor Air Temperature Gages
48. Main Storage Battery Switches
49. Heater and Defroster Switches
50. Oxygen Panels
51. Pilot's Wheel
52. Propeller Switches
53. Intercooler Shutter Switches
54. Pitot Heater Switch
55. Cowl Flap Switches
56. SCR 535 Power Switch
57. Throttle Friction Lock
58. SCR 535 Emergency Switch
59. De-icer Control
60. De-icer Pressure Gage
61. Emergency Ignition Switch Bar
62. Ignition Switches
63. Brake Pedals
64. Elevator Tab Control Wheel
65. Alarm Button
66. Passing Light Switch
67. Navigation Light Switches
68. A C Inverter Switch
69. Rudder Tab Control Knob
70. Landing Light Switches
71. SCR 522 Control Box

RESTRICTED

25

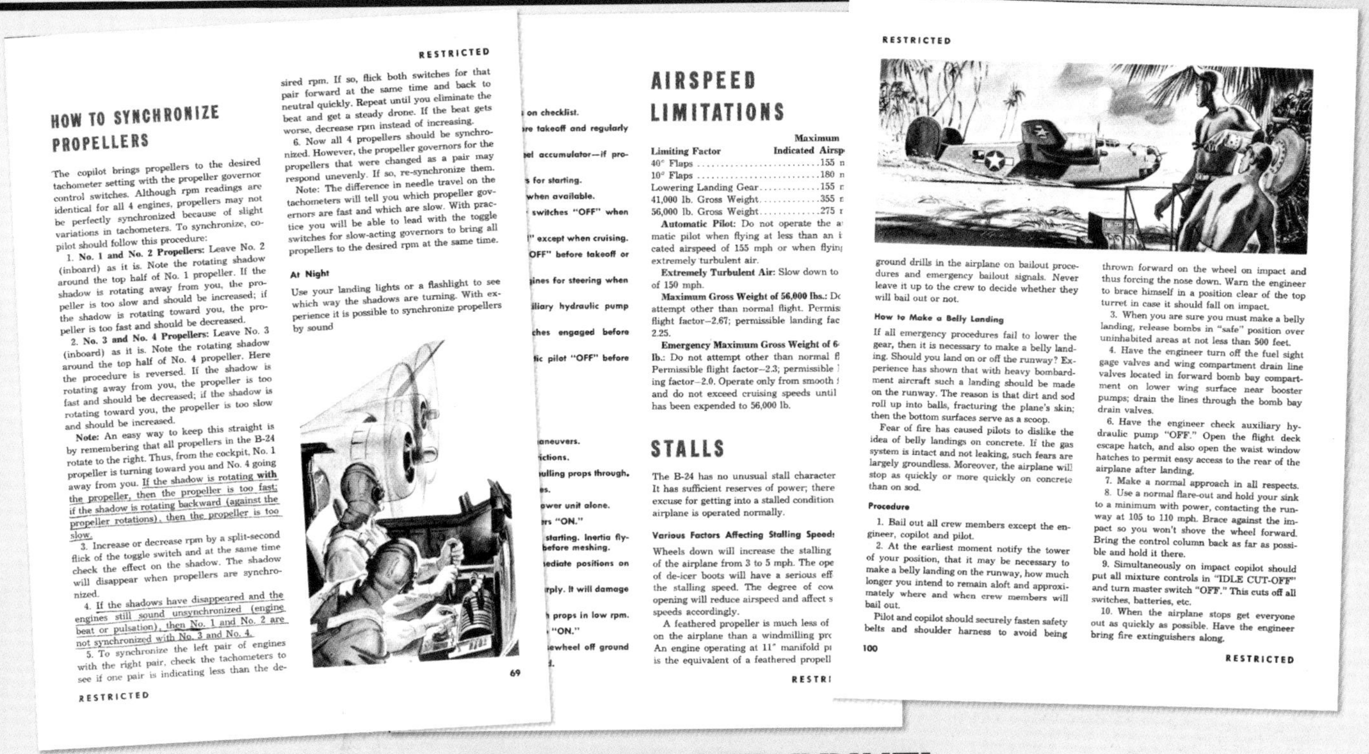

RESTRICTED

HOW TO SYNCHRONIZE PROPELLERS

The copilot brings propellers to the desired tachometer setting with the propeller governor control switches. Although rpm readings are identical for all 4 engines, propellers may not be perfectly synchronized because of slight variations in tachometers. To synchronize, copilot should follow this procedure:

1. **No. 1 and No. 2 Propellers:** Leave No. 2 (inboard) as it is. Note the rotating shadow around the top half of No. 1 propeller. If the shadow is rotating away from you, the propeller is too slow and should be increased; if the shadow is rotating toward you, the propeller is too fast and should be decreased.

2. **No. 3 and No. 4 Propellers:** Leave No. 3 (inboard) as it is. Note the rotating shadow around the top half of No. 4 propeller. Here the procedure is reversed. If the shadow is rotating away from you, the propeller is too fast and should be decreased; if the shadow is rotating toward you, the propeller is too slow and should be increased.

Note: An easy way to keep this straight is by remembering that all propellers in the B-24 rotate to the right. Thus, from the cockpit, No. 1 propeller is turning toward you and No. 4 going away from you. If the shadow is rotating with the propeller, then the propeller is too fast; if the shadow is rotating backward (against the propeller rotations), then the propeller is too slow.

3. Increase or decrease rpm by a split-second flick of the toggle switch and at the same time check the effect on the shadow. The shadow will disappear when propellers are synchronized.

4. If the shadows have disappeared and the engines still sound unsynchronized (engine beat or pulsation), then No. 1 and No. 2 are not synchronized with No. 3 and No. 4.

5. To synchronize the left pair of engines with the right pair, check the tachometers to see if one pair is indicating less than the desired rpm. If so, flick both switches for that pair forward at the same time and back to neutral quickly. Repeat until you eliminate the beat and get a steady drone. If the beat gets worse, decrease rpm instead of increasing.

6. Now all 4 propellers should be synchronized. However, the propeller governors for the propellers that were changed as a pair may respond unevenly. If so, re-synchronize them.

Note: The difference in needle travel on the tachometers will tell you which propeller governors are fast and which are slow. With practice you will be able to lead with the toggle switches for slow-acting governors to bring all propellers to the desired rpm at the same time.

At Night

Use your landing lights or a flashlight to see which way the shadows are turning. With experience it is possible to synchronize propellers by sound

69

RESTRICTED

AIRSPEED LIMITATIONS

Limiting Factor	Maximum Indicated Airsp
40° Flaps	155
10° Flaps	180
Lowering Landing Gear	155
41,000 lb. Gross Weight	355
56,000 lb. Gross Weight	275

Automatic Pilot: Do not operate the automatic pilot when flying at less than an indicated airspeed of 155 mph or when flying in extremely turbulent air.

Extremely Turbulent Air: Slow down to of 150 mph.

Maximum Gross Weight of 56,000 lbs.: Do attempt other than normal flight. Permissible flight factor–2.67; permissible landing factor 2.25.

Emergency Maximum Gross Weight of 6… lb.: Do not attempt other than normal fl… Permissible flight factor–2.3; permissible … ing factor–2.0. Operate only from smooth … and do not exceed cruising speeds until … has been expended to 56,000 lb.

STALLS

The B-24 has no unusual stall character… It has sufficient reserves of power; there … excuse for getting into a stalled condition … airplane is operated normally.

Various Factors Affecting Stalling Speed

Wheels down will increase the stalling … of the airplane from 3 to 5 mph. The ope… of de-icer boots will have a serious eff… the stalling speed. The degree of cow… opening will reduce airspeed and affect s… speeds accordingly.

A feathered propeller is much less of … on the airplane than a windmilling pro… An engine operating at 11" manifold pr… is the equivalent of a feathered propell…

RESTRI…

RESTRICTED

ground drills in the airplane on bailout procedures and emergency bailout signals. Never leave it up to the crew to decide whether they will bail out or not.

How to Make a Belly Landing

If all emergency procedures fail to lower the gear, then it is necessary to make a belly landing. Should you land on or off the runway? Experience has shown that with heavy bombardment aircraft such a landing should be made on the runway. The reason is that dirt and sod roll up into balls, fracturing the plane's skin; then the bottom surfaces serve as a scoop.

Fear of fire has caused pilots to dislike the idea of belly landings on concrete. If the gas system is intact and not leaking, such fears are largely groundless. Moreover, the airplane will stop as quickly or more quickly on concrete than on sod.

Procedure

1. Bail out all crew members except the engineer, copilot and pilot.
2. At the earliest moment notify the tower of your position, that it may be necessary to make a belly landing on the runway, how much longer you intend to remain aloft and approximately where and when crew members will bail out.

Pilot and copilot should securely fasten safety belts and shoulder harness to avoid being thrown forward on the wheel on impact and thus forcing the nose down. Warn the engineer to brace himself in a position clear of the top turret in case it should fall on impact.

3. When you are sure you must make a belly landing, release bombs in "safe" position over uninhabited areas at not less than 500 feet.
4. Have the engineer turn off the fuel sight gage valves and wing compartment drain line valves located in forward bomb bay compartment on lower wing surface near booster pumps; drain the lines through the bomb bay drain valves.
6. Have the engineer check auxiliary hydraulic pump "OFF." Open the flight deck escape hatch, and also open the waist window hatches to permit easy access to the rear of the airplane after landing.
7. Make a normal approach in all respects.
8. Use a normal flare-out and hold your sink to a minimum with power, contacting the runway at 105 to 110 mph. Brace against the impact so you won't shove the wheel forward. Bring the control column back as far as possible and hold it there.
9. Simultaneously on impact copilot should put all mixture controls in "IDLE CUT-OFF" and turn master switch "OFF." This cuts off all switches, batteries, etc.
10. When the airplane stops get everyone out as quickly as possible. Have the engineer bring fire extinguishers along.

100

RESTRICTED

READ THE RED PRINT!

The Liberator Pilot Training Manual isn't so much a flying instruction manual as it is a primer for the crew to begin to understand one of the most complex machines man had ever built.

Like O.C. once said, "The B-24 is difficult to fly, both physically and mentally, but when you add flying over water, at night, with a full bomb bay, at 20,000 feet where it's well below zero, and they're shooting at you, you stay pretty busy!"

RESTRICTED

LANDING WITH ONE MAIN WHEEL UP, OTHER MAIN AND NOSEWHEEL DOWN

If this landing is executed properly, there is much less damage to the airplane and chance of injury to personnel than in a belly landing. Know and try all emergency means to lower the main gear. If you have plenty of gas aboard, ask the tower to call an expert to tell you how to get the gear down. If you can't get it down, use this procedure:

Procedure

1. Bail out all crew members except the engineer, copilot and pilot.
2. Choose a runway on which you can groundloop without running into a hangar or parked aircraft, or going over a cliff.
3. Make a normal power approach and trim for a normal landing.
4. Be sure auxiliary hydraulic pump is off after brake accumulators are charged.
5. Land at a speed 5 to 10 mph faster than usual and use power to keep sink to a minimum. Grease 'er on.
6. Land with the wing on the side of faulty gear slightly high, and immediately after contact raise this wing still higher and … the outboard engine on the bad-gear side … reduce drag.
7. As soon as the main gear is solidly on the ground, raise the nose to a high angle of … to get maximum lift and to reduce sp… rapidly as possible.
8. As lift decreases, the wing on the … gear side and the nose gear will tend … Hold the wing up with ailerons as long … ble; when the wing starts down and … use brake on the good-gear side to … groundloop, which will seldom exc… Damage is usually limited to the outbo… peller, wingtip and vertical fin.

LANDING WITH NOSEWHEEL DAMAGED OR RETRACTED, OR WITH NO BRAKES

There are a number of situations in which it will be desirable to hold the nose high throughout the landing roll and bring the airplane to a stop resting on the tailskid. Examples: When the nosewheel is damaged or the shimmy damper faulty; when the nosewheel tire is flat; when the nosewheel cannot be extended, or when landing with no brakes.

This procedure requires careful load distribution and precise cooperation from the crew. It is the airplane commander's duty to brief his crew thoroughly on the proper procedure for a landing of this kind.

Caution This type of landing is … in a strong crosswind. It is desirable … longest runway, but the pilot mus… ment in balancing the benefits of a l… against the hazard of landing crossw…

Procedure

1. Hold the airplane in level fli… 155 mph (160 mph with nose turr… the load so the airplane will fly le… nose-down trim. Normally this re… stationed between the No. 6 bulk…

102

RESTRICTED

MECHANICAL FAILURES AND PROCEDURES

EMERGENCY LOWERING OF LANDING GEAR

There are 4 ways to lower the gear on a B-24. It is seldom that all 4 fail. Recently a pilot flew around for 2 hours trying to figure out with an ignorant engineer how to get the gear down. Then, with 5 minutes of gas left, he executed a belly landing which did $75,000 damage. Investigation showed that 60 seconds of know-how would have put the gear down.

Know all emergency procedures. Rehearse them with your engineer and copilot. Take an afternoon and crawl around the airplane with them. Read each procedure and dry-run it on the spot. That's the way to get acquainted with your airplane. Then, if an emergency arises, **you'll be ready.**

METHODS OF LOWERING THE LANDING GEAR

1. Normal hydraulic operation.
2. By use of the auxiliary hydraulic pump.
3. By use of the hand hydraulic pump, front star valve open, rear star valve closed.
4. Emergency hand crank method.

Important: First try all hydraulic methods of lowering the landing gear.

Know Your Landing Gear

Know whether the emerge… lowering system in your air… **sign**, with cable connection b… hand crank and nose gear, o… out cable connection. Most … design have been modified; … it hasn't been modified, refer … proper procedure. Successfu… ing of landing gear depends …

Procedures applicable to lat… emergency landing gear h… to main gear only.

LOWERING MA…

1. Place the landing g… pilot's control pedestal … tion.

2. Turn the emergen… until the main gear is … requires approximatel… on the forward side o… be reached from the … the bomb bay catwal…

200

RESTRICTED

BAILOUT DITCHING AND FIRES

BAILING OUT OF THE B-24

It is the responsibility of the airplane commander to make certain on every flight:

1. That a parachute is available and satisfactorily fitted for each person making the flight.
2. That the parachute is conveniently located at the normal position of the person making the flight and that he knows its location, how to put it on, how and where to leave the airplane, how to open the chute and how to land and collapse the chute. (See P.I.F.)
3. That a life vest is worn under the chute harness on all over-water flights and that the crew knows the location, how to attach and how to use the individual seat-type life raft.
4. That all persons aboard know the bailout signals and the bailout procedure to be followed.

The easiest and most effective way to carry out this responsibility is to appoint a parachute officer (usually the engineer) who will make a special study of equipment, its use, approved bailout signals, and the proper method of leaving the airplane. He will assist in conducting bailout drill once each week on the ground until the entire crew is proficient, and as often thereafter as necessary to keep the crew conscious of the proper care and wearing of equipment.

210

RESTRICTED

AUDIO TRANSCRIPT 06:06:26

I'd never seen that snow country. The Colonel would wake up in the morning and snow would be in drifts up against the side of the buildings, it was always blowing so much. It would be snowing like a blizzard out there and the Colonel would say, "Wonderful weather! Everybody up!"

So off we'd go, knock off the snow, get in our airplanes, and take off, right in the middle of a blizzard, 'cause we had to get the experience of flying in the snow and flying with de-icing boots on. We'd get up there and fly a radial above the clouds and fly radio beams and fly instruments and do all the stuff that was required.

I think I was there 90 days and we only flew 105 hours in that 90 days. But every day, all day long, those old bombers were going, somebody up there in them. And they were killing them, too.

Once in a while, one of them would go down and kill everybody on board.

We lost a lot of men, just from training.

ABOVE Bad weather is good practice for pilots, but O.C. saw several classmates lose their lives flying in inclement weather. It must have been sobering for a young man to look at the empty bunk of a friend who had died that day. This was serious business after all.

BELOW In early May, O.C. logs two hours as First Pilot. Now half of his time in the air is spent as Qualified Pilot (Dual). Actual instrument time is also up, as is his time at Liberal. Pilots graduating from Liberal went either east (bound for the European Theater) or west (the Pacific). O.C. wanted to go west for his next stage of training. He soloed on 8 May, and all that was left was an instrument check.

In mid-May his orders came for Lemoore, California, and he flew one of the E series over to Fresno.

INDIVIDUAL FLIGHT RECORD	O.C. KEMP
STATION	LAAF, Liberal, Kansas
FLYING CLASSIFICATION	Plt. 2-8-44
ORGANIZATION ASSIGNED	AAFTC AAFCFTC 34th 2525th AAF B.U. Sec. "H" S.O.D.
MONTH	**May 1944**
AIRCRAFT TYPE	RB-24E
LANDINGS	100
COMMAND PILOT	
CO-PILOT	20:50
QUALIFIED PILOT (DUAL)	19:55
FIRST PILOT (DAY)	:50
FIRST PILOT (NIGHT)	1:15
NON-PILOT DUTY (PASSENGER)	5:40
INSTRUMENT (DAY)	7:30
INSTRUMENT (NIGHT)	9:00
INSTRUMENT TRAINER	
TOTAL TIME THIS MONTH	42:50
TOTAL PILOT TIME TO DATE	322:40

TRANSIT PROCESSING

18 May - 8 June 1944
Hammer Army Air Field
Lemoore, California
461st Army Air Force Base Unit
4th Army Air Force

From Liberal, Kansas, O.C. went west to Hammer Army Air Field in Lemoore, California, which in addition to processing crew transfers, also trained new pilots.

O.C. spent just under three weeks at HAAF awaiting his next orders, which sent him on to Muroc, CA, for further training. Though he did no flying at Hammer, it was there that he was paired with the other officers who would serve with him until the War's end.

BELOW LEFT This photo was taken after a training flight in the desert, where, though it was 100° on the ground, it was freezing at 10,000 feet. From left to right: co-pilot Norman Olson of Dallas, Wisconsin (left) and bombardier Jack Berger of Brooklyn, New York (center).

BELOW RIGHT The first navigator assigned to the crew was replaced during their time at Muroc. Fred Sperling, of Joliet, Illinois, joined the crew there.

BOMBER COMMAND TRAINING

Jun. 8 - Oct. 8, 1944
Muroc Army Air Field
Muroc, California
T-4 Squadron
421st Army Air Force Base Unit
4th Army Air Force

In 1910, Ralph, Clifford, and Effie Corum built a homestead on the edge of Rogers Lake and when a post office was commissioned for the area they named their isolated village Muroc, a reversal of their last name.

In August 1932, General Henry "Hap" Arnold acquired property near the dry lake for a bombing range. The facility became Muroc Army Air Field (MAAF). Over $120 million was spent to develop the base in the 1940s and expand it to 301,000 acres. The main 15,000 foot runway was completed in a single pour of concrete.

LEFT The 4th Army Air Force insignia patch.

BELOW RIGHT During the War, Muroc's primary mission was to provide final combat training for bomber and fighter crews prior to overseas deployment. In addition, due to its remote location, the facility was ideal for the testing of experimental aircraft. The field is in the bottom left of the photo.

But the Muroc installation largely drew attention because nearby Rogers Lake was so flat ("like a giant billiard table," said General Arnold) that it could serve as a giant runway, which was ideal for flight testing. The immense dry lake bed and year-round good weather made MAAF the best location to test America's first jet, the super-secret Bell XP-59A Airacomet.

If you haven't heard of Muroc, never mind. Shortly after the War it was renamed Edwards Air Force Base and was where renowned test pilot Chuck Yeager flew the Bell X-1 faster than sound and where the Space Shuttle landed on occasion.

O.C. was excited to get started. "I'm a B-24 commander now, with all the responsibilities of the job. The crew must learn to work together. We will bomb, give the gunners strafing practice, and go on cross-country flights to give the navigator practice. During all this we'll be getting better acquainted with the B-24 and its little peculiarities."

And it got better: O.C. got two days off every ten days, so he made the 150 mile trip to San Diego whenever he could, driving his Ford Model A. Life was good and getting better. Now he was part of a crew.

B-24J

Consolidated (which became Consolidated-Vultee in March 1943, just a month after O.C. left his work there to be drafted into the Army) re-engineered the G/H model as a starting point for the J model. By then Consolidated had become "Convair," which is a shortening of "Consolidated-Vultee Aircraft." In the 1960s, it changed its name one last time, becoming "General Dynamics," a key NASA subcontractor in the 1960s.

Because of shortages of Emerson nose turrets, a modified version of the A-6 tail turret was used in the first Js. They also had a reconfigured fuel system, a new autopilot and bombsight, and anti-icing equipment. This was the variation produced in the largest quantity, and was so similar to the G and H models that the latter were modified to become Js merely by upgrading the autopilot and bombsight. Sixteen ex-RAF B-24Js remained in service in India until 1967 without a serious accident. There is only one B-24J still flying, the impeccably restored *Witchcraft,* owned by the Collings Foundation of Stow, MA. Rides cost $450.00.

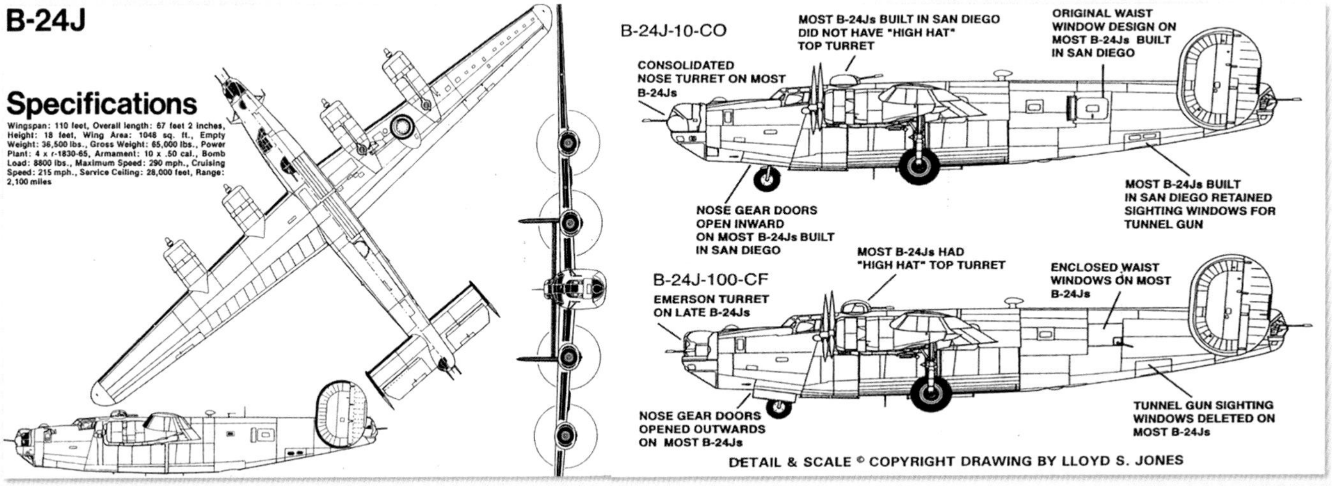

CO-PILOT NORMAN OLSON

Called "Oly" by his fellow officers, Norman J. Olson was an atypical Army Air Force pilot. Raised on a farm near Dallas, Wisconsin, he joined the service years before the War broke out, and in a different country.

Oly was trained as a pilot by the Royal Canadian Air Force but due to U.S. Army regulations was never allowed to captain an American aircraft. He rarely let his disappointment show, however.

Tall, quiet, with a placid personality, he commanded respect and confidence apparently without effort.

And he did it all without knowing how to read. During down time on Angaur Island in the Pacific, bombardier Jack Berger would sit down with Oly and teach him to read by going through a dictionary with him.

Oly was a sun worshiper. "He was always in great shape," remembers Berger. "Really proud of his physique." He was also a tremendously competent and reliable co-pilot. O.C. always mentioned his name with a smile on his face and an occasional tear in his eye. He loved the man like a brother.

After the War, Oly returned to Wisconsin, went to college, and eventually graduated from law school, practicing in Chicago for many years. He never married but remained a bachelor. He died in January 1982.

NAVIGATOR FRED SPERLING

While training at Muroc, after a near-collision with a mountain, O.C. asked that his assigned navigator be replaced—too much was riding on his skills and on the fifteen hour missions they would be flying over the endless waters of the Pacific the navigator was arguably the most important crewman. Fred Sperling, of New Lenox, IL, fit the order perfectly. Dapper and relaxed, he knew his job well and did it right every time.

RIGHT Fred on the left, Oly on the right.

Fred had only one problem: he sometimes got airsick. The other officers used to tease him about it, handing him paper bags before a flight, but he soon got over it. And it never interfered with his work.

Fred was the only officer on the crew who was married during the War. On Valentine's Day 1943 he wed his high school sweetheart Marjorie in Joliet, IL. After the War, Fred remained in the service, serving in Korea and Vietnam. In 1980, after 38 years, he retired a Lt. Colonel but kept on working, then for Rockwell International, finally retiring after thirty years there. He died in 2003.

BOMBARDIER JACK BERGER

Jack Berger is the last of Crew 23A still with us at 94. He describes himself as a "little Jewish kid from Brooklyn," but that's just the beginning. Let Jack tell his story:

"I was the youngest of four kids. We were a rich family: we moved every six months to avoid paying rent. My father was a barber who never made a living. We had nothing. We lived in a sixth floor tenement walk-up. When I was nine, I worked after school making deliveries, getting two cents for each one. And every day I walked four miles to school to save five cents bus fare.

"All my friends were in the service and I knew I'd be called up, so in 1942 I enlisted as an Air Cadet. I was good at math and knew I was a cinch to pass the Air Force tests, even though I had flat feet.

"I wanted to be a pilot, but during training I bounced the plane forty feet off the ground during a landing. On another day I tried taking off when there was another plane already on the runway. Though we did not collide, my instructor said, 'You're a bombardier. Period.'

"During bombardier training, they put us up on a lift about twenty feet high and we sighted through the Norden bombsight, synchronizing on objects that looked like they were 15,000 feet below. It was like dropping a plum into a pickle barrel from a hundred feet above, but when I released my 'bombs' they always hit dead center. I had the knack. In class, when my instructor asked questions I would never raise my hand but he'd look at me anyway and say, 'You, the kid from Brooklyn, what's the answer?' He knew I knew it. After my training, he asked me to stick around and become an instructor, but I turned him down. I came out the winner.

"I met the other officers of our crew in Muroc. We were very gung ho—we always wanted to fly. And I still wanted to be a pilot, so once Omer put me in the co-pilot's seat. I was having fun but I drifted ten miles off course in five seconds.

"When I got out of the service I met my future wife Muriel at a Halloween party. I was still in uniform. Our first date cost $1.20 and I only had $3.00 in my pocket. We got married and I went into the men's furnishings business with Muriel's father. We worked seven days a week and eventually had two stores. 'Pop' Seidman was the gentlest man I ever knew. And I shone in his eyes."

In a letter home, O.C. described Jack as a "quite a card. Everyone on the crew gets along together great. After all, we're going to be spending a lot of time together and it will be easier because we like each other."

Throughout this book, many of the details about O.C.'s crew are given us courtesy of Jack's great memory.

LEFT Jack and Rusty Restuccia (radio/radar operator and prolific nose artist of, among other planes, *Rover Boy's Baby*) in front of *All American*, the last flying B-24J. Rusty helped restore her.

RIGHT O.C. and Jack in the cockpit of *Rover Boy's Baby.*

EXTRA! **Pacific Post** **EXTRA!**

Section One | MONDAY, JUNE 19, 1944 | Ten Cents

IT'S AN EARLY THANKSGIVING!

SAIPAN INVASION AND THE GREAT MARIANAS TURKEY SHOOT

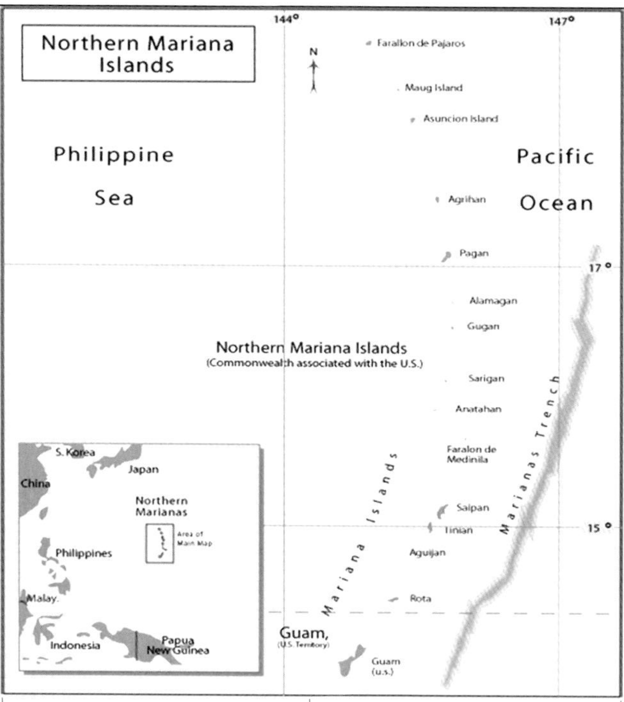

SAVING SAIPAN

MARIANA ISLANDS, Apr. 29 — The Marianas are a 1,500 mile long, arc-shaped archipelago forming the east boundary of the Philippine Sea. The islands are actually the tops of 15 volcanos which stand west of the world's deepest ocean recess, the Marianas Trench, formed as the Pacific tectonic plate slipped under the Asiatic one.

On 7 December 1941, Japan had taken our island, Guam, and we needed it back for its airbase, which we would then use to fly over Tokyo and destroy the Empire. Simple as that.

By this time, we had taken back most Japanese conquests except the Philippines, the Carolines, the Palaus, and the Marianas, so on the day before D-Day in Europe, an Allied invasion fleet left Hawaii bound for Saipan, which it intended to liberate, then retake Guam, from which B-29 Superfortresses with their 5,000 mile range would strike Japan.

On 13 June, the first of 165,000 shells were hurled at the 45 square mile island and landings began at dawn two days later when 8,000 Marines slogged ashore.

The enemy was ready. They had placed flags in the bay to indicate range and their artillery destroyed twenty amphibious tanks while still offshore. Barbed wire, machine guns nests, and mined trenches took many American lives, but by nightfall the Marines had a beachhead along ten miles of shore. That night the Japanese attacked but were driven back with heavy losses.

By 18 June, the Marines had taken the airfield, and like the battle for Kwajalein, an action hundreds of miles away ensured that the Japs would not be able to take it back, though they tried mightily over the next six weeks with several bloody engagements and a final, desperate *banzai* charge on 7 July.

Saipan was our most costly victory thus far: 3,000 dead and 10,000 wounded. The Japanese lost 30,000 men.

THE BATTLE OF THE PHILIPPINE SEA

PHILIPPINE SEA, Jun. 19 – The sea action that enabled victory in Saipan was also one of the greatest air battles in history, the fifth and last carrier-to-carrier battle of the War, and resulted in the almost total destruction of Japanese naval capability.

The small cadre of highly-trained Japanese pilots had been decimated at the Coral Sea and Midway engagements. Meanwhile, America had been training tens of thousands of pilots to exacting standards.

The Japs expected us to attack the Carolines or Palaus first and so were surprised when Saipan came within our sights instead. Undaunted, Admiral Toyoda ordered his fleet east to counter-attack.

But on 15 June, U.S. subs discovered his fleet and Task Force 58 formed a line to meet them. Jap reconnaissance identified the U.S. fleet on 19 June and the battle began as F6F Hellcats engaged Zeros, shooting down 35 as they launched from Orote Field on Guam.

More lop-sided engagements followed, one in which 25 Zeros plunged into the sea, while only one American fighter fell.

A huge sortie of over 100 aircraft was intercepted by U.S. airmen, who shot down 70, and a third raid of 50 fighters was intercepted by 40 Hellcats, who shot down 7, losing none.

The fourth wave could not find the U.S. fleet and headed to Guam to refuel, where they were met by more Hellcats, and 30 of the 50 were shot down, leading one American pilot to exclaim, "This is like an old-time turkey shoot!"

That day the tide of the War turned as the Japanese lost 650 aircraft, two carriers, and any edge their navy had left.

Over the two days of the battle, F6F Hellcats were responsible for 500 kills while losing only 24 planes.

With its best pilots gone, only one option remained for the Japanese fleet: the *kamikaze*.

THE HIGH LIFE

Since Muroc was only 150 miles from San Diego, O.C. went home every ten days during the summer of 1944. Fred Sperling had family in Los Angeles and gadfly Jack Berger made friends everywhere and knew people in L.A., so O.C. gave them both rides there and back in his Ford. They were so free they felt like civilians.

At Muroc, O.C.'s time was spent getting to know his fellow officers and the six enlisted men who had been assigned to his crew, none of whom had ever flown in a B-24 before. It was thus O.C.'s turn to be an instructor, to teach the enlisted men the ins and outs of the world's most complex machine. Though the instruction was a chore to pilots, the practice had a logic about it: crews, learning about the machine that could either save or take their life, respected their instructors. In turn, the officers were forced to review their own knowledge and find answers to the enlisted men's questions.

The officers were warned, however, to maintain military discipline. "When push comes to shove, if they think you're their buddy, they won't obey orders," they were told. "They should always call you 'sir' or 'lieutenant.' You call them by their rank or last name."

O.C. wondered at the formality of it all, but obeyed orders. For his efforts, his crew would come to respect him and follow his lead.

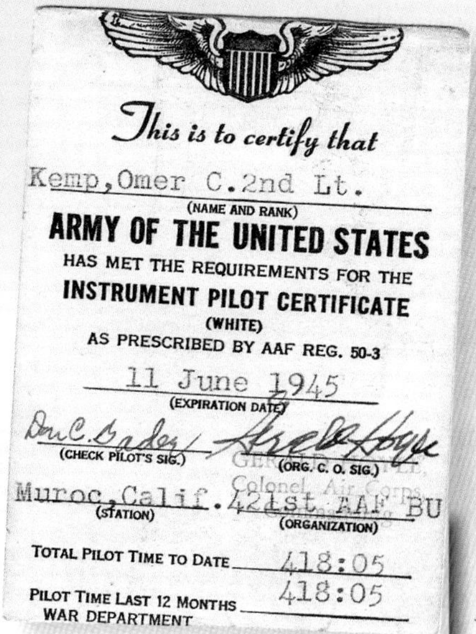

This is to certify that

Kemp, Omer C. 2nd Lt.
(NAME AND RANK)

ARMY OF THE UNITED STATES
HAS MET THE REQUIREMENTS FOR THE
INSTRUMENT PILOT CERTIFICATE
(WHITE)
AS PRESCRIBED BY AAF REG. 50-3

11 June 1945
(EXPIRATION DATE)

(CHECK PILOT'S SIG.) (ORG. C. O. SIG.)
Colonel, Air Corps

Muroc, Calif. 421st AAF BU
(STATION) (ORGANIZATION)

TOTAL PILOT TIME TO DATE 418:05
PILOT TIME LAST 12 MONTHS 418:05
WAR DEPARTMENT

RIGHT O.C. finished his final checkride and receives his Instrument Pilot Certificate, the biggest feather in his cap yet.

AUDIO TRANSCRIPT 07:02:20

In Muroc, we were flying out there on the dry lake. The Air Force field was about three feet above the lake bed. We were flying air-to-ground gunnery. We used to love that. We would fly right up over the Joshua bushes and down through the canyons and we were shooting at the ground. The waist gunners had to learn to strafe. We didn't have any nose turrets or we could have really shot up things.

But some of those guys were flying a little bit low and one guy came in with Joshua trees stuck in his cowling and rocks in the bomb bay! We were supposed to fly at two hundred feet and most of us flew at sixteen.

We'd use these little blue bombs -- hundred pound bombs -- and we had to hit the target and it would shoot off a little puff of smoke when it hit. It wouldn't damage anything much when it went off -- it could land in your back yard. It was sort of a "safe" bomb. We bombed these targets that had big circles white-washed out in the desert and you had to fly over them and practice.

EXTRA! **Pacific Post** EXTRA!

Section One | THURSDAY, JULY 20, 1944 | Ten Cents

FORAGING FOR THE ENEMY

WE SKIP THE CAROLINES AND GO STRAIGHT FOR THE MARIANAS

Following the Marshall and Gilbert campaigns, Operation Forager was launched in the Marianas and Palaus under the command of Admiral Nimitz. It was intended to neutralize Japanese outposts, support our drive to retake the Philippines, and provide bases for the bombing of Japan.

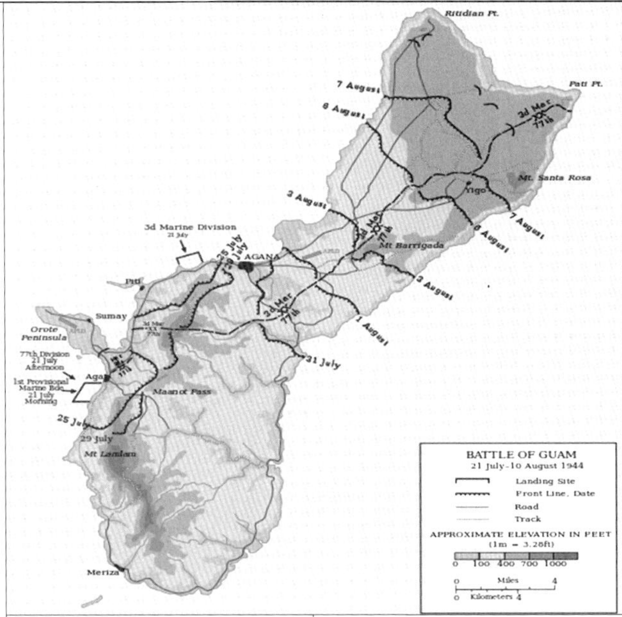

GUAM

MARIANA ISLANDS, Jul. 21 – Located at the southern end of the Mariana chain, Guam had been a U.S. protectorate since before the War. We lost it on 10 December 1941 and we needed it back.

By now we'd learned how to take an island: on 7 July aerial bombardment by carrier aircraft and B-24s began, then, once air superiority was ensured, close battleship bombardment followed.

By the invasion on 21 July, the islands had been pulverized. None the less, when Marines stormed the beaches on both sides of the Orote Peninsula, the Japs fought back fiercely, though by 9:00 A.M. the beachheads were secure and by nightfall our boys had moved a mile inland.

Counter-attacks, mostly at night using infiltration tactics, were ferocious, and the losses on both sides were terrible.

Because of the reefs surrounding the island, ships were anchored hundreds of yards offshore and supplies had to be ferried ashore, often under heavy enemy fire.

The airfield at Orote and the Apra harbor were not secured until 25 July. The Japanese then withdrew to the mountainous northern end of the island, where, cut off from supply, they nevertheless—as we had seen before—fought bitterly to the last man.*

On 10 August, on Mount Barrigada, resistance ended with the ritual suicide of Lt. Gen. Hideyoshi Obata.

Even before the end of hostilities, the Seabees had started building five large airfields for the B-17s and B-24s that would soon go to work softening up the Philippines.

TINIAN

MARIANA ISLANDS, Jul. 24 – Tinian, just 3.5 miles across a shallow strait from Saipan, was needed for airfields, so as soon as Saipan was secured, shelling of the S-shaped, 39-square mile island began.

A feint toward Tinian Town in the south masked the Marine landing on 24 July in the north.

Intense shelling by the Japanese resulted in serious damage to two U.S. ships, and stubborn resistance on land, mirroring the Saipan defense—daytime retreats and nighttime counter-attacks—would have resulted in more Allied deaths if not for the gentle terrain, which permitted the use of tanks and our newest weapon: napalm, an explosive mixture of jellied gasoline which burned away foliage around enemy redoubts.

When the island was declared secure on 31 July, 8,000 Japanese were dead. Only 323 American lives were lost.

Tinian soon became an important base for Allied operations, boasting the busiest airfield of the War.

Latest War Bulletins

KYUSHU, JAPAN, Jun. 15 – Flying from Chinese bases, B-29s attack the Japan homeland for the first time, dropping 200 tons of bombs on steelworks at Yawata.

TOKYO, JAPAN, Jul. 18. – Japanese Prime Minister General Tojo resigns following the IJF defeat at Saipan. General Koiso forms a new government

RASTENBURG, PRUSSIA, Jul. 20 – At his Wolf's Lair headquarters, as the chiefs of staff began their daily meeting, an explosion nearly takes life of Adolf Hitler. Suspicions point to high ranking military service members.

BIAK ISLAND, NEW GUINEA, Jul. 23 – Final mopping up of the Japanese positions in the Ibdi area begins.

CHINA, Jul. 23 – Gen. Chiang Kai-shek gives U.S. Gen. Stillwell command of Chinese Forces but demands that the Communist army recognize the authority of the Nationalist government.

COUTANCES, FRANCE, Jul. 25 – The American 1st Army launches Operation Cobra south of St. Lô.

*Some held out. On 24 January 1972 Sergeant Shoichi Yokoi was discovered by hunters. He had lived alone in a cave for 27 years, believing the War was still on.

THERE'S A WAR ON . . .

In a letter from his folks, O.C. was apprised of a B-24 training crash that appeared in the *San Diego Union* newspaper. "Yes, I knew the pilot," wrote O.C. "He was in Liberal, Kansas with me. I knew him very well."

"I suppose you heard about the accidents here," he wrote a couple of weeks later. "Two ships blew up in mid-air about five minutes apart. Five were killed on one ship and one on the other. They don't know yet what caused it but will before long. I didn't fly that night because my navigator was grounded. The ships were in our section. This is the first accident we have had since we've been here. It's upsetting and a terrible reminder."

. . . BUT NOT HERE, NOT THIS MINUTE

On one of their cross-country flights, O.C. flew to Salt Lake City. "I didn't land, though I flew over downtown and up to Ogden and looked over the lake from about 100 feet."

O.C.'s Model A was running its tires bald. In early August, he invited "Oly" Olson to go to San Diego with him for the weekend. A few days before, he wrote his mom: "He hasn't been off base in a couple of weeks. I hope you will have a big dinner for us when we get there Wednesday, 'cause we'll be plenty hungry. And tell Mavis to get ready for a date with my boy Olson." O.C.'s sister Mavis was still pining for Chauncey Rogers, the young Marine who, after the gruelling New Britain campaign, was on well-deserved R&R in the Russell Islands, but her daily letter-writing to Chauncey didn't mean she couldn't go on an innocent double date with her brother and his co-pilot.

By mid-August O.C. writes, "There is a rumor that we may stay here until the 1st of October. I'm not sure yet so I'll wait and see. Ground school and flying are pretty near wound up, so we don't have anything else to do. They have so many crews waiting to go overseas now that they can't find room for them. I suppose it will take longer than they expected."

BELOW O.C. continues to rack up flight time through August as First Pilot, as well as putting in time on alternate days in the Link Trainer.

INDIVIDUAL FLIGHT RECORD	O.C. KEMP
STATION	MAAF, Muroc, California
FLYING CLASSIFICATION	Plt. 2-8-44
ORGANIZATION ASSIGNED	4th Army Air Force 421st AAF B.U. T-3
MONTH	**August 1944**
AIRCRAFT TYPE	B-24D, B-24J
LANDINGS	20
COMMAND PILOT	
CO-PILOT	1:00
QUALIFIED PILOT (DUAL)	6:00
FIRST PILOT (DAY)	36:55
FIRST PILOT (NIGHT)	1:30
NON-PILOT DUTY (PASSENGER)	
INSTRUMENT (DAY)	5:00
INSTRUMENT (NIGHT)	1:30
INSTRUMENT TRAINER	10:30
TOTAL TIME THIS MONTH	45:25
TOTAL PILOT TIME TO DATE	467:30

AUDIO TRANSCRIPT 08:00:00

One day we finished flight training about two o'clock. That was supposed to be the end of the day but I wanted to fly home and buzz my folks' house, so I signed up for some local time and asked if any of the crew wanted to go to San Diego with me. About half of them did. I had Juan Gutierrez the engineer, Cal Morrow the radio man, Oly, Fred, and Jack.

So I climbed her out and just left it on climb-out power and I went up over L.A. like a shot -- we were really going! I had to get down to San Diego and back in time enough to fly the local. San Diego is about one hundred fifty miles from Muroc, as the crow flies, I guess.

So we came down here about a hundred ninety miles an hour. The old Liberator usually cruises at one-sixty. I could see State College to the east and I could see where my street was. It stuck out from all the other streets around. You could line right up on it and that's what I did.

I stuck the old nose down and put the throttle and the turbos up against the firewall. In a moment I was going close to two seventy, diving the bomber.

I came down over Winona Street so fast that if they would have had forty foot TV antennas like we have now [the 1970s], I would have taken them all out like grass.

Out in the alley behind the house we had these telephone poles that at one time had a double storey of wires on them, which they had long since taken off, but they didn't bother to cut off the poles and they were sticking up high and they were going by my window like a picket fence.

When we passed the street, at first I was quite a ways from the Navy's long-range radio towers out near Chollas, three giant things that stick way up there, about six or seven hundred feet. I looked up and all of a sudden they were right in front of me! I hung back on the wheel and I went right up like a homesick angel, as they say.

Now the secret to making a "buzz-job" is to never come back again. They will be there with their camera taking your number down. I turned around, went back to Muroc, did my local flying, landed, and swore everybody to secrecy. Then I got in my Model A and drove back to San Diego. Three hours later, I'm home.

"Did you guys see a B-24 around here, flying low?"

"No, but an airplane just about crashed!"

"That was me!"

"UP LIKE A HOMESICK ANGEL"

Here we're reminded that O.C. is still a 20 year-old kid, after all. No matter what he's experienced over the last year, he is not above risking his life—and not just his own—for a joyride in an expensive aircraft.

O.C.'s sister Gloria remembers seeing the bomber when it roared overhead, knocking china off shelves, rattling windows, and shaking chimney bricks off neighbors' houses (and their own).

They all ran outside to see that was happening, but her dad hurriedly guided the kids back inside the house and pulled down the black-out curtains, telling them, "We don't know who that was, do we?"

EXTRA! **Pacific Post** EXTRA!

Section One THURSDAY, SEPTEMBER 17, 1944 Ten Cents

OPERATION STALEMATE STALLS

THE BATTLE FOR THE PALAU ISLANDS MEETS STIFF JAP RESISTANCE

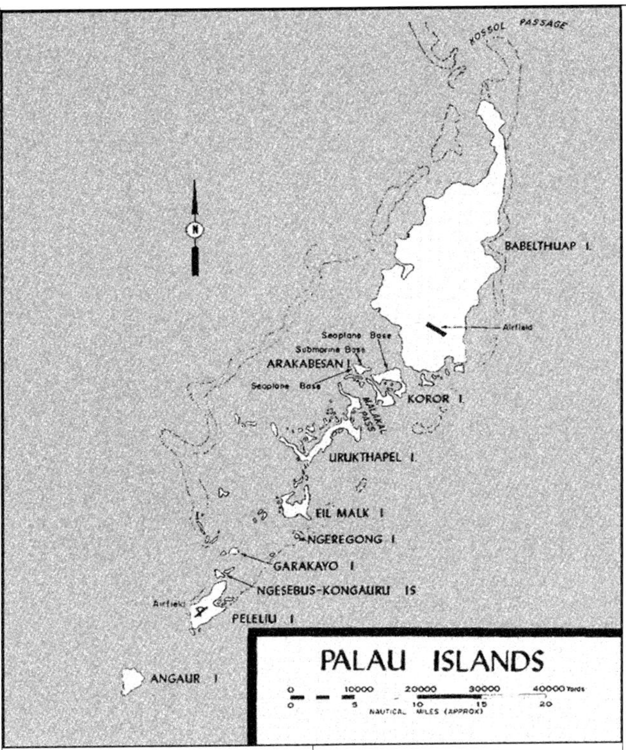

Having pierced Japan's defensive perimeter in the Marshalls and reestablishing our base at Guam in the Marianas, the principal Jap naval base was then moved west to the Palau Islands, just 400 miles east of the Philippines. The Palaus had to be taken to protect MacArthur's right flank when he return to the Philippines, but Admiral Koga had stated that the Palaus must be "held to the death." That they were.

PERIL AT PELELIU

PALAU ISLANDS, Sep. 12 — Learning from their mistakes in the Solomons, Gilberts, Marshalls, and Marianas—where they met the Americans on the beaches—in the Palaus the Japanese focused their defenses inland, where, in the highlands of Peleliu, honeycombed with bunkers, they could wait out the invaders, who, the Japs believed, would soon tire of slow attrition from snipers and infiltrators and move on.

Mt. Umurbrogol, which oversaw the entire island as well as the airstrip, was fortified with miles of tunnels connecting machine gun emplacements. The beaches were covered with obstacles and mines. Taking Peleliu promised to be expensive in blood and treasure.

Unfortunately, we did *not* alter our tactics, and planned three divisions of Marines landing in the southwest near the airfield. As usual, an armada of warships hurled tons of explosives at the six square mile island, which the Navy believed would neutralize the enemy. Tragically, they were wrong.

As the Marines came ashore on 15 September, the Japs opened the steel doors of their gun emplacements and destroyed 60 landing craft, killing scores of men. And when the Marines took the airfield, Jap tanks struck back.

But even though we had lost 200 men and 900 wounded and were still mostly trapped on the beaches, American commanders believed victory was near because they had pierced the Jap perimeter. They were wrong again.

By the third day, the airfield was secure and was being used for spotting enemy aircraft. The Army joined the fray and the long process of weeding out the dug-in defenders began as Navy Corsairs dropped napalm to clear foliage.

And to the north, Mt. Umurbrogol, towering over the tiny island, remained the enemy stronghold, with its sharp ridges overlooking narrow defiles. One such ridge, known after as "Bloody Nose Ridge," was the site of the one of the most horrific battles of the War.

As the Marines moved forward, Jap snipers picked off stretcher bearers, knowing another man would be called to carry the wounded, and thus present another easy target. They also infiltrated foxholes by night, inflicting casualties.

After six days on Bloody Nose, the Marines lost more than half of the division's 3,000 men. They were then withdrawn and replaced by the Army's 81st Infantry, who battled another month more before securing Mt. Umurbrogol at the cost of over 1,800 American lives. Meanwhile, the Japanese lost 10,000 men defending Peleliu.

The battle was controversial due to the high death toll and the island's apparent lack of strategic value. It was never used for staging operation in subsequent invasions. And because Allied commanders had predicted a three-day battle, few reporters followed the invasion and thus America was shocked when the death toll was finally made public.

But we learned a terrible lesson on Peleliu that would save lives in the major battles to come: Iwo Jima and the invasion of Okinawa. Many had died so others would live.

THE LAST FULL MEASURE

Armiger Chauncey Rogers was killed in the Battle of Peleliu on 16 September 1944. Chauncey was a "runner," carrying messages between Marine combat units when he was shot in the head by a Japanese sniper on the second day of battle.

Mavis Kemp received the telegram a few days later. Chauncey had listed her as next of kin. The 17 year-old girl was devastated. "I cried for weeks," she said. "He was the kindest, sweetest boy and I loved him with all my heart. He was the first person I knew personally who died in the War. It took a long time for me to get over his death."

Chauncey was remembered as a high-spirited boy who loved to ride his Indian motorcycle and chafed against his parents' strict rules, often running away from home for short spells when he was young. His brother Newell, ten years his junior, remembers "crying like a baby" at his hero brother's funeral in Pocatello, ID.

Chauncey was 19 years-old when he died along with 1,251 other brave Marines in the taking of Peleliu Island.

OVER THERE OVER HERE

O.C. now adds cross-country "bombing missions" to his training. These flights, including one to Portland, gave Fred Sperling experience finding targets and then getting them home over deserts as featureless as a South Pacific sea under a moonless sky. They were kept an extra month for training. "When I get to the Pacific, I'll be ready to fight," wrote O.C. On some missions flak was actually shot at them. "They came a little close and hit two of the ships this morning," he wrote home.

<u>INDIVIDUAL FLIGHT RECORD</u>	O.C. KEMP
STATION	MAAF, Muroc, California
FLYING CLASSIFICATION	Plt. 2-8-44
ORGANIZATION ASSIGNED	4th Army Air Force 421st AAF BU T-3
MONTH	**September 1944**
AIRCRAFT TYPE	B-24D, B-24E, B-24J
LANDINGS	9
COMMAND PILOT	
CO-PILOT	
QUALIFIED PILOT (DUAL)	16:50
FIRST PILOT (DAY)	13:30
FIRST PILOT (NIGHT)	6:45
NON-PILOT DUTY (PASSENGER)	
INSTRUMENT (DAY)	9:30
INSTRUMENT (NIGHT)	6:45
INSTRUMENT TRAINER	:55
TOTAL TIME THIS MONTH	37:25
TOTAL PILOT TIME TO DATE	556:40

R E S T R I C T E D

SPECIAL ORDERS)
:
NUMBER 258)

MUROC ARMY AIR FIELD
Muroc, California, 8 October 1944

E X T R A C T

1. In acc with par 6, AR 605-145 & par 2a (2), AR 615-200, the fol-named personnel, AC unasgd (HBC), are reld fr atchd 421st AAF BU, Sq "T", are atchd & WP 4 AF Processing Unit, Army Air Base, Hamilton Field, Calif, so as to arrive thereat not later than 1800, 11 Oct '44 for final processing, prior to overseas asgmt. PCS.

Travel by rail and/or Govt motor vehicle is directed. TC will furn the nec T. Meal tickets will be furn for two hundred forty (240) EM for two (2) meals per man under the prov of AR 30-2215, as amended, a/r $1.00 per meal when meals are taken in the dining car, or a/r $.75 per meal if taken elsewhere.

Personnel will not be accompanied by dependents, nor will dependents join personnel at new sta. TPA not atzd.

CREW 425:

P	2d Lt.	1092	OMER C. KEMP	0 710 957	Pilot
CP	F/O	1051	NORMAN J. OLSON	T 192 976	Co-pilot
N	2nd Lt.	1034	FREDERICK C. SPERLING, JR.	02 060 604	Navigator
B	F/O	1035	JACK A. BERGER	T3 712	Bombardier
E	Cpl.	748	Juan F. Gutierrez	39 550 289	Engineer
R	Cpl.	757	Calvin G. Morrow	19 130 002	Radioman
AG	Cpl.	612	Lloyd I. Nygren	39 280 958	Gunner - Belly
G	Cpl.	611	Eugene W. Vaughn	37 616 773	Gunner - Nose
G	Cpl.	611	Charles K. Yetter	37 558 620	Gunner - Upper
G	Cpl.	611	Joseph A. Trasatti	13 133 599	Gunner - Tail

Tr Comdr will carry all records for Officers and EM and present them to Comdt of Crews at destination. TPA is not atzd.

TC will furn nec T. In accordance with AR 30-2215, the QMC will issue one (1) emergency meal ticket a/r not to exceed $1.00 per meal per man, when taken in a dining car to one-hundred and twenty-three (123) EM for any unforeseen delay enroute. TDN. 1-5250 P 431-01, 02, 03, 04, 07, 08 A 0425-24.

By order of Colonel HOYLE:

MILTON H. LEVINE
Capt, Air Corps
Ass't Adjutant

ABOVE O.C.'s transfer to Hamilton Field, CA for final processing before his departure overseas. Here, for the first time, we see the full Crew 425 roster, the nine men who will remain with O.C. throughout the War. Officer's names are capitalized, enlisted men in lower case.

RIGHT Standing, L-R: Jack Berger (bombardier), Fred Sperling (navigator), Norman Olson (co-pilot), O.C. Kemp (pilot), and Calvin Morrow (radioman).

Kneeling, L-R: Joseph Trasatti (tail gunner), Lloyd Nygren (Sperry Ball gunner), Juan Gutierrez (engineer and top gunner), Eugene Vaughn (left waist gunner), and Charles Yetter (nose gunner).

TRANSIT PROCESSING

8 October - 1 November 1944
Hamilton Army Air Field
Novato, California
460th Army Air Force Base Unit
4th Army Air Force

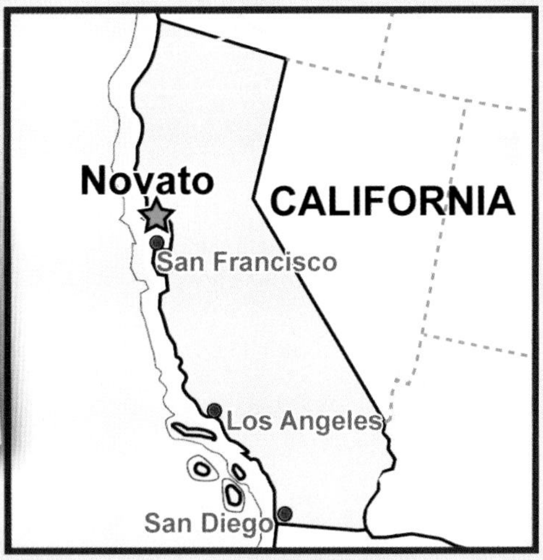

Hamilton Airfield was named after 1st Lt. Lloyd Hamilton of the 17th Aero Squadron, who was awarded the Distinguished Service Cross for heroism at Varssonaore, Belgium, in leading a low level bombing attack on a German airdrome thirty miles behind enemy lines on 13 August 1918. The Air Transport Command (ATC) used Hamilton as a major aerial port and transshipment facility for troops and cargo heading to the Pacific and CBI (China-Burma-India) theaters. Sadly, the first B-17s to travel to Hawaii left Hamilton AAB and arrived in Honolulu on the morning of 7 December 1941. The radar operators, mistaking the oncoming Japanese attack aircraft for the expected American planes, paid no attention when a swarm of them appeared on their scopes.

Novato was only sixty miles from Palo Alto, where O.C.'s Aunt Opal lived, so most weekends he hitchhiked across the Golden Gate Bridge and down the peninsula to visit her family. The three weeks at Hamilton were spent waiting for an aircraft to take overseas. "Most of the new ships are Ls," he wrote home. "I hope I get one from San Diego. We will be so heavily loaded that the bombardier and one of the gunners will go overseas by C-47. We should leave the states within a month from now."

AUDIO TRANSCRIPT 07:01:30 / 07:07:20

Hamilton was an old base. It wasn't a War "spring-up" like many of them were; it was a permanent thing. The generals lived there and it was very nice.

They sent me up a brand-new B-24 from San Diego. It had two hours on the tach. That same bunch that I used to carry parts up and down for had built me an airplane a year later . . . and I was flying it!

In his 24 October letter he mentions for the first time that his family should not share what he has written in his letter about his goings and comings. "Don't broadcast anything I told you as it wouldn't be good until I get overseas. Everything I do is supposed to be secret."

LEFT An artist's rendition of Hamilton AAB circa 1943. Today, the air field is no more. The runway is a bird sanctuary and the hangers have been converted into office space.

EXTRA! **Pacific Post** EXTRA!

Section One | THURSDAY, OCTOBER 20, 1944 | Ten Cents

MACARTHUR RETURNS!

AND A TERRIBLE NEW JAPANESE WEAPON IS UNVEILED

The Philippines were an important source of rubber and also commanded the sea routes by which petroleum was shipped. For the U.S., capturing the Philippines brought us one step closer to Japan. It was also a personal matter for Supreme Allied Commander Douglas MacArthur: two and a half years before, he left the Philippines vowing to return, insisting that we had a moral obligation to liberate the 7,000 island archipelago. So, in September, carrier-borne aircraft began a systematic destruction of Japanese air power on the islands.

LANDING AT LEYTE

LEYTE ISLAND, PHILIPPINES, Oct. 20 – Leyte, north of Mindanao, was chosen for its approachable beaches, existing roads, and relatively weak defenses.

On 20 October, the 6th Army came ashore on Leyte's northeastern coast. Resistance was light and by 13:30 General MacArthur made his dramatic entrance through the surf stating, "I have returned!"

But along with a million Filipinos on the island, there were 70,000 IJF soldiers, and resistance in the mountainous interior was fierce. The north was secured first, and then we pushed south, where four airstrips were under Japanese control. And, unlike recent island engagements, the Japanese sent dozens of air sorties from nearby bases over the invaders, strafing and bombing.

By mid-December, 200,000 Americans hand landed on Leyte and organized resistance was over by 19 December with over 80,000 Japanese dead.

HORROR FROM THE SKY

LEYTE GULF, PHILIPPINES, Oct. 23 – What began for the 3rd and 7th Fleets as a routine support mission for the Leyte landings became history's largest naval engagement as Japan, surprising the Allies with Operation Sho-go ("Victory"), committed its entire fleet in four sea engagements in the waters east of Leyte Island.

Sho-go had three prongs: one task force would lure Admiral Halsey's 3rd Fleet north out of the area while two others sailed down either side of Leyte to prevent the Allied landings. We took the bait, engaging them on either side of Leyte Island, nearly losing both fleets.

On 24 October, Halsey's reconnaissance planes spotted the north decoy force and took the bait there as well, leaving only our escort groups to protect the Leyte landings.

The next day Halsey engaged the Jap fleet, sinking two cruisers, but superior Jap firepower sunk two U.S. carriers. Sailers were then horrified to see fighters and bombers diving straight at them, intent upon crashing into the ships. The *kamikaze* ("divine wind") attack was born.

A Zero plowed into the flight deck of the *St. Lô*, causing fires that spread to the magazine, sinking the carrier. By 26 October, 55 kamikazes had damaged the carriers *Sangamon, Suwannee,* and *Santee,* and escorts *White Plains, Kalinin Bay,* and *Kitkun Bay.* In total, seven carriers had been hit, as well as forty other ships.

Nevertheless, Halsey's task force sunk four Jap carriers. Then he turned his force south to reinforce our landing forces.

Notwithstanding the horrific *kamikaze* attacks, the Battle of Leyte Gulf proved a disaster for the IJN, which lost 28 of 64 warships to America's 6 of 218. The vast superiority of American sea power, proven time and again in the island-hopping campaigns, now made the conquest of the Empire possible, but at an unprecedented and unthinkable cost—to both sides.

R E S T R I C T E D

SPECIAL ORDERS) HAMILTON ARMY AIR FIELD
:
NUMBER 370/5/953) Hamilton Field, California 31 October 1944

SUBJECT: Movement Orders, Shipment No. FC-114-AS, Crew No. FC-114-AS 26

					B-24 L
2nd Lt.	KEMP, OMER C.	0710957	AC 1092	P	AIRPLANE NO.
2nd Lt.	OLSON, NORMAN J.	0192976	AC 1051	CP	44-41501
2nd Lt.	SPERLING, FREDERICK C. JR.	02060604	AC 1034	N	
F/O	BERGER, JACK A.	T3712	AC 1035	B	
Cpl	Gutierrez, Juan F.	39550289	748	ABG	PROJECT NO.
Cpl	Morrow, Calvin G.	19130002	757	ROG	96787-R
Cpl	Nygren, Lloyd I.	39280958	612	AG	
Cpl	Vaughn, Eugene W.	37616773	611	AG	
Cpl	Yetter, Charles K.	37558620	611	AG	
Cpl	Trasatti, Joseph A.	13133599	611	AG	

1. You are reld fr atchd 460th AAF Base Unit and fr TD at Hamilton Field, Calif and are asgd to Shipment No FC-114-AS, with crew no as indicated above, and WP immediately in mil acft indicated above to Fairfield-Suisun Army Air Field, Fairfield, Calif, RUAT to the CO for temp duty, thence to the overseas destination of this shipment by air.

2. This is a PCS with TD enroute. Dependents will not accompany nor join pers at any assembly point, staging area or port of aerial embarkation. TPA is not atzd. Except as may be necessary in the transaction of official business, individuals are prohibited fr discussing their overseas destination even by shipment number. Each indiv has been indoctrinated in matters of security and censorship of all activities if pers under movement orders; and has been instructed not to file safe arrival telegrams with commercial agencies while enroute to or at overseas destination.

3. In lieu of subs, a flat per diem of seven dollars ($7.00) is atzd for C & F/O for travel and for periods of TD enroute to final overseas destination, in accordance with existing law and regulations. Payment of mileage is not atzd.

//

7. Pers will use APO 16655 c/o Postmaster, San Francisco, Calif suffixed by the last two letters of the shipment no and crew no to which asgd (example: APO 16655-AS 5). Immediately upon arrival overseas and upon asmt to an orgn, pers will use the address of the troops at that place and will furnish their perm APO and cable addresses to their friends, relatives and publishers by forwarding WD AGO Forms 971 (V-mail change of address form) and to the theatre postal officer by dispatching WD AGO Form No 204 (Notice of Change of Address).

8. Baggage to be transported by air will not exceed weights as amended, reflected on line e of weight chart List G. Officer baggage not transported by air may be shipped to the Seattle Port of Embarkation for movement to overseas destinations, marked as follows:

TO: PORT TRANS O (PE)
SEATTLE PORT OF EMBARKATION
SEATTLE, WASHINGTON
FOR: FC-114-AS (followed by crew number)

By order of Colonel MELIN:

JAMES J. EILERS,
CWO, USA,
Assistant Adjutant

GET A MOVE ON

O.C. is directed to leave Hamilton Field and go to Fairfield-Suisun AAB in Fairfield, CA, along with his crew, but he's taking something else along as well: a brand-new B-24L, serial no. 44-41501. It has the latest radar equipment and just ten hours on the tach. He's responsible for this aircraft until they arrive at their destination, wherever that is. He and his crew are now known as crew "26" on this cryptically-named Special Project: FC-114-AS 26. Note that they're prohibited from discussing their destination. At this point it is not clear if even *they* know where they're headed.

B-24L

The battle-tested B-24J lacked very little, but went overboard in its armaments. Bristling with defensive weapons, it had become too heavy for high altitudes. With new long-range fighter escorts like the P-51 Mustang now joining the Liberators on missions, the bombers did not have to be so heavily armed. The first thing to go was the Sperry ventral turret, which was replaced by a ring of two .50 caliber machine guns.

The new M-6 "Stinger" tail turret cut 200 pounds. And with less steel plating, the L weighed 1000 pounds less than the J. Waist gun windows were enclosed and a larger observation window was installed in the nose.

Planners knew the War would soon be over and began winding down production in Fort Worth and the Douglas and North American factories. By July 1944, the Ls leaving the remaining factories at San Diego and Willow Run had no rear turrets at all—they had them installed when they reached the particular theater of the War. In total, just 1,667 Ls were built. The Js had proven so successful that the improvements that remained were mostly cosmetic.

Besides, there was a new kid in town who could fly higher, faster, and farther: the B-29, and beginning in late 1944, the Superfortress started eclipsing the mighty B-24.

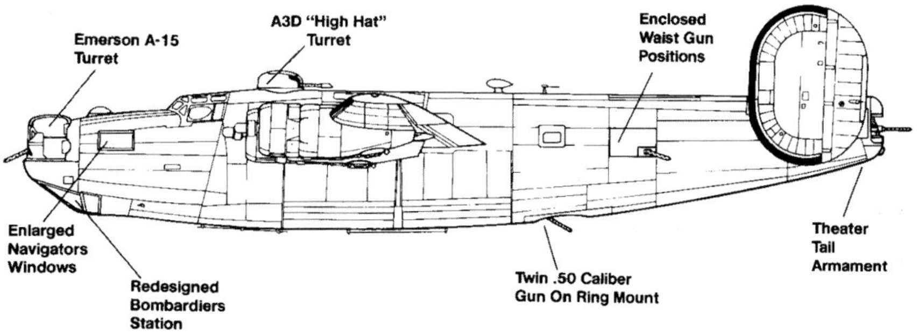

OVERSEAS STAGING

1 - 13 November 1944
Fairfield-Suisun Army Air Base
Fairfield, California
1504th Army Air Force Base Unit
West Coast Wing
Air Transport Command
4th Army Air Force

Fairfield-Suisun Army Air Base was designed to house medium attack bombers, but the 4th Army Air Force never officially occupied the base, though the Navy used it over the summer of 1942 to practice landings on an aircraft carrier deck painted on the runway.

In late 1942, recognizing the base's potential to become a major aerial port and supply transfer point for the Pacific Theater, the War Department assigned Fairfield to the Air Transport Command (ATC). The base soon became the West Coast's largest staging air field, transitioning hundreds of thousands of men and materiel to and from the South Pacific.

O.C. guessed in a letter home that they'd be at Fairfield-Suisun about a week getting acclimated with their new B-24L. And they would have been on their way in that time but for bad weather. "When I find out my APO," he wrote home, "I'll send it to you. I can't tell you any more about what's going on but if you can bear with me for awhile till I can tell where I am legally, I will."

By 1949, the Strategic Air Command was based there, and in 1951 it was renamed Travis Air Force Base after Brigadier General Robert F. Travis, who was killed on 5 August 1950 when his B-29 Superfortress crashed minutes after takeoff, killing Travis and 18 others. Although the aircraft was carrying a Mark 4 nuclear weapon, the bomb's plutonium core was aboard another aircraft, rendering a nuclear explosion impossible.

BELOW LEFT O.C.'s Military Identification Card. "Not a pass. For identification only."

BELOW RIGHT Aerial view of Travis Air Force Base today.

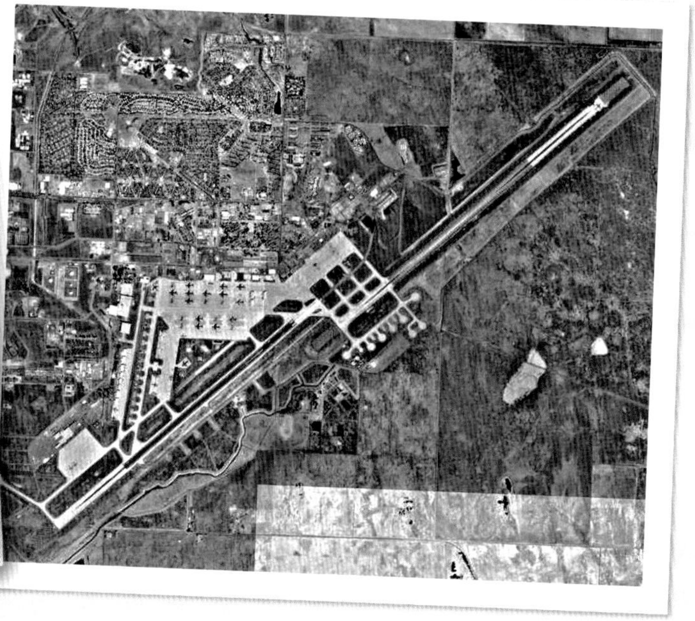

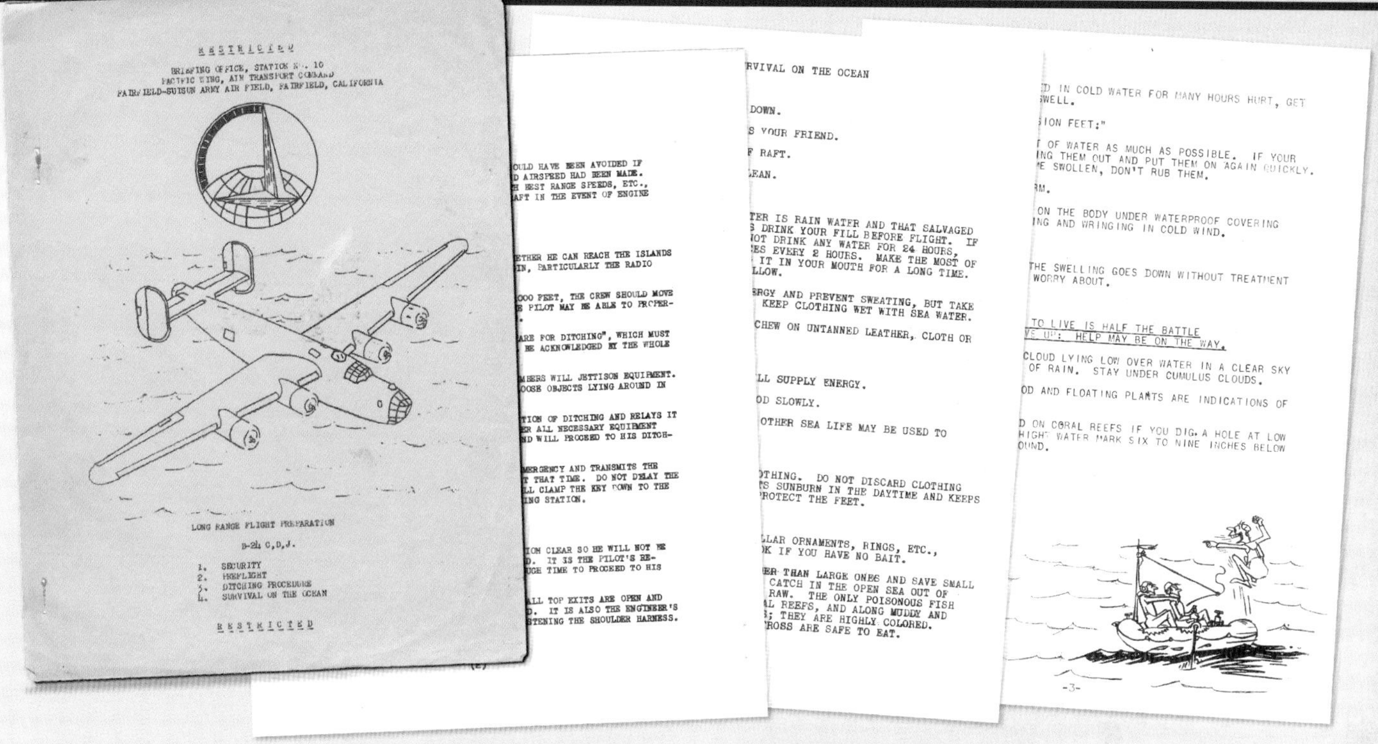

RESTRICTED

BRIEFING OFFICE, STATION N . 10
PACIFIC WING, AIR TRANSPORT COMMAND
FAIRFIELD-SUISUN ARMY AIR FIELD, FAIRFIELD, CALIFORNIA

LONG RANGE FLIGHT PREPARATION

B-24 C,D,J.

1. SECURITY
2. PREFLIGHT
3. DITCHING PROCEDURE
4. SURVIVAL ON THE OCEAN

RESTRICTED

OULD HAVE BEEN AVOIDED IF
D AIRSPEED HAD BEEN MADE.
H BEST RANGE SPEEDS, ETC.,
AFT IN THE EVENT OF ENGINE

ETHER HE CAN REACH THE ISLANDS
IN, PARTICULARLY THE RADIO

OOO FEET, THE CREW SHOULD MOVE
E PILOT MAY BE ABLE TO PROPER-

ARE FOR DITCHING", WHICH MUST
BE ACKNOWLEDGED BY THE WHOLE

MBERS WILL JETTISON EQUIPMENT.
OOSE OBJECTS LYING AROUND IN

TION OF DITCHING AND RELAYS IT
ER ALL NECESSARY EQUIPMENT
ND WILL PROCEED TO HIS DITCH-

MERGENCY AND TRANSMITS THE
T THAT TIME. DO NOT DELAY THE
LL CLAMP THE KEY DOWN TO THE
ING STATION.

ION CLEAR SO HE WILL NOT BE
D. IT IS THE PILOT'S RE-
UGH TIME TO PROCEED TO HIS

ALL TOP EXITS ARE OPEN AND
D. IT IS ALSO THE ENGINEER'S
STENING THE SHOULDER HARNESS.

RVIVAL ON THE OCEAN

DOWN.

S YOUR FRIEND.

F RAFT.

EAN.

TER IS RAIN WATER AND THAT SALVAGED
S DRINK YOUR FILL BEFORE FLIGHT. IF
NOT DRINK ANY WATER FOR 24 HOURS,
ES EVERY 2 HOURS. MAKE THE MOST OF
IT IN YOUR MOUTH FOR A LONG TIME.
LLOW.

RGY AND PREVENT SWEATING, BUT TAKE
KEEP CLOTHING WET WITH SEA WATER.

CHEW ON UNTANNED LEATHER, CLOTH OR

LL SUPPLY ENERGY.

OD SLOWLY.

OTHER SEA LIFE MAY BE USED TO

OTHING. DO NOT DISCARD CLOTHING
TS SUNBURN IN THE DAYTIME AND KEEPS
ROTECT THE FEET.

LLAR ORNAMENTS, RINGS, ETC.,
OK IF YOU HAVE NO BAIT.

ER THAN LARGE ONES AND SAVE SMALL
CATCH IN THE OPEN SEA OUT OF
RAW. THE ONLY POISONOUS FISH
AL REEFS, AND ALONG MUDDY AND
; THEY ARE HIGHLY COLORED.
ROSS ARE SAFE TO EAT.

D IN COLD WATER FOR MANY HOURS HURT, GET
SWELL.

SION FEET:"

T OF WATER AS MUCH AS POSSIBLE. IF YOUR
ING THEM OUT AND PUT THEM ON AGAIN QUICKLY.
E SWOLLEN, DON'T RUB THEM.

RM.

ON THE BODY UNDER WATERPROOF COVERING
ING AND WRINGING IN COLD WIND.

THE SWELLING GOES DOWN WITHOUT TREATMENT
WORRY ABOUT.

TO LIVE IS HALF THE BATTLE
VE UP: HELP MAY BE ON THE WAY.

CLOUD LYING LOW OVER WATER IN A CLEAR SKY
OF RAIN. STAY UNDER CUMULUS CLOUDS.

OD AND FLOATING PLANTS ARE INDICATIONS OF

D ON CORAL REEFS IF YOU DIG A HOLE AT LOW
HIGH WATER MARK SIX TO NINE INCHES BELOW
OUND.

-3-

OH, TAKE THIS . . . JUST IN CASE

Before his flight overseas, O.C. was given this pamphlet containing advice regarding security, preflight procedures, ditching procedures, and surviving on the ocean. The last page is telling with its no-nonsense, honest qualifier: THE WILL TO LIVE IS HALF THE BATTLE. DON'T GIVE UP: HELP MAY BE ON THE WAY.

STRIPPED FOR ACTION

As we've seen in his orders, O.C. was given temporary command and responsibility for a brand new B-24L with serial number 44-41501. But as he says elsewhere, it was taken from him the moment he arrived at Hickam Field on O'ahu and he only saw it once again, late in the War.

The plane, featuring some of the most salacious nose art to appear in the Pacific theater (obviously painted by an aficionado of renowned 1940s pin-up artist Gil Elvgren), served in the 431st squadron of the 11th Bomb Group, a sister group to the 494th that O.C. served in. Both were a part of the 7th Air Force, but the 11th had its headquarters on Guam in the Mariana Islands.

Sometime late in the War *Stripped for Action was* apparently in Agra, India, where the photos at right were taken. Sadly, in December 1945 she was termed "excess" and destroyed.

C O N F I D E N T I A L

HEADQUARTERS
1504TH AAF BASE UNIT, WEST COAST WING
PACIFIC DIVISION, AIR TRANSPORT COMMAND
FAIRFIELD-SUISUN ARMY AIR BASE, CALIFORNIA

OPERATIONS ORDER)
: 7 November 1944
NUMBER 79)

E X T R A C T

2. PAC Ltr, WD Hq. AAF;, Wash D.C. File 370.5, Sub: "Movement Orders, Shipment FC---AS" dated 5 Oct 44, and Ltr. ATC, WOW, PD, Hamilton Fld, Calif, File 300.4, Sub: "Authority to Issue Travel Orders and Instructions Governing" dated 4 Dec 43, and Ltr, File 370.5/953, Air Base Hq. Hamilton Fld, Calif dated 31 Oct 44, the below listed Offs and EM WP in designated mil acft in connection with Project 96787-R, Shipment FC---AS, from Fairfield-Suisun AAB, Calif, to Hickam Fld, Hawaii, RUAT to COMMANDING GENERAL, SEVENTH AIR FORCE, Hickam Fld, Hawaii for asgmt to the Seventh Air Force. This is a PCS.

B-24L #44-41501 Crew #FC---AS 26
APO #16655 AS 26

2D Lt.	KEMP, OMER C.	0710957	P
2D Lt.	OLSON, NORMAN J.	0192976	CP
2D Lt.	SPERLING, FREDERICK C. JR.	02060604	N
Cpl.	Gutierrez, Juan F.	39550289	E
Cpl.	Morrow, Calvin G.	19130002	RO

Except as may be necessary in the transaction of official business, indiv are prohibited from discussing their oversea destination even by shipment number. They will not file safe arrival telegrams with commercial agencies while enroute and at domestic or oversea destinations.

From time of departure from Continental US until arrival at perm oversea sta, pmt of per diem is atzd for a maximum of forty-five (45) days.

Auth is granted to make variations and to proceed to such other places as may be necessary for the completion of this mission.

Clo and Equip is prescribed in accordance with List G, Indiv Clo and Equip 15 Nov 43, as amended by AAF Ltr 65-4, 19 May 44, AAF Ltr 65-RA, 16 June 44, TWX WARX 78321, 9 Aug 44, TWX 4147 and 4148, 15 Aug 44. Baggage to be transported by air will not exceed weights, as amended, reflected on line e of weight chart of List G.

TDN 501-31 P 431-02-03 212/50425.

By order of Lt. Col. STEPHENSON:

JOHN L. TEMPLETON,
Major, Air Corps,
Ex. for Operations.

YOU ASKED FOR IT

O.C. left Muroc over a month ago and has been champing at the bit to get overseas since then. His orders finally came in on 7 November and remind him to be circumspect about his destination. But they are mysteriously silent about the exact date of his departure.

His Flight Record, however, indicates a 14 hour flight on 14 November, nine daylight hours and five at night, so it's likely he took off mid-morning and arrived at Hickam Field in Honolulu around midnight on that day.

Going to Hawaii wasn't a surprise; everyone heading to the South Pacific passed through there, but O.C. still didn't know his final destination. The San Francisco-Honolulu leg was the world's longest uninterrupted flight and considered the most dangerous for that reason, which is why he got the pamphlet on the preceding page.

AUDIO TRANSCRIPT 09:00:45

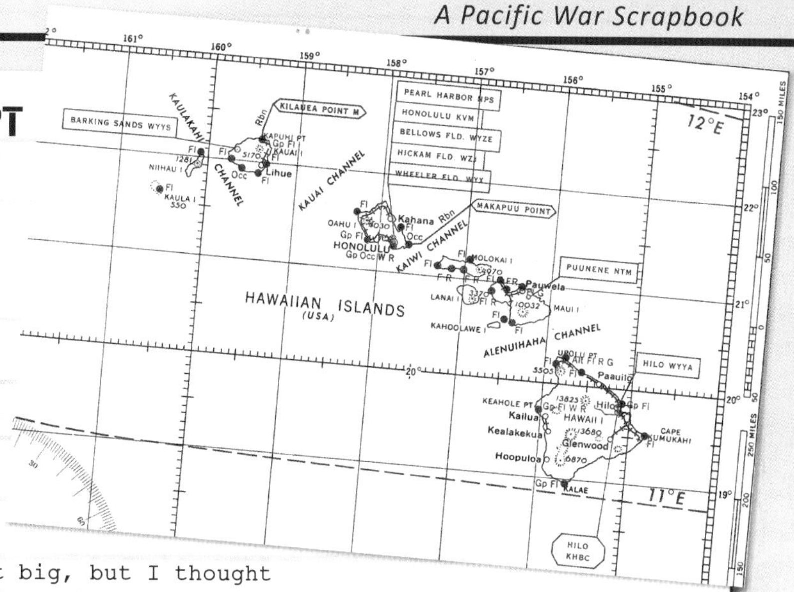

So we started out, a twenty year-old kid and a brand-new airplane. And all this training they put everybody through wasn't really necessary because the navigator was the most important guy, and the airplane had to be built right.

But I still started our flight to Hawaii with an uneasy feeling. The Hawaiian Islands are five hundred miles wide and it's pretty hard to miss something that big, but I thought about Columbus. So after about fifteen hours I thought, Well, we've got to be getting pretty close now.

Then there was a puff of clouds on the horizon and somebody yelled, "There it is!"

We were right on course. Good old Fred Sperling had it nailed down. And he was kind of happy too because he had done all this training and the only thing he had was that sextant that he shot the stars with and his charts. He always was a really good navigator.

I didn't know how to do it. No way could I have done it. If Fred would have died out there we would have really been in trouble.

ABOVE O.C.'s navigation chart of Hawaii with its principal military airports, towns, and radio towers. As noted, the San Francisco–Hawaii flight was the world's longest flight leg and required pin-point accuracy. If you missed the Islands, there was no more land for 1,000 miles—which is why O.C. got rid of the navigator back in Muroc who almost flew them into a mountain. Out here there was no room for error.

AUDIO TRANSCRIPT 10:00:05

As we got closer to Pearl Harbor we could see that, sure enough, the Japs had fled. They had heard I was coming (laughs).

We landed at Hickam Field in Honolulu. There were two fields: a Navy field and an Air Force field right next door to each other. And of course, as we were landing, we could see all the pock marks from the War, although they had been cleaned up and there was very little real evidence of the destruction there in Pearl Harbor.

And they said, "Oh, we're so glad to see you! We want your airplane." So they took my brand new B-24 away from me and sent it overseas. I never saw the poor thing again until many months later. The War was nearly over and it was coming in with an engine on fire. I think they finally junked it. By this time they had many thousands of hours on it. It had been flown constantly by many crews.

The only thing I had to remember it by was the steering wheel button. I still have it in my trunk. Everybody took one off because they disappeared so fast. You had to get one fast or you didn't get one at all.

AIR COMBAT REPLACEMENT

14 - 16 November 1944
Hickam Army Air Field
Honolulu, O'ahu, Terr. of Hawaii
91st Airdrome Squadron
7th Army Air Force

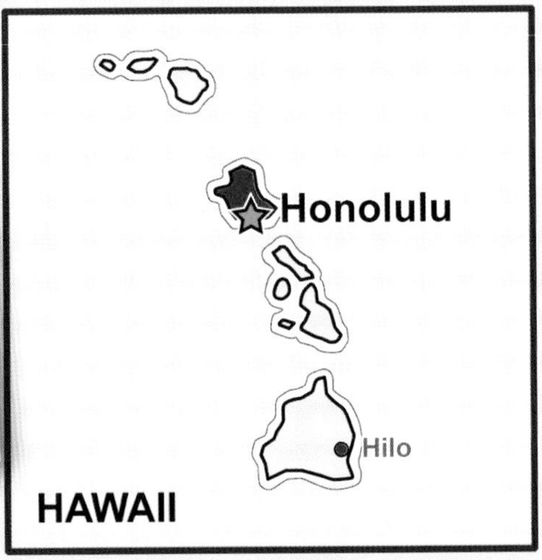

In the late 1930s, when Luke Field on Ford Island in the middle of Pearl Harbor proved too small to handle the increasing air traffic, Hickam Army Air Field was built on the eastern arm of the bay entrance. It was named in honor of Lt. Col. Horace Hickam, a pilot who was killed in Galveston, Texas when his Curtiss A-12 Shrike hit an obstruction during a night landing. (They seem to always name air fields after pilots that crash.)

Hickam soon became the principal Army airfield in Hawaii and the only one large enough to accommodate the B-17 Flying Fortresses, which were brought to Hawaii in 1941 in preparation for potential hostilities.

The first mass flight of bombers (21 B-17Ds) from Hamilton Field, California arrived at Hickam on 14 May 1941. By December, the Hawaiian Air Force had been an integrated command for slightly more than one year and consisted of 754 officers and 6,706 enlisted men, with 233 aircraft assigned at its three primary bases: Hickam, Wheeler Field, and Bellows Field, all on O'ahu Island.

When the Japanese Navy attacked O'ahu's military installations on 7 December 1941, Hickam was bombed and strafed to eliminate air opposition and prevent U.S. planes from following them back to their aircraft carriers. Hickam suffered extensive damage and aircraft losses, with 189 people killed and 303 wounded.

During the War, the base became the hub of the ATC Pacific aerial network, supporting aircraft ferrying troops and supplies to forward areas—a role it would reprise during the Korean and Vietnam wars, earning it the nickname "America's Bridge Across the Pacific."

BOTTOM LEFT A trio of B-17s salutes the main gate at Hickam Field.

BOTTOM RIGHT Hickam Army Air Field, 1941, prior to the attack on Pearl Harbor.

AIR COMBAT REPLACEMENT

16 November - 31 December 1944
Barking Sands Army Air Field
Kauai, Terr. of Hawaii
91st Airdrome Squadron
6th Air Service Area Command

In June 1943, the 7th Air Force moved into an airfield on the northwest shore of Kauai at the far western end of the Hawaiian Islands, using it to stage overseas transfers and as a holding area for crews waiting for their planes to be outfitted for use in the Pacific Operations Area (POA).

The name "Barking Sands" reputedly comes from an old story that long ago a native fisherman left his dogs staked on the beach while he took his boat fishing some distance offshore. A storm came up and when he returned, his dogs were gone, but their ghostly barking has continued ever after.

Or it might just be the crunchy sound the sand makes when you walk on it.

LEFT 6th Army Air Force emblem.

AUDIO TRANSCRIPT 10:01:33

At Hickam they took my airplane away and we were flown to Barking Sands on Kauai, which is about 150 miles to the northwest of O'ahu. It had a boomerang-shaped runway that ran along the coast. We spent an entire month there and all we had to do was just lay on the beach. There wasn't anything to do, no nightclubs or anything around to see at all. There weren't any girls, and that made it kind of dull.

BOTTOM LEFT A B-24, a C-47, and C-45 run up their engines prior to taking off circa 1944.

BOTTOM RIGHT Today Barking Sands is known as the Pacific Missile Range Facility.

ON THE GARDEN ISLAND

"We went swimming," O.C. wrote home, "and really had a swell time. The weather out here is nice after leaving California and the rain. I'm liking it better every day. We have quite a few mosquitoes but our quarters are fine and most of them seem to stay outside.

"I'm thinking of going wild boar hunting in the mountains one of these weekends. Should be interesting.

"We went to the pineapple cannery and drank pineapple juice from a fountain, if you can believe that. I've just about lived on pineapple juice since I got here."

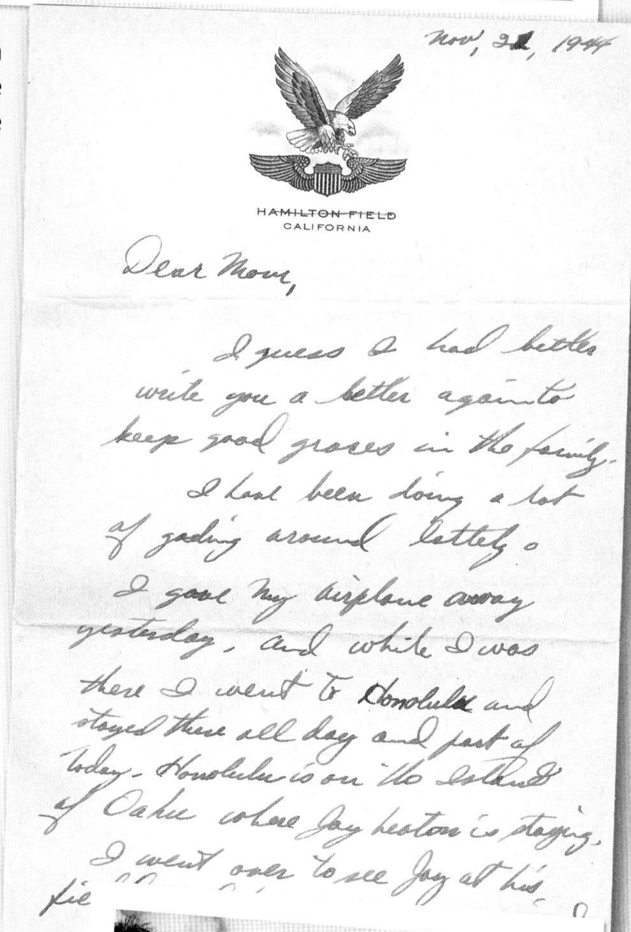

Nov, 2d, 1944

HAMILTON FIELD
CALIFORNIA

Dear Mom,

I guess I had better write you a letter again to keep good graces in the family.

I have been doing a lot of gadding around lately. I gave my airplane away yesterday. and while I was there I went to Honolulu and stayed there all day and part of today. Honolulu is on the Island of Oahu where Jay Heaton is staying. I went over to see Jay at his fie

And—shock of all shocks—he actually approved the sale of his beloved Model A. His dad got $100 for it. O.C. figured by the time he got back (if he did) it wouldn't be worth half that anyway. "It's just a rattle-trap," he told a friend. "Lucky I never got killed in it."

Out on the ramp he admired the silver perfection of 44-41501, the ship he'd brought over from the States, hoping they would let him keep it. But within days he was ordered to fly it back to O'ahu and turn it in to the modification team.

"I wanted to see Jay anyway," he wrote. (His cousin Jay Kemp was a parachute technician in a Navy fighter squadron on O'ahu.) "He was on charge of quarters [guard duty], but I got the sergeant to let him off and we hitched a ride on an Army truck, which is about the only way to get around the island. We went to Laie to see the temple. It was beautiful with the lights at night. We stayed out there and went back to Honolulu the next day."

"Back in Honolulu, we rented bicycles so we could get around town. We went to Waikiki Beach and a number of beautiful places. You can't even tell they ever dropped bombs here because they have cleaned it up so well. It's hard to believe we're so far away from the States, with all the modern improvements. Only gas and tires are rationed here and you can get anything you could have gotten in peacetime. Seems funny that this is where the war started and yet it seems farthest from it now."

HOME OR SOMETHING LIKE IT

He hasn't gotten a letter in almost a month. It took the Army Post Office a while to track down a serviceman, and O.C. was getting lonesome. But he discovered that five other fellows in his barracks were also Mormons, so they asked the Barking Sands C.O. if they could borrow a command car one Sunday to drive to Kapa'a on the eastern side of the island to attend church.

"The meeting was very much like home and we enjoyed it very much," wrote O.C. "Afterwards, they had a luau. We ate *poi,* which is made from the breadfruit plant, and a barbecued pig. I tried the raw fish but I wasn't much good at eating the bones and heads like the natives were. The fish was good, at least the edible part. After dinner we learned how to weave a number of tricky things out of coconut palm leaves. I can honestly say that it was the best day I've spent in the Islands so far."

BELOW Though the people of that era are often decried as baldly racist, these young men, who were being sent overseas to kill Japanese, had no problem worshiping with them. Our differences—as well as our similarities—are truly in our hearts, not in the color of our skins.

WAITING AND WAITING . . .

"Yes! I'm still here. I guess it will be next year sometime before we get out of here. The war news looks plenty bad. I guess Luxembourg is taken by now. Sure seems like this will never get over with. I'll be an old man before this war is over. I may be over here for a couple of years. I sure hope not but it may take that long or more. Just about everyone I meet has been here from two to three years without leave. I guess I sound kind of gloomy, but can you blame me? I'm going crazy waiting to get into the excitement. We are flying just enough to get our flying pay, which requires four hours a month. That isn't enough for me."

MELE KALIKIMAKA

"Well, it's only four more days until Christmas. It might as well be the Fourth of July, it doesn't seem at all like Christmas here. I tried to get a tree but couldn't. We are going to attend a Christmas program at the church next Sunday. Wish you could see it. The Japanese and Hawaiian children are very cute when they do their parts on stage. They have very good memories. When I was that age I couldn't remember anything except when dinner was."

After attending the Christmas program, he wrote home: "Santa Clause showed up with a package for each child that contained candy, nuts, dried prunes, an apple, and an orange. The kids really went for that. After, we four servicemen were invited over to a member's home for a traditional Christmas eve. After eating we decorated the Christmas tree they had saved for us to fix. (We only broke one ball.) Then we all formed a line and wiped the dishes so fast the dish washer couldn't keep up. We finished the job double quick."

BELOW But the day after Christmas he got his orders: He had been assigned to the VII Bomber Command, Angaur Island, Palau group, Caroline Islands.

R E S T R I C T E D

HEADQUARTERS
ARMY AIR FORCES, PACIFIC OCEAN AREAS
APO 953

26 December 1944

S Y M B O L S

SPECIAL ORDERS) (FAGAT - 1st Available Govt Air T)
: (FAGWT - 1st Available Govt Water T)
NUMBER 128) (EDD - Effective Date of Departure)
(EDCMR - Eff Date of C on M/R

E X T R A C T

15. Following-named Offs AC and EM (B-24 Crews) Shpmt Nos indicated are reld from asgmt and dy 63rd Adrm Sq APO 966 and asgd VII Bomb Comd APO 244 for dy. WP. TDN. Tvl via orgn acft and FAGAT. Per diem auth UP Sec II Cir 356 WD 44 as amended. 67-414 P 431-02 03 A 0425-25. EDCMR 29 Dec 44.

B-24L 44-41501
2d Lt (1092) OMER C KEMP 0710957
2d Lt (1055) NORMAN J OLSON 0927583
2d Lt (1036) FREDERICK C SPERLING JR 02060604
Cpl (737) Juan F Gutierrez 39550289
Cpl (757) Calvin G Morrow 19130002

By order of Lieutenant General HARMON:

J. R. ANDERSEN,
Colonel, AC,
Chief of Staff.

AUSTRALIA HAS A POLL-TAX. IT COSTS $6.00 NOT TO VOTE
AN INSECT KEPT AUSTRALIA FROM BEING SETTLED EARLIER. THE CORAL "INSECT" BUILT THE GREAT BARRIER REEF WHICH SCREENS THE FERTILE COAST OF QUEENSLAND FOR 1200 MILES. EXPLORERS FOUND THE REEF AND OVERLOOKED THE CONTINENT BEHIND IT
HOW AUSTRALIA GOT ITS NAME
A SPANISH EXPLORER WHO HAD NEVER SEEN THE GREAT SOUTH CONTINENT NAMED IT "AUSTRIALIA DEL ESPIRITU SANTO" IN HONOR OF AUSTRIAN-BORN PHILIP III OF SPAIN. IN TRANSLATION THIS WAS MISSPELLED AUSTRALIA.

MINIMUM WAGES FOR BIG INDUSTRIES IN AUSTRALIA HAVE BEEN ESTABLISHED BY ARBITRATION COURTS EVER SINCE 1907.
DINKUM OIL
DOESN'T COME OUT OF A WELL. IT'S SIMPLY AUSTRALIAN SLANG FOR THE REAL TRUTH, THE STRICT LOWDOWN. (SEE SLANG GLOSSARY AT END OF THIS BOOK)

Prior to leaving Kauai, they were issued a dozen or so palm-sized pamphlets giving the background of the cultures they would encounter in the Pacific War theater. The guides are filled with interesting facts, a sort of mini-geography and culture lesson detailing peoples from Hawaii to Australia to India and China.

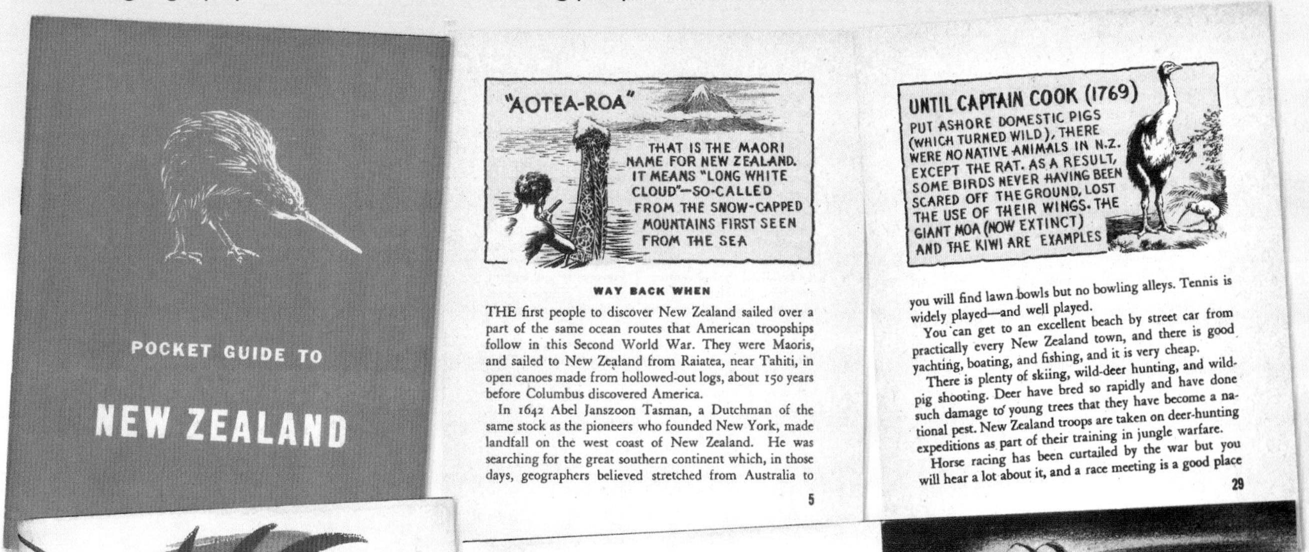

POCKET GUIDE TO
THERE ARE 120 MILLION SHEEP IN AUSTRALIA - 40 SHEEP FOR EVERY SQUARE MILE. NO WONDER IT'S THE NO. 1 WOOL PRODUCING COUNTRY IN THE WORLD!
1/3RD OF ALL THE SEVEN MILLION PEOPLE IN AUSTRALIA LIVE IN THE TWO GREAT CITIES OF SYDNEY AND MELBOURNE!
NORTHERN TERRITORY IS DOTTED WITH WHITE ANT (TERMITE) NESTS SHAPED LIKE A SKYSCRAPER AND USUALLY TALLER THAN A MAN. THEY ALWAYS POINT NORTH AND SOUTH!
NEW ZEALAND
"AOTEA-ROA"
THAT IS THE MAORI NAME FOR NEW ZEALAND. IT MEANS "LONG WHITE CLOUD"—SO-CALLED FROM THE SNOW-CAPPED MOUNTAINS FIRST SEEN FROM THE SEA
WAY BACK WHEN
THE first people to discover New Zealand sailed over a part of the same ocean routes that American troopships follow in this Second World War. They were Maoris, and sailed to New Zealand from Raiatea, near Tahiti, in open canoes made from hollowed-out logs, about 150 years before Columbus discovered America.
In 1642 Abel Janszoon Tasman, a Dutchman of the same stock as the pioneers who founded New York, made landfall on the west coast of New Zealand. He was searching for the great southern continent which, in those days, geographers believed stretched from Australia to
5
UNTIL CAPTAIN COOK (1769) PUT ASHORE DOMESTIC PIGS (WHICH TURNED WILD), THERE WERE NO NATIVE ANIMALS IN N.Z. EXCEPT THE RAT. AS A RESULT, SOME BIRDS NEVER HAVING BEEN SCARED OFF THE GROUND, LOST THE USE OF THEIR WINGS. THE GIANT MOA (NOW EXTINCT) AND THE KIWI ARE EXAMPLES
you will find lawn bowls but no bowling alleys. Tennis is
widely played—and well played.
You can get to an excellent beach by street car from
practically every New Zealand town, and there is good
yachting, boating, and fishing, and it is very cheap.
There is plenty of skiing, wild-deer hunting, and wild-
pig shooting. Deer have bred so rapidly and have done
such damage to young trees that they have become a national pest. New Zealand troops are taken on deer-hunting
expeditions as part of their training in jungle warfare.
Horse racing has been curtailed by the war but you
will hear a lot about it, and a race meeting is a good place
29

A POCKET GUIDE TO NEW GUINEA
never tear them off, as a bad sore may result. A lighted
cigarette, a cigarette lighter, a spit of tobacco juice, soapy
water, gasoline, or a pinch of salt are used to make
leeches let go. Don't scratch the spot afterwards, or it may
become a sore. 'Tis said old residents miss all such vermin
when they leave the islands.
As for fish, they are common in the streams and along
the coasts, and the underwater life of the coral reefs and
lagoons is just as colorful and fascinating as that of the
jungles.
FOOD AND TRAVEL
IN a region such as this, knowing what to eat and where
to get it becomes more than just a matter of interest. It may
mean the difference between life and death. So, too, may
knowing how to travel. There's always a chance that you
may get off by yourself, or be in a small party that is cut
off from supplies.
Island Foods. Every bit of food brought into the islands
takes up valuable shipping space. Local foods in the South
Seas are mostly both good and tasty. Some tropical fruits
and vegetables are familiar enough to you in home
markets—like coconuts, sweetpotatoes, bananas, and pine-
apples. Others you've probably only heard about.
In place of our wheat and potatoes, most islanders use
32
taro and yams. Taro is the bulbous root of a kind of lily,
and is usually a light purple when cooked. The yam is
like a giant potato. Both have a high food value, and may
be eaten roasted or steamed. Breadfruit is prepared in the
same way. The breadfruit tree has leaves something like
giant fig leaves, and the knobby yellow-green fruit is
often almost the size of a football. Nowadays many native
communities grow corn and manioc (cassava, from which
tapioca is extracted). Sugarcane is widely grown, and,
incidentally, New Guinea is the original home of this plant.
The coconut palm is a larder in itself. You are probably
used to getting coconuts only at the ripe stage when the
flesh is hard and white. The soft jelly-like flesh of a half-
33

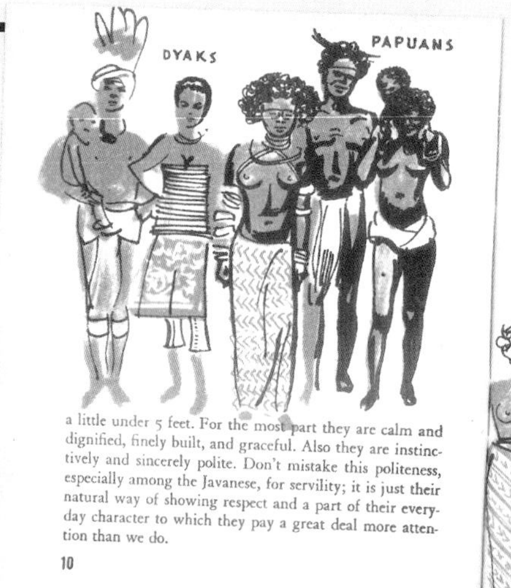

a little under 5 feet. For the most part they are calm and dignified, finely built, and graceful. Also they are instinctively and sincerely polite. Don't mistake this politeness, especially among the Javanese, for servility; it is just their natural way of showing respect and a part of their everyday character to which they pay a great deal more attention than we do.

10

If you except some tribes in Sumatra and in the eastern part of the island the chief Indonesian characteristic is to live in peace and harmony with his fellows, his god, his surroundings, and himself. He doesn't want to push other people around, conquer more land or offend the beliefs of others. Intolerance, oppression or an overbearing attitude he dislikes strongly, and is very likely to get tough about it. This world needs, and will always need, more people like that.

As do most quiet people, the Indonesians have a well-

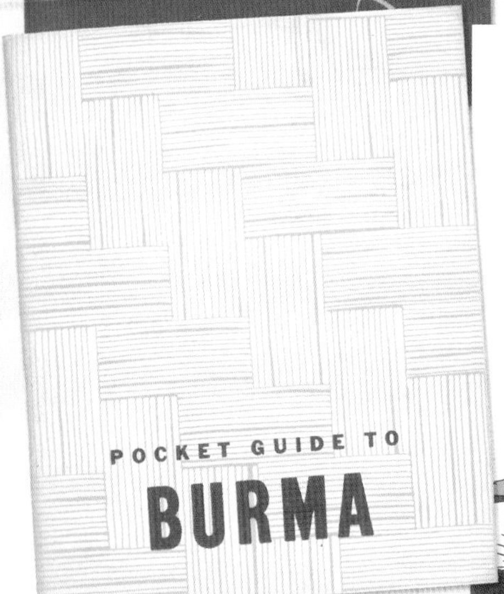

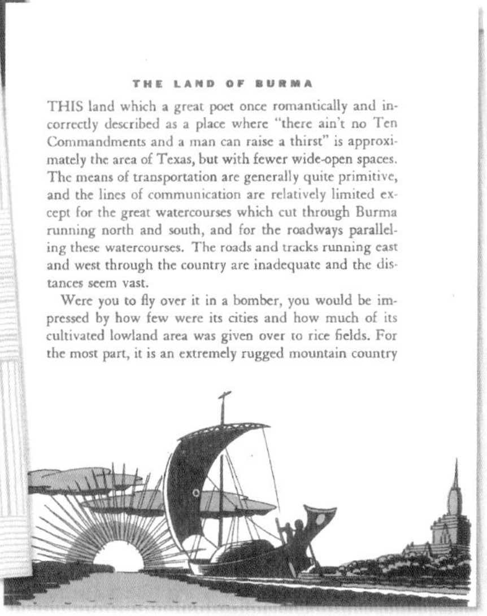

THE LAND OF BURMA

THIS land which a great poet once romantically and incorrectly described as a place where "there ain't no Ten Commandments and a man can raise a thirst" is approximately the area of Texas, but with fewer wide-open spaces. The means of transportation are generally quite primitive, and the lines of communication are relatively limited except for the great watercourses which cut through Burma running north and south, and for the roadways paralleling these watercourses. The roads and tracks running east and west through the country are inadequate and the distances seem vast.

Were you to fly over it in a bomber, you would be impressed by how few were its cities and how much of its cultivated lowland area was given over to rice fields. For the most part, it is an extremely rugged mountain country

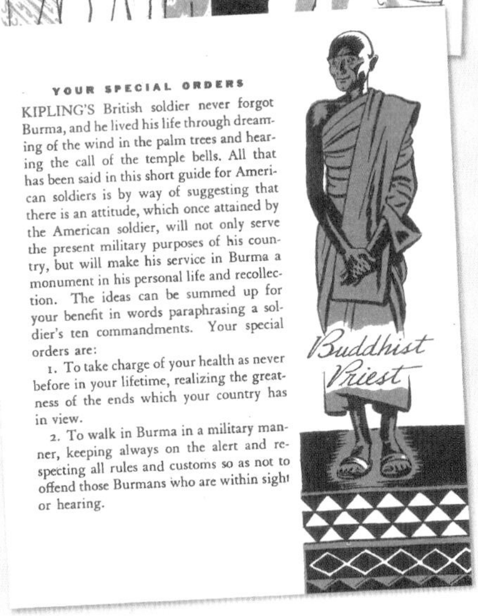

YOUR SPECIAL ORDERS

KIPLING'S British soldier never forgot Burma, and he lived his life through dreaming of the wind in the palm trees and hearing the call of the temple bells. All that has been said in this short guide for American soldiers is by way of suggesting that there is an attitude, which once attained by the American soldier, will not only serve the present military purposes of his country, but will make his service in Burma a monument in his personal life and recollection. The ideas can be summed up for your benefit in words paraphrasing a soldier's ten commandments. Your special orders are:

1. To take charge of your health as never before in your lifetime, realizing the greatness of the ends which your country has in view.

2. To walk in Burma in a military manner, keeping always on the alert and respecting all rules and customs so as not to offend those Burmans who are within sight or hearing.

The guides demonstrate sensitivity to our Allies' cultures and accurate (if not politically correct) descriptions of the physical characteristics of each ethnic group. They counsel servicemen to be knowledgeable about, and respectful of, the cultures. They are cautioned about taking photos, showing anger, and manifesting racism: "Remember, it's Hitler who harps on the superiority of his own color, his own people, his own country."

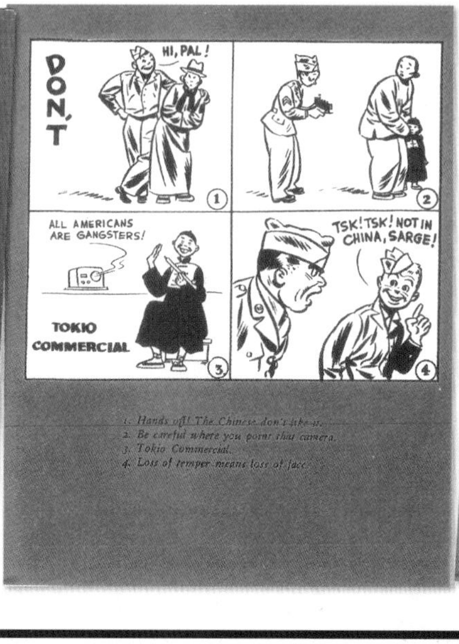

1. Hands off! The Chinese don't like it.
2. Be careful where you point that camera.
3. Tokio Commercial.
4. Loss of temper means loss of face.

dividing up China's territory when she was too weak to resist. The planes we have been able to send them have carried far more than their own weight in good will for us.

It is up to you not to spoil that fine feeling. To the Chinese people you stand for all of us here at home as well as for yourself. It depends on you whether China will like us, and whether they will trust us in the future.

CHINESE MONEY

THE basic unit of currency in China is the Chinese dollar. One United States dollar will buy about 20 Chinese dollars (19.71). However, the actual value varies a good deal from time to time and this official exchange rate can only be used for general guidance.

45

JUST ANOTHER LOUSY DAY IN PARADISE

The reason for the month on Kauai was a bottleneck created by the new B-24s themselves: the Ls had to be modified to satisfy 7th Air Force combat requirements: the installation of a Plexiglas tail turret with greater visibility, twin .50-caliber tail guns, storage racks for life rafts, a navigator's cubby on the flight deck, and fifty more minor modifications requiring 1,000 man-hours per plane. The modifications were performed at Hickam, so O.C.'s flight time was restricted to flying 44-41501 over to Pearl and bringing a modified B-24 back to Kauai, which would be flown into the combat theater by another crew while he waited for an aircraft to be completed so he could fly it to wherever he would be stationed.

Meanwhile, life on Kauai wasn't too bad: the base boasted a movie theater, an officer's club, an exchange, and a post office. A survey found a nearby beach suitable for swimming and lifeguard towers were built and manned from 1400 to 1930 hours daily. Athletic equipment included fishing tackle, boxing gloves, ping-pong, baseball and softball equipment (there was a fierce rivalry between the four squadrons). Local guides led tours around the island to the famous Na'Pali coast and Waimea Canyon.

RIGHT While waiting for modifications, ground crews often painted nose art on the aircraft. 865th Squadron ground echelon members gather around as Al "Rusty" Restuccia puts the finishing touches on 752 *Rover Boy's Baby* at Barking Sands. Rusty painted nose art on a number of planes in the 494th.

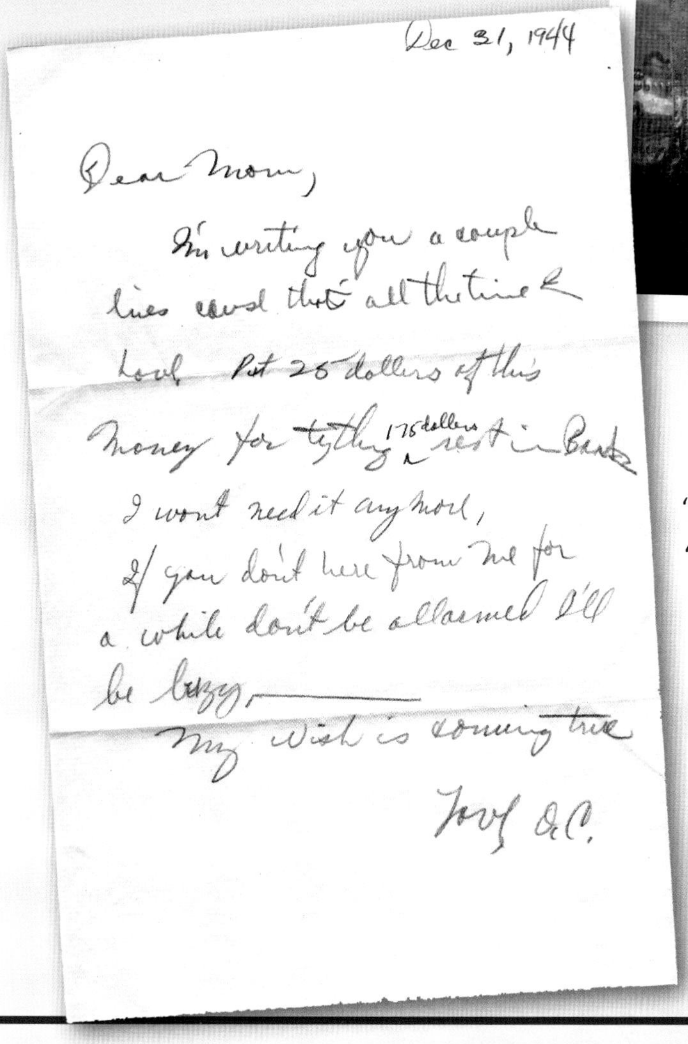

Dec 31, 1944

Dear Mom,

I'm writing you a couple lines cause that's all the time I have. Put 25 dollars of this money for tything 175 dollars rest in Bank I wont need it any more,

If you don't here from me for a while don't be allarmed I'll be busy, ——

My wish is coming true

Love O.C.

MY WISH IS COMING TRUE

"Dec 31, 1944

"Dear Mom,

"I'm writing you a couple of lines 'cause that's all the time I have. Put 25 dollars of this money for tithing and 175 dollars in Bonds.

I won't need it any more.

"If you don't hear from me for a while, don't be alarmed. I'll be busy.

"My wish is coming true.

Love, O.C."

GETTING OVER THERE

The ground and air crews, separated at Hamilton for their trip to Hawaii—the ground crews by ship and the aircrews flying new B-24s—were reunited in Kauai until orders came for the ground echelon to board another ship for the trip to the Palau Islands, stopping at Kwajalein, Los Negros, and Saipan islands on the way. When they arrived at the tiny island of Angaur there was no dock and they had to climb down rope ladders into landing craft with their field bags, 3-day supply of C-rations, and their carbines.

The air crews flew their modified Liberators 2,360 miles to Kwajalein Island where they spent the night. The four officers had the singular distinction of crossing the International Date Line on January 1st. The next morning, they flew 300 miles to Eniwetok atoll and spent the night there. The third day they flew 1,000 miles more to Saipan in the Marianas Islands, refueled, then landed on Angaur in the Palaus.

Crew 23A arrived at APO 264 on 5 January 1945. In the two months since Angaur had been taken, it had been transformed into the bustling hub of the 494th Bomb Group. Each of the four squadrons had their own bivouac area with enlisted men's quarters, officers' clubs, mess halls, and administrative area. Because he was still in Kauai in December, O.C. missed a Christmas dinner of roast beef, mashed potatoes, asparagus, and cake flown in from Australia. He also missed out on the first B-24 loss when *The Bull* ditched in the ocean after two engines quit during landing, killing most of its crew. When O.C. arrived in early January, the 494th was still reeling from the loss.

AUDIO TRANSCRIPT 10:01:33

After a month at Barking Sands they took us back to Hickam Field. I got this old airplane that didn't know how to fly square and I flew it overseas. It used a lot of fuel.

We landed on Kwajalein Island and I began to realize what the war was like because it was shredded, the trees were all burned out and shot off with pools of water around because every time you turned around it would rain. We spent the night there and there was an air raid. We heard the sirens go off and we were all supposed to do something, but we didn't know what. But no bombs fell and we figured it was just some guy coming back without his IFF on. [IFF: Identification, Friend or Foe, a transponder that transmits a code if the aircraft is friendly. Without the correct code, you will be fired upon.]

Then we flew to Saipan and then on to Angaur to replace crews that had finished their duty. And when we got there, they said, "Glad to see you! We want your airplane," and they took that one from me and gave me an even older one to fly.

PACIFIC OPERATIONS AREA

5 January - 27 April 1945
Angaur Army Air Field
Angaur, Palau Islands
865th Bombardment Squadron
494th Bombardment Group (H)
7th Army Air Force

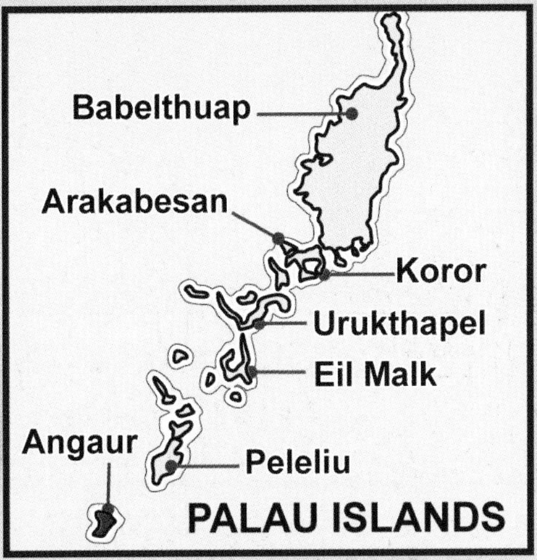

APO 264 TO YOU, BUB

For security reasons, names of destinations were not used in the War. All orders referred to the Army Post Office (APO) number only.

Only half again as long as its 7,000 foot runway, Angaur covers barely three square miles and sits at the southern end of the Palau chain in the western Caroline Islands. Its key feature was its proximity to the Philippines just 400 miles due west. Just six miles across the shallow channel from the furious fighting at Peleliu, Angaur saw its own bitter battles the previous September and October.

R E S T R I C T E D

SO 3 THIS HQ DTD 4 JAN 45 CONTAINED 14 PAR.

SPECIAL ORDERS 4

HQ 494TH BOMB GROUP (H)
APO #264
5 January 1945

E X T R A C T

15. The fol named O and EM having been asgd this orgn per pars 2 and 3 SO 2 Hq VII BC dtd 4 Jan 45 are hereby further asgd 865th Bomb Sq (H) and will rpt to CO thereof for dy. Auth: Ar 315-200.

2D Lt (1092) OMER C KEMP 0710957
2D Lt (1055) NORMAN J OLSON 0927583
2D Lt (1036) FREDERICK C SPERLING JR 02060604
2D Lt (1035) JACK A BERGER 0928139
Cpl (737) Juan F Gutierrez 39550289
Cpl (612) Joseph A Trasatti 13133599
Cpl (757) Calvin G Morrow 19130002
Cpl (611) Eugene W Vaughn 37616773
Cpl (611) Charles K Yetter 3758620
Cpl (612) Lloyd I Nygren 39280958

16. The fol named EM 865th Bomb Sq (H) this sta are hereby detailed to participate in regular and frequent aerial flights untl reld by comp auth per VOVO 4 Jan 45. Auth: AR 35-1480 and AAF Reg 35-20.

Cpl (737) Juan F Gutierrez 39550289
Cpl (612) Joseph A Trasatti 13133599
Cpl (757) Calvin G Morrow 19130002
Cpl (611) Eugene W Vaughn 37616773
Cpl (611) Charles K Yetter 3758620
Cpl (612) Lloyd I Nygren 39280958

By order of Colonel KELLEY:

SYLVESTER J. PETRINE,
Major, Air Corps,
Adjutant

7th AIR FORCE

The Hawaiian Air Force was the first unit of the Army Air Force to see action in the War when it lost a third of its 230 planes to Japanese Zero fighters and Val dive bombers in the attack on Pearl Harbor.

Its first offensive mission was in January 1942 when a B-17 Flying Fortress flew to Midway, refuelled, went on to Wake island for reconnaissance photos, and returned—a 4,000 mile journey typical of the duty it would later make a routine occurrence.

The Hawaiian Air Force was redesignated as the 7th Air Force in February 1942 and by May its 5th and 11th Bomb Groups took up station at Midway Island to prepare for the strike against the Japanese fleet in early June which we had decoded from their secret radio transmissions. Eventually, the 7th Air Force had a territory covering 16 million square miles, five times the area of the U.S.

The prime task of the 7th was to assist the Navy in denying the enemy his forward bases. While the Navy was building ships and the Army was drafting soldiers, the 7th was waiting for the arrival of the only aircraft that could accomplish its mission: the new Consolidated B-24 Liberator heavy bomber, which had a range of over 3,000 miles.

Until the B-24 bombers arrived, the 7th sent its P-39 and P-40 fighters south to the Phoenix Islands to disrupt enemy movements in the South Pacific.

In July 1942, 35 B-17s of the 11th Bomb Group set up in New Caledonia and Fiji. By August they had advanced to the New Hebrides. The 11th and 5th Bomb Groups were then assigned to the 13th Air Force, where they participated in the attack on Guadalcanal in August.

Back in Hawaii, the 7th activated the 318th Fighter Group and in November it received the 307th Bomb Group B-24s fresh from the States. The 307th used Midway to stage B-24 bombing runs on Wake island.

In early 1943 both squadrons moved to the new 13th AAF forward base on Guadalcanal. In June, the 307th flew 2,300 miles from Hawaii to strike the phosphate plants on Nauru island in the Gilberts.

In July, the 7th became the land-based aviation arm of Admiral Nimitz's island-hopping campaign, moving with the Navy while still retaining responsibility for the protection of the Hawaiian islands. The 30th Bomb Group (B-24s) and 41st Bomb Group (B-25s) bulked up the 7th, and the 11th Bomb Group (B-17s) was retrieved from the 13th AAF. With its full complement of fighter and fighter bomber squadrons, the 7th was now ready to take the fight to Japan.

In September, flying from Hawaii, B-24s struck Tarawa in the Gilberts, as well as Mille and Maloelap in the Marshalls. Next came Operation Flintlock and the taking of Kwajalein from bases in the Gilberts.

In January 1944, the 11th and 30th Bomb Groups left the Ellice islands and set up HQ at Tarawa and Abemama, assaulting Kwajalein, Wotje, and Maloelap. After Operation Flintlock, the invasion of Eniwetok atoll in the western Marshalls was next on the list. In just over three months, from November 1943 through February 1944, the Japanese defensive perimeter in the Central Pacific—an area of 800,000 square miles—crumbled and numerous large fleet anchorages and airfields were secured.

In March, the 7th made Kwajalein its forward base, pummeling Dublon Island in the Truk atoll, which had been the Japanese fleet headquarters but which was abandoned when we invaded the Marshalls. With the taking of Eniwetok, the distances became too great for fighter escort of the bombers, and the fighters were sent back to Hawaii. With the neutralization of Truk (though the Japanese retained control of the atoll), the Caroline Islands were skipped and instead the Mariana Islands, 1,000 miles further west, became the goal of Operation Forager: the taking of Saipan and its nearby neighbors to the south, Guam and Tinian, in the summer of 1944.

After Saipan was taken, the 7th took up residence there, turning its sights southwest: the Palau Islands, which were invaded in September. By November, the southernmost island Angaur became the base for the 494th Bomb Group and thus, in January 1945, Angaur became O.C.'s home.

BOMBERS OF THE 7th AIR FORCE

BOEING B-17 "FLYING FORTRESS" The B-17 was first used during daylight precision bombing raids over Germany with great success. The aircraft was legendary for its ability to suffer great damage and still keep flying. It also saw action in the Pacific in the Battle of the Coral Sea and Midway, and between the two theaters, the B-17 dropped more bomb tonnage than any other bomber of the War. Prior to the arrival of the larger and heavier B-24, which also had a higher service ceiling and greater range, the B-17 was the primary workhorse of Allied heavy bombers.

MARTIN B-26 "MARAUDER" The B-26 was a medium bomber used primarily in the Pacific theater. Early models were nicknamed the Widowmaker because of their often fatal stalling characteristics on take-off and landing, which were rectified in later models with increased wing area, fin and rudder. The 7th's Marauders took part in the Battle of Midway, fitted as torpedo bombers. As the Allies advanced across the great distances of the Pacific, the B-26 was of lesser use due to its limited range and smaller bomb capacity. In early 1944, Marauders were phased out in favor of the B-25 Mitchell.

NORTH AMERICAN B-25 "MITCHELL" Achieving notoriety as the plane Jimmy Doolittle flew in his one-way attack on Japan in early 1942, Mitchells were used in every theater of the War. Its utility as a low-level medium bomber in situations unsuited to high-altitude bombing made the B-25 an important player. B-25s participated in the battles for Papua New Guinea and Burma, and its formidable forward guns made its strafing capability a terror for Japanese shipping. Built to withstand heavy enemy fire, many B-25 aircraft flew scores of missions in the Pacific.

CONSOLIDATED B-24 "LIBERATOR" By now you're familiar with the Liberator, but you may not know that though almost 19,000 were produced during the War, by the time the D version appeared, its "boxcar" design had already been superseded by the proposed B-29 with its extended ceiling, payload, and range. But the numbers of bombers required, and the proven performance of the Liberator, meant it would serve until the B-29 could be produced in adequate numbers, which wasn't until late 1944.

FIGHTERS OF THE 7th AIR FORCE

LOCKHEED P-38 "LIGHTNING" Named the "fork-tailed devil" by the Germans and "Two Planes, One Pilot" by the Japanese, the P-38 was a formidable fighter, serving in all theaters as a night bomber, level bomber, night fighter, and long-range escort. Its twin engines gave it added reliability over water, and its maneuverability and heavy armament were superior to all enemy fighters and thus P-38 pilots scored the most aces of the War. It wasn't until the P-51 Mustang appeared late in the War that the P-38 had an equal. Its gorgeous lines made it a favorite of collectors after the War.

BELL P-39 "AIRACOBRA" One of the few aircraft designed and built by Bell for the War, the P-39 had a radically innovative design, with the first tricycle gear on a fighter and a liquid-cooled V-12 engine placed in the fuselage *behind* the pilot. A 10-foot driveshaft passing along the cockpit floor spun the prop. A 37 mm cannon fired through the prop hub, capable of piercing .8" of metal at 500 yards, more powerful by far than any other fighter weapon. Its small self-sealing wing gas tanks and an inefficient turbocharger limited it to low-altitude flights, but its 400 mph top speed meant it could compete ably with Japanese Zeros in combat.

CURTISS P-40 "WARHAWK" Used by most Allied powers throughout the War, the P-40 was the third most-produced American fighter after the P-51 and P-47. Its lack of a two-stage supercharger made it poor competition for German Me-109s, but it fared well in the South Pacific against the Japanese. It was agile at high speeds and lower altitudes, and had one of the tightest turns of any monoplane fighter, though it was inferior to Japanese Zeros and Oscars. Its 1,000 hp engine was not impressive, but it weathered the brutal conditions in the Pacific better than most aircraft and was relatively simple to maintain and repair.

REPUBLIC P-47 "THUNDERBOLT" The P-47 was the largest, heaviest, and most expensive fighter aircraft in history to be powered by a single piston engine. It was armed with eight .50-caliber machine guns, four per wing. It could carry a 2,500 pound bomb load, more than half of what a B-17 bomber could carry. It was an effective short-to-medium range escort fighter in high-altitude air-to-air combat and, when unleashed as a fighter-bomber, proved especially adept at ground attack in both War theaters.

494th BOMBARDMENT GROUP (H)

In December 1943, under orders from the 7th Air Force, Colonel Laurence B. Kelley began putting the 494th Bomb Group (H) together. ("H" stands for "heavy," as distinguished from medium- and light-bomb groups.) They were assigned to Wendover Field in western Utah, and Kelley, a West Point graduate with extensive flying credentials, began selecting officers for his group, which was to take to the field within six months. Appropriately, it chose as its motto "Ultimum Fit Primum," The Last Shall Be First.

In January 1944, fifty three B-24 crews began training at Wendover and on 30 April, the Group was transferred to Mountain Home Army Air Field, forty miles south of Boise, ID, which was better equipped for training. In May, new B-24Js began to arrive. In early June, the 494th was transferred to Barking Sands Air Field on the western shore of Kauai island, Territory of Hawaii, where the men waited for their planes to be modified before the Group could be transferred to Angaur Island in the Palau chain, not yet secured. Angaur had been chosen because it was just 400 miles east of the Philippines, MacArthur's stated destination.

The 494th, known as "Kelley's Kobras," was comprised of four bomb squadrons numbered 864, 865, 866, and 867. Each squadron was assigned between fifteen and twenty B-24s and each plane had a crew of ten, resulting in an air echelon of about 700 men, with a ground echelon (maintenance, support, and staff) of about three times that many, so by the time the 494th reached its full strength, there were 3,000 men living on a three square mile island.

The 865th and 867th squadrons arrived on 21 September and Col. Kelley arrived a month later. By then, pyramid tents had replaced pup-tents, the island had been dusted with DDT to forestall an incipient malaria outbreak, and a water-treatment plant was in operation. The first Quonset huts had been constructed. Each man now had two gallons of water per day and the first beer rations were dispensed.

In November 1944, the 865th and 867th squadrons went to work, targeting the nearby islands of Yap and Koror. They flew thirteen missions amidst heavy anti-aircraft fire but no fighter resistance. On 22 November, the 864th and 866th squadrons arrived, bringing the total to sixty Liberators on the tiny island.

With the Palaus largely subjugated, the 494th then turned its sights to the Philippines. Their first target was Legaspi Airdrome on Luzon Island, and while the Palau missions had been uneventful, the Philippines were hot with flak and fighters. Crews wondered how long their luck would hold out, and for two weeks in December it did.

Then, returning from a successful bomb run on Lahug Airfield on Cebu Island, flying just 400 feet above the water to get under a violent thunderstorm, two engines of *The Bull* suddenly died. With no time to prepare for ditching, Capt. Richards rang the ditch bell and the B-24 plowed into the water, breaking up. The next day, Richards and three crewmen were rescued, but seven others were lost.

Overall though, in its first seven months of operation, the 494th was extremely fortunate: between 15 August 1944 and 15 March 1945, it flew 68 missions, dropping 2,900 tons of bombs with a 74% hit rate, losing only six planes (two shot down and four from operational failure). Of the 38 men who went down, 27 were saved.

COLONEL LAURENCE KELLEY

Laurence Browning Kelley was born in Hemple, MO, in 1909. He graduated from West Point in 1933, became a pilot, and in May 1943 became chief of the Unit Training Division of the Army Air Force. He took command of the 494th Bomb Group in January 1945 and in November took it to the Pacific. After the War he served with War Department and graduated from the Air War College and the National War College. Promoted to general, he took command of the Wiesbaden Air Base in Germany in 1951. He became director of logistics at Air Force HQ in Washington in 1957 and died in 1979.

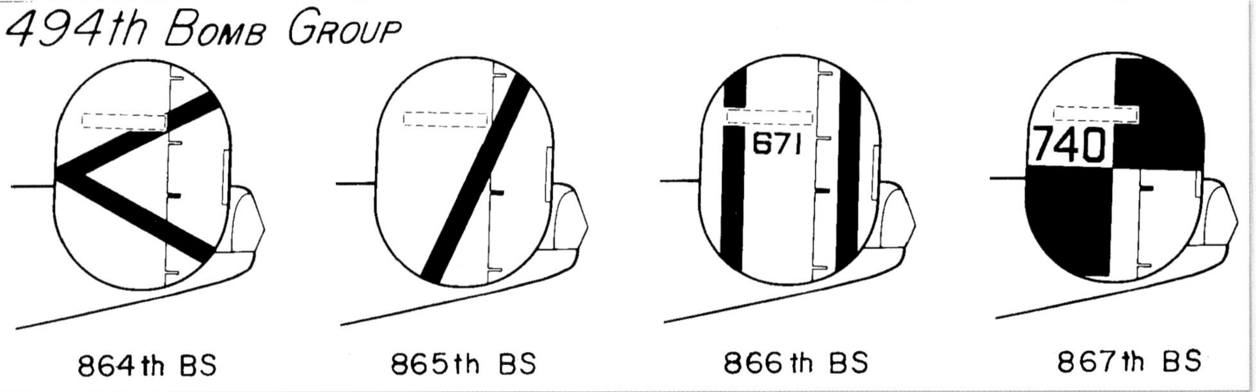

ABOVE Each squadron had unique markings that were painted on the tail vanes of their assigned B-24s.

BELOW Corresponding squadron emblems.

"Kobras"

"The Flak Pak"

"Monkey Business"

"Playboys"

RIGHT Col. Kelley was no desk-jockey. He not only loved to fly, but had his own B-24, *The Missouri Mule*, in which he flew missions with the 494th. On 10 April 1945 he led the Group in a bomb run on Cotabato on Mindanao Island in the Philippines. Japanese ack-ack was thick, and the *Mule's* left landing gear was shot away. When he returned to Angaur, Kelley was forced to make a belly landing. As you can see, the plane sustained minimal damage and everyone walked away with an even greater respect for their "fighting" C.O.

ASSAULT ON ANGAUR

Because O.C. was destined to spend the first half of 1945 on this tiny island in the western Carolines, a short history of the taking of Angaur is in order.

Angaur, mandated to Japanese after WWI, is a harp-shaped limestone and coral island just three miles square, rich in inorganic phosphate, which is important in agriculture and armaments. The island is mostly flat—making it ideal for the 6,000 foot runway required by B-24s—except for a 200' tall caldera (the eroded top of an ancient, inactive volcano) in the northwest of the island where the phosphate mines were located.

As a part of Operation Forager, the assault on Angaur began five days after the initial landings at Peleliu and after six days of shelling and bombing by the Navy. When the Army's 81st Infantry came ashore on 17 September 1944 at the north end of the island, they encountered a now familiar sight: absolute devastation caused by the shelling. But they also knew that Lt. Gen. Inoue had dug in his 1,400 troops and would be hard to defeat.

We knew resistance would be strongest near the phosphate factory outside Saipan Town, the only island village, which is why we chose to land elsewhere. But the Japanese had fortified the entire island, mining the lagoons and beaches.

At the landing sites, enemy fire was light and ineffective, with the 81st pushing the defenders south and west, pressing the bulk of them into the caldera, nicknamed the "Bowl," a heavily jungled area with just one entrance, a narrow defile carved out of the Bowl's southern coral rim to permit a narrow-gauge railroad access to haul phosphate ore from mines to the processing plant near the harbor at Saipan Town a half-mile away.

To make matters worse, during the assault a typhoon blasted the Palaus, wafting huts and tents into the air, snapping palms like matchsticks, and pummeling the invaders with sheets of hot rain, turning the topsoil into a morass of mud, swallowing up boots and vehicles and leaving the jungle a steaming, dripping sauna. Hordes of insects descended on the sweating GIs slowly chopping their way through the dense undergrowth. Giant land crabs invaded soggy sleeping rolls, and lizards and snakes were everywhere. It was hellish.

At the southern tip of the island, it took two days of intense fighting to defeat the 400 Japanese defenders. From there on, attention turned to the Bowl, where the last echelon of Japanese were intent on making their final stand.

TOP RIGHT The devastation wasn't limited to the shelling. A typhoon also erupted during the assault.

CENTER LEFT The remains of the phosphate processing plant outside Saipan Town after the shelling.

BOTTOM LEFT Two GIs of the 81st Infantry Division—known as "Wildcats"—take a break during the fighting.

TAKING THE BOWL

By the end of D-Day plus 3, General Mueller of the 81st reported, "All organized resistance ceased. Island secure." This was true because the remaining 350 Japanese had retreated to the caldera and were completely surrounded and could not impact the construction of the airfield just a mile away. Yet little did Mueller realize that the battle for Angaur would drag on for another month.

The coral terrain was nearly impassable and the Japanese had made the caldera a virtual fortress, digging caves on the ridges, giving them a tactical advantage. In addition, a 75 mm cannon mounted on rails could be rolled out of a cave, fired, and then rolled back, escaping not only destruction but detection as well. And because the Japanese used smokeless and flashless powder, trained observers could not ascertain the source of the firing.

We knew a frontal assault would be costly, so we blared warnings in Japanese over a P.A. and reconnaissance planes dropped pamphlets advising surrender, but only a few saw reason. The rest waited for the frontal assault which would undoubtedly come through the fifty yard-long railroad cut—now called "Bloody Gulch" because of the losses incurred getting through it.

Days passed with little progress. When a Sherman tank named *Sea Breeze* rolled through the gulch, Japanese artillery knocked off its treads. Soldiers could not get around the stranded tank. A demolition team had to blast the hulk out of the way. Eventually, however, tanks were able to enter the Bowl and the final fight began. When Major Goto, commander of Japanese forces, was killed by mortar fire, a few Japanese soldiers made a bid for escape but most remained behind and fought to the last man.

In the taking of Angaur, the 81st Infantry killed 1,338 Japanese and captured 59. 260 of our men died and 1,354 were wounded.

TOP LEFT The Bowl, looking to the northwest.

CENTER LEFT Soldiers attempt to gain ground among the vertical ridges surrounding the Bowl.

BOTTOM LEFT Soldiers wait for grenade smoke to clear before they enter Bloody Gulch.

BUILDING THE AIR FIELD

UPPER LEFT A reconnaissance photo taken prior to the assault on Angaur Island. At this time, the island is still covered with dense jungle. In the shelling and intense bombing to follow, many areas of the island were blasted bare.

CENTER UPPER LEFT Angaur Air Field was begun on D+3 when the 1884th Engineer Aviation Battalion followed the troops ashore. Reefs prevented Amtracks from reaching the beach, so a gangway of men passed supplies.

CENTER LOWER LEFT When engineering crews surveyed the field, shells still screamed overhead. The 81st Infantry was battling fighters in the Bowl less than a mile away.

As the Engineers bulldozed jungle, filled swamps, downed palms, and pulverized and graded coral, they encountered sniper and mortar fire, land mines, booby traps, and unexploded bombs. They had been given just thirty days to finish the field. Intelligence reports indicated that there were 35,000 Japanese soldiers still occupying Koror and Babelthuap islands a few miles away and they too knew the importance of Angaur Island. In addition, the battle for Peleliu Island, just six miles to the north, would rage on for another two months.

BOTTOM LEFT Within two weeks, the Engineers had finished the air field, complete with hardstands for the B-24 Liberators arriving shortly.

RIGHT Two engineers manned each tractor and grader, one to level the runway, the other to watch for snipers shooting from the tree line.

BOTTOM RIGHT On 21 October 1944, the first B-24, *Hay Maker*, touches down on Angaur Air Field. Shortly thereafter it would make its first bombing run on nearby Yap and Koror islands.

MAKING DO

While the Aviation Engineers were blasting and grading for the airfield, they were also building a base that would eventually house thousands of men. Doing this on a coral and limestone outcrop with only a foot of topsoil was quite a chore. But they'd done it many times as Admiral Nimitz island-hopped across the Pacific, and they'd do it a few times more before the War ended.

Unfortunately, nature didn't want us at Angaur. A typhoon struck during the landing, turning the island into a muddy morass. The first night on land, soldiers pitched their pup-tents under trees near the beach. In the morning they awoke to find every imaginable insect sharing their sleeping rolls, along with giant land crabs. Ants, worms, lizards, and snakes were everywhere. The brooding sky daily unleashed sheets of rain followed by the brilliant disk of the sun that baked everything to dust in 110 degree heat.

UPPER LEFT Rough seas made unloading equipment and supplies difficult and field kitchens weren't set up for a month. As a result, Ten-In-One rations (food for ten men for one day) were the fare during October, with occasional C rations of three cans containing entrees of ham, eggs and potato, or chicken and vegetables, and three cans with biscuits, cereal, coffee, and cubed sugar.

When the new kitchens finally started serving meals in late November, 866th Squadron Flight Surgeon Dr. Coppes noticed the men air-drying their mess kits after washing. He ordered the squadron cooks to provide a drum of boiling water for the men to rinse their mess kits in before use. He also prohibited his squadron from sharing meals with other squadrons, which made him unpopular. But when an outbreak of hepatitis hit every squadron *but* the 866th, Coppes was hailed as a hero.

BOTTOM LEFT GI inventiveness is legendary. In December, the fresh water supply problem was licked after a well was dug and the fresh water pumped to the surface with the motor from an old clothes dryer. Airmen also used wind power to turn agitators to wash clothes.

BOTTOM RIGHT Airmen fill a converted oil barrel with water to stock a newfangled type of island shower. Note the pipe exiting the bottom of the barrel ending in a can with a pierced bottom and a valve: the shower head.

865th SQUADRON: "THE FLAK-PAK"

The 494th Bomb Group had been underway for a couple of months when Col. Kelley started a contest to choose mascots for each of the four squadrons. The winner for the 865th was a cartoon wolf wearing an engineer's cap slung low over his brow and eagerly licking his chops for combat. Though the wolf was never named, his squadron was: The Flak Pak.

In August, while the Group was still stationed at Barking Sands in Kauai, the 494th got orders for Angaur Island in the Palau group. It would be another month before the 81st Infantry took the island, but the ground echelon started by sea transport on 17 August. In early October they arrived just days after the island was deemed secure and got right to work preparing for the arrival of the B-24s, clearing ground and planning the layout of the camp. The first bombers of the 865th and 867th arrived on 24 October after a gruelling fourteen hour flight from Kauai.

In early November, the Flak Pak flew its first mission, sending twelve aircraft over Yap and Koror islands in the Palaus. They returned the next week and bombed Koror and Arakabesan islands to put enemy airfields and communications out of service.

The 865th flew missions to the Philippines, focusing on Luzon in advance of the invasion scheduled for January 1945. They bombed the neighboring island of Masbate and were harassed with ack-ack fire and Zeros. Weather was a factor and occasionally pilots had to jettison their payload without reaching their objective because clouds obscured the target. O.C.'s favorite plane, *Rover Boy's Baby*, made its first combat mission in November.

ABOVE LEFT Col. Kelley welcomes the first replacement crews to Angaur.

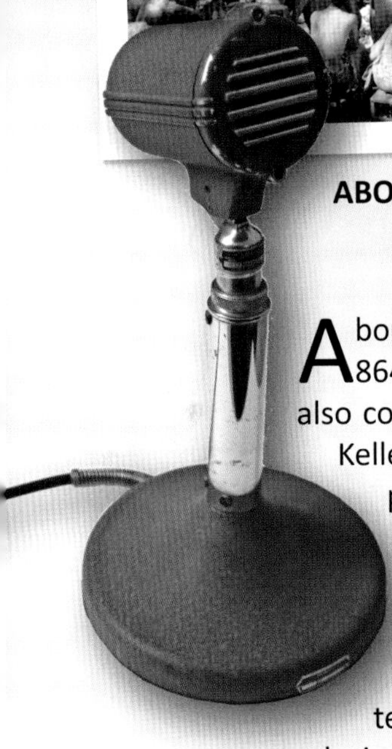

NOW HEAR THIS . . .

About this time the Angaur got a radio station and a D.J. Cpl. Carter Reynolds of the 864th broadcast the news at noon, including world, theater, and squadron updates. He also concocted joke-commercials such as one for Kelley's Kots ("Be kind to your belly—use a Kelley"). In addition, the men listened to Tokyo Rose on shortwave radio. While most of her program was laughably propagandistic, she played popular American music and hearing a woman's voice—even if she *was* the enemy—was somehow comforting.

In December, 2x4 pyramid tent frames started going up, replacing the pup-tents airmen had been using. A Quonset hut was built for Group administration, and the dispensary and mess hall were completed and the first hot meals were served.

RIGHT The first replacement crews arrived in January 1945. O.C. is in the middle of the front row.

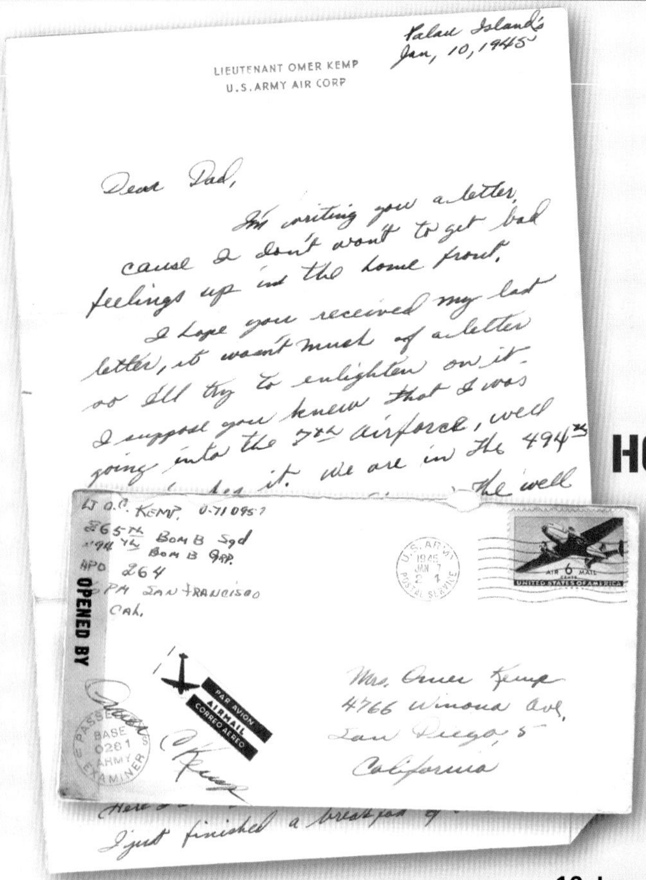

Palau Island's
Jan, 10, 1945

LIEUTENANT OMER KEMP
U.S. ARMY AIR CORP

Dear Dad,

I'm writing you a letter, cause I don't want to get bad feelings up in the home front.

I hope you received my last letter, it wasn't much of a letter so I'll try to enlighten on it. I suppose you knew that I was going into the 7th airforce, well ... it. We are in the 494th ... the well

...

I just finished a breakfast of ...

HOPE THIS PASSES THE CENSOR

7 January "When we arrived we had to pitch our tent, but we made it all right. It's the first one I've pitched since I've been in the Army. It is temporary till we get a wood floor and a frame built by the engineers. We live about 100 feet from the ocean which has no waves due to the reef. We take a swim every night in the warm water—and I do mean *warm*.

"I hooked up the electricity today and we are listening to the radio, a broadcast from Hawaii. We also get China, Australia and Palau Radio, which is run by some GIs here.

10 January "I just finished a breakfast of pancakes and wheat cereal. We also had grapefruit juice. Our food is not too elaborate, but I would say it was very well put together with the time and available materials. We have powdered milk and eggs sometimes. I will never complain about Mom's food when I get back!

"We are living in a tent now. We have a nice sand floor. Every night we are visited by either a crab or a lizard. We have flies and ants (I just killed an ant on my leg). The mosquitoes don't pass malaria since they've been spraying DDT, but we still use the netting just in case.

"The latrine is a real masterpiece. It doesn't take long to get through with what one has to do in there and get out!

"I don't have any spare time because I'm always dickering around with something. I'm sure glad I've got a good tool kit with me, because I use it all the time. I haven't been on a mission yet, but it won't be long now. The boys have been on missions to Manila on the island of Luzon in the Philippines.

"I have to cut the legs off my pants, 'cause it's too hot for the darn things. Also my sleeves. I hope you are all well. Don't worry about me. This deal is going to be a snap if we ever get started. Lots of love, O.C."

EXTRA! **Pacific Post** EXTRA!

Section One | THURSDAY, JANUARY 9, 1944 | Ten Cents

FIGHT FOR THE PHILIPPINES

THE BIGGEST LAND BATTLE IN MILITARY HISTORY UNFOLDS

General MacArthur's landing at Leyte Island in October lit the powder keg that exploded with the Battle of Leyte Gulf, resulting in a decisive victory for the U.S. Navy and destroying the remainder of the Imperial Japanese Navy.

The 6th Army, supported by Filipino guerilla fighters, pushed west across Leyte, reinforced by the 5th Air Force. In December, after Leyte was deemed secure, the 6th moved north to Mindoro Island to prepare for air attacks on Luzon.

Unlike the rest of the Philippines, Mindoro is relatively dry, allowing aircraft to fly regularly with little concern for weather. Immediately after airfields were constructed, U.S. bombers began shellacking Clark Air Field, Manila, and Corregidor Island on Luzon Island. Reconnaissance and bombing flights focused on southern Luzon. Parachute drops with dummies fell to the earth, resistance fighters conducted sabotage operations, and mines were cleared from southern shores—all of which were efforts designed to mask the true landing point: halfway up the west coast of Luzon at Lingayen Gulf.

LANDING AT LINGAYEN

LUZON ISLAND, PHILIPPINES, Jan. 9 – But General Yamashita was not fooled. When General Krueger's 6th Army landed 175,000 soldiers on the south shore of the Gulf, they met stiff resistance, including *kamikaze* aircraft aimed at the ships disgorging the invaders.

General MacArthur had chosen Lingayen because it was only forty miles from Clark Air Field. For three years the Japanese had used Clark as a staging area for air operations. Not only did we need to retake Clark to ensure our own air superiority over the Philippines, but it was a crucial step on our continuing march to Japan.

But stiff Japanese resistance was no match for the sheer numbers of Americans pressing inland and Clark was retaken in late January 1945.

A second amphibious landing took place southwest of Manila on 15 January. More die-hard resistance took place but by 4 February we were on the outskirts of the city. The Japs had blown all bridges and were holding up in Manila, using its citizens as human shields. When we entered the city, street-by-street battles resulted in many civilian casualties.

Army units had also moved south from Clark and by 11 February units from the north and south met up and surrounded Manila. It took several weeks before the last fires of resistance were staunched.

In the end, 1,000 American soldiers died taking Luzon Island and though the Japanese lost 12,000 soldiers, many of the hardier holdouts would not surrender until the War's end.

BATAAN "DEATH MARCH"

BATAAN PENINSULA, LUZON, PHILIPPINES – After General MacArthur was forced to abandon his headquarters at Corregidor Island in March 1942, 60,000 Filipino and 15,000 American GIs were taken prisoner and marched up Bataan Peninsula to the regional capital of Balanga. Because their captors believed surrender stripped a soldier of honor, they determined to thin the ranks long before their prisoners finished the 80 mile forced march. The atrocities began when 400 Filipinos were summarily executed after they surrendered.

For the first three days, prisoners had no food or water. Many died of heat exhaustion. Many others were beaten and bayoneted. If they refused to participate in burial details, they were killed and their bodies added to those awaiting burial. Many were beheaded. Some were even forced to bury their comrades alive.

Thousands of men died on the trek, and even after arriving at the internment camp they died at a rate of fifty a day due to disease and malnutrition.

LIBERATORS FLOWN BY THE 865th SQUADRON

The 865th usually had between 16 and 18 planes in its arsenal, 13 of which appear below. These are all J models manufactured by Convair in San Diego in 1944 (as indicated by the "44" in the serial number). Call numbers (used by air and ground crews and traffic controllers) were the last three digits of the serial number.

44-40563 *Double Trouble*

44-40645 *Super Chick*

44-40654 *Bugs Bunny Jr.*

44-40705 *The Sniffin' Griffin*

44-40711 *Sittin' Pretty*

44-40732 *Flyin' Pay*

44-40733 *Innocence A-Broad*

44-40742 *The Flying Fifer*

44-40748 *The Early Bird*

44-40750 *Sluggin' Sal*

44-40756 *Crash Kids*

44-42057 *The Bull II*

GOOD COMEBACK

Jack Berger recalls that one morning as they were doing the engine run-up before taking off for a mission, O.C. hesitated to move forward when it was his turn—he didn't like the sound one of the engines was making.

Line Officer Lt. Bishop roared up in his Jeep, shouting for them to get a move on. O.C. got out of the plane and said, "I don't like the sound of this engine."

Bishop was having none of it. "You're just yellow," he shouted. "Get going!"

O.C. turned and looked at Bishop. "Okay," he said, grabbing Bishop's arm and hauling him toward the aircraft. "Then you're coming with us."

44-40752 *Rover Boy's Baby*

They flew the mission that day, but in another plane.

CALL TO DUTY

During training, being captain is a lot of perks and few responsibilities as there is always someone aboard the aircraft who outranks even the captain. Not so in combat; the captain is the pilot in command and his word is final. To stress this, everyone on board the aircraft is required to use the formal address: "Yes, sir," or "Yes, Captain."

In this little pamphlet, the need for this hierarchy is explained:

"Not many months ago two bombers were shot out of formation by fighters attacking from about 5 o'clock, slightly high but not out of the sun or clouds. Neither bomber had opened fire, nor was there any fire from other formation planes. On another day an attacking [German] Me-109 almost crashed into a bomber from about 6 o'clock level. There was no fire from the tail gunner. When the plane got back to base, his boxes were full of ammo, but his guns were not loaded. The gunner was dead at his station. Another time a gunner explained that he had not shot at a sure kill because he was up in the waist and couldn't get back to his turret in time. And from yet another plane a nose gunner said he never fired for two reasons: first, if he didn't fire, he wouldn't have to clean his guns; and second, if he did fire, he didn't think he would have hit anything anyway."

In each case, the pamphlet places the blame on the aircraft commander. He alone is responsible for the discipline, competency, and safety of his crew. It goes on to list qualities of a good airplane commander:

1. You are in charge, the last link in the chain; flying the aircraft is just part of your responsibilities.
2. You must work harder than everyone else and you must know their job as well as they do.
3. Never assume; discover the weaknesses and strengths not only of your aircraft, but of your crew.
4. You literally represent the President, the Commander-in-Chief; take charge, give orders, review results, reward achievement and punish failure. Once you relinquish command, you never get it back.
5. Invite your crew's advice; your men will soon know how much or how little you know, and they will respect a man who knows his limitations. Seek advice from your superiors on how to help your men.
6. Get to know each man individually. Tell him your expectations, but keep your remarks to a minimum.
7. Your example matters. Your initiative, determination, loyalty, honesty, dependability, understanding, executive ability, physical fitness, and presence all bear on whether men will follow you into combat.
8. Discipline is the outcome of how you achieve the foregoing; if you fail, your crew will not function in combat; if you succeed, they will act as a team and everyone's chances of survival will increase.

Commanders are required to know the duties of each crew member at least well enough to understand if there is a problem; he needs to understand the engines and their limitations as well as the engineer does, the engineering duties of his co-pilot, the principles of weather and navigation methodology of his navigator, the knowledge of bombing procedure, bombsight usage, and payload preparation of his bombardier, the capabilities and limitations of the radioman's equipment and procedures (including competency in Morse Code and security procedures), and the capabilities and limitations of the gunners' weapons.

O.C.'s crew knew him as a competent commander who led by example. In most photos herein, he wears his crusher cap and wings, a reminder that he was never really off duty but was responsible for his men at all times. And they loved him for it. In the words of bombardier Jack Berger: "He brought us home every time."

FLIGHT GEAR

Unlike famous general Curtis Lemay, who wore his officer's cap with the wire insert stiffeners in place, causing it to stand tall on his head, most pilots removed the wires because their radio communication headsets would not fit over the cap otherwise. Without the wires, the caps were easily crushed and were thereafter called "crusher caps." O.C.'s is above right.

Though it was unbearably hot seven degrees north of the equator on the ramp at Anguar, at 20,000 feet it got downright chilly, and O.C. wore the insulated flight suit he'd worn a year ago in January at Pampa, Texas, which meant possible heat stroke as he ran the checklist and prepared to take off.

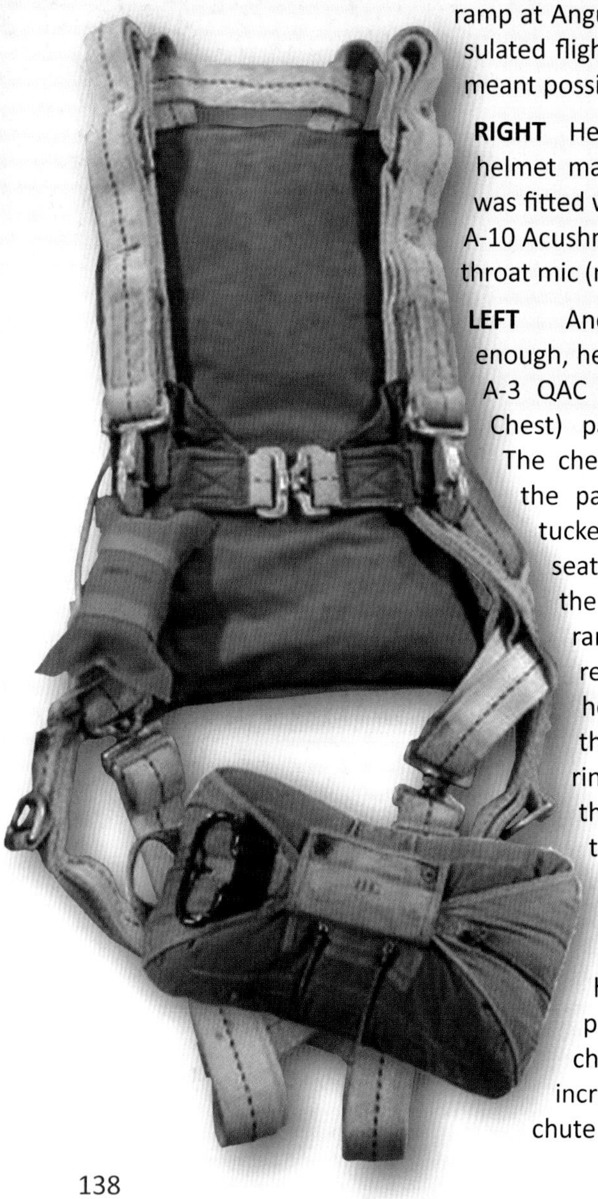

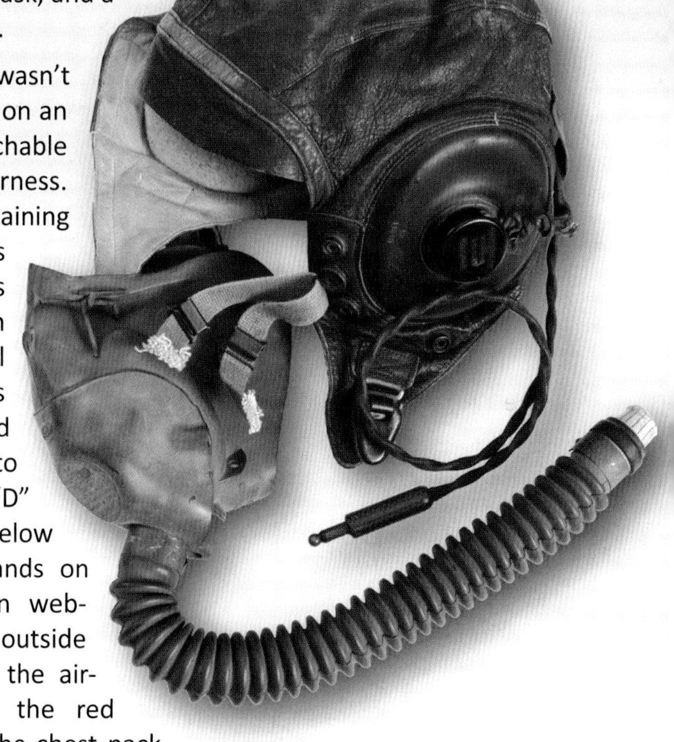

RIGHT He also wore an A-11 leather flight helmet made by Shelby Shoe Co. which was fitted with an ANB-H-1 receiver, an A-10 Acushnet oxygen mask, and a throat mic (not pictured).

LEFT And if that wasn't enough, he also belted on an A-3 QAC (Quick Attachable Chest) parachute harness. The chest pack containing the parachute was tucked under his seat and when the bailout bell rang, it was retrieved and hooked onto the two steel "D" rings located below the yellow bands on the extension webbing. Once outside the aircraft, the airman pulled the red handle and the chest pack popped open, releasing the pilot chute, followed by the main chute. At the same time, the tension on the extension webbings increased and they popped loose, clearing the airman from the chute lines and wafting him safely down. That was the idea anyway.

JAPANESE FIGHTERS

MITSUBISHI A6M "ZERO-SEN" (Type 0 Carrier Fighter) aka "ZERO" (U.S. airmen gave Japanese aircraft "hillbilly" names to make them more memorable.) The Zero (aka Zeke and Hamp) was the best carrier-based aircraft produced by either side. It traded armament and armor for maneuverability and range, which resulted in an impressive 12-1 kill ratio that endured until 1943 when the P-38 Lightning and F6F Hellcat appeared. The Zero developed only 1,000 hp but had a 3,000'/min climb and a 10,000' ceiling. Those were Zeros screaming from the clouds to attack Pearl Harbor.

NAKAJIMA Ki-43 "HAYABUSA" (Peregrine Falcon) aka "OSCAR" The Army's version of the Zero was a daunting dogfight opponent, though its armament was poor and it lacked self-sealing gas tanks. Allied pilots reported that Oscars were difficult targets, but burned easily and broke apart with a few hits. In spite of its drawbacks, the Oscar shot down more Allied aircraft than any other Japanese fighter and almost all of the Japanese aces achieved their kills in it. 6,000 were produced, many of which were used during the last months of the War for *kamikaze* missions.

KAWANISHI N1K2-J "SHIDEN" (Violet Lightning) aka "GEORGE" A land-based fighter that was considered by pilots on both sides to be one of the best planes of WWII, the George had heavy armaments and was designed to counteract the advantages of the P-51 Mustang and the VBF-10 Corsair. Unfortunately, the engine was unreliable, the aircraft had a poor climb rate, and handled poorly at altitude. Notwithstanding these drawbacks, in the hands of an expert pilot, the George could give as well as it took. But only 1,500 of two variants were produced due to B-29 strikes on mainland Japan that crippled production.

MITSUBISHI J2M "RAIDEN" (Thunderbolt) aka "JACK" In late 1943, the makers of the potent Zero went into production with the Jack, an aircraft designed to intercept the high-altitude bombers expected to appear soon in the skies over Japan, as well as engage their escorts. It thus relied on speed, climb performance, and armament at the expense of maneuverability. But supercharger design problems limited its power development at altitude, though its 20 mm cannons made it a real factor until the Allies switched to night bombing in March 1945, thus reducing its effectiveness.

NANKING
LAHA
MANILA
BATAAN
PALAWAN
BURMA
CHANGJIAO
MANCHURIA
SOOK CHING
BANKA
KALAGONG
PARIT SULONG
WAKE
WUHAN
YICHANG
JAVA
SANDAKAN
15,000,000

THE COLD, HARD TRUTH

The stomach-churning atrocities on the previous page should instill a righteous outrage in anyone, but as the following letter reveals, our soldiers still had difficulty realizing they were at war. I have included it here, just before O.C.'s first bomb run—where he would undeniably kill people—because I am certain he pondered that terrible truth as he lay sleeplessly in his bunk before his first 2:00 a.m. wake up call.

RESTRICTED RESTRICTED

Headquarters
AAF Gulf Coast Training Center
Randolph Field, Tex.

3 August 1943

SUBJECT: Psychology

TO: Commanding General 33rd FTW, BAFS, Waco, Texas

1. The following extract was taken from a Regimental Intelligence publication which was written by Private Frank B. Sergeant and was noted by his Division Commander, Major General Charles W. Ryder. General Eisenhower was so impressed by it that he published it to the Allied Forces in North Africa. A copy was brought to the United States by General Marshall personally, who ordered it distributed to the Army at Large:

THE SUGGESTED PSYCHOLOGICAL TRAINING FOR INTELLIGENCE PERSONNEL

In the training of the American soldier there is one point which, unfortunately so far, has been overlooked. We may call it "psychological preparation for combat."

We had the general impression, at the front, that newly arrived American soldiers did not realize the nature of war; neither did they have a conception of the psychology of the enemy. American soldiers are innocent and trusting; good-hearted and confiding. They are not at all aggressive. Unlike the British and French, Americans have never seen enemy actions in the raw. Maybe they saw ruins of bombed buildings in England, but they regarded them as if they were remains of ancient Pompeii or Carthage. The young soldiers could never visualize the human beings who used to live in those buildings and who were now dead. Americans never had to drag the torn bodies of loved ones out of smashed buildings, or to fight for survival. Unlike the French, they were never subjected to terror. In other words, Americans never had any reasons to hate anybody. When American troops first came to the front they did not hate their enemy. But if you don't hate your enemy, you will fear him if his determination to kill you is stronger than your determination to kill him.

Psychology of hate.

The British and French know what they are fighting for because they have been in this war for a long time, and the Germans believe that they do too. The British fight for their very lives; they fight to stop the Germans from bombing their homes; to stop them from killing their families. The British front line soldier slashed forward without mercy. He hates the enemy. The American soldier is different. He is fair minded and thinks that the enemy will be fair too. He does not really want to kill, because he does not hate, yet. Subconsciously he thinks of war as a game where the umpire's whistle will stop it before it gets too rough. He cannot imagine anybody wanting to kill him, and so he commits all the mistakes which have cost so many lives already. Enemy prisoners marvel at the thoughtlessness with which American soldiers move. They cannot understand why Americans never think of taking cover; why they don't follow through; why they can be bluffed and trapped so easily.

I know so well those men who were cut into ribbons at the KASSERINE PASS and I know why they were thrown into confusion, panicked by attacks, and accepted their fate almost paralyzed. When they jumped into foxholes to let the tanks roll over them, and were bayonetted in these foxholes by the infantry that came behind the tanks, they died with an astonished look on their faces, as if they wanted to ask: "Could that be possible, would they really do that?"

We are prone to regard the Italians with a mixture of contempt and pity. But the boys I knew, who were blown to bits by Italian hand grenades would not think so. If they could come to life again they would not feel pity for the poor, coerced Italians; they would go after them until they had killed every last one. So would the medical orderlies I knew, who went to treat German casualties and lost their arms by booby traps.

The psychology of hate is such:

Until John Doe learns to hate he will be no good. As long as he regards his opponent as a good fellow, a man who, after all, does not really want to fight and kill him, John Doe will go into combat carelessly and not aggressively. He won't go and look for the enemy; he won't want to kill, to destroy; to win. When the enemy proves to be stronger, John Doe will not hold out and counter attack; try to beat the enemy with the last ounce of energy, beat him by his stronger will. John Doe will probably give way, get panicky, and want to leave well enough alone in order to be let alone. He will fall into traps and never lay any traps himself. He will trust anybody and never suspect. His slogan will not be "get the B . . . s" but "let's give away our positions." When lead starts flying thickly, he'll want to run.

It is in the nature of hate that it can be instilled or acquired. It was instilled into the German, Italian or Japanese soldiers until it became a habit with them. Then, of course, they went ahead and nothing could stop them. They whistled when they threw hand grenades. Then it was too late, and we lost so many unnecessarily.

Hate is like gin. It takes awhile, and then, suddenly, it hits you. After you have seen your buddies killed; after you see bodies, or what's left of them, piled up for burial; when you realize that they are after you, too; when it finally connects in your mind that moral code does not exist in this way, then you will begin to hate and want to retaliate. A soldier has to develop the primitive instinct to kill anybody who threatens him or his own. Beyond that he must learn to kill before the other can get at him.

Until he hates the enemy with every instinct and every muscle, he will only be afraid.

This is primitive psychology, a cruel and inhuman one. But war is all that. Hate must become first nature to a soldier and make him want to use every trick. We went out for days to look for the enemy, we fired at everything that moved, we laid booby traps all over the front, because we wanted to kill.

2. It is believed that a good purpose will be served if the above extract should be reproduced at stations under your command and a copy given to each graduating student.

By command of Major General BRANT:

M. GIESENSCHLAG
Captain, Air C.
Act-Asst. Adjutant Gen.

MISSION BRIEFING

By January 1945, the Japanese Navy had been greatly reduced. The best pilots and planes of their Air Force had been destroyed, and those that were left now engaged in terrible and tragic *kamikaze* strikes, a pointless and wasteful maneuver, no matter what side you were on.

Two replacement crews had been lost in early January and so Col. Kelley sat everyone down and gave them the word: The War was still very much on, especially in the Philippines, their current target. Their missions would be fifteen hours long, flying to and from the targets over open sea, and bombing amidst incredibly heavy flak. They would leave in darkness and return in darkness. Anyone who did not take that seriously was a fool, he said. As a training measure, he was putting an experienced pilot in each replacement crew for a while to see if the new crews were up to snuff. Anger percolated in the crowd—their training was just fine, they believed.

Col. Kelley ignored the glares and continued: Anti-artillery fire over the Philippines was deadly. Ack-ack had struck the right wing of *Rip Snorter* of the 866th Squadron over Clark Field days earlier, ripping the wing right off—but that was no excuse for breaking formations on bomb runs. No excuse whatsoever.

In addition, Jap fighters, reluctant to approach B-24s bristling with .50 caliber machine guns, were now flying above formations and dropping bombs which exploded in mid-air, sending white tendrils streaming down like fireworks—except they were composed of white-hot phosphorus, which if it hit a plane, would burn right through the thin aluminum skin—and one phosphorus bomb threw hundreds of tendrils. (Another reason taking Angaur was important: to diminish Japan's ability to make phosphorus bombs.)

"Oh," continued Col. Kelley: "We've found that doing our runs at 10,000 feet yields the most accuracy." A groan rose from the crowd. Kelley continued: "I'm aware that this new altitude is in the overlapping zone of medium and heavy artillery, but it's unavoidable. Greater bombing accuracy means fewer return missions. It will be hot when you're up there, but you won't be up there as often."

No one cheered. Everyone wanted to fight, to kill the enemy and destroy his safe havens. And the more missions flown, the sooner they'd get R&R.

Kelley knew what they were thinking. "The veteran crews are now taking turns heading to Australia for some well-deserved R&R. They've done their share—they've flown their twenty missions—now it's time for the replacement crews to step up."

That got a cheer. They were eager to get into the thick of it.

CARL NORDEN'S "BLUE OX"

Dutch emigre engineer Carl Norden began work in the U.S. on ship gyrostabilizers in 1904. During WWI, his aircraft gyroscope resolved leveling and wind bombing issues. At that time, both pilot and bombardier had identical connected pilot direction indicator (PDI) dials. As the bombardier sighted, his PDI changes were reflected on the pilot's PDI and the pilot matched the bombardier's course. Norden proposed using the entire bombsight as the indicator, utilizing mechanical linkages from the sight (called a "football" because of its shape) to an autopilot module which controlled aircraft flight axes.

The football contained a telescope attached to a gyro that would keep the sight pointed at the same azimuth regardless of aircraft movement. (Azimuth is an angular measurement in a spherical coordinate system (right).) The vector from an observer to a point of interest (star) is projected perpendicularly onto a reference plane (the horizon); the angle between the projected vector and a reference vector (north) on the reference plane is the azimuth, usually measured in degrees.)

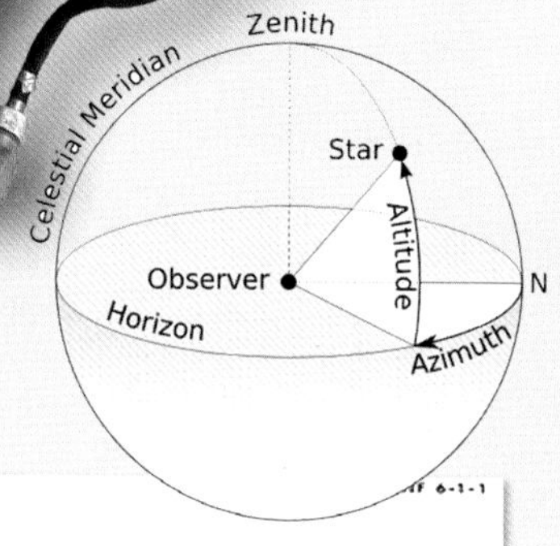

To time bomb drops, Norden refined the "equal distance" concept, based on the observation that the time needed to travel a certain distance over the ground remains relatively constant during the bomb run. After locating the target in the sight, the bombardier makes fine adjustments with two control wheels. An internal calculator settles on a solution in just a few seconds, reducing the required length of the bomb run to just thirty seconds.

But there were practical problems. When bombers flew tight formations, each using his own bombsight, the autopilots vectored the planes toward each other as they approached the target, threatening collision. This was resolved by having just the lead bomber use the Norden. The rest salvoed their bombs when they saw the lead drop his.

Real-world results were mixed. The bombsight required visual contact. In addition, jet stream winds at high altitude overwhelmed the mechanism. Even the shape of the bomb affected its trajectory. Nevertheless, the Norden bombsight was a piece of remarkable technology that helped win the War.

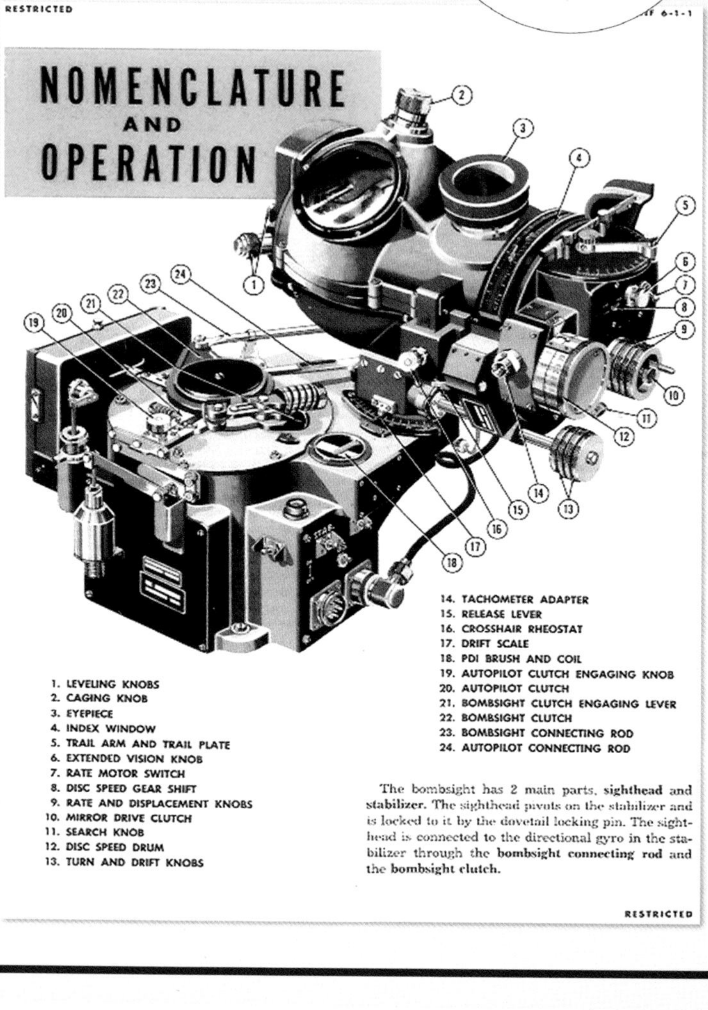

RESTRICTED F 6-1-1

NOMENCLATURE AND OPERATION

1. LEVELING KNOBS
2. CAGING KNOB
3. EYEPIECE
4. INDEX WINDOW
5. TRAIL ARM AND TRAIL PLATE
6. EXTENDED VISION KNOB
7. RATE MOTOR SWITCH
8. DISC SPEED GEAR SHIFT
9. RATE AND DISPLACEMENT KNOBS
10. MIRROR DRIVE CLUTCH
11. SEARCH KNOB
12. DISC SPEED DRUM
13. TURN AND DRIFT KNOBS
14. TACHOMETER ADAPTER
15. RELEASE LEVER
16. CROSSHAIR RHEOSTAT
17. DRIFT SCALE
18. PDI BRUSH AND COIL
19. AUTOPILOT CLUTCH ENGAGING KNOB
20. AUTOPILOT CLUTCH
21. BOMBSIGHT CLUTCH ENGAGING LEVER
22. BOMBSIGHT CLUTCH
23. BOMBSIGHT CONNECTING ROD
24. AUTOPILOT CONNECTING ROD

The bombsight has 2 main parts, **sighthead** and **stabilizer**. The sighthead pivots on the stabilizer and is locked to it by the dovetail locking pin. The sighthead is connected to the directional gyro in the stabilizer through the **bombsight connecting rod** and the **bombsight clutch**.

RESTRICTED

7TH BOMBER COMMAND MISSION REPORT

MISSION NUMBER 1 — 494th B.G. 866th B.S.

PILOT Kemp, Omer C. CREW ---
A/C TYPE & T/N B-24J 748 GP. MISSION NO. 494-042
DATE 14 Jan 45 PAYLOAD 6 - 500#
DESTINATION Cabanatuan, Luzon, P.I.
OBJECTIVE supply dump & aircraft
TIME 12:55 DISTANCE 2,000 HITS 60%

NOTES Commander: Harrah

Target: dispersed airplanes and revetments.

U.S. ARMY AIR FORCE FORM 1066-AB Rev. 45-01 DISPOSITION RESTRICTED

BY THE SKIN OF THEIR TEETH

You may have heard of the Great Raid. Hundreds of survivors of the Bataan Death March were imprisoned in a camp near the hamlet of Cabanatuan in central Luzon and were rescued by the 6th Rangers in late January 1945. But on January 13th, the 7th AAF didn't know there were American POWs in that camp. Aerial reconnaissance indicated that it held Japanese soldiers and they were going to destroy it the next day.

Five days earlier, Allied troops landed in the Lingayen Gulf fifty miles to the east. As they pressed inland, they linked up with Filipino guerillas and were informed that the Cabanatuan Penal Colony billeted Japanese soldiers, yes, but it also held 500 American POWs. Word was sent to the 494th, which moved its target five miles west to Cabanatuan Town. O.C. learned about the objective change—and the near tragedy they almost inflicted upon 500 U.S. POWs—just the night before this, his first bombing run.

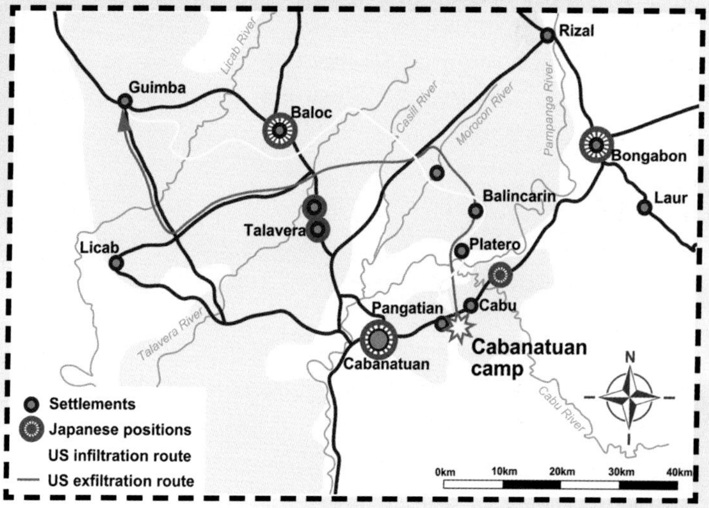

At 2:00 a.m. on 14 February, O.C. was awakened. He would fly co-pilot on this mission, to get the lay of the land. After a quick breakfast of dehydrated eggs and coffee, the officers had a 2:45 a.m. briefing where they saw aerial photos of the new target and received flight, navigation, and emergency instructions.

At 4:15 a.m. they took off with 26 other B-24s and flew in loose formation for four hours. Everyone except the pilots and navigator could grab a nap, but no one slept. The navigator directed them to the rendezvous point and then the bombers turned to their target, which never appeared in the official records.

The Mission Report does not detail their raid on Cabanatuan Town. It only contains their original objective, the Penal Colony, which had, in addition to Japanese troops and American POWs, dispersed aircraft and revetments (munition storage bunkers with gently sloping earthen sides). They dropped six 500 pound general purpose bombs on the town and scored a 60% hit rate, encountering no enemy aircraft and no anti-aircraft fire. Then they turned south and refueled on Leyte Island before heading home. The trip took 13 hours.

On 29 January, in a daring surprise night raid thirty miles behind enemy lines, the Rangers, Alamo Scouts, and Filipino guerillas attacked Cabanatuan Penal Colony, wiped out the Japanese garrison, and freed 500 POWs, losing just two men in the process. It was the greatest military rescue in U.S. history—but it was almost the War's greatest tragedy.

DANGEROUS ISLAND

After he settled into his new quarters and flew his first mission and survived, O.C. heaved a huge sigh of relief and looked around to see where he'd landed.

On Angaur, what hadn't been hauled ashore, chopped down, bulldozed, or burned away with flamethrowers was little more than concrete and steel wreckage, blasted palm trees, and impenetrable jungle. There were still a few snipers and infiltrators lurking about who sneaked into camp at night to steal shoes and rations. O.C. heard stories about wild-eyed, rabid Japs running into tents and exploding grenades to kill an American or two along with themselves. Like everyone on the island, he slept with his service revolver under his pillow.

But some stories were just strange. An intelligence officer awoke to find his tent ransacked. He reported that the thief had stolen some top secret papers from his locker. Later, a Japanese encampment was raided and the secret papers were recovered. The officer examined them, relieved, until he noted Japanese writing on the back of several sheets, which he rushed to a translator who considered them gravely. Finally, he handed them back. "This guy is writing a detective story," he laughed. "A lousy detective story, I might add."

O.C. also heard the famous story about the avid Japanese baseball fan who—from a safe distance—watched the engineering squadron games, cheering the players and shouting in Japanese something that needed no translation when calls went against them. When a well-hit ball down the third base line was called foul, the Jap soldier wound up and beaned the umpire with a piece of coral and then took off over the hill, followed only by the cheers of the engineers.

TOP LEFT O.C. goes exploring—with his sidearm, of course.

TOP RIGHT The new frame-walled tents were a vast improvement over the pup-tents everyone had lived in for two months.

LEFT CENTER A few buildings at the phosphorus plant were the only structures left standing after the invasion.

RIGHT CENTER The .45 caliber Colt M1911A1 was the standard Army issue sidearm during the War (and long after) because of its simple, trustworthy design and deadly stopping power.

RIGHT BOTTOM When Germany controlled the Palaus, workers at the phosphate plant kept macaque monkeys as pets and several escaped captivity. Years later, hundreds of feral monkeys roamed the island, like the one O.C. caught on film crouching on his tent roof, waiting for an opening to steal food or even a shiny wristwatch. For this reason Angaur to this day is still known as "Monkey Island" by the natives.

FED UP WITH IT

All through January, O.C.'s folks did not get a letter from him. He was writing three or four lines every few days, but it took him three weeks to finally finish a letter and send it off. He just couldn't bring himself to relate such bad news. On 1 February, after receiving a batch of letters from home and feeling guilty, he dashed off a letter, which was little more than a litany of gripes:

"I'm pretty well disgusted with this outfit I'm in," he wrote. "They've only sent me on one mission and that was as a co-pilot. It looks like I'll be over here forever. If it's anything I hate, it's waiting around when I could be flying. It makes me very mad and I sure wish I could get going so I could get home.

"Of course we are just replacements and so we get nothing. The veteran crews have ships that they've already named. I guess it will be a while yet before we get very many missions because there are no extra ships."

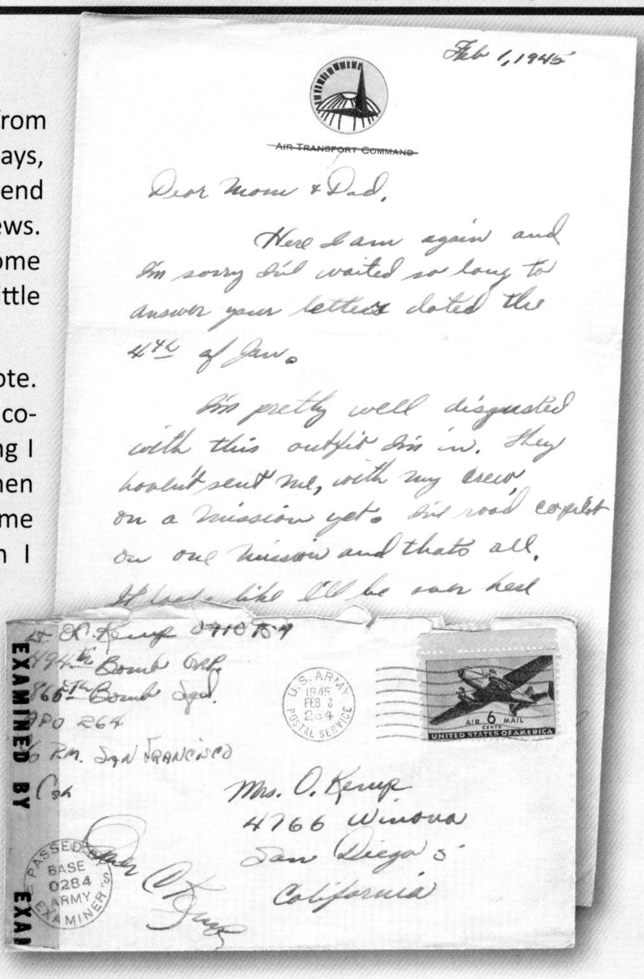

Feb 1, 1945

~~AIR TRANSPORT COMMAND~~

Dear Mom & Dad,

Here I am again and I'm sorry I've waited so long to answer your letters dated the 4th of Jan.

I'm pretty well disgusted with this outfit I'm in. They haven't sent me, with my crew, on a mission yet. I've rode copilot on one mission and that's all. It looks like I'll be over here

Lt. O.C. Kemp 0718759
494th Bomb Grp.
865th Bomb Sqd.
APO 264
c/o P.M. San Francisco
Calif.

U.S. ARMY 1945 FEB 2 264 POSTAL SERVICE

AIR 6 MAIL CENTS UNITED STATES OF AMERICA

Mrs. O. Kemp
4766 Winona
San Diego 5
California

EXAMINED BY

PASSED BY BASE 0284 ARMY EXAMINER

THE REPLACEMENT CURSE

O.C. wasn't the only airman who as frustrated with the meager number of missions he was being assigned. In the Army Air Force, the more missions flown, the more points a flight crew earned. In the 494th, the magic number for leave was twenty missions. To go home, you had to log forty successful combat sorties. So when replacement crews arrived, their presence was considered an impediment by the veteran crews.

Replacement crews were identified by a letter after their number. From the beginning, Crew 23A struggled to get missions. While favored veteran crews got up to three missions a week, O.C.'s crew got nothing.

And they were not alone. As a member of another replacement crew put it:

> *We were treated like bastards at a family reunion. First, they decided to let their co-pilots be the First Pilots on our crews and made our First Pilots co-pilots on old crews. At least we might have gotten our fair share of mission assignments that way. They also threatened to make us drill. Like in marching. We raised hell and even threatened to quit flying. They finally decided to let us be, but never were equitable in giving out mission assignments. From 12 January to 8 May 1945 our crew flew 14 missions. The older crews flew some 25 during the same time.*

It's also true that some of the new crews had difficulty and two were lost in January. Group command wondered whether replacement crews were being properly trained in the States so all replacement crews were grounded until a complete investigation could be completed. As a result, experienced pilots took over some of the replacement crews for awhile. This greatly damaged the morale of the new crews.

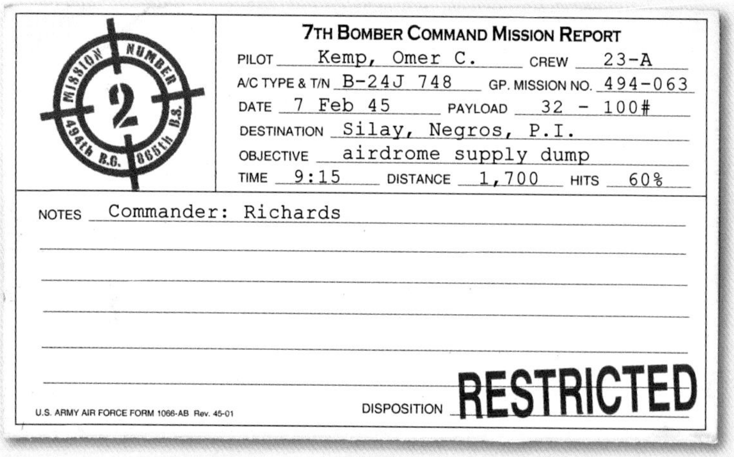

7TH BOMBER COMMAND MISSION REPORT

PILOT Kemp, Omer C. CREW 23-A

A/C TYPE & T/N B-24J 748 GP. MISSION NO. 494-063

DATE 7 Feb 45 PAYLOAD 32 - 100#

DESTINATION Silay, Negros, P.I.

OBJECTIVE airdrome supply dump

TIME 9:15 DISTANCE 1,700 HITS 60%

NOTES Commander: Richards

U.S. ARMY AIR FORCE FORM 1066-AB Rev. 45-01

DISPOSITION RESTRICTED

OPERATION VICTOR I

General MacArthur had been tasked by the Joint Chiefs to provide staging for 22 divisions of American soldiers who would invade Japan by November 1945 and he needed ports and airfields to do so.

The Visayas, a group of islands in the central Philippines, were made up of Panay, Negros, Cebu, and Bohol islands. Filipino guerillas controlled most island interiors, but 30,000 Japanese held the coastal towns, including Silay on the west side of Negros Island, which had a busy air field from which it launched Zero fighters and Betty bombers. It had to be destroyed before the ground offensive could begin on 18 March 1945. Operation Victor I was aimed at Panay and Negros islands; Victor II at Cebu and Bohol.

On 7 February Crew 23A joined 21 other bombers heading toward Silay Airdrome, the main Japanese fighter and bomber base on Negros. They rained 32 100 lb. bombs on the field and supply dump and scored a 60% hit rate. They had been instructed that if they were downed by flak they should bail out over the southern half of the island and head for the hills and hope to be picked up by the Filipino guerillas. The Japanese reportedly had 17,000 men defending Negros, so their escape would be dicey.

Negros Island was plenty pock-marked by the time the 185th Infantry came ashore near Bacolod City on 29 March. They surprised the Japanese and quickly seized a key bridge, then moved north almost unimpeded before meeting real resistance near Talisay. When they arrived at Silay Airdrome, they found over 200 destroyed enemy aircraft. The 494th had done its job well.

They pushed on and by 2 April, the western coastal plain was in Allied hands and the defenders had withdrawn to the fortified highlands to the east.

The island was not declared secure until 4 June and it wasn't until a full two months later that the 40th Division—a California National Guard detachment—overcame the last organized resistance.

RIGHT Actual aerial reconnaissance photo of Silay Airdrome. Look closely: can you find the airdrome? If not, you're in good company. I couldn't find it either.

THE RAMP

For every airman, there are several men on the ground, and their work begins long before the air crews arrive to take the ships into the sky. Then they go back to work repairing damaged planes and when the bombers return, they swarm over them, patching flak holes and repairing engines in blazing heat and stunning downpours that leave standing water where mosquitoes flourish and the acrid smell of DDT fills the nostrils, along with the lingering odor of gasoline and motor oil that is napalm.

TOP LEFT Mechanics service the #1 and #2 engines of 729 *Hay Maker.*

TOP RIGHT In just two months, the air field is complete, with hardstands (parking areas) for 100 aircraft and miles of taxiways.

CENTER LEFT & RIGHT The ordnance crew loads 500 pound GP (general purpose) bombs onto a trailer for transport to the ramp.

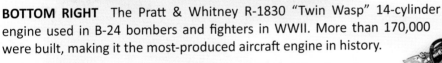

BOTTOM RIGHT The Pratt & Whitney R-1830 "Twin Wasp" 14-cylinder engine used in B-24 bombers and fighters in WWII. More than 170,000 were built, making it the most-produced aircraft engine in history.

BOTTOM LEFT A ground crew rebuilds two "Twin Wasp" engines.

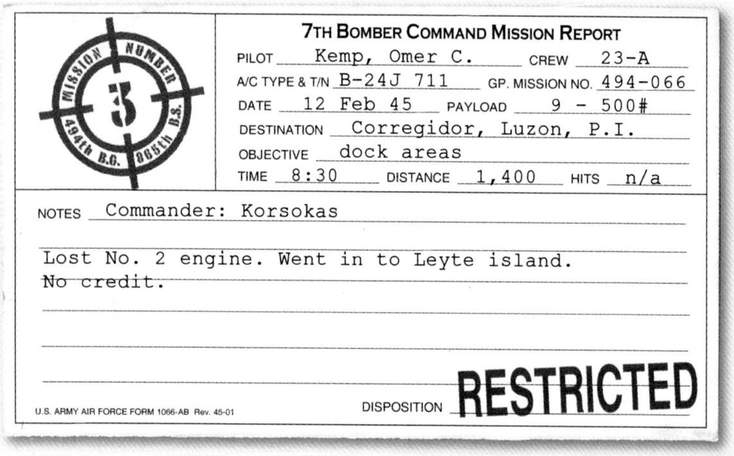

7TH BOMBER COMMAND MISSION REPORT

PILOT Kemp, Omer C. CREW 23-A
A/C TYPE & T/N B-24J 711 GP. MISSION NO. 494-066
DATE 12 Feb 45 PAYLOAD 9 - 500#
DESTINATION Corregidor, Luzon, P.I.
OBJECTIVE dock areas
TIME 8:30 DISTANCE 1,400 HITS n/a

NOTES Commander: Korsokas

Lost No. 2 engine. Went in to Leyte island.
~~No credit.~~

U.S. ARMY AIR FORCE FORM 1066-AB Rev. 45-01 DISPOSITION RESTRICTED

SEIZING THE CROWN

Corregidor, the tadpole-shaped island at the entrance of Manila Bay, was MacArthur's headquarters when he was Field Marshall of the Philippine Army. But it could not withstand the Japanese artillery onslaught from the Bataan Peninsula to the north in early 1942. Though MacArthur was ordered to leave the Philippines, 10,000 American and 60,000 Filipino soldiers made their last stand, first on the island, then evacuating to Bataan and holding out for two more months. They were eventually captured and the horror of the Bataan Death March, a forced slog 80 miles north to POW camps, ensued. Tens of thousands died in that war crime.

MacArthur's famous declaration, "I shall return!" uttered as he reluctantly left Corregidor, had echoed in his mind for three long years of exile in Australia. He opposed Admiral Nimitz's "island-hopping" plan to retake the Central Pacific, preferring instead the slow land march through New Guinea, the Celebes and Borneo (and cutting off Japan's access to Sumatran oil fields in the process), finally retaking the Philippines and then using Clark Field on Luzon Island to stage bomber runs on the Japanese mainland. But the Joint Chiefs, playing it safe, approved both plans, and MacArthur had to do with less and make progress anyway.

That he did. And when his Army came ashore at Lingayen Gulf on Luzon Island on 9 January 1945, he pointed them south to Manila, repeating the same tactic the Japanese used in 1942 to secure the island. But Corregidor, now the HQ of Japanese forces in the South Pacific, received the brunt of his anger and he intended to utterly destroy the island once considered invincible. He told Gen. Douglass, commander of the 7th AAF, to "Give 'em hell—flatten it," and Douglass did just that. Starting in late January 1945, the 494th pitched in, sending daily formations of B-24s to silence Corregidor's 56 gun batteries.

BELOW LEFT The aerial reconnaissance photo O.C. used on this mission, with clouds obscuring the targeted dock areas at the neck of the island. Unless it was socked in, it would be hard to miss this dramatic objective.

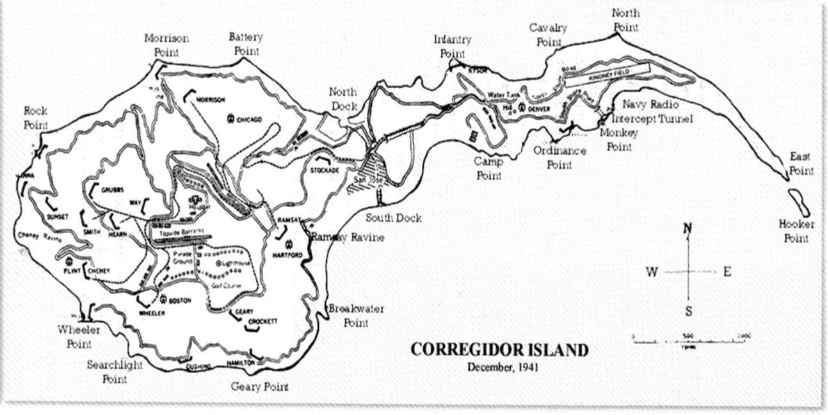

COMPLICATIONS ON MISSION 3

Crew 23A was to be a part of the attack on Corregidor on 12 February, but was unable to complete the mission. On the way to Luzon Island, the #2 engine in *Sittin' Pretty* developed problems. It wasn't long before it quit and O.C. feathered the prop and considered his options. An engine out made their participation in the run on Corregidor Island problematic. He would not be able to keep up with the others, and if they were attacked—and they were more likely to be attacked over this target than any other in the Philippines—his plane would be less maneuverable than the others.

He had no choice but to drop out.

He radioed command pilot Col. Korsokas and told him his decision: he would fall out of formation and attempt to land at Tacloban Airdrome on the eastern shore of Leyte Island, still far ahead in the pre-dawn darkness. Korsokas wished him well and O.C. told his crew to check their parachutes and review ditching procedures.

At night, over the ocean, without a moon, the sea and sky are indistinguishable. Because his own senses cannot be trusted, a pilot must trust his artificial horizon and attitude indicator instruments to tell him if he's flying straight and level. So O.C. kept one eye on the other engine gauges to see how they were handling the added strain of the lost engine and the other eye on his instruments.

When the sky began to lighten and Leyte appeared on the horizon, O.C. peeled off and headed for the airdrome. He radioed ahead that he had an engine out and declared an emergency. As he landed, he side-slipped his plane to compensate for the non-functioning engine and brought the behemoth down heavily, finally stopping safely after a long rollout. Fire and emergency crews surrounded the plane and a jeep full of mechanics roared up with their tool boxes.

In a few hours the engine was repaired—it was an oil leak, common in B-24s engines, which had starved the power plant, causing it to seize—and Crew 23A climbed back aboard. It was a short hop home to Angaur, only 400 miles, but each man on that three hour trip hoped this was the one and only mechanical problem they would encounter on their missions.

Unfortunately, it would not be.

ABOVE LEFT In a situation similar to O.C.'s, a B-24 from the 865th Squadron lands without engine #4 as evidenced by the stationary, or feathered, prop.

ABOVE RIGHT The most famous vehicle of the War was the Willys-Overland MA (Military Model A) light utility 4x4. Ford also produced the design, though its version was called the "GPW" or Government Passenger Willys. The "W" was dropped as the moniker evolved into "Jeep."

EXTRA! **Pacific Post** EXTRA!

Section One SATURDAY, FEBRUARY 17, 1945 Ten Cents

THOSE FANTASTIC FILIPINOS

"HOW CAN YOU THANK A WONDERFUL PEOPLE LIKE THAT?"

MINDANAO, PHILIPPINES, 17 Feb. – B-24 pilot John Lampe and Crew 14 had been at it since the first, and Mission 69, aimed at a Japanese troop bivouac near Ising City, was just the next mission. Or so they thought.

During "bombs away," engine #2 was suddenly flame, likely from small arms fire. Lampe feathered the prop and noticed that #1 and #2 engines had no fuel pressure. The right aileron was inoperative and the interphone was out. Soon the bomb bay and rear compartment were on fire and without waiting for the bell, the crew had begun bailing out. Lampe stayed behind, trying to maintain control during several wild loops, but he finally gave up and bailed out too. *I'll Get By* went down into the jungle in a red roar.

Eleven parachutes drifted to the ground, fired upon by Japanese at the nearby Davao Penal Colony. Engineer Floyd Swain saw he was coming down over the camp and tugged his shroud in an attempt to steer his chute outside the walls. He landed just thirty yards from the stockade, shucked the harness, and hobbled into the jungle on a broken ankle.

He heard footsteps and reached for his .45, but he'd left it on the plane. He crawled into the foliage and tried to make himself invisible. Looking back, he saw a Filipino boy standing in the path, looking straight at him. "You come America?" asked the boy. Swain nodded. The boy helped him to his feet and they lurched down the path away from the penal colony. Swain, with everyone else on his crew, had landed in Filipino guerilla-controlled territory.

For a week, the Japanese and the Filipinos competed in a silent contest to see who could find the American airmen first. The Japs never saw the Filipinos, but the Filipinos kept tabs on the Japs through a telegraph of swift-footed boys who memorized messages and slipped quietly through the dense jungle to deliver them.

Four other men were found immediately and taken by villagers to the guerilla HQ. Most had landed in trees 200 feet tall and a couple still had their sidearms. Bombardier James Smith had the most difficult time. He landed in a tree, slid to the ground and found himself in a chest-deep swamp and was soon covered with leaches. Birds screeched every time he took a step, as if calling out his position to the enemy. In the jungle Smith encountered nose gunner Foster Derr and they pushed their way through a jungle so thick they could not see six feet in front of them in midday.

Two days later they saw a shack in a clearing on a rise with a dozen men milling around it. As they were deciding what to do, they heard a noise. Smith turned, pulling his pistol. Ignoring it, a young boy smiled and said, "You wait," and ran toward the men in the clearing. When the men approached them, the airmen saw one carrying an American rifle and heaved a sigh of relief. Another was wearing homemade sergeant's stripes and was about to take Smith's gun when he saw his lieutenant's bars. Suddenly, the raggedy line of men snapped to attention and presented arms—to the Americans.

They were the Philippine Infantry Division: 5,000 men fighting the Japanese on Mindanao, and they found all of Crew 14. Smith later said, "They were the best fighting outfit I ever saw. I never saw such spirit and morale. Everyone was cheerful and eager and friendly. They treated us like kings even though they were starving and ill-equipped. You couldn't call it a shoestring army—this army did not even have shoes, let alone shoestrings."

But the guerillas *did* have a short-wave radio and word soon came that a Navy PBM would fly in and pick them up.

When Crew 14 arrived back on Angaur, they knew they had one last job to do. As they told their buddies about their guerilla rescuers, money was quietly pressed into their palms. Clothing, rations, and ammo began to pile up outside their tents. Medical supplies mysteriously disappeared from the dispensaries. Cooks and supply personnel threw regulations to the wind. Engineers "lost" an alarming number of shovels, axes and saws. Ammo dump guards walked only one side of their posts at pre-arranged hours. The top brass on Angaur got stiff necks from looking the other way.

And when two big Liberators left Angaur, scheduled for a practice navigation run, they somehow went off course and wound up over a clearing on Mindanao, which just happened to be directly over the headquarters of the Philippine Infantry Division.

Sgt. Swain put it best: "How can you thank a wonderful people like that for saving your life, and then insisting they were honored to do so?"

THE FOXHOLE FAITHFUL

In the 1940s, America was still a deeply religious nation. Most people not only believed in God, but also attended religious services. The young men who came of age at that time had a powerful sense of faith, family, and fealty to country. As children of the Depression, they had been taught at their mother's knees to believe in God, to respect authority, and work with others for common goals. The era of the narcissistic young person demanding rights while eschewing concomitant responsibilities was happily still decades away. In addition, the War reminded them of life's fragility. Everyone knew someone who had died serving their country. With most of their peers in the service, young men eagerly enlisted to do their part. But once in the war zone, the reality of death filled their minds and hearts. Thus it was that wherever American soldiers went, one of the first structures they erected was a house of worship.

TOP LEFT Chaplain Milton Dowden leads the men in a hymn during a Protestant meeting. He also led Catholic and Jewish services.

TOP RIGHT The 494th Bomb Group chapel was available for use by any religious group on the island.

CENTER LEFT The chapel, built by 494th volunteers, proves too small for the overflowing crowd on a Sunday morning. Later, when Theater #1 was built, services were held there.

MIDDLE RIGHT The Angaur cemetery and memorial chapel. Most of the bodies of the men buried there were later moved back to the States.

BOTTOM LEFT O.C. joins fellow Mormon servicemen outside the 494th Chapel after their church services. "We have about 25 members for church," wrote O.C. to his mom. "So that makes it nice."

ALL IN A DAY'S WORK

Armament crews and mission planners have been up all night, doing their job. Now, in the pre-dawn darkness, the bomber crews are awakened to do theirs.

They learn about their mission at the briefing: target, number of planes, payload, escorts (if any), and emergency procedures.

Then it's off to a light breakfast and a short drive to the flight line, where the ground crew has the aircraft prepped and ready.

The captain and the crew do a quick walk around, discussing the mission.

Chaplain Dowden trots over and leads the crew in a short prayer.

Inside the aircraft, the pilot reviews his checklist and fires up the four Twin Wasp engines, raising clouds of coral dust and moving slowly out onto the ramp. He lifts off one minute after the plane before him.

The long flight is busy. The navigator takes regular celestial sightings, the radio operator checks frequencies, the engineer tends his engine gauges, and the gunners load the ammo into their .50 caliber guns.

Leaving the rendezvous, they slip into a single file "trail" formation. Gunners don flak vests and man their machine guns.

A minute out and the pilot gives control of the aircraft to the bombardier, who lines up the cross-hairs on the Norden bombsight.

At bombs away, they peel gracefully off, and the tail gunner reports smoke rising from the target. Relief floods the plane.

Course is set for home, flak vests are shed, and coffee and smokes are shared. Stress gives way to humor and the crew slowly realizes they've lived to fight another day.

It's evening and the ground crew waits near the tower, listening for the crackling speaker to announce the arrival of *their* aircraft, hoping the flyboys didn't damage her too much. Otherwise, their work day, which just began again, will be a long one.

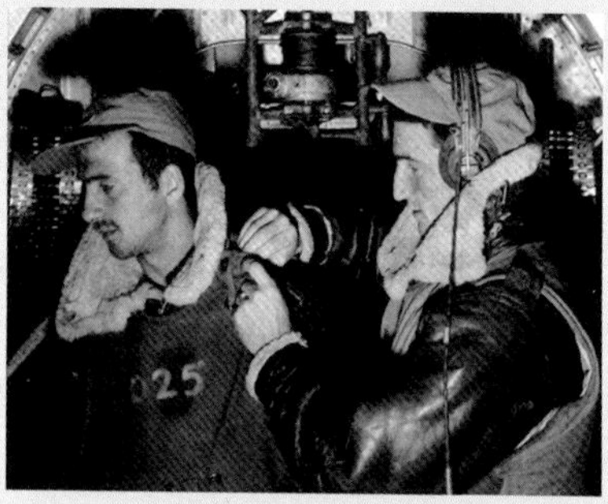

SHORT TAKES

Once O.C. was on Angaur, the number of letters he wrote home decreased dramatically. He was somewhat disappointed that more people didn't write him, but he was no great shakes at sitting down and scratching out a letter either. He averaged about one a week for the first couple of months, then his letters home dropped off drastically as he started flying more missions. A sample of some of his observations:

MISSIONS "We're still not getting many missions. It's tough because other crews are and we just sit here. Of course, one reason is we don't have our own ship yet. We're hoping an older crew gets its 40 missions in and hands off their plane to us."

WEATHER "If the sun isn't pounding 100°, it's raining to beat the band, though when it's not raining, nights are cool and comfortable. The rain seems to stir up typhoons offshore. So far they've avoided the island, but we still get some high surf and some tents built too close to the shore got washed away. Our officers' club got washed out to sea. I'm not worried about our quarters. Since we were late getting here, we're 100 yards from the beach, so I guess we're okay."

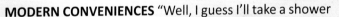

ROMANCE "I received a letter from Verna today. I'm sure it's all over on that battlefront. I guess I'm going to give it up as a bad policy, this female business."

SPORTS "The LDS fellows put together a basketball team to play other groups. We lost our first game, but we're practicing more so maybe next time we'll make a better showing."

NATIVES "There seem to be about 150 natives on the island, families mostly. Many were killed in the assault last September. There are a few kids but hardly any women and no white women at all."

MODERN CONVENIENCES "Well, I guess I'll take a shower in our nice outdoor bathroom. It's quite a contraption, right out in the open, with no doors or anything. You just stand out there naked as a jay bird and soap up."

REQUESTS "If you really want to send me something, send me some brown and white fudge and some fruit cake. There, that ought to keep you busy!"

AIRCRAFT "Most of the ships we fly were made in San Diego and they only have about 400 hours on the best of them so they are in pretty darn good condition as of yet. I just hope I get to fly one before the war is over."

EXTRA! **Pacific Post** EXTRA!

Section One | MONDAY, FEBRUARY 19, 1945 | Ten Cents

STRIKING AT THE HOMELAND

TAKING IWO JIMA NOW PUTS JAPAN WITHIN BOMBER REACH

IWO JIMA, VOLCANO ISLANDS, 19 Feb. – By now, the outcome of island battles is no longer in doubt. Because of our superior numbers, armament, and control of the seas and skies, we are confident we will win.

The only question is: At what cost?

Operation Detachment was designed to help the B-29s bombing Japan from bases in the Marianas by securing a forward base for their P-51 Mustang fighter escorts. Admiral Nimitz chose Iwo Jima, a 5 mile-long island just 750 miles south of Tokyo as the best location for the base.

Thinking our invasion of Japan would stage through Formosa, the Japanese High Command had not adequately reinforced Iwo Jima, even removing its fighter planes just days before the invasion.

But General Kuribayashi still had eight infantry battalions, a tank regiment, two artillery and three heavy mortar battalions—a total of almost 23,000 men. And Mt. Suribachi, a dormant volcano at the southern tip of the island, overlooked the most likely landing beaches on the eastern shore. Artillery from its imposing 550 foot height would without doubt devastate Allied landing forces.

His plan was, as we had seen before, to allow us to land and then wear us down in a war of attrition which the Japanese military, steeped in propaganda about American cowardice, were certain they could win.

Knowing this would be the toughest fight of the War thus far, the 7th Air Force bombed the island for eight months, but the dense network of 11 miles of tunnels throughout the island protected the defenders.

When the Navy arrived with 500 ships and disgorged the 4th and 5th Marine Divisions onto Blue and Red beaches, the men were prepared for battle (many of the 5th were veterans of Peleliu and Guadalcanal), but not only were they faced with a towering bank of soft black sand on the beach, they were soon raked with flanking fire from nearby concrete machine-gun nests and devastating artillery fusillades from high atop Mt. Suribachi.

The first day, 500 Marines died on that beach, but 30,000 of their comrades came ashore and began their assault on Mt. Suribachi.

On D+2 the triangular airstrip in the middle of the island was captured and Mt. Suribachi succumbed four days later after huge losses on both sides, at which point the famous flag-raising photo was taken. This was actually the second photo, as the Secretary of the Navy had requested the first-raised flag as a memento and that event went unphotographed. When the flag was replaced, a photographer was there to record the moment for posterity.

With Suribachi secured, the Marines turned their attention to the fortified bunkers on the north slope containing most of the dug-in defenders.

Because Iwo forms a part of Japan proper, the Japanese troops were instructed to give no quarter. The Marines had to fight for almost every square foot of the rocky island. Almost every gorge and cave was heavily defended and had to be cleared out with explosives and flame-throwers. Even when flushed out into the open, the Japanese threw themselves boldly at the Marines rather than surrender.

It wasn't until the final ten-day battle of "Bloody Gorge" at Kitano Point that the island was declared secured after a brutal *banzai* charge by 300 Japanese, many armed only with sticks, swords, and stones clutched in their hands.

Though the battle was largely over by 26 March, by June 2,000 more Japanese had been killed as their hiding places were discovered. Only 250 were taken prisoner.

The Marines lost almost 6,000 dead and over 17,000 injured, one-third of their host, in the bloodiest battle of the War thus far.

Fighter aircraft began operating from Iwo within days of the assault and the first B-29 Superfortress landed on 4 March. With the arrival of the B-29s and their fighter escorts, the Japanese mainland would soon feel the fury of American anger.

In the end, knowing it could no longer stop the U.S. in its march toward the homeland, Japan used defenders' lives merely to buy time to prepare for the invasion of Japan itself.

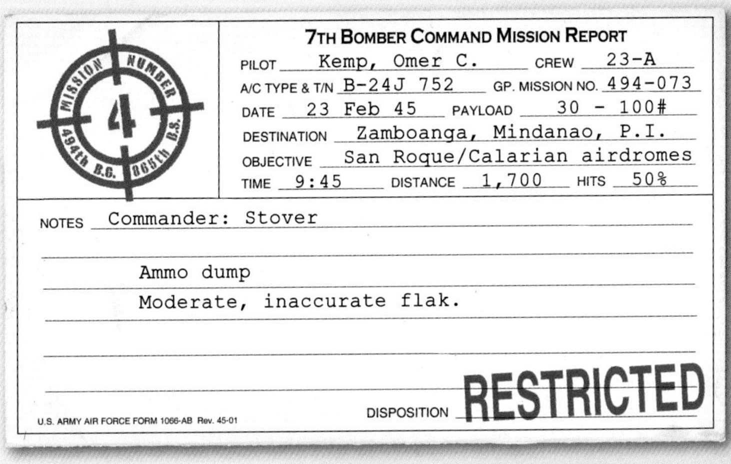
MISSION NUMBER 4 — 494th B.G. 865th B.S.

7TH BOMBER COMMAND MISSION REPORT

PILOT Kemp, Omer C. CREW 23-A
A/C TYPE & T/N B-24J 752 GP. MISSION NO. 494-073
DATE 23 Feb 45 PAYLOAD 30 - 100#
DESTINATION Zamboanga, Mindanao, P.I.
OBJECTIVE San Roque/Calarian airdromes
TIME 9:45 DISTANCE 1,700 HITS 50%

NOTES Commander: Stover

Ammo dump
Moderate, inaccurate flak.

DISPOSITION RESTRICTED

U.S. ARMY AIR FORCE FORM 1066-AB Rev. 45-01

FROM ANGAUR TO ZAMBOANGA

The Zamboanga Peninsula is an arm sprouting from the western coast of Mindanao Island. It was occupied by the Japanese early in 1942 and was used thereafter to stage aircraft strikes against Borneo to the south. As MacArthur's forces approached the Philippines in late 1944, it became a prime target for our bombers.

San Roque Airdrome, just inland from the port city of Zamboanga on the southern tip of the Peninsula, was the 494th's first area target, but they had been bombing eastern Mindanao for some time, losing the bomber *I'll Get By* to ground fire less than a week before. (See "Those Fantastic Filipinos," page 152.) As of 23 February, it was still not known whether anyone had survived the crash. Everyone in the 494th was on edge: Mindanao was proving to be a difficult objective with flak batteries defending the targets and Col. Kelley's order of 10,000 foot altitude bombing runs put them squarely in the sights of even medium-sized artillery.

That day, 24 planes made the ten hour round trip to drop a total of eighteen tons of bombs on San Roque, scoring 50% hits. Though no enemy fighters were seen, they did encounter moderate flak and five planes returned to Angaur with flak holes.

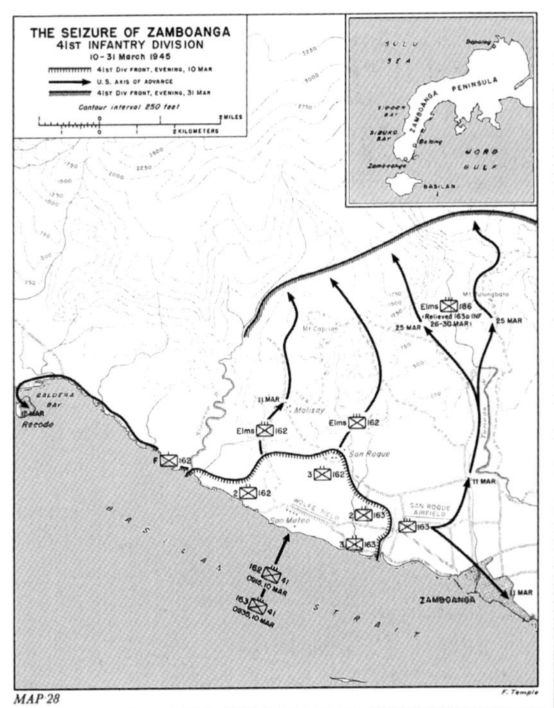

RIGHT Two weeks later, on 11 March, as a part of Operation Victor V, Zamboanga was liberated by the Army's 163rd Infantry. Engineers soon repaired and lengthened the runway. The airdrome was officially renamed Moret Field after Lt. Col. Paul Moret, a Marine pilot who was killed in a 1943 airplane crash at New Caledonia. Today, San Roque is known as Zamboanga International Airport. Nearby Calarian Airfield (Wolfe) was used for fighters.

ABOVE LEFT Photo taken at "bombs away." The target is beyond the bottom of the frame. But if you look closely you can see the bombs arcing silently toward their target.

EXPLORING ANGAUR

Raised by explorers who literally turned over every rock in their path, as soon as he got settled in, O.C. went exploring himself. At the small harbor on Angaur he met a couple of seamen, Swain and Dickinson, and they soon became pals. O.C. told them he'd originally joined the Navy—they were no doubt surprised—and they were of course interested in planes. Their forays started at the air field where O.C. proudly showed off the various aircraft, including the B-24 he'd just flown on a mission.

CENTER RIGHT On one excursion they requisitioned a jeep and headed to where the fiercest fighting of the battle of Angaur had occurred just three months before: the Bowl in the northwest corner of the island. Travel off marked roads was discouraged as there were still many unexploded bombs and mines lying about.

BOTTOM LEFT The gang poses before an area devastated by the battle.

BOTTOM RIGHT The burned out hulk of a Sherman tank squats near the mouth of Bloody Gulch—the same crippled tank the engineers had to blow up to get out of the way so the 81st Infantry could move into the Bowl the previous October.

BOTTOM CENTER While he was poking around, O.C. found an unfired 6.5mm shell from a Japanese Arisaka rifle.

NORTH AMERICAN P-51 "MUSTANG"

Two requirements led to the development of the P-51: (1) a fighter aircraft to better the P-40 Tomahawk's altitude and maneuvering, and (2) a long-range escort fighter to protect bombers. It was probably the first computer designed aircraft in that its wing design used laminar-flow wind-tunnel tests and its body was designed using conical-section technology resulting in a sleek, low-drag fuselage. It may also be the first jet aircraft due to its use of heated air exiting the radiator to produce a slight amount of thrust.

B-17 missions over Europe were meeting stiff resistance. P-38 and P-47s were incapable of protecting the bombers due to their respective maintenance and range issues. The P-51 had both a simple, reliable engine and room for a huge fuel load; it could accompany the Fortresses to the target and back. It made its appearance in Europe in early 1944 but instead of escorting the B-17s, went in before them, intercepting German fighters while they were still forming up. As a result, the Luftwaffe lost 17% of all its fighters in just over a week, literally changing the course of the war in Europe. The B-17s were now free to bomb Germany with impunity.

Mustangs made their first appearance in the Pacific in the American Volunteer Group over China, but came on in numbers once Iwo Jima was taken. The 750 miles to Tokyo was within their range. The B-29 Superfortresses had been hitting the Japanese mainland since Thanksgiving 1944 and though these raids had achieved devastating destruction, the bomber echelons were also swarmed by up to 300 enemy fighters at a time. Dozens of bombers were lost in the mismatched air battles over Japan. They needed fighter protection.

The Mustangs arrived on Iwo Jima on D+15 and flew their first sorties five days later. The Japanese knew what the arrival of the fighters meant and on 26 March, five troop transports landed on the main airstrip, intent upon destroying as many B-29s and P-51s as possible. The Mustang pilots found themselves shooting at the enemy, not with machine guns but with pistols. Several pilots were killed in the battle and when their comrades took off on 6 April for their first B-29 escort mission, they were spoiling for revenge. They got it in the greatest aerial battle in history in which 136 Japanese fighters were downed, the Mustangs receiving credit for an amazing 37 kills. More than one pilot became an "ace" (five kills) in a minute or less. Most importantly, just five B-29s and two Mustangs failed to return. The P-51 had arrived in the nick of time.

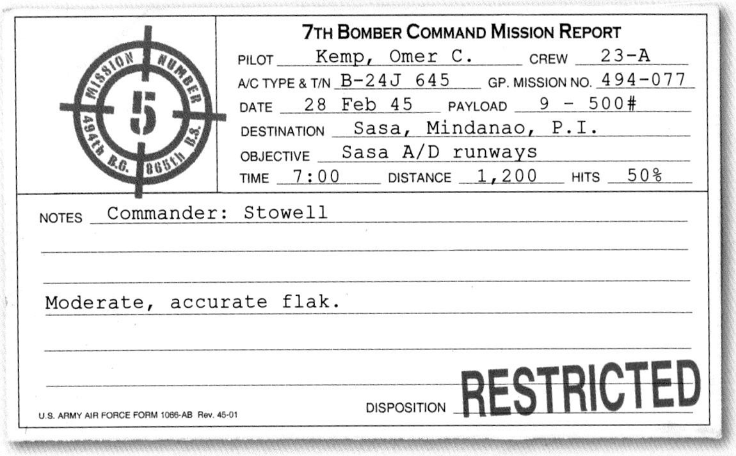

7TH BOMBER COMMAND MISSION REPORT

PILOT Kemp, Omer C. CREW 23-A
A/C TYPE & T/N B-24J 645 GP. MISSION NO. 494-077
DATE 28 Feb 45 PAYLOAD 9 - 500#
DESTINATION Sasa, Mindanao, P.I.
OBJECTIVE Sasa A/D runways
TIME 7:00 DISTANCE 1,200 HITS 50%

NOTES Commander: Stowell

Moderate, accurate flak.

DISPOSITION RESTRICTED

U.S. ARMY AIR FORCE FORM 1066-AB Rev. 45-01

SACKING SASA

Leap year babies only get a birthday every four years, so O.C. always celebrated his on 28 February. This year he would be 21, but he was apprehensive about the gift he was getting: a mission to the Davao Gulf of Mindanao, which was where *I'll Get By* was shot down ten days earlier and whose crew was still missing and presumed dead.

Sasa Airdrome, located near Davao City, was the largest Japanese air and sea base on Mindanao and was surrounded by powerful anti-aircraft batteries. It housed the 1st Kokutai, a flying group that epitomized the word's meaning: "national character." Sasa would put up stiff resistance to the assault and its ack-ack batteries would fill the sky with flak.

But there was one bright spot: O.C. would be flying his favorite plane, *Rover Boy's Baby*. That had to count for something.

CENTER RIGHT A string of 500# general purpose bombs lines up for loading into a Liberator by the armaments crew.

RIGHT O.C. pored over this reconnaissance photo and knew it would be a long day. Because the mission was to destroy the Sasa Airdrome runways, he carried 500 pound bombs designed to make holes fifteen feet deep. Like most missions over Mindanao, there would be no fighter cover. If they met Zeroes, the ten .50 caliber machine guns onboard were their only defense. Ack-ack would be deadly accurate, and the batteries on the nearby hills would hurl 120 mm shells at them, shells that could tear a wing off.

The Mission Report is silent about the outcome, which is good news for the crews.

Happy birthday, O.C.

EXTRA! **Pacific Post** EXTRA!

Section One | SATURDAY, MARCH 3, 1945 | Ten Cents

AT LAST: LUZON LIBERATED!

BLOODY BATTLE OF MANILA CAPS BRUTAL ISLAND CAMPAIGN

MANILA, LUZON ISLAND, PHILIPPINES, 3 Mar. – By mid-1944, Allied forces were within 300 miles of Mindanao, the largest island in the south Philippines and B-24s were hitting the island regularly. Admiral Nimitz's 7th Fleet had swept up the Central Pacific, capturing the Gilbert and Marshall chains.

And Supreme Commander of the Southwest Pacific Douglas MacArthur had isolated or destroyed Japanese resistance on New Guinea and the Admiralty islands.

Starting in June, the Marianas were taken and soon B-29s began bombing runs on Japan.

Rabaul on New Britain, the largest Japanese base in the Southwest Pacific after Manila, was isolated and impotent.

In the Philippines, a pincer movement was closing. In September, as Nimitz pushed west past the Carolines to the Palaus, MacArthur struck northward from Morotai in the Dutch East Indies.

The Pacific campaign was going so well it was decided to move the invasion from Mindanao north to Leyte, so in mid-October, U.S. troops assaulted Leyte a full two months ahead of schedule. Though they met stiff opposition from Gen. Yamashita's 60,000 troops, their numerical superiority simply overwhelmed the Japanese.

In an attempt to prevent the landings, the Japanese Navy steamed toward Leyte, but were met by the Fast Carrier Task Force. In the Battle of Leyte Gulf, four Japanese carriers and scores of other ships were lost. Never again would the IJN threaten American advances in the Pacific.

Above, the Philippines capitol is barely standing after the American bombing. Below, ample evidence of the battle for Manila is seen in waterfront structures.

MacArthur's next objective was Mindoro Island, northwest of Leyte and just south of Luzon. MacArthur needed its runways for fighter support during the Luzon campaign. Mindoro was invaded in mid-December and secured a month later.

Meanwhile, the 6th Army landed at Lingayen Gulf in northern Luzon Island and began their march south toward Clark Air Field and the capital at Manila.

At the same time, the notorious Bataan Peninsula was secured and 500 POWs rescued.

For the most part, Yamashita kept his army sequestered in the mountains, forcing U.S. forces to fight them in situations favoring the defenders. Japan sent no reinforcements to Yamashita after mid-January and so he ordered his troops to fight to the death.

Admiral Iwabuchi held out in Manila until 3 March as Allied forces besieged the city, shelling it with artillery fire. Over 100,000 Filipinos were killed by artillery, conflagrations, and murder by their Japanese oppressors before the fight ended with the death of almost 16,000 Japanese soldiers. America lost 1,000 men in the battle.

Once Manila was secured, we turned our eyes toward Corregidor Island at the mouth of Manila Bay, the site of MacArthur's 1942 expulsion. The Japanese held up against furious bombardment in Mantilla Tunnel on the island, but they too, finally succumbed.

With the main islands now in hand, MacArthur ordered the freeing of the smaller islands. The 8th Army, with help from Filipino guerillas, made almost 40 landings in various islands in the archipelago, including Mindanao on 17 April, followed by Panay, Cebu, and Negros islands in the Visayas.

Some isolated Japanese units held out on Mindanao and Luzon until the end of the War.

America lost over 10,000 men in the Battle for the Philippines, 36,000 wounded, and 100,000 casualties from sickness and accidents.

Ten U.S. and five Allied divisions engaged in the Battle, second only to the Normandy invasion in terms of the number of men involved.

AUSSIES ASSIST

BORNEO, DUTCH EAST INDIES, Mar. 3 – The Dutch East Indies (Sumatra, Java, Celebes, western New Guinea, and Borneo) were Japan's most coveted war prize for their rubber and oil reserves, and while MacArthur was clearing out the Philippines, Australian troops took back these islands in a bloody but largely unheralded campaign. Aided by local guerillas, Aussie forces engaged in some of the most terrible battles of the War. And like their countrymen from Gaudalcanal to Iwo Jima, few Japanese soldiers surrendered, most fighting bravely to the bitter end.

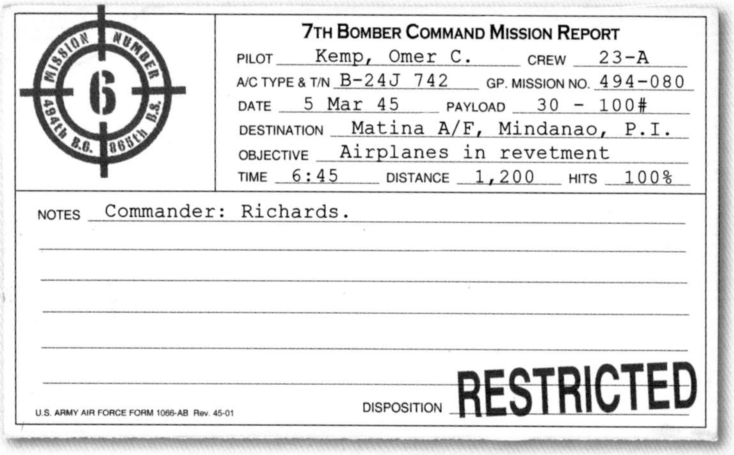
MISSION NUMBER 6 494th B.G. 865th B.S.

7TH BOMBER COMMAND MISSION REPORT

PILOT Kemp, Omer C. CREW 23-A

A/C TYPE & T/N B-24J 742 GP. MISSION NO. 494-080

DATE 5 Mar 45 PAYLOAD 30 - 100#

DESTINATION Matina A/F, Mindanao, P.I.

OBJECTIVE Airplanes in revetment

TIME 6:45 DISTANCE 1,200 HITS 100%

NOTES Commander: Richards.

U.S. ARMY AIR FORCE FORM 1066-AB Rev. 45-01

DISPOSITION RESTRICTED

MATINA TAKES A MAULING

O.C. had been on Angaur for two months. He was finally getting some missions, which was good, but there was a critical shortage of aircraft engines and personnel to repair them, which was bad. This problem would reach a head on this mission.

RIGHT CENTER Matina Airdrome was just 5 miles southwest of Sasa, their previous mission. It housed the Imperial Navy's Nakajima J1N1 "Irving" twin-engine fighters used for reconnaissance, night fighting, and *kamikaze* missions. The 494th's orders were to destroy each and every one of them.

They rendezvoused at Lawigan Point, fifty miles east of the target. Just before reaching the rendezvous, 864th squadron bomber *Blunder Bus* lost power in the #3 engine. Capt. Mackie tried unsuccessfully to feather it and had to leave the formation. The closest Allied base was Tacloban Airdrome on Leyte Island, 400 miles away across 100 miles of open water. Mackie turned north, skirting the Mindanao coast, both pilots literally standing on the left rudder pedals to maintain the heading. Mackie ordered everyone to lighten ship. Bombs, flak suits, gas tanks, armor plate, and even the Sperry turret were jettisoned. They slogged along above an unbroken blanket of clouds below. Just when they reached the strait between Mindanao and Leyte and Mackie thought they might actually make it, his #2 engine quit. He rang the bail-out bell. The radio operator sent out the SOS and tied down the radio key so rescuers could get a bearing on the plane as long as possible, then he jumped. As he descended, he counted chutes and saw everyone had made it. *Blunder Bus* was last seen on fire, streaking toward the jungle. Fortunately, everyone landed safely on Leyte, which was in Allied hands and Filipino natives helped them find Tacloban Airdrome.

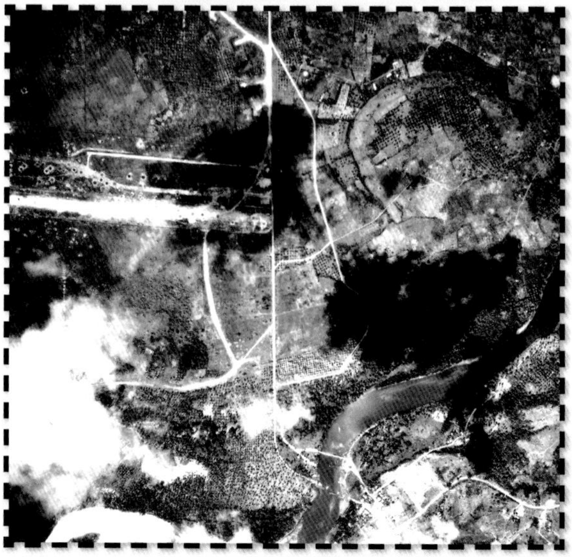

BOTTOM RIGHT The other bombers, including O.C.'s Crew 23A in *Super Chick*, were able to continue to the target and scored an unprecedented 100% hit rate, as evidenced by this photo taken moments after the strike. The airstrip is the pock-marked horizontal white line in the upper left quarter.

IT'S THE BEST SEAT IN THE HOUSE . . .

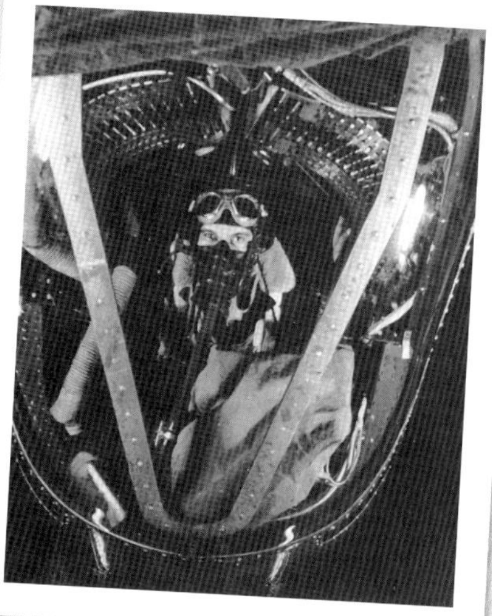

Unless they're shooting at you. Jack Berger tells us what being a bombardier in a B-24 entailed:

"A bombardier had to be good at math because he had to consider velocity, speed, and altitude before saying, 'Bombs away!'

"The Norden bombsight functioned like a carpenter's level. If the bubbles were off center by a fraction, at high altitudes the bombs could go way off target. Bumps or shifts in wind could move the bubbles.

"The pilot and navigator would get us within fifteen minutes of the objective and then I'd try to get visual contact of the target and surroundings. As we approached, I'd go back and pull the safety pins from the bombs, activating them. Then the bomb bay doors would be opened and I'd zero in with the bombsight, making quick compensations to get those bubbles back on dead center and stay there.

"Some of the bombardiers 'toggled,' dropping their bombs when the plane in front of them dropped his. I never did—I did my own calculations and cross-hair sighting and though it may have looked like I dropped my bombs when the lead plane did, my drop was always based on *my* calculations.

"One time, the lead bombardier dropped all his bombs in the water, completely missing the target, but he still claimed 50% hits. I learned to never, ever depend on the lead.

"Each bombardier was supposed to sight the target through his Norden. Usually, we dropped the bombs within one second of each other that way, even though it looked like we toggled on the release of the plane in front of us.

"One time—and I have the pictures to prove it—another plane's bombs went 100% into the water, but in interrogation after the mission, the captain claimed 50% hit target, which was a lot of bull."

UPPER RIGHT A bombardier poses in his forward position. Note the .50 caliber cartridge belts curving overhead.

CENTER LEFT Jack had a true bird's-eye view on their missions over the Palau Islands.

BOTTOM RIGHT 7th AAF bombardiers on Kwajalein Island send wishes home for Mother's Day 1944. Tomorrow, they'll use these same 500 pound bombs to send a distinctly different message to the enemy.

BRIEF

brief was a bi-monthly magazine published by the Army Air Forces Pacific Operations Area (AAFPOA) which focused on the airman's life. It featured articles about the progress of the War, aircraft mishaps, stateside sports updates, advice columns, editorials, comics, poetry, and griping letters to the editor—all presented with cleverness and good cheer, like the article on the next page, "Heroes Don't Win Wars."

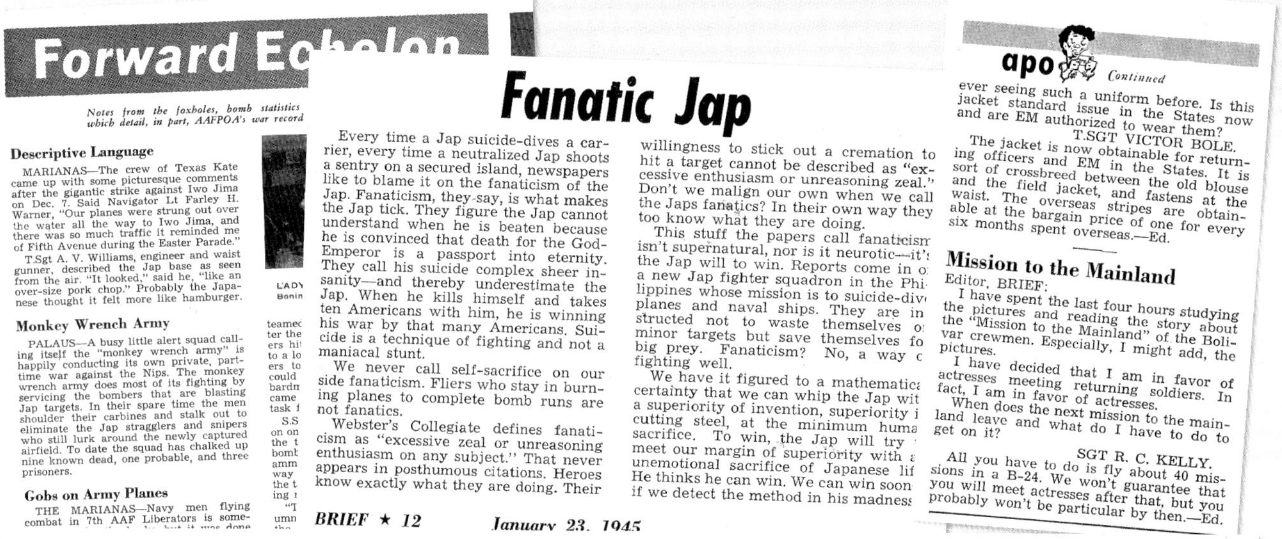

Forward Echelon

Notes from the foxholes, bomb statistics which detail, in part, AAFPOA's war record

Descriptive Language

MARIANAS—The crew of Texas Kate came up with some picturesque comments after the gigantic strike against Iwo Jima on Dec. 7. Said Navigator Lt Farley H. Warner, "Our planes were strung out over the water all the way to Iwo Jima, and there was so much traffic it reminded me of Fifth Avenue during the Easter Parade."

T.Sgt A. V. Williams, engineer and waist gunner, described the Jap base as seen from the air. "It looked," said he, "like an over-size pork chop." Probably the Japanese thought it felt more like hamburger.

Monkey Wrench Army

PALAUS—A busy little alert squad calling itself the "monkey wrench army" is happily conducting its own private, part-time war against the Nips. The monkey wrench army does most of its fighting by servicing the bombers that are blasting Jap targets. In their spare time the men shoulder their carbines and stalk out to eliminate the Jap stragglers and snipers who still lurk around the newly captured airfield. To date the squad has chalked up nine known dead, one probable, and three prisoners.

Gobs on Army Planes

THE MARIANAS—Navy men flying combat in 7th AAF Liberators is some-

Fanatic Jap

Every time a Jap suicide-dives a carrier, every time a neutralized Jap shoots a sentry on a secured island, newspapers like to blame it on the fanaticism of the Jap. Fanaticism, they say, is what makes the Jap tick. They figure the Jap cannot understand when he is beaten because he is convinced that death for the God-Emperor is a passport into eternity. They call his suicide complex sheer insanity—and thereby underestimate the Jap. When he kills himself and takes ten Americans with him, he is winning his war by that many Americans. Suicide is a technique of fighting and not a maniacal stunt.

We never call self-sacrifice on our side fanaticism. Fliers who stay in burning planes to complete bomb runs are not fanatics.

Webster's Collegiate defines fanaticism as "excessive zeal or unreasoning enthusiasm on any subject." That never appears in posthumous citations. Heroes know exactly what they are doing. Their willingness to stick out a cremation to hit a target cannot be described as "excessive enthusiasm or unreasoning zeal." Don't we malign our own when we call the Japs fanatics? In their own way they too know what they are doing.

This stuff the papers call fanaticism isn't supernatural, nor is it neurotic—it's the Jap will to win. Reports come in of a new Jap fighter squadron in the Philippines whose mission is to suicide-dive planes and naval ships. They are instructed not to waste themselves on minor targets but save themselves for big prey. Fanaticism? No, a way of fighting well.

We have it figured to a mathematical certainty that we can whip the Jap with a superiority of invention, superiority in cutting steel, at the minimum human sacrifice. To win, the Jap will try to meet our margin of superiority with an unemotional sacrifice of Japanese life. He thinks he can win. We can win sooner if we detect the method in his madness.

BRIEF ★ 12 January 23, 1945

apo *Continued*

ever seeing such a uniform before. Is this jacket standard issue in the States now and are EM authorized to wear them?

T.SGT VICTOR BOLE.

The jacket is now obtainable for returning officers and EM in the States. It is sort of crossbreed between the old blouse and the field jacket, and fastens at the waist. The overseas stripes are obtainable at the bargain price of one for every six months spent overseas.—Ed.

Mission to the Mainland

Editor, BRIEF:

I have spent the last four hours studying the pictures and reading the story about the "Mission to the Mainland" of the Bolivar crewmen. Especially, I might add, the pictures.

I have decided that I am in favor of actresses meeting returning soldiers. In fact, I am in favor of actresses.

When does the next mission to the mainland leave and what do I have to do to get on it?

SGT R. C. KELLY.

All you have to do is fly about 40 missions in a B-24. We won't guarantee that you will meet actresses after that, but you probably won't be particular by then.—Ed.

Heroes Don't Win Wars

BY PFC BUD NELSON

MARIANAS—We were sitting around the tent on C-ration boxes, a flickering candle pointing the flame-tip at the whim of the breeze. We had saved our beer, borrowed some more, cajoled even more and even wrangled a piece of ice from the Mess Sergeant.

For the first few rounds we discussed things in typical GI style. For the next few, the conversation ("gentlemen, shall we talk about women now—or later?") drifted to the pleasures of life of which we are now deprived.

Somewhere around the even dozen mark, when the buzz was definitely noticeable, one of the group, a many-times busted cook, said: "You know, Bud, that *brief* is a pretty good magazine. But it's like all the others—all you read about are noble characters with ribbons and medals drooling down their chests and relating amazing stories of capturing hundreds of prisoners, escaping certain death, jumping out of planes without parachutes, and generals slushing out double-talk about when the war is going to end. Why don't you write about a guy who is just a soldier? Why don't anybody ever mention the poor bastard who got dragged into the Army, got stuck out here on one of these godforsaken holes and is doing nothing but his job?"

"What is there to write about him?" I asked. "Something's got to happen to a guy before you can write a story about him."

"That's what I'm bitching about. Ninety-nine percent of the guys in the Army never had anything happen to them. Why don't you write about a guy who never had anything happen to him?"

"And what would I say?"

"Hell, I don't know. That's your racket. But you take, for example, that guy Chuck who was on KP today." My pal drained his beer and lit another butt. "Now there's a guy that nothin' ever happened to. He doesn't even get into trouble. He's too damn dumb."

"What's he do all day? He drives a truck. He goes back and forth on this island 100 miles a day. He eats three meals. He goes to the movies at night. He writes a gushy letter to some babe that probably has thrown him over a year ago. He lays in his slit-trench during air raids. He goes on KP every fifth day.

"He sure as hell isn't going to get any medals or citations. He won't kill any Japs or knock down any Zeros. He won't do a damn thing to get his name in the paper. He won't even get a rating. But somebody's got to drive that truck. Somebody's got to pull KP, or be latrine orderly, or clean up the dayroom, or file letters, or type special orders, or drive some major over to the hospital to see a nurse."

My friend the cook was warming up now. "Hell, Nelson, I personally think it's just as dangerous to light one of those damn field stoves as it is to go over a target. A lot of cooks have been blown to hell-and-gone by them. And a hell of a lot more burned to a crisp. But can you imagine a general pinning a medal on a guy and saying, 'for heroism in lighting a stove, field, M1937, day after day for two years'? Or a guy getting a citation which reads: 'for typing out correspondence eight hours a day, every day, for two years without making a mistake'?

"Don't you think those guys would like to see their names in print, saying how they're fighting the war, too? Don't you think they're just as fed up with this war, just as disgusted with all the crap they have to put up with? Don't you think a mechanic down on the line thinks what he's doing is just as important as what the gunner or the pilot are doing? Don't you think a cook feels he's winning the war just as much as some jerko who snagged himself some bars, wrangled flying pay for putting in four hours cruising over a deserted island and spends the rest of his time censoring mail and sacking?

"Can you blame a guy if he gets a good racket?" I asked.

"Hell, no. More power to him. But once in a while somebody ought to make the hero-worshippers realize heros don't win wars. The guys who win wars are the guys who have to lug reams of paper around, or open cans of C-rations, or clean pots and pans, or grease jeeps or dig sump pits or do any of a thousand jobs that nobody ever heard of except the poor bastard that has to do it.

"I've been in this Army a long time. I been up and down the ladder like a paperhanger. I've had a dozen different jobs and I've lived with all sorts of guys. But the more I think about it, the more convinced I am that it's the guy who's just a serial number, the guy who says, 'Yes, Sir' like an automaton, the guys whose jobs are so monotonous and regulated that they can do them while their minds are 10,000 miles away, who are really the heroes of this war.

"He's got nothing to look forward to except the day of his discharge, nothing to think back on except before he got in. He's told down to the twitch of his shoulders just how he should do whatever he's doing, and he damn well better do it that way whether it's the best way or not.

"He's the guy, Nelson, that is winning this war—if it is being won. And he's the guy I think somebody ought to write about. Maybe some of those poor, rationed, over-worked—for a hundred bucks a week—civilians, by the grace of a lucky number, or flat feet, or some pull with a doctor, will realize fightin' a war is nothing but damn drudgery and a hell of a waste of a man's life—not a thrill-packed series of flights over some damn atoll nobody ever heard of until he got stuck on one of 'em."

"You got an idea there," I said. "And I think somebody ought to do it."

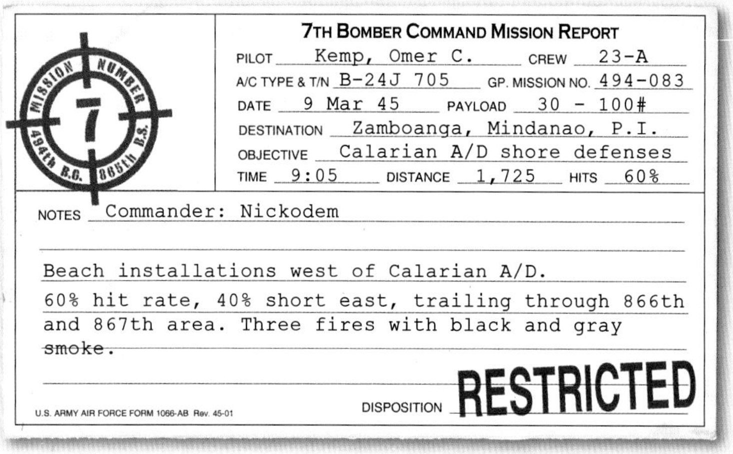
7TH BOMBER COMMAND MISSION REPORT

MISSION NUMBER 7 494th B.G. 866th B.S.

PILOT Kemp, Omer C. CREW 23-A
A/C TYPE & T/N B-24J 705 GP. MISSION NO. 494-083
DATE 9 Mar 45 PAYLOAD 30 - 100#
DESTINATION Zamboanga, Mindanao, P.I.
OBJECTIVE Calarian A/D shore defenses
TIME 9:05 DISTANCE 1,725 HITS 60%

NOTES Commander: Nickodem

Beach installations west of Calarian A/D.
60% hit rate, 40% short east, trailing through 866th and 867th area. Three fires with black and gray smoke.

DISPOSITION RESTRICTED

U.S. ARMY AIR FORCE FORM 1066-AB Rev. 45-01

CALAMITY AT CALARIAN

On Mission #4 on 23 February, Crew 23A bombed San Roque Airdrome, so they were familiar with their 9 March target, shore installations at Calarian air field, a dirt airstrip just two miles west of San Roque. There were no enemy fighters and little flak that day, but they witnessed a horror that gave every man something new to worry about on missions crowded with scores of bombers converging over tiny objectives.

On the Calarian run, 24 planes of the 494th were joined by a couple dozen more from the 5th and 30th bomb groups. Just after bombs away, 5th Bomb Group pilot Ken Gutheil looked up to see a formation of 307th B-24s about two thousand feet above him... and they were dropping *their* bombs.

Gutheil was certain he was finished. A bomb hit the wing of the plane directly in front of him and there was a huge explosion, damaging three other aircraft, including Gutheil's, which suffered seven holes in one wing, a damaged stabilizer, and a burned off left aileron and rudder. He was able to limp home to his base on Samar Island, but his plane was a total loss.

At the time of the explosion, Lt. Kanduros, bombardier of the aircraft that was struck, had just checked his watch to note the time of impact of his own bombs. A wing tank behind him exploded and he saw a ball of flame rolling toward him. The aircraft went into a violent spin and suddenly the nose section separated from the rest of the plane and Kanduros was pinned to the ribbing as the bomber spiraled toward the earth. He saw his parachute hanging to his left and grabbed it, but knew he couldn't get it on because he was wearing his bulky flak vest. Moving slowly so as not to be thrown from the spinning nose section, he managed to slip off the flak vest and don the parachute. He turned slowly. The entire aft of the plane was gone. A moment later he was sucked out and he pulled the rip cord, gratefully watched his chute blossom overhead, and looked down. The water was only two hundred feet below and he hit it at almost terminal velocity. Somehow, he found himself alive, kicking toward on the ocean surface.

He was only a couple hundred yards from shore, but rather than risk capture, he swam for a group of ships three or four miles away. Soon a float plane landed to pick him up and within an hour he was having a cup of coffee aboard the *USS Phoenix,* part of the invasion fleet which would come ashore two days later.

Lt. Kanduros was the only survivor of his aircraft.

AUDIO TRANSCRIPT 14:00:40

The custom was that we'd fly in a squadron over a target in a line, one after the other and the lead bombardier would put the cross hairs on the target and the Norden bombsight would take over control of the airplane and all the bombardier had to do was keep the cross hairs lined up. When he twisted the knobs on the bombsight, the plane would turn left or right. He was flying it for the last few seconds before bombs away and when he had the target within the cross hairs at the right speed and altitude, the bombs would drop automatically.

The bombardier in the following plane would watch for the bombs starting to drop and when he'd see them he'd just press his own release button, and away they'd go. He was literally "salvoing" his bombs on that other guy's sighting. Same for the guy behind him.

At Calarian on Mindanao, we were trying to bomb an airfield and the lead bombardier was coming up to the target, lining it up, and he turned away and bumped the bomb release toggle switch and all the bombs went below – and all the rest of the crews bombed right along with him. So all the bombs fell into the jungle short of the runway by three or four miles, just bombing the devil out of the jungle. So we scratched that off as a complete abort for the whole squadron. We missed the target completely and didn't even come close.

A couple of months later we got word that we'd killed four hundred Japanese. They had their whole billet right where our bombs went. They were all hiding up in the jungle instead of being anywhere near the airfield. They thought we knew just where they were, but we didn't know a thing.

COINCIDENCE AT CALARIAN

ABOVE Sometimes good luck and bad collide and both survive. During Mission #7, O.C.'s squadron had some rather amazing good luck, which was also bad luck for the enemy.

From this account we see that the reported hits on Mission Report #7 must either have been for the Group as a whole and not O.C.'s individual crew or his squadron, or the brass later perhaps termed the misplaced bombs accurate, in which case the rest of the Group must have done quite poorly. Killing 400 enemy soldiers with just a 60% accuracy rate is, by any standard, notable work.

RIGHT When Allied troops took the Zamboanga Peninsula a few days later, this was the sort of destruction they encountered at the port, much of it courtesy of the 494th Bomb Group.

BOEING B-29 "SUPERFORTRESS"

The B-29 Superfortress is a four-engine heavy bomber with advancements over the B-24 Liberator such as a pressurized cabin and remote-controlled machine-gun turrets. In the late 1930s, Boeing won the bid to build a pressurized derivative of its B-17 with a nose wheel undercarriage. The result was Model 334, a bomber capable of cruising at 32,000 feet, delivering a 20,000 pound payload, a 5,800 mile range, and a speed of over 350 mph—all of which made it nearly impossible for an enemy fighter to catch. However, it had problems with its engines, which often caught fire. Many early photos of the plane starting its engines show ground crews standing by with fire extinguishers.

Starting in mid-1944, B-29s in China began bombing Japan but to little effect. More successful were the missions staged from the Marianas Islands in early 1945: the bombing of military installations, the mining of harbors, and the later controversial incendiary bombing of major Japanese cities, burning large portions thereof and leaving hundreds of thousands of civilians without homes. And yet Japan did not capitulate. It wasn't until the *Enola Gay* dropped the atomic bomb "Little Boy" on Hiroshima on 6 August 1945 that Japan even considered surrender, and did not do so until days after *Bockscar* dropped "Fat Man" on Nagasaki on 9 August.

Even the most die-hard B-24 fan must admit the B-29 is an elegant, beautiful, and capable aircraft.

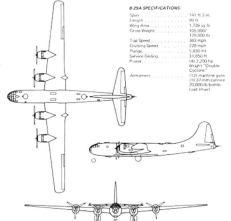

B-29 SUPERFORTRESS The Boeing B-29 Superfortress was built for a single primary purpose—to help end the war in the Pacific. It was built in absolute secrecy. Classified as a heavy bomber, 3,970 Superforts were built for the U.S. Air Force.

During World War II, B-29s flew more than 100 million miles in the Pacific, dropping 171,060 tons of bombs. The first XB-29 flew on September 21, 1942; Boeing's Wichita Division completed the first production model April 15, 1943. B-29s also were license-built by Bell and Martin. B-29As came from Boeing's Renton factory.

In the spring of 1945, B-29 production peaked with Boeing building eight of the four-engine bombers in one day. In the same spring, attacks by as many as 1,000 B-29s were directed against Japan. On August 6, 1945, the B-29 Enola Gay dropped an atomic bomb on Hiroshima and the end of World War II was in sight.

In the first 3 months of the Korean War, 130 Superfortresses flew 41,957 combat hours and dropped 28,201 tons of bombs. Later modifications gave the B-29 added usefulness on photo-reconnaissance missions, as typhoon hunters, weather watchers, rescue planes, and aerial refueling tankers.

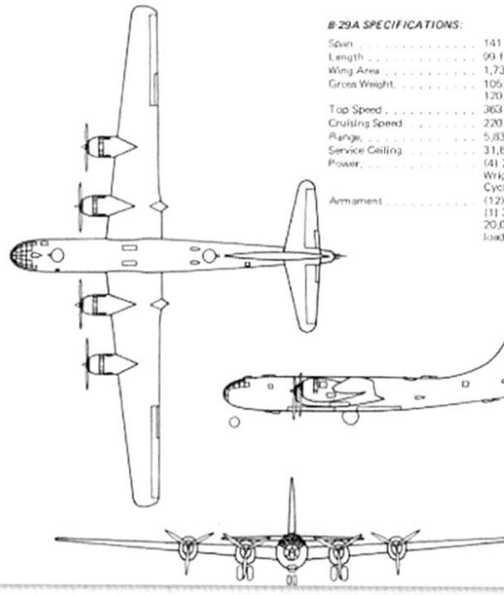

B-29A SPECIFICATIONS:

Span	141 ft 3 in.
Length	99 ft
Wing Area	1,739 sq ft
Gross Weight	105,000/ 120,000 lb
Top Speed	363 mph
Cruising Speed	220 mph
Range	5,830 mi
Service Ceiling	31,850 ft
Power	(4) 2,200 hp Wright "Double Cyclone"
Armament	(12) machine guns (1) 37 mm cannon 20,000-lb bomb-load (max)

EXTRA! **Pacific Post** EXTRA!

Section One SATURDAY, MARCH 10, 1945 Ten Cents

HELL RAINS DOWN ON HIROHITO

HUNDREDS OF B-29S SHOWER TOKYO WITH INCENDIARY BOMBS

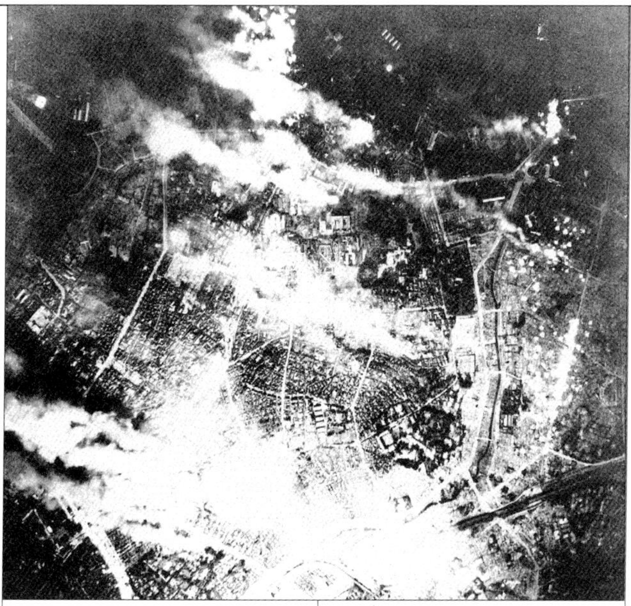

TOKYO, HONSHU, JAPAN, 10 Mar – We believed once our bombers got within range of the Japanese homeland, they would capitulate. We should have remembered Guadalcanal, Tarawa, Peleliu, Iwo Jima, and Okinawa. It seemed no amount of destruction would quell the Japanese will.

The bombing began a year ago, when the range of the new B-29s—2,000 miles farther than a B-24—made possible sorties from China, but they still could not reach Tokyo.

But when we took the Mariana Islands, 1,500 miles from Japan, the round-trip was not only conceivable, it was possible. Shortly after the first Superforts landed in Saipan in October 1944, they went to work attacking Japanese steel production and aviation plants with general purpose bombs.

But success was limited by distance, poor weather, and heavy anti-aircraft and fighter harassment. The planes that the Empire had removed from Iwo Jima and other islands were re-purposed to protect Japan and the B-29s were huge targets. And when we made our first raid on Tokyo on 24 November, effects of the bombing were negligible.

In January 1945, Hap Arnold, head of Army Air Forces, brought in Curtis LeMay to solve the problem. LeMay, a veteran of the Battle of Britain, knew first hand the effects of strategic bombing of civilian populations. He advocated low-level, night time bombing of urban areas using the new M-69 firebomb, believing that when the largely wood-and-paper homes in Tokyo went up in flames the people would be demoralized and demand that their government surrender.

So on the night of 9 March, under the auspices of Operation Meetinghouse, over three hundred B-29s streaked toward Tokyo at an altitude of between 4,000 and 9,000 feet. They met little resistance as the anti-aircraft were calibrated for their usual appearance at 30,000 feet, though fourteen aircraft were lost in the attack.

As they dropped over 1,700 tons of munitions on the target area, crews noted that the M-69 bomb was incredibly destructive. The ensuing firestorm burned 16 square-miles of Tokyo and killed an estimated 100,000 people. The next day, a million people were homeless and a quarter of all residences had been destroyed.

It was the single most destructive bombing raid in history, greater in its immediate effect than Dresden, Hiroshima or Nagasaki.

Over the next six months, in addition to the thousands of conventional bombings by the Air Force, the Superfortresses returned again and again, destroying almost 60 cities and inflicting half a million deaths.

And still the Japanese did not surrender.

Even at the time the attack was controversial. Some argued that targeting the civilian population made us little different than our enemies.

LeMay answered that the Musashino factory, where the Nakajima aircraft engine (the powerplant of Japan's newest, most dangerous fighter, the J1N1 Irving) was made, was in Tokyo. The city also had dozens of plants that produced machine tools, electronics, precision instruments, aircraft and aircraft parts.

After the War, it was revealed that though heavy industry was little affected by the bombings, light industry and the homes of workers—as well as workers themselves—in heavy industry were destroyed by the firebombings. In addition, 50% of Tokyo's industry was in residential and commercial neighborhoods and the bombing cut the city's war output in half.

Though the Imperial Palace was specifically declared off limits to bombing, it took some damage. But it was surrounded by neighborhoods decimated by the bombings. When the Emperor made a rare appearance outside the palace, for the first time he was made personally aware of the hell America was about to unleash on his Empire.

brief

There were pinups on the back of every issue of *brief* and an address inside for a soldier to send away for a signed photograph from the model's agent.

No wonder so many of the planes were adorned with beautiful women—it's what they were fighting for.

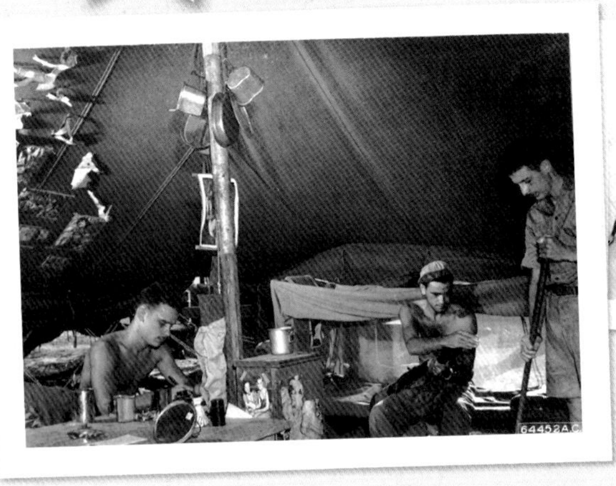

LEFT Enlisted men's tent, 865th Squadron. Note the girlie cut-outs pinned to the tent wall.

RIGHT The most popular pin-up girl of the time was inarguably Betty Grable because of her provocative pose (for the time) and shapely gams.

BOTTOM LEFT A young Ava Gardner demonstrates her girl-next-door appeal.

BOTTOM CENTER Believe it or not, the striking Yvonne De Carlo grew up to play Mrs. Munster on the quirky 1960s television sitcom.

BOTTOM RIGHT And of course, Lana Turner, believed by many at the time to be Hollywood's most beautiful actress, as evidenced by the fact that she was chosen by 400 of her most ardent fans in the 494th as "Miss Angaur" (unfortunately in absentia).

CENSOR DUTY

Speaking of things requiring censoring... every squadron in the Army Air Force had a censor, and the thankless job in the 865th fell to O.C. Kemp. It was not a job he wanted; he was not interested in the private lives of others, but perhaps that is why he was chosen.

RIGHT Seagram distillers contributed to the War by donating this poster, which made famous a phrase still in use today.

TOP LEFT War Dept. Pamphlet No. 21-1 details prohibited subjects:

War Department Pamphlet No. 21-1 29 July 1943

WHEN YOU ARE OVERSEAS

THESE FACTS ARE VITAL

Writing home

THINK! Where does the enemy get his information—information that can put you, and has put your comrades, adrift on an open sea; information that has lost battles and can lose more, unless you personally, vigilantly, perform your duty in SAFEGUARDING MILITARY INFORMATION?

CENSORSHIP RULES ARE SIMPLE, SENSIBLE.—They are merely concise statements drawn from actual experience briefly outlining the types of material which have proved to be disastrous when available to the enemy. A soldier should not hesitate to impose his own additional rules when he is considering writing of a subject not covered by present regulations. He also should guard against repeating rumors or misstatements. It is sometimes stated that censorship delays mail for long periods of time. Actually, mail is required to be completely through censorship within 48 hours.

There are ten prohibited subjects

1. Don't write military information of Army units—their location, strength, matériel, or equipment.
2. Don't write of military installations.
3. Don't write of transportation facilities.
4. Don't write of convoys, their routes, ports (including ports of embarkation and disembarkation), time en route, naval protection, or war incidents occurring en route.
5. Don't disclose movements of ships, naval or merchant, troops, or aircraft.
6. Don't mention plans and forecasts or orders for future operations, whether known or just your guess.
7. Don't write about the effects of enemy operations.
8. Don't tell of any casualty until released by proper authority (The Adjutant General) and then only by using the full name of the casualty.
9. Don't attempt to formulate or use a code system, cipher, or shorthand, or any other means to conceal the true meaning of your letter. Violations of this regulation will result in severe punishment.
10. Don't give your location in any way except as authorized by proper authority. Be sure nothing you write about discloses a more specific location than the one authorized.

INCLOSURES IN LETTERS.—Do not inclose anything in a letter that would violate any of the foregoing rules.

PHOTOGRAPHS, FILMS.—Special rules apply to the transmission of photographs and films. Do not send them until you have ascertained what regulations are in effect in your area.

540677°—43

1. Don't write military information of Army units—their location, strength, materiel, or equipment.
2. Don't write of military installations.
3. Don't write of transportation facilities.
4. Don't write of convoys, their routes, ports, time en route, naval protection, or war incidents occurring en route.
5. Don't disclose movements of ships, naval or merchant, troops, or aircraft.
6. Don't mention plans and forecasts or orders for future operations, whether known or just your guess.
7. Don't write of the effects of enemy operations.
8. Don't tell of any casualty until released by proper authority and then only by using the full name of the casualty.
9. Don't attempt to formulate or use a code system, cipher, or shorthand, or any other means to conceal the true meaning of your letter. Violations of this regulation will result in severe punishment.
10. Don't give your location in any way except as authorized by proper authority. Be sure nothing you write about discloses a more specific location than the one authorized.

BOTTOM LEFT But it wasn't just the contents of their letters home they were cautioned against; it was their speech and conduct as well. And there, under the caption "Capture," we see the famous order to divulge no more than your "Name, Rank, & Serial Number."

Talk

SILENCE MEANS SECURITY.—If violation of protective measures
serious within written communications it is disastrous in conversation
Protect your conversation as you do your letters, and be even more caref
A harmful letter can be nullified by censorship; loose talk is direct delive
to the enemy.
If you come home during war your lips must remain sealed and y
writing hand must be guided by self-imposed censorship. This ta
guts. Have you got them or do you want your buddies and your coun
to pay the price for your showing off? You've faced the battle front;
little enough to ask you to face this "home front."

Capture

Most enemy intelligence comes from prisoners. If captured, you a
required to give only three facts: YOUR NAME, YOUR GRADE, YOU
ARMY SERIAL NUMBER. Don't talk, don't try to fake stories, and u
every effort to destroy all papers. When you are going into an area whe
capture is possible carry only essential papers and plan to destroy the
prior to capture if possible. Do not carry personal letters on your perso
they tell much about you, and the envelope has on it your unit a
organization.

Be sensible; use your head

7TH BOMBER COMMAND MISSION REPORT

MISSION NUMBER 8 — 494th B.G. 865th B.S.

PILOT Kemp, Omer C. CREW 23-A

A/C TYPE & T/N B-24J 711 GP. MISSION NO. 494-088

DATE 16 Mar 45 PAYLOAD 30 - 100#

DESTINATION Sarangani Bay, Mindanao, P.I.

OBJECTIVE Area #5

TIME 7:35 DISTANCE 1,200 HITS

NOTES Commander: Richards

Area #5: storage and housing units.

U.S. ARMY AIR FORCE FORM 1066-AB Rev. 45-01

DISPOSITION RESTRICTED

A DIRECT CONNECTION

On the southeast shore of Mindanao, Sarangani Bay is the open mouth above a jaw formed by the Davao Gulf to the east. At the north end of the Bay was the town of Makar, with an airfield and troop bivouacs. For the previous three days, the 494th had been hitting Makar, and today 24 bombers (six from each 494th squadron), including O.C. and Crew 23A, were assigned Area #5, which contained storage and housing units, as their primary target.

On Mission #7 a week earlier, O.C. and company had blasted Japanese airfields on the southern tip of the Zamboanga Peninsula. The next day, Allied forces made amphibious landings there and soon pushed the defenders north. Now the Japanese were trucking material and reinforcements 200 miles west to the Peninsula via the road leading out of Makar. If the 494th could disrupt these shipments, they would be saving American lives on the peninsula.

But they were reminded that on Mindanao, like the rest of the Philippines, they were to bomb only assigned targets. Filipino guerillas, with their extensive intelligence network, knew where to hit the enemy, and their target suggestions were taken seriously, as were their warnings about places *not* to hit. "So, when in doubt, haul 'em out," said Capt. Richards, their mission commander, referring to the thirty 100 pound bombs in the B-24 bellies.

But their alternate target was the north road out of Makar, which headed toward the Zamboanga Peninsula. Just four days before, a crew from the 866th, tarried after their bomb run over their primary target to do photo reconnaissance. They spied a convoy of twenty trucks heading north along the road and regretted having already dropped their bombs. But the pilot was unwilling to miss this golden opportunity, though he knew if he approached the convoy at their current altitude of 10,000 feet they'd see him in time to scatter. So he took the *Queen of Hearts* down to the deck and well beyond the redline speed of 260 mph. When he popped up over a hill at 500 feet just a half mile south of the convoy, he crabbed to the right and dropped his left wing, giving his port gunners a clear target. They unloaded their .50 caliber machine guns on the convoy. Once past, he stood the plane on its right wing, did a 180° turn, and made another pass so his starboard gunners could join in. When they were safely away, he asked for an aircraft damage report. There was none.

Crew 23A reported no incidents during this mission. Indeed, we don't even know if they hit anything or not.

GET THE PICTURE? NOT OUT HERE WE DON'T

Aside from gambling, drinking, and swimming, there wasn't much to do on Angaur, and so shortly after their tents were up, the men started building movie theaters, most featuring a sheet hung against a tent. Eventually there were thirteen makeshift theaters on the island, one for each squadron and engineering unit.

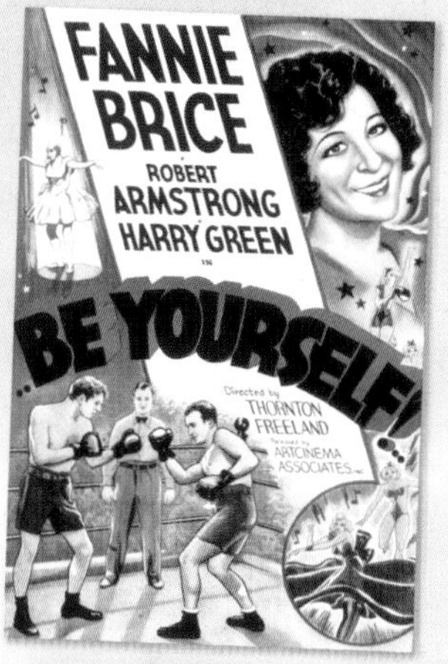

TOP AND RIGHT CENTER The hit movies of the day did *not* play on Angaur; instead, during February 1945, the men watched relics like *Be Yourself,* a 1926 musical/boxing melodrama time and time again. And they weren't happy about it.

BOTTOM LEFT So they decided to build a real theater with a cement stage and a large screen. On their way back to the island from missions in the Philippines, pilots routinely stopped to refuel at Tacloban Air Field on Leyte Island. While there, they filled their empty bomb bays with lengths of Marsden mat, perforated lengths of steel used until muddy runways were paved. The matting was welded up into seating and though it still rained during many shows, the raised benches kept behinds out of the mud. Theater No. 1 served nicely, especially when a USO troupe stopped in. The elevated stage, shaded by Quonset hut sections, made the dancing girls easier to spot, with or without field glasses.

BOTTOM CENTER Projectors were hard to come by. Here a captured Japanese projector is rigged for sound.

BOTTOM RIGHT It wasn't until March that a current movie, *A Tree Grows in Brooklyn,* made it to Angaur. Featuring an all-star cast, it tells the story—from the point of view of 16 year-old Francie—of a poor Irish-American family struggling to get ahead in New York tenements in the early 1900s.

ORPHAN ANN ON "ZERO HOUR"

Every evening during the War, American soldiers across the Pacific tuned their shortwave radios to hear "The Zero Hour," a 75-minute broadcast featuring the latest in American big-band music, humorous skits, and news of the War they couldn't get from their own military—even though it *was* blatant propaganda. The key personality on the show was a woman with a silky, confiding voice and an impeccable American accent who called herself "Orphan Ann."

Americans called her "Tokyo Rose."

Servicemen listened to her to broadcasts to get a sense of the effect of their military actions by reading between the lines. Rose was sometimes unnervingly accurate, naming units and even individual servicemen. And her voice, warm and sometimes even tender, reminded many a lonely soldier that he was far from home and might never return there.

But who was she? Though over the years twelve women had the job, Iva Toguri D'Aquino, an American citizen born in Los Angeles to Japanese immigrants, was the most likely suspect.

America also used the airwaves. Walter Kaner broadcast as "Tokyo Mose." He had a theme song, "Moshi, Moshi Ano-ne," sung to the tune of "London Bridge is Falling Down," which became so popular with Japanese children and GIs alike that it was called "the Japanese occupation theme song."

And on every island with American servicemen and a generator, someone played records over a ten-watt radio station. When official use ended for the night, enterprising GIs took to the airwaves and played music and chatted with their comrades. In the Mariana Islands, Radio F-I-G came on late, saying, "Men, it's your nightly musicale, brought to you by F-I-G. We'll be on from now until we get tired and hit the sack." Emphasis was on soft, sweet music, the kind that put men in the mood to write love letters. With a broadcast reach of one mile, the station played requests, which were often hollered out from tents. When the brass tried to usurp the time to broadcast squadron announcements, the DJs rebelled. "Who'd bother to tune in for the KP roster?"

ABOVE RIGHT GIs imagined Tokyo Rose as a beautiful geisha.

BOTTOM RIGHT How Tokyo Rose really looked. Iva Toguri was detained for a year after the War, but the Justice Department finally admitted that her broadcasts were for the most part innocuous. But when Toguri tried to return to America, public outcry led to her prosecution and conviction for treason, though key witnesses later claimed their testimony had been compelled. In 1977, Toguri was pardoned by President Gerald Ford.

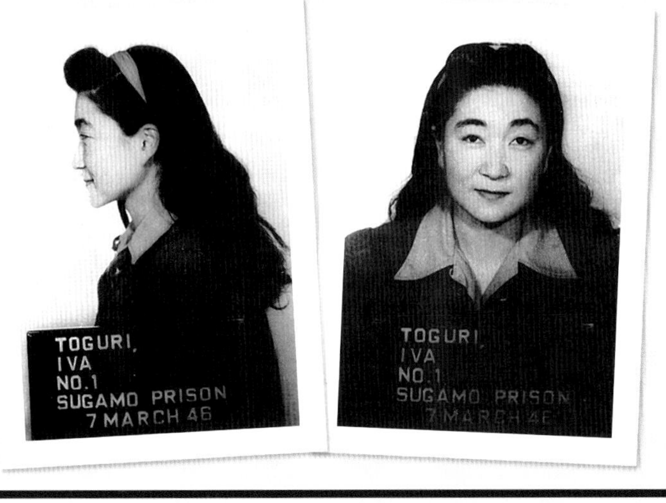

EYES IN THE SKY

"Make it in triplicate!" was the war cry of the typewriter corps in the War, and the visual analog was the Combat Camera Unit which took thousands of photographs of flight crews, their habitations, duties, and the planes they flew. During the month of November 1944, Detachment F of the 7th CCU joined the 494th and many of the photos seen in this scrapbook come from crisp 4x5 negatives stored for seventy years in cool, dark government archives—photos not of generic scenes but of the men of the 494th.

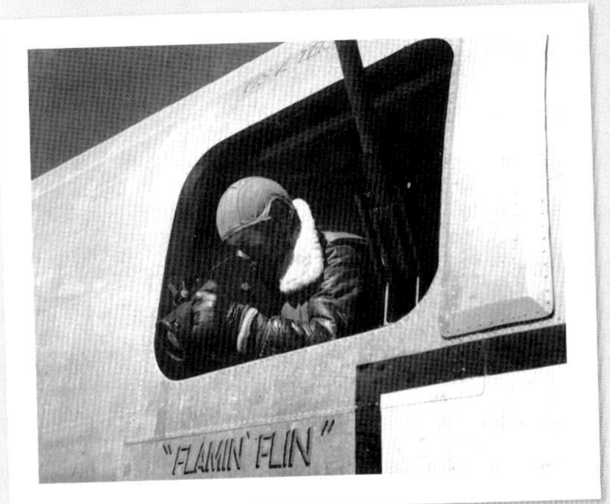

LEFT Technical Sergeant Will Bond, wearing his cold weather gear, sights his Fairchild K-20 still camera out of the starboard waist gunner's window. By February 1945 most of the B-24s in the 494th Bomb Group had been equipped with rear turret still cameras that were automatically triggered a certain number of seconds after bombs away to record the accuracy of hits.

CENTER RIGHT Will Bond points his Filmo A-7 16 mm motion picture camera down the escape hatch just forward of the waist gunner position for a bombing record shot. Early B-24s had mirror-image waist windows which impeded the gunners' movements. Later versions offset the windows by a couple of feet, resolving the issue.

CENTER LEFT Mimicking how pilots paint bombs on their aircraft to signify successful missions, Sergeant Antone Bruns stencils the 11th bomb on his A-7 case, indicating the number of photo missions he's been on.

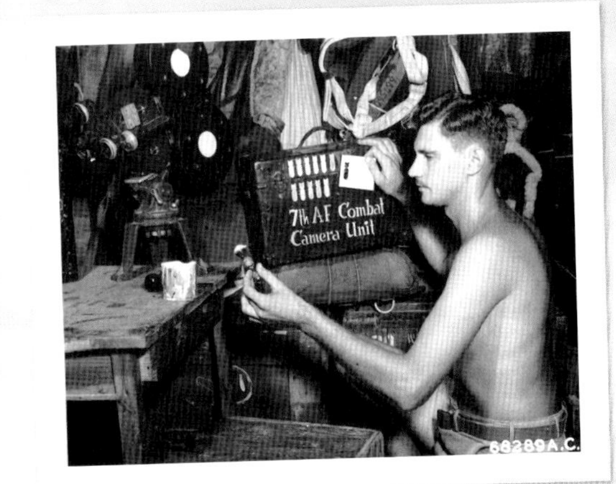

BOTTOM RIGHT A Fairchild K-17 4x5 aerial still camera of the type which photographed many of these crystal clear images.

BOTTOM LEFT 494th Group intelligence officer Capt. Briton Martin (right) examines aerial reconnaissance photos with Lt. Friedlander.

NOTE The 494th had its own Group photographers as well, though they weren't as well outfitted as the 7th CCU. Once, when they ran out of developer, they substituted a strong floor soap solution, which produced good prints, though they were brown in color. Vinegar from the mess was used for stop baths, but the prints soon turned gray if exposed to light for an extended period of time.

EXTRA! **Pacific Post** EXTRA!

Section One FRIDAY, MARCH 23, 1945 Ten Cents

ON THE DOORSTEP IN OKINAWA

LONGEST AND BLOODIEST BATTLE OF THE WAR ECLIPSES IWO JIMA

OKINAWA, RYUKYU ISLANDS, 23 Mar. – Perhaps the irony was intentional, but Operation Iceberg would be the hottest battle of the Pacific War and it gave us pause about the invasion of Japan scheduled for 1 November, dubbed "Operation Downfall," which was hoped to be anything *but* ironic.

Taking this long, slender island would be more difficult than the Philippines, which were filled with anti-Jap guerillas. Okinawa was loyal to the Empire, having long been a Japanese protectorate.

The invasion was on the same scale as Overlord in Normandy: 180,000 men, including General Buckner's 10th Army, comprised of four Army divisions and the 1st and 6th Marines, would take the island from the western shore, supported by 1,200 ships.

The Japanese, led by General Ushijima, numbered 100,000, including 20,000 Okinawan militia. Ushijima knew the island's strengths: caves and tunnels in the limestone hills in the south and the dense forested terrain on the Motobu Peninsula were where he concentrated his defenses.

The Allies knew, too, and planned to cut the island in half, then turn the Marines loose in the north while the Army hit the southern hills.

Task Force 50 under Admiral Mitscher began bombardment on 23 March and on 1 April

General Buckner's men began the amphibious assault.

As was now the custom, there was little resistance on the beaches and troops moved inland with little difficulty, capturing the airfields. By D+2 they had split Okinawa in half.

Then all hell broke loose. Between 6 April and 22 June, 1,465 *kamikazes* swarmed over the Allied fleet, sinking 38 ships and damaging 368, as seen in the photo above of the carrier *USS Bunker Hill.*

In addition, a Japanese strike force of ten vessels, including the world's largest battleship *Yamato*, steamed to Okinawa. Fortunately the *Yamato* was sunk long before it reached the island.

The land battle was a different story. The 6th Marines moved north, sealing off Motobu, trapping Ushijima's forces on the peninsula, which was covered with wooded mountains, rocky ridges and ravines. It took two weeks to clear the peninsula as soldiers endured several *banzai* attacks, some by women armed only with hand-made spears.

Meanwhile, the Army encountered stiff opposition near Shuri Castle in west-central Okinawa, suffering 1,500 casualties while killing or capturing three times that many. But the battle had just begun.

South of Shuri, they encountered fortified caves which had to be cleared one at a time. In addition, the Japanese used civilians as human shields and bombs, strapping TNT to them and sending them out to the American lines.

There were also highly organized night infiltrations which resulted in brutal hand-to-hand fighting and astonishing casualties.

By 19 April, a new Allied offensive opened on the southwest coast, supported by over 300 ship-borne guns and 650 Navy planes. But, like Iwo Jima, the defenders merely waited out the barrage then emerged from their hiding holes to mortar American soldiers working their way up steep hillsides. One particular bloody engagement took place on Kakazu Ridge, called "Hacksaw Ridge" by the GIs who lost 720 men taking it.

And yet the bulk of the defenders were still further south.

Monsoon rains arrived in May, turning the island into a muddy morass. Soldiers, under constant enemy fire, were forced to hunker down for weeks in foxholes full of water, feces, and dead bodies, the battlefield turned into a combination latrine, garbage dump, and graveyard.

The downpour aided the Japanese withdrawal of 30,000 men to their last stand at Kiyan, where General Buckner was killed by enemy artillery fire just four days before the last Japanese resistance collapsed on 20 June.

In the end, Gen. Ushijuma committed *harakiri.* 75,000 IJF soldiers died, 150,000 Okinawans (a quarter of the native population), and 14,000 U.S. soldiers and Marines.

But Okinawa was ours and we now stood inside Japan's front door.

DOWN TIME

Once the mines and iron tetrahedron obstacles were cleared from the lagoon, the men now calling Angaur home looked around and said, "If it wasn't for the heat, the snipers, the insects, the undrinkable water, and the malaria, this place wouldn't be half bad."

But there was still danger. Most young men of that time did not know how to swim and so lifeguard towers were immediately erected as the soldiers frolicked in the waves clutching their inflated rubber mattress covers under their arms like enormous water-wings.

It wasn't long before someone noted that since most of the trees on the island had been blown up, they would need some shade, so they scrounged wood planking from the shipping crates holding everything from ammo to replacement engines and built a cabana and a couple of Adirondack chairs. Suddenly things started feeling downright *civilized*.

Some mechanic looked at a P-38 wing tank, noted that those two oxygen bottles over there weren't being used for anything, that the sail of that ruined life raft might find use again, and the first entry in the Angaur regatta was built.

Beach volleyball soon followed, as did beer and chips and a girly magazine or two. The only thing missing was the girly. For the first six months of its existence, Angaur did not see a single female. When the first nurses arrived, the men all mysteriously came down terrible cases of love sickness.

Raised on the beaches of southern California, O.C. felt at home and got to right work on his tan. A torn life raft was cut up and glued together with rubber cement, and a comfortable one-man raft was born, perfect for lounging in the lagoon on a warm evening under a setting sun.

brief

HOW LONG IS A MISSION?

It's a long, trackless road across the vast emptiness of the Pacific. Always over water, the flights are the most monotonous in the world. But many a pilot and crewman has admitted to fearing the sea as much as the opposition he is sure to meet. They know there are no auxiliary airfields where they may land in case of trouble. Crews fly anywhere from eight to fourteen hours over the wastes of the Pacific only to spend a few seconds, or at most minutes, of destruction over targets.

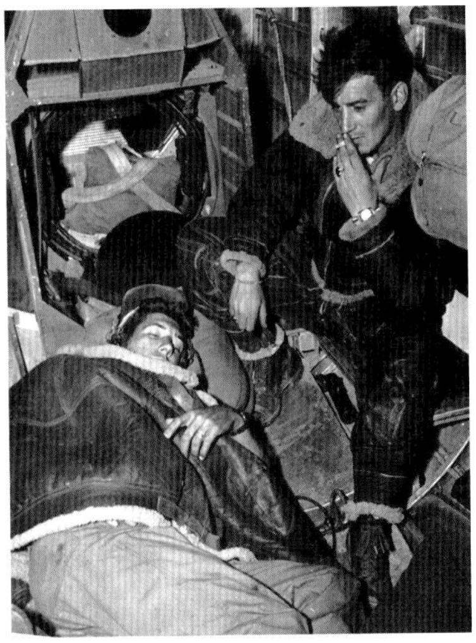

Of course, nearing the target, the tone changes. Suddenly, the senses are guy-wire taut, alert for the slightest puff of flak or the muffled echo of anti-artillery fire. The navigator, his job of getting them to the target finished, mans the nose gun, nervously awaiting a possible head-on fighter attack. The radio operator now grips the machine gun in the "high hat" turret. The two waist gunners, clad in bulky flak vests, point their .50 caliber machine guns out the large open windows, presenting themselves as prime targets for a Zero swooping down out of the sun.

After lining up on the objective, the pilot flips a switch, handing control to the bombardier, who guides the aircraft to target. The pilot now sits helplessly, a spectator. One can only imagine the heart-stopping fear he gulps back when the sky before him turns black with flak and yet he cannot touch the yoke to bank away from the danger.

But once the bombs are away and they are safely on the road home, the tenseness gives way to relief, sometimes even hilarity if the going was particularly rough. There is food on the way back and sometimes the crew loosens up enough to break into a songfest. Pictured here is one crew of one B-24 on the way to and from Iwo Jima.

TOP RIGHT Pilot Lt. Warren Sutterfield turns the controls over to his co-pilot to read a few pages of *A Tree Grows in Brooklyn*.

CENTER LEFT Sgt E. Bespolka eats a Dagwood sandwich and guzzles tomato juice.

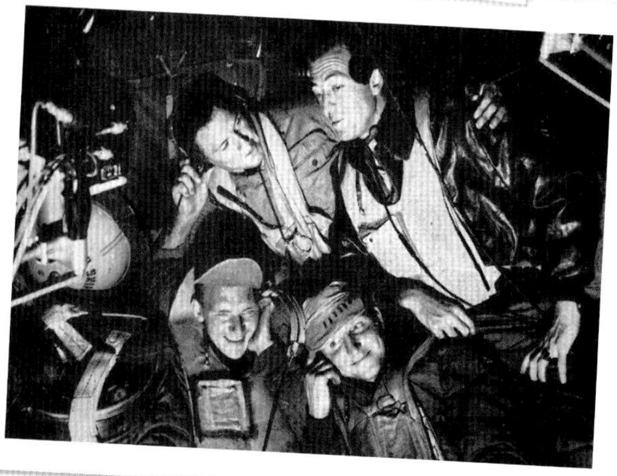

BOTTOM LEFT Bombardier Lt. Bill Verbeek croons through his throat mike as his shipmates listen doubtfully.

BOTTOM RIGHT Sgt. Lyle Leber scrawls a tender missive to his wife.

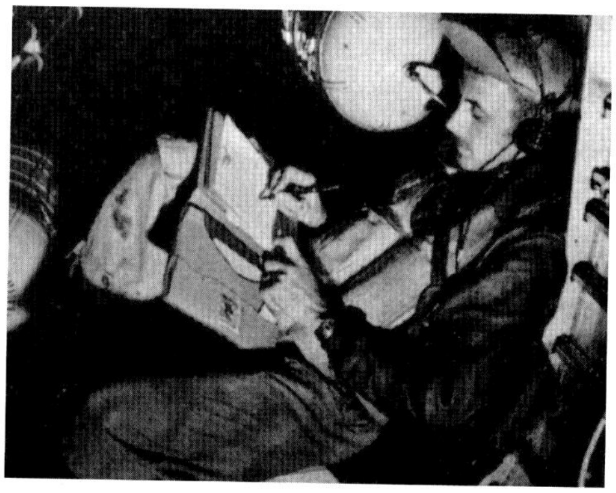

EXTRA! **Pacific Post** EXTRA!

Section One | THURSDAY, APRIL 12, 1945 | Ten Cents

PRESIDENT ROOSEVELT DEAD!

CEREBRAL HEMORRHAGE PROVES FATAL; TRUMAN SWORN IN

WARM SPRINGS, GEORGIA, Apr. 12 – Franklin D. Roosevelt, President for twelve of the most momentous years in this country's history, died at 3:35 P.M. Central Time today in a small room in the "little White House" here in Georgia.

Mr. Roosevelt had been in Warm Springs—which he liked to call his "second home"—since 30 March. The week preceding he had spent in his home in Hyde Park, N.Y.

He was 63 and had served as President longer than any other American.

Less than three hours after the President died, Harry S. Truman was sworn in as 32nd President.

With the President at the time of his death of cerebral hemorrhage were Comdr. Howard G. Breunn and Dr. James P. Paulin of Atlanta.

News of Mr. Roosevelt's death came from Secretary William D. Hassett. He called in three press association reporters who had accompanied the President here and said:

"It is my sad duty to inform you that the President died at 3:35 of a cerebral hemorrhage."

The news was simultaneously telephoned to the White House in Washington and announced there, too.

In Washington, where the news of the President's death at first produced shocked disbelief, officials immediately wondered what effect the tragedy would have on the many domestic and international projects the President was guiding.

Whether it would cause postponement of the United Nations security conference at San Francisco remained to be seen. No one knew in the confusion of the tragic moment. But the conference was perhaps the project closest to the President's heart, and there was some belief that in tribute to him the United Nations would carry it through.

Truman Takes Oath

WASHINGTON, Apr. 12 – Vice-President Harry S. Truman of Missouri was sworn in as 32nd President of the United States today at 7:00 P.M. Eastern Time.

He solemnly repeated the oath of the nation's highest office just three hours after Franklin Delano Roosevelt died of a cerebral hemorrhage in Warm Springs, Ga.

Truman is 60.

It was a moment of significance to America and a warring world. The transition in the nation's leadership came when Allied might was nearing victory in Europe and when preparations for permanent peace now are under way.

Yanks Near Berlin

PARIS, Apr. 12 – American 9th Army tank forces crashed over the Elbe River today and were reported approaching the suburban area of Berlin tonight. One semiofficial report placed the Yanks within 49 miles of the Reich capital.

A strict security blackout, lifted temporarily to reveal that the 9th Army's 2nd Armored Division had bridged the Elbe in the Magleburg area, hid movements of the tank forces beyond the river—the last natural barrier before Berlin.

Charging in from the east, the Russians were meeting fierce resistance on the approaches to Berlin, Radio Moscow said, but in the west the American tanks were believed speeding along virtually unopposed down the homestretch.

Yanks Storm Bohol Island

MANILA, Apr. 13 – Under cover of naval and air bombardment, Yanks landed Wednesday on Bohol Island, last of the Central Philippines still in enemy hands, Gen. Douglas MacArthur reported today.

Maj. Gen. William Arnold's Americal troops landed at Tagbiliran on the southwestern shore and quickly drove inland "in an endeavor to secure control of the island before the surprised enemy could rally his strength," MacArthur said.

PRESIDENTS NAMED EVERY 20 YEARS DIE IN OFFICE

NEW YORK, Apr. 12 – President Roosevelt's death today carried on a tradition that Presidents elected in 20 year-intervals die in office. The list includes:

1840—William Henry Harrison
1860—Abraham Lincoln
1880—James A. Garfield
1900—William McKinley
1920—Warren G. Harding
1940—Franklin D. Roosevelt

GETTING THERE . . . AND BACK AGAIN

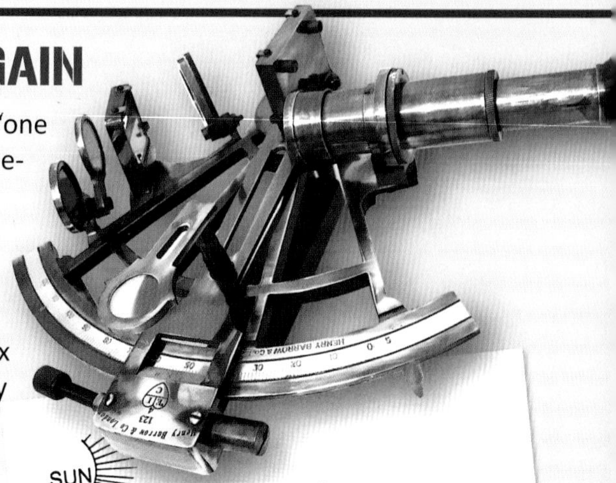

Developed in the mid-1700s, a sextant (*sextans* is Latin for "one sixth"—60° being one-sixth of a circle) measures the angle between any two objects, usually the sun and the horizon.

RIGHT Readings are optimally taken at high noon. The viewer sights the horizon through the telescope (C) and slowly moves the index arm (his left thumb is on it) forward until the sun (its glare reduced by a choice of tinted glasses), reflected by the index mirror (A) and the horizon mirror (B) (which is divided vertically in two, the left side unsilvered to reveal the horizon, the right mirror receiving the sun's image) align. He then reads the angle on the graduated arc (E). Knowing the angle, the time, and date, he then consults a nautical almanac to find his latitude. At night Polaris can be used instead of the sun. Longitude is found by measuring the distance between the moon and a star or planet at a certain time and consulting a Greenwich time chart.

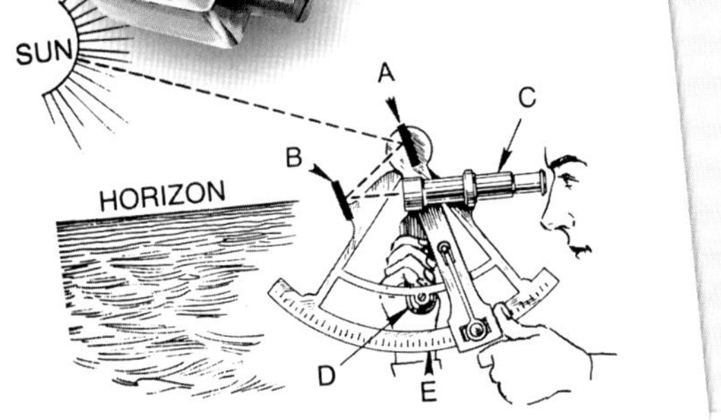

LOWER LEFT By the War, sextants had advanced greatly, utilizing battery-driven drum micrometers, gyroscopes, bubble gauges, and artificial horizons. Because an airplane moves quickly through space, these new sextants took several successive readings, averaging the results to get location fixes. This version of the Fairchild Model A-10-A is used by the navigator in the photo to take a night sighting.

CENTER RIGHT Celestial navigation is subject to weather conditions and a cloudy sky renders it useless. For this reason, the military developed a land-based radio navigation system, **Lo**ng **Ra**nge **N**avigation, or LORAN, which used repeating signals broadcast from two or more antennas on the 1850-1950 kHZ spectrum. The receiver calculates its position by measuring the time difference between the arrival of the signals. The first receivers were too heavy for aircraft, but the APN-9 weighed only 40 pounds. Unlike sextants, LORAN worked in any weather, but required transmitters, which were built as we moved across the Pacific. By May 1945 there was an operating LORAN station on Angaur, Peleliu, Iwo Jima, Okinawa, Guam, and Saipan islands. By the War's end there were 75 LORAN installations across the globe. The technology was not superseded until the advent of GPS.

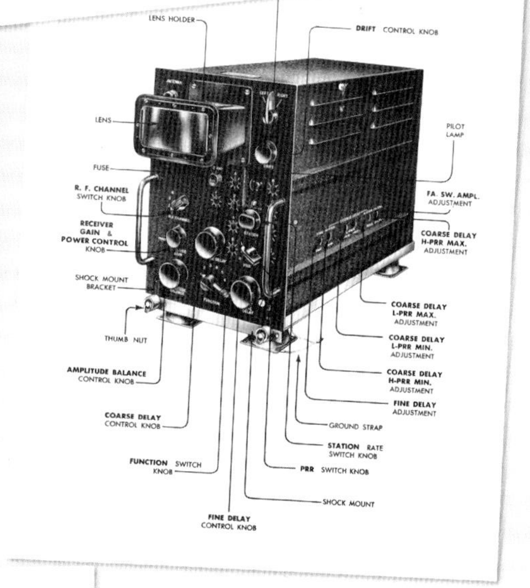

Fortunately, the Japanese did not or could not jam LORAN transmissions. Without LORAN, those 1,500 mile flights O.C. made would have been markedly more dangerous.

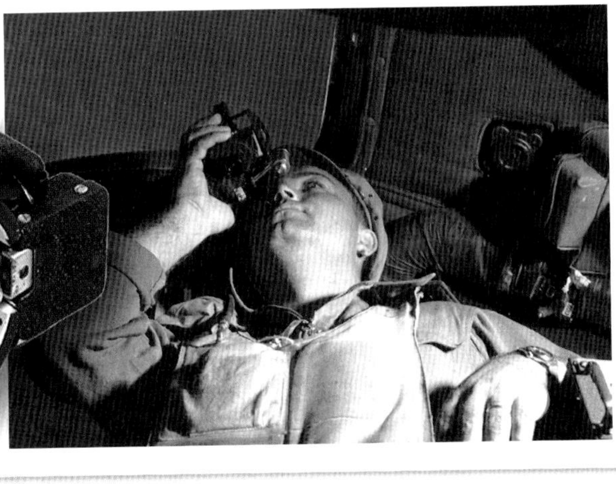

MISSION NUMBER 9 494th B.G. 865th B.S.

7TH BOMBER COMMAND MISSION REPORT

PILOT Kemp, Omer C. CREW 23-A
A/C TYPE & T/N B-24J 711 GP. MISSION NO. 494-101
DATE 13 Apr 45 PAYLOAD 30 - 100#
DESTINATION Sapakan, Mindanao, P.I.
OBJECTIVE troop housing
TIME 7:45 DISTANCE 1,300 HITS 0%

NOTES
Commander: Taylor

U.S. ARMY AIR FORCE FORM 1066-AB Rev. 45-01 DISPOSITION RESTRICTED

FRIDAY THE 13TH

With the Mindanao troop landings just four days away, the 494th engaged in its final sorties over the island, which it had been pummeling in 24 plane missions since mid-February. Surely there could be no more enemy still alive down below. But just four days earlier on a raid on Kabacan, twenty miles to the east, the crew of *Short Run* saw three Japanese Bettys strafing guerilla positions and were attacked by two Zekes. It was still busy over Mindanao, and the date of today's mission gave even the most non-superstitious pilot (of which there are *none*—the checklist itself is a quietly intoned mantra) pause. As they left the briefing at 4:00 a.m. and were trucked to *Sittin' Pretty*, O.C. wondered if he had already used up the meager amount of luck that seemed stingily doled out to air crews.

LOWER RIGHT The target was tiny: troop housing in the lower right quadrant of the reconnaissance photo. No runway to aim for, just tiny rectangles, indistinguishable from civilian housing—and often interspersed therewith. Pinpoint accuracy was needed, which may explain the 0% hit rate—a miss was as good as a mile.

In a letter home a few days later, O.C. exults, "They finally gave us our own ship! Her name is *Rover Boy's Baby* and she's one of the best. Now we feel like we're really in this war with our own airplane and finally our fair share of missions." Crew 30 had just finished their forty missions in the ship two days before, handing her over to Crew 23A in exchange for a promise to take care of her. They crossed their hearts and hoped (not) to die.

WHAT YOU DON'T KNOW . . .

A pilot is strangely isolated from the most important moment of a mission: when he's directly over the target. Japanese fighters might harass prior to and following bombs away, but they prefer to let the anti-aircraft batteries pester the bombers when they're dropping their bombs. But they come back strong when the B-24s break formation bombs away.

One pilot, realizing that in two dozen missions he'd never seen his bombs hit the ground, turned the yoke over to his co-pilot as they neared the objective and craned his neck to see red and white flashes all over the target area. He suddenly realized that every gun down there was firing at him and wished he'd never looked.

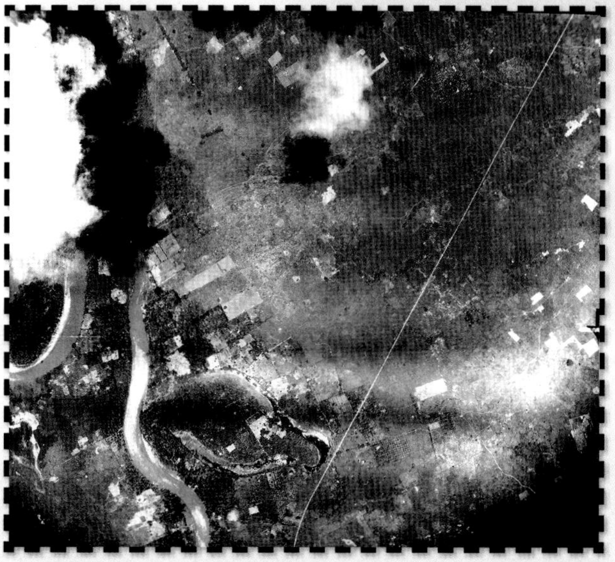

BELL P-59 "AIRACOMET"

Wait a minute. Everyone knows there were no jets in WWII. Or were there? It was well-known that the Germans were developing jet aircraft, which prompted U.S. aviation engineers to do the same. Major General "Hap" Arnold learned of jet propulsion technology from the Brits in 1941. He obtained the power plant specs and, back in the U.S., asked General Electric to build an American version. He also approached Bell Aircraft to build a fighter to house the engine. By spring 1942, Bell had produced a prototype which was shipped to Muroc Air Field in California for testing, equipped with a dummy prop to disguise its top-secret capabilities. Unfortunately, there were problems with engine response and reliability, roll axis stability, and performance. Test pilots were unimpressed with the P-59's speed, but overwhelmed by its smoothness during flight.

CONSOLIDATED PB4Y-2 "PRIVATEER"

The U.S. Navy had long used the B-24 Liberator as a patrol bomber, calling their unmodified version the PB4Y-1. Entering service in late 1944, version 2 of the Privateer had a longer fuselage and a tall vertical stabilizer, along with two additional .50 caliber machine guns, bringing the total to twelve guns in six turrets. It had no turbo superchargers because Navy missions were not usually flown at high altitude. Originally designated the B-24N, it was to be built by Ford for the Army, but the order was cancelled in May 1945. The Navy, however, continued forward, taking delivery of 739 planes, most after the end of the War.

KILLING TIME

As noted, soldiers are inventive, and never more so than when it comes to entertaining themselves. They couldn't swim and write letters home all the time. Sometimes they just had to forget where they were and Uncle Sam was there to help. He gave each enlisted man a daily beer and officers a monthly bottle of whisky. Cigarettes were ubiquitous and used for barter. Spotter Cards featuring silhouettes of enemy aircraft killed two birds with one stone: you got educated about the enemy and lost money to a friend at the same time.

TOP LEFT A crew in O.C.'s squadron opened a store in their quarters selling booze and cigarettes.

CENTER LEFT A craps table was built in the enlisted men's area. They tossed dice for cigarettes.

BOTTOM RIGHT Notwithstanding the competition for free time, the men still turned out in droves to watch the squadrons compete at baseball.

BOTTOM LEFT The Engineer's camp featured a dirt basketball court and, if you note, a movie screen at the far end under the trees.

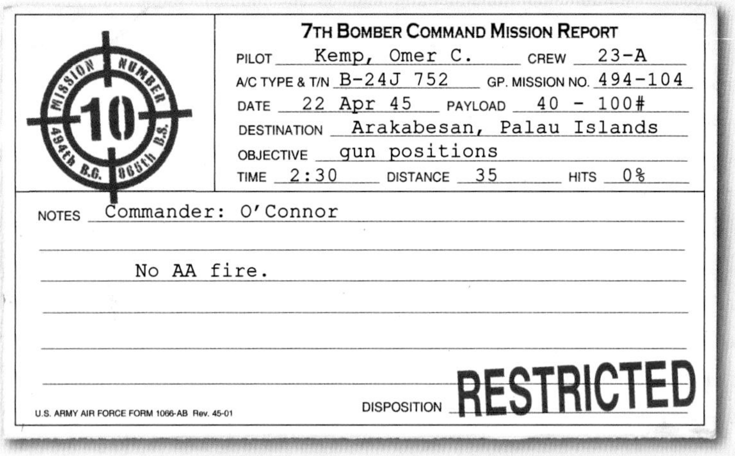

7th Bomber Command Mission Report

PILOT Kemp, Omer C. CREW 23-A
A/C TYPE & T/N B-24J 752 GP. MISSION NO. 494-104
DATE 22 Apr 45 PAYLOAD 40 - 100#
DESTINATION Arakabesan, Palau Islands
OBJECTIVE gun positions
TIME 2:30 DISTANCE 35 HITS 0%

NOTES Commander: O'Connor

No AA fire.

U.S. ARMY AIR FORCE FORM 1066-AB Rev. 45-01 DISPOSITION RESTRICTED

MOPPING UP THE PALAUS

In the push west across the Pacific, many islands had been skipped that still held Japanese defenders, now cut off from any hope of victory or even supply, but they were not dampened in their desire to harass nearby shipping and overflights. Though they were not a priority, when the Mindanao land invasion began and the work for heavy bombers was done, Col. Kelley turned his attention to quieting the remaining Japanese in the Palaus.

So for the next three weeks they hit Koror and Arakabesan, two islands linked by a short bridge in the middle of the chain north of Angaur, the shortest flights of the War, though not necessarily the easiest. Let O.C. tell it:

AUDIO TRANSCRIPT 11:03:10

We went on "milk runs," as we called them, to bomb the bypassed Palau islands. We had to fly upward in a spiral until we got high enough to drop our bombs, because the target was only 35 miles from Angaur.

We had cut the Japs off from resupply, so they were saving their ammo and normally didn't fire at overflights. But if they saw us coming in with our bomb bay doors open, they knew they were in for it and would start shooting their heads off.

LEFT In a picture taken November 1944, Arakabesan Island can be seen off the Liberator's left wing tip, its seaplane base smoking from the bomb strike. Arakabesan lies across a short causeway from Koror Island, which was the center of Japanese Southwest Pacific presence until it was cut off entirely in late 1944.

Crew 23A's mission that day was to hit the gun emplacements surrounding the seaplane base, but they were unsuccessful and did not register any hits.

Unfortunately, the artillery on Koror and Arakabesan would continue in operation and would eventually down *brief*, an 867th bomber, a month later.

TRAINED ON TARGET

When engaging in bombing runs involving two dozen aircraft over great distances, little time was wasted grouping together for the long flight to the objective, so planes roared off the runway once a minute. One pilot described the line of B-24s waiting their turn as a "phalanx of elephants that, while lumbering on the ground, were elegant fliers."

RIGHT The traditional diamond formation flown to and from objectives was abandoned once they neared the target. Lack of intercepting fighters meant they did not need mutual fire support, and a "trail" formation, with a lead plane gauging target and bomb-drop timing, meant the following aircraft dropped their bombs in succession, known as "toggling." Not everyone did this—Jack Berger refused to toggle as a matter of principle—but most other bombardiers had no such compunction. The result was either near-perfect hit rates or mission-wide misses.

THE THACH WEAVE

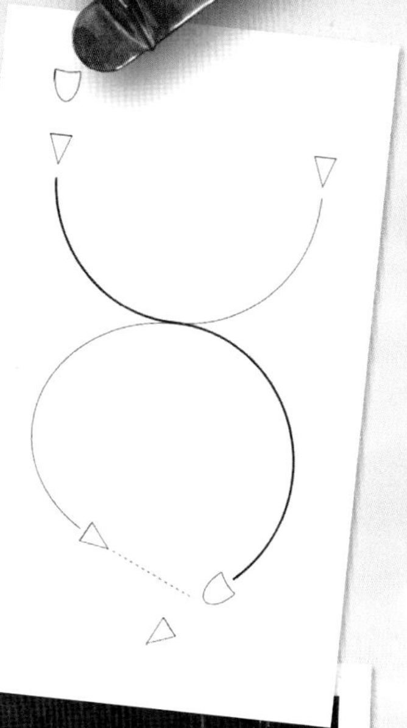

Early in the War, the faster and more maneuverable Zeros made mincemeat of Navy 4F4 Wildcats in dogfights. In response, aviator John Thach, working out the details with matches on a desktop, developed what he called the "Beam Defense Position," but which shortly became known as the "Thach Weave."

It was executed by two aircraft flying side-by-side. Whichever one found himself with a Zero on his tail became the "bait." The other was the "hook." They would suddenly turn toward each other and cross paths, each fighter drawing a wide arc and then heading back toward the other with the effect that suddenly the Zero would find himself head-on with the hook and little chance of escape.

Saburō Sakai, the famous Japanese ace, after encountering the tactic over Guadalcanal, said, "Two Wildcats jumped Commander Nakajima's plane. He had no trouble getting on the tail of an enemy fighter, but never had a chance to fire before the teammate roared at him from the side. Nakajima was raging when he got back to Rabaul; he had been forced to dive and run for safety."

First used at Midway, the Thach Weave worked successfully throughout the War. It is still an effective dogfight tactic today.

HALF-WAY THROUGH THE ALPHABET

They were still improving the B-24. By December, the Group had 53 J models, though they were eagerly awaiting the arrival of the Ls, which reduced weight by replacing the Sperry ball dorsal turret with a pair of ring-mounted .50 caliber machine guns and a tail turret with improved visibility. In February 1945, the Ms started arriving with even more weight-saving characteristics, a better rear turret (right) and a retractable Sperry ball ventral turret. The M was the last variant produced in quantity (1,600) and the last ones flew only between the factory and the scrap heap after the War.

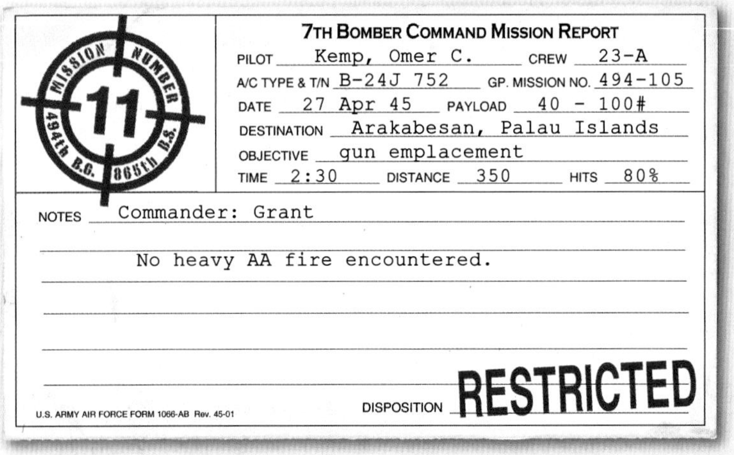

MISSION NUMBER 11 494th B.G. 865th B.S.

7TH BOMBER COMMAND MISSION REPORT

PILOT Kemp, Omer C. CREW 23-A

A/C TYPE & T/N B-24J 752 GP. MISSION NO. 494-105

DATE 27 Apr 45 PAYLOAD 40 - 100#

DESTINATION Arakabesan, Palau Islands

OBJECTIVE gun emplacement

TIME 2:30 DISTANCE 350 HITS 80%

NOTES Commander: Grant

No heavy AA fire encountered.

U.S. ARMY AIR FORCE FORM 1066-AB Rev. 45-01

DISPOSITION RESTRICTED

GOING BACK FOR SECONDS

As they turned their attention to the northern Palaus, which had been bypassed when the Army and Marines invaded the two southernmost islands of Peleliu and Angaur the previous September, the 494th was reminded that the enemy was still capable of delivering a knock-out punch.

On this particular mission, seven out of 25 planes returned with flak damage, though none were damaged beyond repair. This made the brass decide evasive training was in order and the final mission, taking place 28 April, benefitted from the training and flak hits were avoided.

The Mission Report says they carried forty 100# bombs. The usual complement of bombs is thirty, so they were likely dropping M-31 incendiary cluster bombs with fins that spun the bomb on descent, creating centrifugal force that popped the canister open, releasing 38 sub-munitions charges over a wide area, initiating fires upon impact. They scored an 80% hit rate in keeping with the 494th's highest-in-the-Pacific bombing accuracy rate.

UPPER RIGHT Arakabesan Island as seen from 10,000 feet. The causeway to Koror island at the right is clearly seen. The seaplane base and its gun emplacements are on the southwest side of the island, already reduced to rubble from dozens of previous bombing runs, but when reconnaissance photos showed repairs to buildings, runways, or docks, more missions were scheduled to drive the defenders back into the caves they inhabited.

WELCOME, YANKEE

"With considerable surprise and amusement," said Major General Willis Hale, "we noted this greeting placed for us by the Japs on one of their runways." As seen by the craters in the photo at right on either side of the message, the 494th had a message of their own.

brief FILE 13

Editorial by Sgt Roger Angell

The war, it would seem, is being cleaned up, just like burlesque. In Europe higher-ups have complained about the charms of Toni Seven, the pinup queen, whose photos are said to be interfering with the war effort. And out here censorship took the form of an order to remove all pinup girls, names, and cartoons from the Superforts.

We don't know the reason for this—probably some women's club wrote from home that the dear boys were being corrupted by pictures of undressed women on the noses of bombers—but it marks the end of a great tradition and means the loss of one of the last personal touches in an already impersonal war. Most of the bomber crews we know named their planes at first only because it was expected of them, but after a couple of rugged missions, the plane became as close to them as anyone in the crew and they would rather have parted with their wings than with their insigne.

Most of the names mean something only to the crews. But occasionally they became outlets for GI humor. One crew, with no illusions about its job, named its bomber *A Tisket, A Tasket—Ten Men in a Flying Casket.* Then there was the takeoff of the usual Varga-Petty girl—the Liberator with the drooping squatty Indian squaw named *Consolidated Mess* (left). There's a fighter called *Is This Trip Necessary?* And one crew thought for weeks with no success, finally said the hell with it and named their plane *Eat at Joe's Place.*

We think there are two contributing factors to the ruling about the B-29s. First, the Superfortress crews really went all out and painted up some super-naked queens with names to match. *Luscious Lucy* and other B-29s with more unprintable names were more likely to arouse official action than *Suzy-Q* and some of the innocent B-17s back at the beginning of the war. But even more telling, we think, was the fact that the '29s are really long-range planes that can fly into combat from islands far to the rear. The B-25s and even the Liberators had to be quite close to the enemy to bomb him and there was less chance of having Red Cross girls around the flight lines to see and be shocked by the bomber insignia.

If the action was taken because of complaints about morality, we'd like to point out that there's nothing so likely to have a permanent effect on an innocent young gunner as a Jap anti-aircraft shell. And any weapon, whether it is a flak suit for his torso or a nude for his morale, should be made available to him.

RIGHT SECOND FROM BOTTOM O.C. and friends try to act casual while posing with *Hay Maker.*
BOTTOM RIGHT The B-29 flight crew removes newly unacceptable nose art from *Wheelin' Deal.*
BOTTOM LEFT Anticipating the censors, the *Eight Ball* artist worked the restrictions into his art.

DEALING WITH IT

One of the chief causes of what we now call Post-Traumatic Stress Disorder (PTSD) but was then simply called "combat fatigue" is the emotional chasm between the unrelenting boredom on base and the super-charged pressure of combat, which for bombing crews in the South Pacific might only last for the few minutes they were over the target, but were nevertheless astonishing in their intensity, leaving many men unable to even remember what had happened, though they retained the sick-gut feeling of seeing the sky in front of them fill with smoky clouds of bursting flak.

Lower bombing altitudes, exposing them to small arms fire (which could easily pierce the thin aluminum skin and puncture a hydraulic line and turn the plane—which was nothing more than a flying bomb anyway—into a fireball hurtling toward the earth) only increased the pressure.

So in a time when men did not readily admit fear, you've got a lot of bottled-up suffering and the reader might better understand the following transcript that relates a seemingly banal activity as actually quite effective therapy, with the added benefit of pleasing the girl back home for whom the airman believed he was making this sacrifice.

AUDIO TRANSCRIPT 10:06:55

The enlisted men lived close by in one tent, but we four officers had quarters on the beach. It was great because there was a lagoon about three feet deep right in front of us and no waves because of the reef, which stood about a hundred yards offshore. We had snorkels and masks that our folks sent us and we used them to find these little shells to make necklaces for our girlfriends at home.

And all the stainless steel wire, instead of being used for securing bolts on engines, was being used to make necklaces. Stainless steel wire, of course, won't rust, and so it was nice stuff to make jewelry out of. I guess the War Department wondered how could they be safetying so many bolts down out there?

We'd go out there with a coffee can and our masks and float along and gather these shells up. Most were small, though there were a few brown ones with speckles about an inch and a half long, but they were rare. The lagoon was pretty well picked over by the time I got there.

Back on the beach, we'd poke holes in the can and set it by the base of a palm tree and the ants would find it and in about two weeks they'd systematically scour those shells as clean as a hound's tooth. We'd always keep a bunch of shells in process while we were stringing others into necklaces.

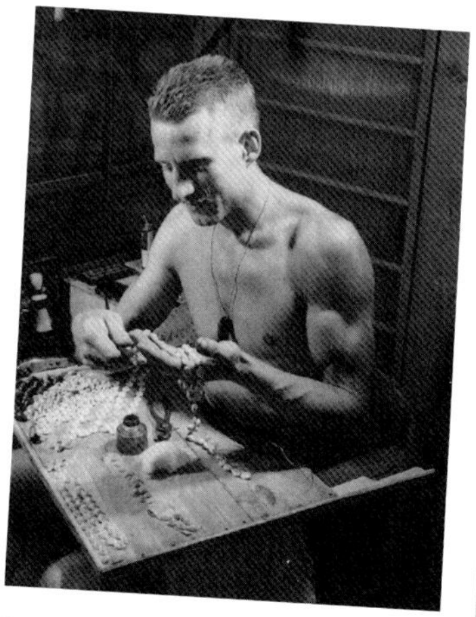

We'd take a pair of long-nosed pliers and make a loop of stainless steel wire and bend the wire down inside this little slit in the shell and then pull it taut. Then make another loop at the other end of the shell and poke it down inside the shell, and then take airplane glue and glue the slit closed so the wire couldn't pull out.

That was what we did to waste time while we waited for flying shifts.

THE MALES HERE!

In 1945, only 20% percent of American homes had a telephone. That was fine; they didn't have much time to chat anyway, what with only 2% having refrigerators (which meant Mom went to market *every* day) and only 3% owning washing machines (and wash day was *all* day).

For national news, everyone read the paper and listened to the radio. For family news, everyone wrote letters. There were so many that the Post Office delivered mail twice a day. A first class stamp was 3¢; air mail 6¢.

But outside the U.S., delivery schedules were slow. It might take months for letters to reach GIs. But when they did, it was like manna in the desert. Besides Tokyo Rose, it was often the only news of home servicemen got.

MILTON CANIFF, PATRIOT

Milt Caniff, creator of two hugely popular adventure comic strips in the 1930s aimed at boys young and old ("Dickie Dare" and "Terry and the Pirates"), was 4F but still found a way to serve, creating "Male Call," which appeared only in military newspapers during the War. He lifted the mysterious and exotic "Burma" from "Terry and the Pirates," adapting her into the beautiful and secretly savvy "Miss Lace," who seemed to live near every military base and enjoyed the company of enlisted men, whom she always addressed as "General."

Caniff said Miss Lace's function was to remind servicemen what they were fighting for, and while the strip brimmed with double entendre, Miss Lace was not a loose woman, though she certainly knew the score. "Male Call" was notable for its honest depiction of what servicemen were up against. The sample below depicts not only Caniff's excellent illustrative abilities, but his big heart and respect for his country's defenders.

SNAFU, SUSFU & FUBAR

These words are acronyms for well-known salty phrases that epitomize the often incomprehensible nature of military life: a million ways things could go wrong: an engine out, inclement weather, disorientation at night over water, and the just plain inexplicable combinations of human and material failings that were responsible for so many pointless deaths during the War. As far as the Army Air Force went, bad luck was probably responsible for more deaths than actual combat.

O.C. had witnessed a number of these on Missions 5 & 7 and had a couple of close encounters himself on later missions. The one he talks about on tape (below) wasn't identified with any particular mission, but it's included here because "pilot error" is often a chief contributing factor to a SNAFU. As O.C. once famously said, "The reason they call it 'pilot error' is you get just one of 'em."

AUDIO TRANSCRIPT 13:05:50

One time I took off and #3 engine quit and so I said, "Well, that's it," and I yanked the release handle by my seat and salvoed my bombs. And then I realized, "Gee, I should have looked to see if there was anyone below."

Luckily, I just bombed the ocean.

After I went around and landed, I realized that the #3 engine toggle switch had stuck. All I had to do was push it forward and the engine came right back on.

But when you're having engine trouble you can't mess around. Besides, I didn't want to go on that mission anyway.

These events were so commonplace that every crew had harrowing stories like this to tell at the mess table. Of course most men survived, but the records are full of situations where lives were lost due to miscalculations, a bad wheel bearing, lack of proper planning, incorrect intelligence, and even downright carelessness.

And as for carelessness, remember that the average age of these crews was twenty years old and they thought they were indestructible.

AUDIO TRANSCRIPT 13:06:00

A crew was taking off from Angaur at night and they were rolling down the runway when the #4 engine quit. They were busy trying to straighten the thing out and they pulled it off the runway because they ran out of ground. They were loaded with a bunch of airplane parts in boxes [the Group was moving to Okinawa and the B-24s were transporting materials] that they couldn't salvo like we would bombs. They didn't even have time to get the gear up. They were at maximum power, speeding off the end of the runway into the darkness, and were going to swing around and land, but just as they started making their crosswind turn, the #1 engine quit and after that they were just like a streamlined brick. They went right into the ocean.

The engineer was standing on the catwalk [the narrow walkway between bomb racks in the bomb bay] when the plane hit the water with the wheels down. It just disintegrated, throwing him out in the water. He got a gash on his leg and that's all. But about half of the crew died.

Those were some of our most dangerous flights, not even against the enemy, just ferrying parts or people or just going from one point to another.

AUDIO TRANSCRIPT 09:03:18

The engines have to be synchronized. If every engine isn't trimmed to the exact same RPM, they make a strange cycling sound. So you look at the gauges and see one that's a little high or a little low and you nudge the switch until it smooths out.

Every once in a while when the engines are singing along like that, one will start to pitch up in sound, cycling faster, and you'll kind of wake up and look and set the trim and quiet it back down. You're supposed to keep an eye on the gauges anyway. And Engineering comes up to see if the cylinder head pressure is up or not and you check the manifold pressure and the RPM.

You also have to pitch the propeller. If the pitch is too shallow, it spins faster and won't do as much work so you back it off to get a bigger bite of air. Props run at about 2150 RPM for cruising speed. If you want to go faster, you bring it up between 2200 and 2400 RPM by putting more throttle on, but you burn a lot of gas that way.

You get the settings right, use the right amount of gas, and you get there. One plane coming over from Hawaii crashed because the crew didn't pay attention to their settings. They didn't know what they were doing and they all died.

HONOR FROM A GRATEFUL NATION

BELOW With the Philippines now freed, the grateful nation awarded the Allied participants the Liberation Ribbon. The only blemish on the honor was that only airmen received it; ground crews were excluded and hard feelings ensued, including the following: "Aren't we just as responsible for dropping those bombs as the bombardier that hunched over the bombsight? Aren't we just as essential?" Nevertheless, the brass, in its wisdom, did not extend the honor to them. Note also that, due to his efforts, O.C.'s crew of six enlisted men have all been promoted. Instead of lowly corporals they are all now "buck" sergeants.

R E S T R I C T E D

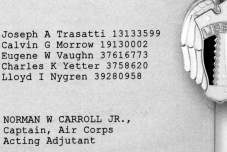

SPECIAL ORDERS 79

Hq 494th Bomb Group (H)
APO #264
26 April 1945

E X T R A C T

3. Under the provisions of General Order #23 Hq US Army Forces in the Far East APO 501 dtd 5 Feb 45 awarding Service Ribbons of the Commonwealth of the Philippines the fol Officers and EM, are, under the provisions of par 2b (1) (b) of the above cited order authorized to wear the Philippine Liberation Ribbon for participation against the enemy over Philippine territory and under enemy fire during the Liberation Campaign. Commanders concerned will make appropriate entries in Service Records, Soldier qualification Cards (WD AGO Form 20) and Officer's Qualification Card (WD AGO Form 66-2) referring to the service rendered by the individual and the General Order cited herein:

865th Bomb Sq (H)

2nd Lt	(1092)	OMER C KEMP 0710957	Sgt	(612)	Joseph A Trasatti 13133599
2nd Lt	(1055)	NORMAN J OLSON 0927583	Sgt	(757)	Calvin G Morrow 19130002
2nd Lt	(1036)	FREDERICK C SPERLING JR 02060604	Sgt	(611)	Eugene W Vaughn 37616773
2nd Lt	(1035)	JACK A BERGER 0928139	Sgt	(611)	Charles K Yetter 3758620
Sgt	(737)	Juan F Gutierrez 39550289	Sgt	(612)	Lloyd I Nygren 39280958

BY ORDER OF COLONEL KELLEY:

NORMAN W CARROLL JR.,
Captain, Air Corps
Acting Adjutant

DISTRIBUTION "A" PLUS
1 ea 201 file.

APRIL ON ANGAUR

PERSONNEL STRENGTH By the end of the month, there were 606 officers, 2029 enlisted men assigned and six officers and forty enlisted men attached to the 494th. They also shared the island with the 20th Bomb Group.

OPERATIONAL LOSSES Two B-24s were lost, both to operational causes. One was taxiing and broke through the coral surface, its wheel penetrating the roof of a Japanese bunker that had not been properly backfilled during grading of the airfield. Seven enemy aircraft were shot down.

MISSION Continued guerilla support on Mindanao through destruction of Japanese personnel and supplies. Also, neutralized northern Palau Islands of Koror and Arakabesan. Fourteen missions occurred, involving an average of 24 aircraft per mission.

CONTROL After serving under the Far East Air Forces under the 13th Air Force since December 1944, control of the 494th reverted to the 7th Air Force.

BLIND BOMBING TRAINING Twenty aircraft are now radar-equipped. Crews were trained in radar bombing techniques through overcast clouds using live bombs over Yap island. The target island was changed after the enemy on Yap started firing on the planes, making the experience a little bit too real for a training mission.

ENGINE SHORTAGE The Group now has 70 bombers, including ten M variants. Three "war weary" planes were retired and the critical engine shortage in March was overcome with the delivery of 150 new engines.

MORALE War news was good, fresh food was available, and the beer ration rose to twelve cans per enlisted man per week. The USO show "Girl Crazy" arrived on the island along with seven female dancers and singers, the first women seen on Angaur in eight months. Better movies were shown. The 494th baseball team lost to the All-stars of the Palau Island League in three well-played games.

RELIGION 1,100 men showed up for Easter sunrise services and gave a record missionary offering of $1,600. Attendance at services continued to be large. Twelve men were baptized in the ocean by Chaplain Dowden.

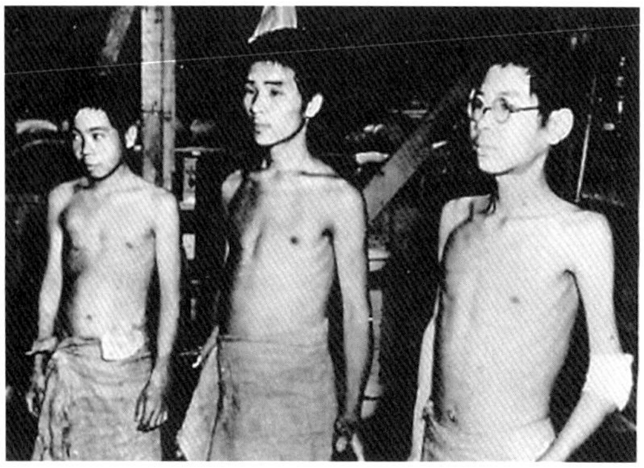

JAPANESE PRISONERS Though the island was declared secure in November, there were still some Japanese fighters in hiding, infiltrating at night to steal food and occasionally sniping from the jungle. Some were even seen watching baseball games from a safe distance and movies at night. When encountered, most of them fought and had to be killed, but a few were captured. The photo at left shows just how young some of these fighters were.

PACIFIC OPERATIONS AREA

27 April - 14 May 1945
Depot Army Air Field
Guam, Marianas Islands
DETACHED SERVICE
11th Bombardment Group (H)
7th Army Air Force

Depot Field was one of five airfields built by the Seabees after the conquest of Guam in mid-August 1944. It was later named Harmon Field after General Millard F. Harmon who died on a flight to Hawaii in March 1945. Despite an intensive search, no trace of his aircraft was ever found.

But when O.C. and Crew 23A landed there, it was still called Depot Field and served as the HQ for the XXI Bomber Command and later the 20th Air Force, which directed the B-29 strategic bombing campaign against mainland Japan. It was also the major B-29 aircraft depot and maintenance facility in the Western Pacific during the War, a mission that continued until it was subsumed into the new Won Pat International Airport in 1949.

"Dear Mom," wrote O.C. "I'm doing a bit of traveling. We flew up to the Marianas and right now I'm at [CENSORED]. We've bombed Truk atoll for two days straight. I'm living with four crews of officers in a Quonset hut. I like it here."

YOU ONLY SHOOT THE ONES YOU LOVE

Jay Kemp was an ordnance man in Navy fighter squadron VF-99, stationed on Guam at Orote Field, about ten miles west of Depot Field. He and his cousin O.C. kept in touch during the War and when O.C. flew in on 27 April for detached service with the 11th Bomb Group for a few missions, O.C. looked Jay up. Jay tells the story this way:

> We were getting ready to hit the sack, writing letters home, cleaning our guns and shooting the breeze. The camp was quiet and our flaps were closed. Someone was telling a story of a Jap who was sneaking into camp at night to steal food. One night he lifted a tent flap and cut the throat of a sleeping sailor. We all shivered, wondering if that could happen to us. We often heard gun shots at night, but it was usually someone shooting a rat. If you got one, you put a rat silhouette above your tent entrance to show how many you'd killed. By the time we left Guam, we had three.
>
> Just then we heard muffled voices outside and someone started messing with the tent flaps. We all lunged for our pistols. The flaps flew apart and a guy wearing an Army pilot's cap thrust his head into the tent. "Is Jay Kemp in here?" he asked nervously, seeing all our guns pointed at him.
>
> I laid down my pistol and gave my cousin a big hug.

SIDE-STEPPED ISLANDS

The Caroline Islands, a 2,000 mile wide archipelago north of New Guinea, contains 500 tiny islands, not one of which you've heard. It is bracketed on the east by the Marshalls and on the west by the Marianas. In February 1944, during Operation Hailstone, between the assaults on Kwajalein and Eniwetok in the Marshalls, the Navy pushed another 800 miles west to make a daring daylight raid on the 120 square mile Truk atoll, which for good reason was called the "Gibraltar of the Pacific" as it was dotted with command centers, seaplane bases, naval bases, air fields, and repair facilities, all protected by daunting anti-aircraft emplacements.

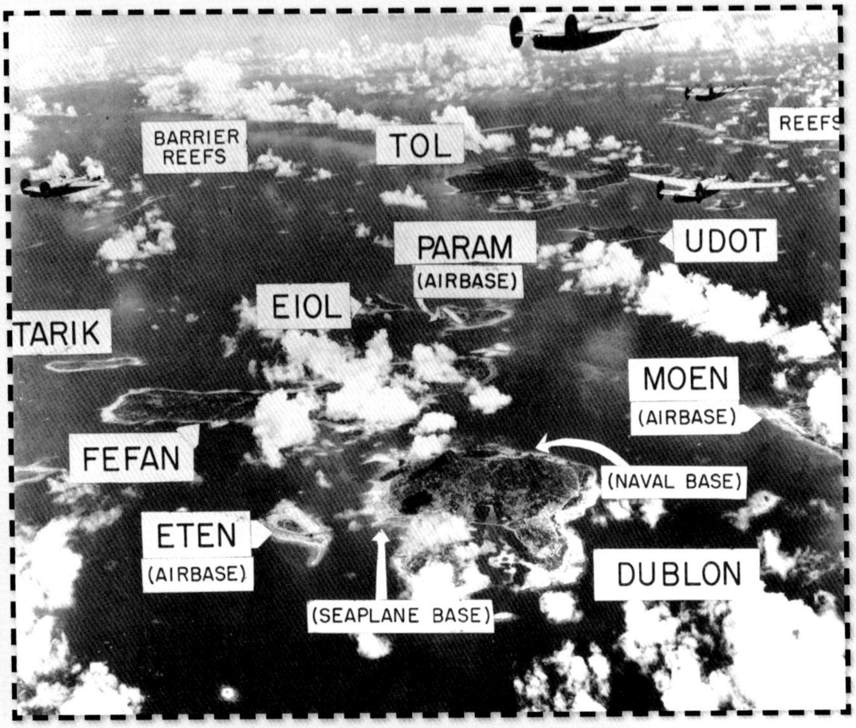

But luck was with us and on 17 February our surprise attack destroyed 50 ships and 250 aircraft (most still on the ground), ending Truk's threat to Allied operations in the Central Pacific. And when we invaded Eniwetok atoll the next day there was no hope of resupply for the defenders.

The Japanese knew Truk was next in line after the Marshalls and had already moved most of their operations south to Rabaul on New Britain Island, but they later sent 100 aircraft back to hold the atoll. A month later U.S. carrier forces destroyed most of them.

With Truk isolated, we skipped the rest of the Carolines, leapfrogging west to the Marianas to take Saipan and Guam, then turning south to the Palaus and north to the Volcanic Islands and Iwo Jima.

Truk still harassed overflights and attacked passing convoys, but was mostly ignored until April when the Philippines campaign ended. With the battle for Okinawa also coming to a close, the 494th and the 11th bomb groups would be moving their bases to the Ryukyu Islands, south of Japan.

So with the time that remained, they set about mopping up the Carolines. On 28 April, 48 planes of the 494th flew to Guam to assist the 11th in terminating Truk resistance once and for all. Over the next two weeks, the two bomb groups alternated daily strikes. By the time Japan surrendered in August, the cave-dwelling Truk survivors were starving.

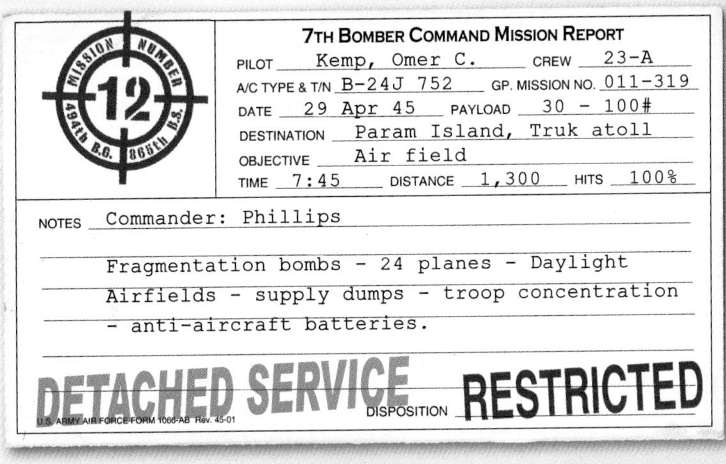

MISSION NUMBER 12 — 494th B.G. 865th B.S.

7TH BOMBER COMMAND MISSION REPORT

PILOT Kemp, Omer C. CREW 23-A
A/C TYPE & T/N B-24J 752 GP. MISSION NO. 011-319
DATE 29 Apr 45 PAYLOAD 30 - 100#
DESTINATION Param Island, Truk atoll
OBJECTIVE Air field
TIME 7:45 DISTANCE 1,300 HITS 100%

NOTES Commander: Phillips

Fragmentation bombs - 24 planes - Daylight
Airfields - supply dumps - troop concentration
- anti-aircraft batteries.

DETACHED SERVICE
DISPOSITION RESTRICTED

U.S. ARMY AIR FORCE FORM 1066-AB Rev. 45-01

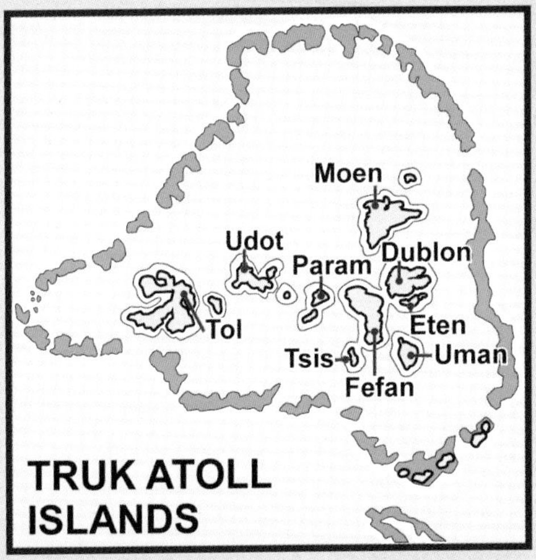

BULLS EYE

Param is a small island in the center of Truk atoll, a perfect target and easily picked out from the others because it has the same pork chop shape as Angaur.

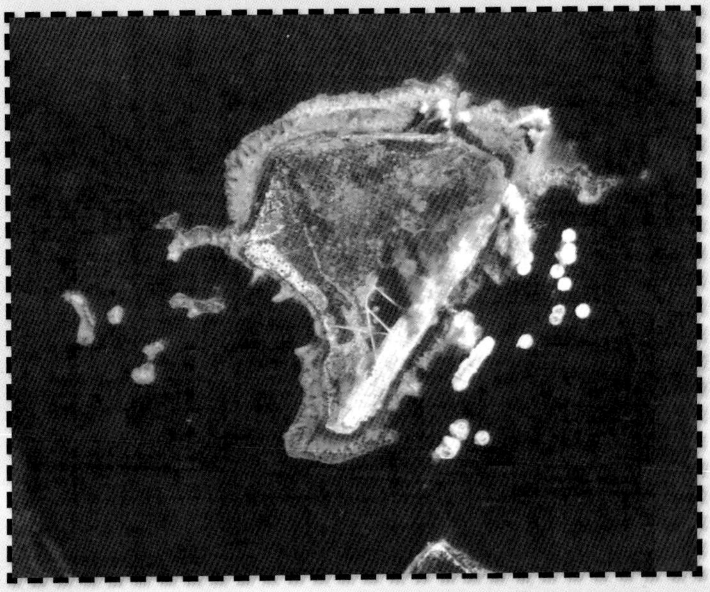

RIGHT The single runway on the southern side of the island has been hit time and time again. This time the targets are wooded areas in the island's center shielding ammo dumps and troop billets. The jungle has been heavily pock-marked by previous bombing runs.

BELOW LEFT Photo Intelligence revealed Japanese fighters nestling in semi-circular revetments near taxiways which were repaired after the last strike, which meant the fighters are flying sorties and must be stopped from leaving the ground again. The island is heavily fortified by numerous anti-aircraft batteries.

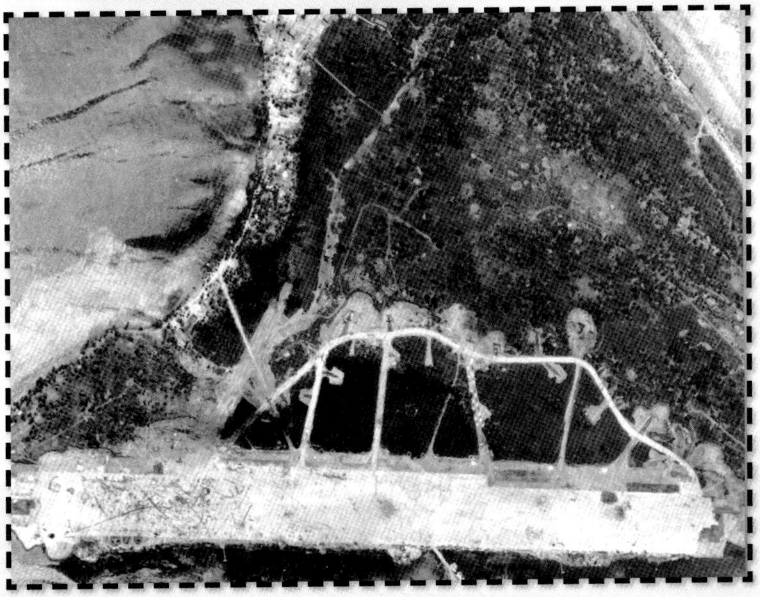

The mission priority is destroying the aircraft, but none were sighted during the last two missions. As they approached the tiny island at about 10:00 a.m., the weather was clear. No flak or artillery fire was reported. The island looked like it was asleep.

They would wake it up.

A few miles out, O.C. turned the controls over to Jack Berger, who guided the plane over the target. At the precise moment, he toggled the "bombs away" switch and let loose with thirty 100 pound fragmentation bombs. As always, Berger's aim was good. 100% of his bombs hit their target.

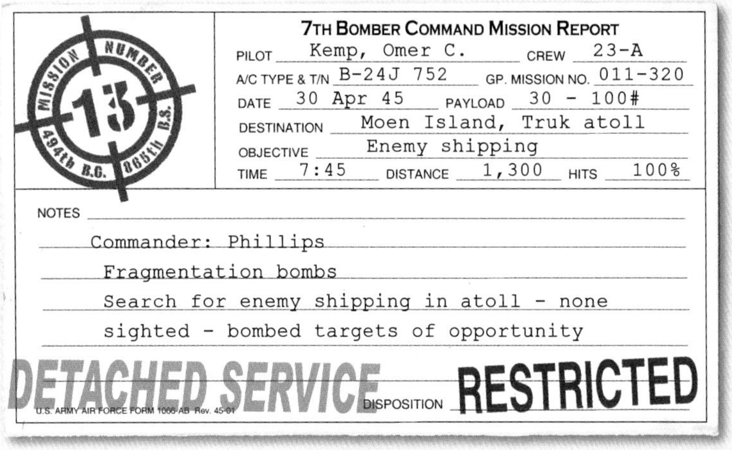

MISSION NUMBER 13 494th B.G. 865th B.S.

7TH BOMBER COMMAND MISSION REPORT

PILOT Kemp, Omer C. CREW 23-A

A/C TYPE & T/N B-24J 752 GP. MISSION NO. 011-320

DATE 30 Apr 45 PAYLOAD 30 - 100#

DESTINATION Moen Island, Truk atoll

OBJECTIVE Enemy shipping

TIME 7:45 DISTANCE 1,300 HITS 100%

NOTES

Commander: Phillips

Fragmentation bombs

Search for enemy shipping in atoll - none sighted - bombed targets of opportunity

DETACHED SERVICE

DISPOSITION RESTRICTED

U.S. ARMY AIR FORCE FORM 1066-AB Rev. 45-01

TARGETS OF OPPORTUNITY

Moen Island, just north of the main base on Dublon Island, supports two large airfields. Airstrip #1 in the foreground of the photo below is also a seaplane base, as seen by the ramp extending into the water from the runway. Airfield #2 is in the upper left corner, the objective for this mission.

It would be attacked in a raid featuring 24 aircraft from the 494th. Fragmentation bombs were placed aboard each aircraft to maximize damage to machinery, buildings, and any nearby aircraft. If there were no aircraft present on the air field and no evidence of repair thereof, pilots were encouraged to search the 120 square mile atoll for Japanese activity and to bomb "targets of opportunity" that presented themselves. The Mission Report notes that they saw little activity in the atoll and so they dropped their bombs on the airfield.

BELOW LEFT Craters have been filled in. Tractor marks indicate the job was not complete when 7th AAF Liberators salvoed another cluster of quarter-ton bombs on the right end of the strip.

RIGHT Bomb bursts blanket shops, hangars and aircraft hardstands on Airstrip #2 as *Madame Pele* leaves its target. The B-24 was bought with the proceeds from Honolulu school children's war bond purchases and named after the Hawaiian goddess of fire.

INDIVIDUAL FLIGHT RECORD	O.C. KEMP
STATION	APO 264 (Angaur Army Air Field)
FLYING CLASSIFICATION	Plt. 2-9-44
ORGANIZATION ASSIGNED	7th AAF, 494th BG, 865th BS
MONTH	**April 1945**
AIRCRAFT TYPE	B-24J, B-24L
LANDINGS	15
COMMAND PILOT	
CO-PILOT	20:55
QUALIFIED PILOT (DUAL)	
FIRST PILOT (DAY)	21:15
FIRST PILOT (NIGHT)	
NON-PILOT DUTY	
INSTRUMENT (DAY)	
INSTRUMENT (NIGHT)	
INSTRUMENT TRAINER	
TOTAL TIME THIS MONTH	42:10
TOTAL PILOT TIME TO DATE	707:50

ABOVE O.C. flew five missions in April, but also did training runs on islands in the Palaus, which accounts for the fifteen landings. He also got his first ride on a B-29 while in Guam. "It really is a slick plane," he wrote home. "I hope to get one of those when I get back to the States. If I can't, then I'll take jet propulsion!"

BELOW No one is raising his pay and he's still sending $150.00 a month home to his folks. In addition, he tithes ten percent of his pay to his church while he is overseas. Flight insurance, perhaps?

WAR DEPARTMENT

PAY AND ALLOWANCE ACCOUNT

(Commissioned Officers, Army Nurses, Warrant Officers, Contract Surgeons)

CREDITS:	Amount
(6) For base and longevity pay from 1 April, 19 45, to 30 April, 19 45	$ 150.00
(7) For additional pay for Foreign Service, from 1 April, 19 45 to 30 April, 19 45	15.00
(8) For pay for Flying Pay, from 1 April, 19 45, to 30 April, 19 45	82.50
(9) For subsistence allowance from 1 April, 19 45, to 30 April, 19 45	21.00
TOTAL CREDITS	$ 268.50

DEBITS:		
(12) Class "E" Allotment of $150.00 per mo eff 1 Jan 45.................	$ 150.00	
(13) Class "N" National Service Life Insurance $6.50 Apr 45....................	6.50	
(14) Due United States for 93 meals fur during Apr 45 @ .25 per meal...	23.25	
TOTAL DEBITS		$ 179.75
NET BALANCE		$ 88.75

(18) Paid by Cash, $ 88.75, on 30 April, 19 45.

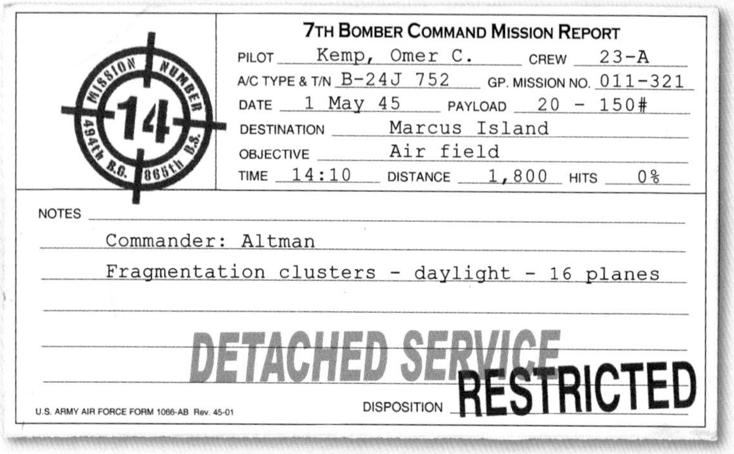

7TH BOMBER COMMAND MISSION REPORT

MISSION NUMBER 14 — 494th B.G. 865th B.S.

PILOT Kemp, Omer C. CREW 23-A
A/C TYPE & T/N B-24J 752 GP. MISSION NO. 011-321
DATE 1 May 45 PAYLOAD 20 - 150#
DESTINATION Marcus Island
OBJECTIVE Air field
TIME 14:10 DISTANCE 1,800 HITS 0%

NOTES
Commander: Altman
Fragmentation clusters - daylight - 16 planes

DETACHED SERVICE
DISPOSITION RESTRICTED

U.S. ARMY AIR FORCE FORM 1066-AB Rev. 45-01

MISSION TO MARCUS

Here we have a first person report in the form of an English paper O.C. wrote in college after the War:

We were staging through Depot Field in Guam against by-passed islands which needed a good going over. The previous days we had hit Truk atoll twice with a perfect score—no flak holes—and were ready for Marcus, a tiny island farther from land than any other island in the Pacific. It was hardly bigger than the chevron-shaped air field on it, and if you could locate it, it made a very satisfying target. But finding it was always a problem.

Our planes did not have radar and since there was no LORAN signal coming from Marcus (the Japanese didn't want us to find it either), we had to navigate by celestial observation, risky because the tiniest error over 1,000 miles could mean missing the target by 50 miles. But Fred Sperling was our navigator and we were not worried. (We should have been, though what happened that day was no fault of Fred's.)

But finding Marcus was just the first problem. Once found, we would face what were reported to be the most accurate flak batteries in the entire Pacific. Some of Japan's best gunners must have been stuck out there on that lonely coral triangle with nothing to do but shoot B-24s out of the sky. And they had done it more than once.

Our element of five Liberators (out of a flight of 16) left Guam at 7:00 A.M. (Six were scheduled but one had problems with his #3 engine and aborted.)

About two hours into the flight, huge storm clouds rose before us. The other thirteen planes went into the typhoon but Lt. Altman, our element leader, decided to go around. I wasn't happy about skirting the storm, which would cost precious time and fuel, but in the Air Force you follow the leader. "We're right behind you," I said and eased *Rover Boy's Baby* into a gentle right bank.

As we rounded the storm, which towered over us like immense breaking waves, we scanned the air for the rest of the mission aircraft and the ocean for Marcus. We saw neither. Dead reckoning indicated we were about fifteen minutes out. We should be seeing it by now but it was nowhere in sight. Just then Altman called, saying his navigator's sextant had gone out and asked if Fred could get a fix on where we were.

While Fred searched for a patch of blue in the clouds above us for a sighting, I banked gently, starting a "square search," a kind of widening spiral where each revolution is five miles bigger than the previous one, searching for Marcus. But there were just as many clouds below us as above. It was starting to look hopeless when the interphone crackled. "Captain," said Fred, anger heating his words. "We're twenty miles west of the target."

I asked engineer Juan Gutierrez how we looked for fuel. "Not good," he said. "We used up a lot going around the storm."

"How much left?" I persisted.

"Less than a third."

"And we're not even to the target!" someone said.

"Quiet!" I said, trying unsuccessfully to keep my voice flat and calm. "We're almost there. Bombing stations."

I relayed the information to Altman and we both turned eastward. Within minutes we were socked in again and Altman's plane, which had been off my left wing, had disappeared in the clouds.

As we approached the target, I silently calculated our odds of getting home and when I glanced over at Oly I saw his face change from concern to alarm. He'd read my thoughts in my eyes. "Lose the bombs, lose two tons," I said, turning and staring straight ahead.

"Ton and a half," said Oly, leaning the engines.

I rested my hand on the bomb bay door lever, ready to salvo our bombs and go home, when Jack Berger, our bombardier, said, "I see it."

"Where?" I asked. We were enveloped in clouds; I couldn't see a thing out my window.

"It's gone now," said Jack. "Socked in again."

"Well," I said. "Give it your best guess."

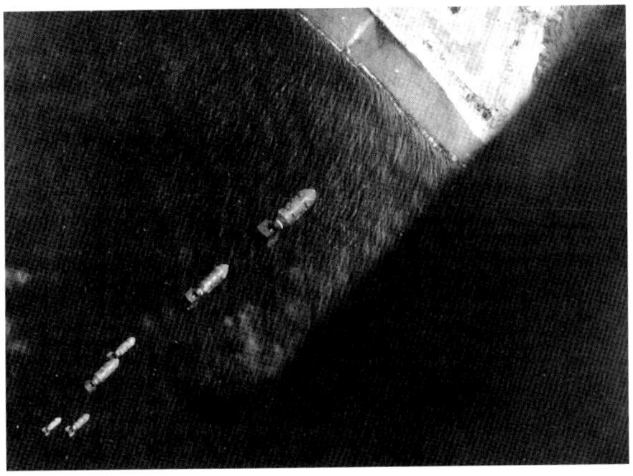

"Guessing," said Jack, and suddenly our aircraft shot upward, released from our heavy bomb load.

Suddenly Altman's plane filled my left window, so close I could see the startled expression on his co-pilot's face. I hauled the yoke back and to the right, and we narrowly avoided a midair collision. In another second he was gone, hidden again by the clouds.

"Holy cow!" said Oly.

"Let's get out of here," I said, and put the plane into a steep right bank. I was about to ask Fred for a vector when he spoke first: "Bearing one eight zero, distance niner seven zero miles, Skipper. Let's go home."

"Okay, boys," I said, "Let's lighten this bird."

Out went the ammo, the waist guns, and the oxygen tanks. If we could have pried off the belly turret, it would have gone too. Each pound we dropped gave us another minute, but we soon ran out of things to drop out the bomb bay doors. I cautioned the men to not throw the life rafts overboard. Someone laughed but I wasn't joking.

I raised the nose to a near stalling speed of 135 mph; cruise is around 160. After a long stretch, we emerged from the clouds. There were no other planes anywhere. The sun was setting in the west. Oly and I took our headsets off and started talking quietly between ourselves. Should we bail out and hope we'd be found or risk a night ditching?

I told Cal Morrow, our radio operator, to contact the Navy and give them the scoop. There must be Navy ships down there somewhere. He got a hold of them and the Navy said they'd track us and send up a Dumbo if we had to ditch.

I did not want to ditch; I'd heard too many horror stories about rough seas and cartwheeling airplanes, killing everyone on board. No, we would hazard it to Saipan, which would shave an hour from our flight. If we made it that far.

I asked Gutierrez about our fuel situation. "The sight gauges are just as inaccurate now as they were five minutes ago, sir," he said, "They show twenty five for each engine."

A B-24 burns 100 gallons an hour. Didn't Fred say we were still 200 miles out?

"Anything else we can throw out?" I asked.

"How about Trasatti?" said someone.

"Hey!" said our tail gunner.

The sun had set and Oly and I dimmed the instrument panel and peered into the darkness. With no moon, we could not tell where the sea ended and the sky began. Occasionally we'd see a light on the ocean but it would turn out to be a fishing boat or our imagination. Finally, we saw a string of lights on the horizon that had to be Saipan. (Like I said, we trusted Fred.)

If oxygen were fuel, we wouldn't have used an ounce those last fifteen minutes—everyone held their breath. Morrow contacted the Saipan tower, saying casually, "We're kind of low on fuel, so don't let anybody jump in line in front of us."

That drew nervous laughter from the crew.

I lined up the approach and heaved a sigh of relief as we passed over the fluorescent surf just fifty feet below us. When our wheels hit the coral runway with that familiar nails-on-chalkboard screech, everyone breathed again. I taxied to the apron and braked to a stop. Oly cut the engines. Soon we were enveloped in darkness and silence. I shivered, a bead of sweat trickling slowly down my spine.

Then we heard sirens and in a minute we were surrounded by fire trucks and emergency vehicles, followed by a lumbering fuel truck. We got out of the plane, its aluminum skin reflecting in the trucks' headlights. I flexed my knees, feeling the firmness of the taxiway under my feet. Yes, we were alive.

Suddenly everyone was lighting up and the fuel crew was shooing the smokers away from the plane. As we stood in the darkness watching them fuel *Rover Boy's Baby,* the same unspoken question was on everyone's mind.

When they finally coiled the black ribbed hose onto the rear of the truck, the fuel boss walked toward me, filling out a form on his clipboard. "Didn't know they held that much," he said, handing me the receipt and giving me a you-are-one-lucky-son-of-a-gun look.

"Three thousand two hundred nineteen gallons," said Oly, reading over my shoulder. "Oh my Lord."

"Just twenty five left," whistled Gutierrez.

I smiled. "That's fifteen minutes' worth. You call that close?"

Nine guys glared at me.

Back on Angaur, they'd given us up for dead but when we radioed that we'd made it to Saipan safely, they planned a warm welcome for us. When we returned to our base on Angaur a few days later, three thousand men lined the runway, cheering and saluting us. Crew 23A and *Rover Boy's Baby* had made it home.

BACK ROW, L TO R O.C. Kemp (p), Norman Olson (cp), Fred Sperling (n), Jack Berger (b)
FRONT ROW, L TO R Joe Trasatti (tg), Juan Gutierrez (e), Lloyd Nygren (g), Charles Yetter (g), Eugene Vaughan (g), Calvin Morrow (r)

. . . IS THERE A THIRD OPTION?

It's an age old debate: ditch or bail out? And it's not a "lady or tiger" choice; neither alternative is appetizing. Most fighter pilots know it's best to jump, as fighters ditch badly. Some bombers can belly land on a mild sea. Or so they say.

RIGHT Over 100 planes went down in the Pacific during the War and much was learned. To begin with, better life vests were developed, surpassing the traditional "Mae West." In addition, a life raft for every crew member made sense. Safety straps stretching from wall to wall protected crew members who sat under them from crashing into the ceiling on impact and, since they sat facing rearward, the sudden loss of momentum bent them back at the waist, thus reducing injury.

One of the most obvious changes in procedure was teaching men to swim. A surprising number could not, and thus drowned. Oxygen bottles were not to be jettisoned; they were good makeshift rafts. But everyone agreed on one thing: coming in, wheels down, on a long, dry, paved airstrip was the preferred landing for any plane.

NEVER FEAR, DUMBO'S HERE!

A grown man can be forgiven for crying when he sees Dumbo, especially if he's a downed flier floating in the ocean after a harrowing crash. The Navy's PBY Catalina float planes were named after the floppy-eared Disney cartoon character and they shadowed bombing missions, responding when needed. When fliers went down, they were instructed to not pop the canister of green marker dye into the water until they saw a Dumbo overhead. They also had signal mirrors, but in choppy seas, aiming the sun's reflection at an aircraft was difficult at best. By early 1945, Dumbos, the #1 goodwill ambassador between the Army and Navy, had rescued over 130 men and given many more confidence during missions across the seemingly endless seas.

YES, IT IS A SPACESHIP

It has room for an entire bomber crew. Dropped from a plane at 500 feet, this plywood motorboat glides to the water on three parachutes, rights itself after impact using rubber bladders, and ignites flares and rockets, making itself visible at night. It has two gas-powered motors plus a mast, mainsail and jib, a compass, and an eight-day clock. A small still operates whenever the motors are running, turning out a gallon of fresh water for every gallon of gas used. Heat from the engine provides warmth and comfort for injured men. A waterproof Gibson girl radio emits an automatic SOS or keyed signals. Gunnel lockers contain clothing, raincoats, blankets, a first-aid kit with dried plasma, and food for thirty days. A waterproof tarp, blue on one side to avoid detection from the air and yellow on the other to signal rescue craft, acts as a sun shield and a rain-catcher in wet weather. So yes, the clever innovations packing this 25-foot life-saver qualify it as a true space craft.

A BRIEF LIFE

It's pretty obvious that B-24M *brief* was named after the weekly 7th AAF magazine, and the moniker—as well as the titillating pin-up—was a sure-fire way to get mentioned therein.

But there were other ways too.

It was strange. You could stand on the Angaur runway and see the bombs dropping on Koror Island, where the Japanese were still in business. The planes would spiral upward for an hour, fly north for ten minutes, drop their bombs, return, and spiral down to land. Though there was some sporadic, inaccurate flak thrown up from Koror, the missions there were actually getting kind of boring.

But on 4 May, Floyd Bennett, a cook in the 867th mess, was anything *but* bored. He had spent months listening to the flyboys talk about their exciting missions and was eager to find out what he'd been missing, so he finagled a ride on *brief* for that day's sortie. On the flight line, he was so excited he could hardly stand still.

Thirty minutes later, 22 Liberators clustered at the rendezvous and swung to the appointed heading. Thirty seconds before bombs away, the AA positions opened up. Black flak bursts bruised the sky around the seven planes in the first element, rocking numbers 5 and 6 with near misses. The first planes were already past the target, but in the middle, an instant after bombs away, pilot Lt. Glen Custer of *brief* suddenly felt his aircraft shudder. He looked out his left window and saw fire eating through the aluminum skin between engine #2 and the fuselage. Suddenly the wing bent straight up, separating from the craft, and spiraled lazily away. The plane immediately flipped over and hurtled toward the lagoon north of Koror Island. Only one parachute was seen.

A Korean POW who was on Koror at the time said two men survived. After the War, nine bodies were found in a pit. The body of the navigator was found elsewhere on the island in a separate grave. He was likely executed by a Japanese officer who was later found guilty of war crimes and served time in prison.

Cook Floyd Bennett had only days to go before reassignment to the States when he "sandbagged" onto the *brief* flight. This plane was the first and only loss of a crew on a combat mission for the 867th squadron thus far in the War. And, predictably, it was detailed in the 5 June 1945 issue of *brief*.

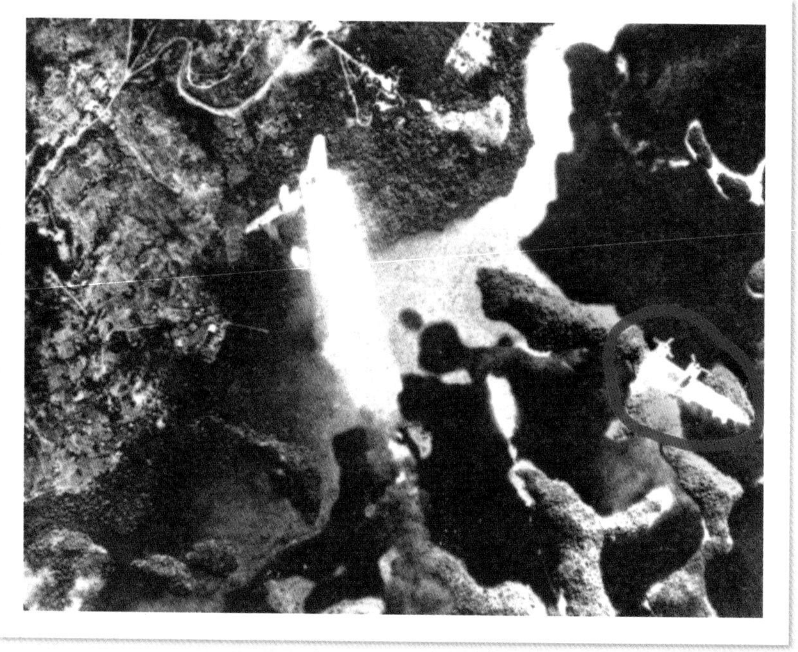

RIGHT On board *Armed Venus,* flying above *brief*, Will Bond was filming the raid when he heard the explosion and caught the shocking moment on film. The fuselage has turned belly up and the left wing is spiraling away at center right of his famous photo.

HONOR FROM A MAN AMONG MEN

General Douglas MacArthur, who had one of the most—if not *the* most—illustrious careers in U.S. military history (West Point - Tampico - WWI - 1928 Olympics - Civilian Conservation Corps - Philippine Field Marshall - WWII Supreme Commander, Southwest Pacific Area - rebuilding Japan - U.N. command in the Korean War - chairman of Remington Rand), at the conclusion of the Philippines campaign made a special commendation to Colonel Kelley of the 494th Bombardment Group:

> *Please accept for yourself and extend to all officers and men involved my heartiest commendation for their brilliant execution of the Visayan* Campaign. It is a model of what able, light, but aggressive command can accomplish in rapid exploitation.*

* The Visayans are four mid-sized islands in the center of the Philippine archipelago: Panay, Negros, Cebu, and Bohol.

BELOW In recognition of their contribution to the War, President Truman authorized the 7th Air Force to issue the Air Medal. Air crews got the medal for their first five missions, and an oak cluster for every five missions after that. Gen. Robert Douglass, Jr., commander of the 7th Army Air Force, personally came to Angaur to award the medals. O.C., like all the men, was counting points: "My crew got 35 points for the medal alone," he wrote home. "I'll send the medal home along with some other junk I have around here."

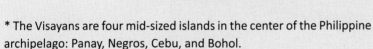

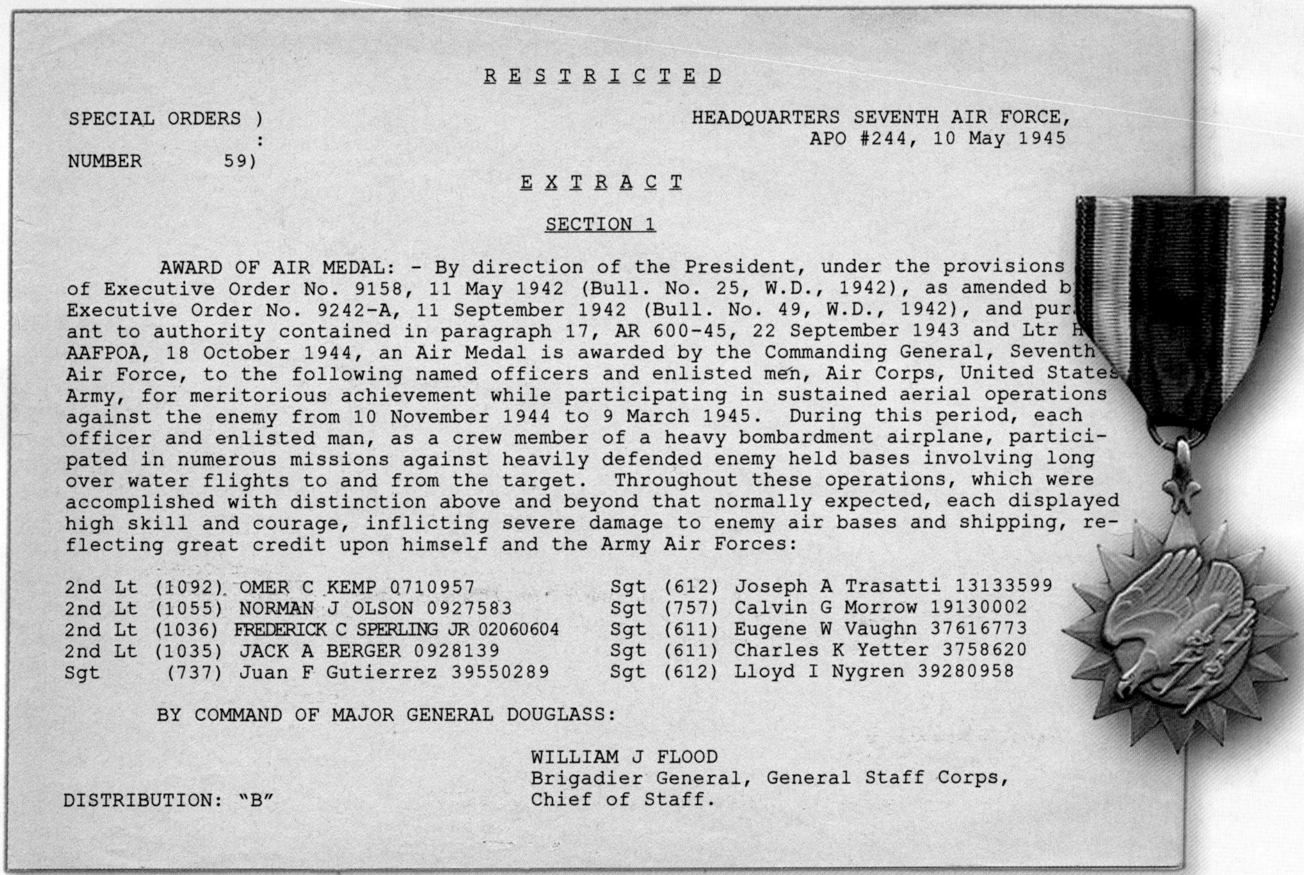

R E S T R I C T E D

SPECIAL ORDERS)
:
NUMBER 59)

HEADQUARTERS SEVENTH AIR FORCE,
APO #244, 10 May 1945

E X T R A C T

SECTION 1

AWARD OF AIR MEDAL: - By direction of the President, under the provisions of Executive Order No. 9158, 11 May 1942 (Bull. No. 25, W.D., 1942), as amended by Executive Order No. 9242-A, 11 September 1942 (Bull. No. 49, W.D., 1942), and pursuant to authority contained in paragraph 17, AR 600-45, 22 September 1943 and Ltr Hq AAFPOA, 18 October 1944, an Air Medal is awarded by the Commanding General, Seventh Air Force, to the following named officers and enlisted men, Air Corps, United States Army, for meritorious achievement while participating in sustained aerial operations against the enemy from 10 November 1944 to 9 March 1945. During this period, each officer and enlisted man, as a crew member of a heavy bombardment airplane, participated in numerous missions against heavily defended enemy held bases involving long over water flights to and from the target. Throughout these operations, which were accomplished with distinction above and beyond that normally expected, each displayed high skill and courage, inflicting severe damage to enemy air bases and shipping, reflecting great credit upon himself and the Army Air Forces:

2nd Lt (1092) OMER C KEMP 0710957	Sgt (612) Joseph A Trasatti 13133599
2nd Lt (1055) NORMAN J OLSON 0927583	Sgt (757) Calvin G Morrow 19130002
2nd Lt (1036) FREDERICK C SPERLING JR 02060604	Sgt (611) Eugene W Vaughn 37616773
2nd Lt (1035) JACK A BERGER 0928139	Sgt (611) Charles K Yetter 3758620
Sgt (737) Juan F Gutierrez 39550289	Sgt (612) Lloyd I Nygren 39280958

BY COMMAND OF MAJOR GENERAL DOUGLASS:

WILLIAM J FLOOD
Brigadier General, General Staff Corps,
Chief of Staff.

DISTRIBUTION: "B"

EXTRA! **Pacific Post** EXTRA!

Section One | MONDAY, MAY 7, 1945 | Ten Cents

V-E DAY!

NAZIS SURRENDER UNCONDITIONALLY TO ALLIED POWERS

REIMS, FRANCE, May 7—At 2:41 A.M. French time, Germany surrendered unconditionally to the western Allies and Russia.

The surrender took place at a little red school house which is the headquarters of Gen. Dwight Eisenhower.

The surrender which brought the war in Europe to a formal end after five years, eight months, and six days of bloodshed and destruction was signed for Germany by Col. Gen. Gustav Jodl, new chief of staff of the German army.

It was signed for the supreme Allied command by Lt. Gen. Walter Bedell Smith, chief of staff for Gen. Eisenhower.

German B'casts Confirm

LONDON, May 7 — German Foreign Minister Ludwig Schwerin von Krosigk broadcast today over German airwaves the following statement: "German men and women! The high command of the armed forces has today, at the order of Grand-Admiral Doenitz, declared the unconditional surrender of all fighting German troops."

Doenitz broadcast submarine crews this message: "Crushing superiority has compressed us into a very narrow area. Continuation of the struggle is impossible from the bases that remain."

Goebbel's Body Found

LONDON, May 7 — In a Moscow dispatch today, Reuters reported without confirmation that the bodies of German Propaganda Minister Joseph Goebbels and his family had been found in an air raid shelter near the Reichstag Building in Berlin.

But Where Is Hitler?

MOSCOW, May 7 — Russian troops, systematically examining the bodies found in the Nazi Chancellery in Berlin, have not yet reported finding Adolf Hitler's body, although the bodies of many members of the general staff, leading Storm Troopers and high-ranking Nazis—all suicides—have been found. The Russians believe that the report of Hitler's death is a Nazi trick, and that the Fuehrer is in hiding.

Celebrations Begin

LONDON, May 7—In anticipation of an early announcement of V-E Day, pennants and flags were strung across the fronts of hotel and office buildings in many parts of London today. For the first time since the War began, factory whistles sounded this morning to mark the start of the working day. The whistles previously had been banned to prevent confusion with air-raid warnings.

War Is Just Half Over!

(Editorial)

V-E Day has arrived.

Organized resistance by Germany is ended. The Allies have paid the terrible price of suppressing the mad terror unleashed by Adolf Hitler. Germany herself is paying the awful penalty of having been led into a depravity of cruelty almost unequaled in the world's history.

Yet our task is not finished. We are but at the halfway mark. Japan still remains, the Japan which raped Manchuria in 1931, leaped upon China in 1937, and indulged in the infamy of Pearl Harbor in 1941.

We have no time to dwell upon the past. We must look ahead to a total victory and the building of a new and safer world order upon the ruins of the old.

Yet so titanic a victory as was signaled by the arrival of V-E Day cannot pass without a backward glance at the blood upon the hands of the aggressors and at the long rows of white crosses of those brave men of ours who made this surcease possible. The world should not soon forget the execrable name and the loathsome acts of Adolf Hitler. It should not forget the fair promises and the red stains upon the soil of Poland and Czechoslovakia and Norway and France and Belgium and the Netherlands and all the other innocent countries when those fair promises were treacherously broken.

Germany is beaten. Let us see to it now that a like fate speedily is visited upon Japan for her part in this horrific war.

brief

THEY DID THE DIRTY WORK

EDITORIAL . . .

JOE AND WILLY*

Joe and Willy turned the trick. The gaunt, unshaven, unhappy infantrymen walked in and took the ground and smashed the lines and broke the back of the German army. The Navy brought them over, the Quartermaster troops supplied them, and the Air Forces softened things up. But to the individual doughfoot, with zero hour ahead, all these things faded away. He still faced the individual enemy soldier; the advance hinged on how far he could drive his weary legs. So when the barrage lifted, Joe and Willy started walking.

They walked from Oran to Berlin, and that is quite a hike. They walked through the cold rain and sand of Tunisia. Then they walked through Sicily, and finally all the way up Italy to the Swiss border. Sometimes they just sat for a while—at places like Anzio or Bastogne where the situation precluded more walking—and Joe and Willy had a chance to watch the Germans try out some interesting theories of massed artillery fire. Sometimes they didn't walk—they waded. That was the way they got to Normandy. Sometimes they swam—across the Meuse and the Aisne and the Rhine.

They crawled on their bellies through the Hertgen Forest and the hedgerows of St. Lô and up the heights of Cassino. They crawled in so many different kinds of mud and through so many battles that sometimes Joe and Willy couldn't remember them all. The way they remembered most places was: "That was where Ed got it; that was where Capt. Herman lost his leg; that was where we got that third cluster on the Purple Heart." There were times when Joe and Willy took a licking and stumbled back for a breather before they tried again. But they kept on walking somehow until somebody told them they could stop. It seems they had won.

The guys in the Air Forces went over Berlin and Hamburg and Cologne in 1,000-plane formations and left desolation where they passed. They knocked the Luftwaffe off Joe's and Willy's backs, but there still were artillery and mortars and machine guns and tanks. When the Air Force had done its best, it was still up to Joe and Willy to do the dirty work, to take and hold the ground, to keep on walking until the Nazis cracked. To Joe and Willy and the rest of the doughfeet go the laurels for the victory.

---

* Joe and Willy were the bedraggled and stoic creations of cartoonist Bill Mauldin. They appeared weekly in the *Stars and Stripes*.

V-J DAY MASTER PLAN

With the end of the European war, a fearsome plan of disaster for Japan went into high gear. In May 1945, the new C.O. of the Army Air Forces Pacific Operations Area, Gen. Barney Giles, laid out the points in a *brief* interview:

- Japan can look forward to the most tremendous aerial pounding in the history of warfare—a shattering, all-out crescendo of annihilation that will begin where the air assault on Germany left off.
- The cream of European air veterans, in vast numbers, will augment existing Pacific air forces in the assault, employing types of fighters and bombers that have not yet seen action and utilizing the most effective firebombs and general purpose bombs ever developed.
- The air strategy worked out over Europe and already started in the Pacific will be carried on until Japan's war industries and military potential have been utterly obliterated.

WHAT BECAME OF THE 97TH INFANTRY?

You will recall that O.C. Kemp started his service in the 97th Infantry at Camp Swift, Texas. After he transferred to the Aviation Cadets and began his adventure as an Air Force bomber pilot, the 97th Infantry had a pretty amazing adventure of its own.

On 2 March 1945, the men of the 97th landed at Le Havre, France and fought in the battle of the Ruhr Pocket. When they crossed the Sieg river on 7 April, they suffered an astounding 80% casualties from a German ambush, yet they went on to capture the German cities of Cologne, Düsseldorf, and Solingen.

On 23 April they stumbled across and then liberated Flossenbürg concentration camp. Two days after that nightmare, they entered Czechoslovakia to protect the left flank of the Third Army on its southern drive, taking Chem and then attacking one of the last pockets of German resistance on 29 April.

They were in Czechoslovakia when they got the cease-fire order on 7 May.

Redeployed to the Pacific, they arrived at Cebu, Philippine Islands, on 16 September and then sailed to Japan for occupation duty, arriving at Yokohama on 23 September 1945.

O.C. wrote home, happy about V-E Day: "It sure is great to have the Germans off our mind, isn't it? I hope the Japs will take the hint. Maybe it means I won't have to do another tour after this one is over."

I'M AN 85! (IN POINTS, NOT I.Q.)

Because the Philippine campaign was basically over, and all that was left to do before Okinawa was pacified was to secure the remaining islands in the Palaus and Carolines, the 494th flew just 13 missions in May 1945. And even though there were usually about twenty planes per mission—that's over two hundred and fifty individual crew assignments—most replacement crews flew rarely during May. O.C.'s crew didn't fly at all.

By then many veteran crews were getting close to going home, either nearing 40 missions or amassing their 85 points in the Army's new point system, so they pushed hard to fly, not only because they felt they'd earned the missions but because they knew what was on the horizon: Soon all the bombing runs would be over Japan. Part of the reason O.C. rarely saw a Zero or encountered heavy ack-ack on his missions was because by spring 1945 the Empire had pulled most of its aircraft, ships, and troops to the home islands to make their last stand.

The more experienced crews on Angaur knew that Group losses, currently running at two or three planes a month, would rise to that many a week once they started bombing Japan, and they wanted no part of it. They had tempted fate dozens of times and they wanted to go home.

To hell with the new guys—let 'em fend for themselves.

PACIFIC OPERATIONS AREA

14 May - 20 June 1945
Angaur Army Air Field
Angaur, Palau Islands
865th Bombardment Squadron
494th Bombardment Group (H)
7th Army Air Force

After three missions in three days on Guam, then waiting around another two weeks with constant stand-by alerts for additional missions that never materialized, the 494th detached crews were both bored and jumpy. So they were glad when the orders came to return to Angaur, where at least the boredom wasn't constantly interrupted. In fact, if you weren't scheduled to fly, it was *never* interrupted. They were so bored they got some seeds and planted a garden. "We have two inch high corn shoots," O.C. wrote home. "Some farmers, eh?"

RIGHT Angaur Island, looking north. In just six months, an island that had been bombed into the Stone Age has become the bustling hub of bomber activity in the Pacific, with docks, a 7,000 foot runway, and living quarters for 5,000 men.

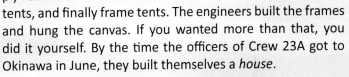

LEFT First came pup tents, then pyramid tents, and finally frame tents. The engineers built the frames and hung the canvas. If you wanted more than that, you did it yourself. By the time the officers of Crew 23A got to Okinawa in June, they built themselves a *house*.

BOTTOM LEFT Chow time for the enlisted men.

BOTTOM RIGHT During daily sick call hour, men of the 865th Squadron patiently await treatment by the medical staff.

THE FAMILY'S PRIDE

His father bought a dozen pigs
And sent him out to milk the cows;
"This boy of mine," he proudly said,
"Must have no part in all these rows."

And then he planted lots of 'taters
An acre more to be exact.
"The dear sweet boy must be deferred,"
He vowed, "and that's a certain fact."

"Why he's not like the other boys
Who chase around and do mean things;
He likes to drive his car about
And just have fun like sporting brings."

His mamma said, "He's such a dear,
I couldn't bear to see him go.
Let other boys the fighting do.
They're more that way as all must know."

And so the boy he got deferred
While all his pals went off to war;
They did their part to save the Land
In many climes both near and far.

The stay-at-home now hangs his head;
He goes about as if in shame.
But dad and mom are proud because
He's holding up the family name.

TO THOSE WHO DIDN'T GO . . .

Many people who did not live through WWII believe that the entire nation was gung-ho to go to war. Not true. There has long been a strain of isolationism in America, and the War raged in Europe for over two years before America was finally compelled to enter the conflict by the events of Pearl Harbor and the Nazi declaration of war against America the next day.

But once American blood was spilled on our own soil, the nation became almost instantly galvanized, and the U.S. entered the War with a steely-eyed determination that shocked the Japanese. It did not surprise Hitler; he never wanted to go to war with America and correctly calculated the country's technological and manufacturing might. He knew the best he could do against the United States was a draw.

Most veterans of the War speak little about those who did not go for whatever reason, though the poem at left, written at the time, gives a fair estimation about how they felt about those who obtained deferrals... and how the deferees may have felt about themselves.

. . . FROM THOSE WHO DID

GI humor is always trenchant and colorful. Below are a few jokes O.C. thought were good enough to write down and hold on to.

Discipline: What a man learns in his first six weeks in the Army or in his first six months of marriage.

A necking party is an affair that lasts until somebody gives in, gives up, or gives out.

Girl: Sorry, but I don't go out with perfect strangers.
Soldier: That's all right, baby. I ain't perfect."

It's all right for a soldier to sit in the dark and tell his girl a story, providing he can hold his audience.

Don't complain if you aren't getting what you want. Be thankful that you aren't getting what you deserve.

Political Candidate: A man who stands for what he thinks the people will fall for.

GETTING A PASS

A GI reprieve,
A pass or leave,
Is a thing that's so simple to get.
If you've got the time,
And committed no crime,
And the CO's your friend, then you're set.
Providing of course
Your absence's no loss
And there's no one else going that day.
Don't feel too secure,
And never feel sure,
That you're going - till well on your way.

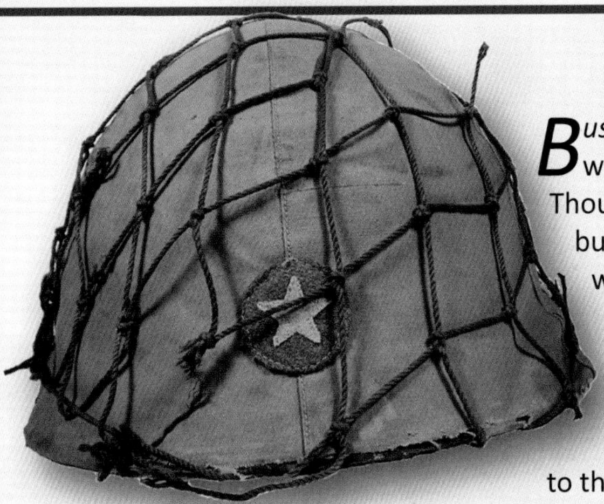

LEFTOVER JAPS

Bushidō ("the way of the warrior") is an ancient Japanese philosophy which promotes war as purifying and death in war as an honor. Though suicide attacks are not generally considered coincident with bushidō, desperation made them acceptable and Imperial soldiers were instructed to fight to the end and "bloom as flowers of death."

As we moved across the Pacific, many Japanese soldiers remained on otherwise "secure" islands. They were a menace mostly to Aviation Engineers who were working in the very heart of the country where the enemy made his last desperate stand. In addition to their regular duties, engineers eliminated enemy fighters on patrols.

On Angaur, a patrol was working its way up a jungled hillside when they heard hammering. A work party of sixteen Japs were building a pillbox of palm logs. Spreading out in skirmish formation, the engineers crept forward until they were within ten yards of the workers before they were spotted. The Japs dropped their tools, grabbed rifles and clubs, and charged with shrieks of "Banzai!" firing blindly over the GI's heads. Within a few seconds it was over and the survivors retreated into the dense jungle. Four were dead.

Captures were rare. On one occasion, two engineers saw a Jap standing in a jungle clearing. He saw them but did not move. As they advanced, they signaled for him to strip naked as a precaution against booby traps. He had trouble getting his pants off because of his wire-wrapped makeshift shoes, so they gestured for him to hold the pants with one hand while holding the other hand in the air. He reached, but not for the sky, instead jerking a grenade from his back pocket. The GIs yelled and the soldier, with an apologetic shrug, tossed the grenade into the bushes. He was brought in without a shot being fired.

Two engineers were scavenging for tools in an abandoned blacksmith shop. Returning to camp, one of the soldiers took a practice burst with the machine gun they carried. Moments later, five Japanese soldiers stepped out of the nearby jungle, carrying a white flag. The engineers' target practice had scared them into surrender.

These holdouts were more of a menace than a nuisance. Trucks traveled about island interiors, blaring messages about the hopelessness of resistance and promising food if the Japs surrendered. Leaflets were dropped into the jungle by aircraft. But though a few came forward and a few were caught, most, trapped by the inflexible tenets of bushidō, starved to death or had to be killed.

CENTER RIGHT A Japanese Type 97 fragmentation hand grenade. Its pineapple-shaped, segmented body dispersed lethally sharp pieces of shrapnel when it exploded.

LOWER RIGHT Engineers on Angaur await the disposition of the body of a Japanese soldier killed while he was infiltrating. Their faces reflect both the utter tragedy and numbing banality of war.

MAY ON ANGAUR

LOSSES IN ACTION One aircraft, #058 *brief*, lost in action over Koror Island, Palaus. (*See p. 202.*)

OPERATIONAL LOSSES *Norman Mackie* crashed on take-off from Depot Field on Guam at the start of a mission against Marcus Island on 1 May, causing the death of four and injury of six. This was the mission (#14) where O.C. and Crew 23A had the low fuel scare.

MISSION Most time was spent preparing for the move to the new operations theater on Okinawa. Training continued as well as aid to the 11th Bomb Group in neutralizing Truk atoll and Marcus Island. Bombing the Japanese anti-aircraft gun positions on Koror and Arakabesan continued until they were silenced. Thirteen total missions were flown, involving an average of 20 aircraft per mission.

RAMP ACCIDENT On 25 May, while the fuel truck was fueling 711 *Sittin' Pretty,* the truck caught fire, scorching the plane's nose.

POINT SYSTEM After a Group check, it was found that 45 enlisted men had 85 or more points and would be rotated home under the new partial demobilization orders.

ENGINEERING With the new engines that came in last month, all required engine changes to Group planes were made so they would be ready for Okinawa. An engine has about a 350 hour life under conditions in the theater.

MOVEMENT TO OKINAWA On 25 May the ship *Jeremiah Daily* arrived and was loaded with cargo in just 2.5 days. It departed on 31 May with a detachment of Group personnel to set up operations on Okinawa.

HEALTH Men began taking the bitter little yellow Atabrine pills, a new anti-malarial drug. The ideal dosage was still unknown so side effects such as jaundice, vomiting, and in some cases a yellow skin sometimes resulted. A common though unfounded belief among the men was that Atabrine caused sterility and so some had to be supervised to take it. And yet the most effective preventative for malaria proved to be DDT, which is relatively nontoxic to mammals but was deadly to malaria-carrying mosquitoes. It was liberally dusted over the entire Palau chain.

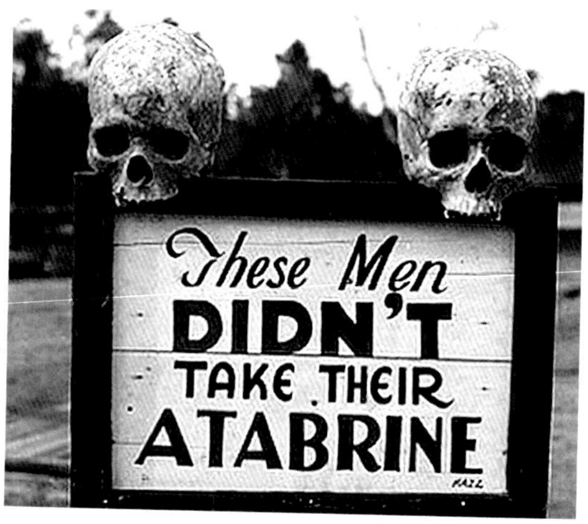

MORALE Morale was high. The defeat of Germany and plans for partial demobilization under the point system helped. But with fewer missions, boredom set in. Fresh food, a liberal beer ration, and a well-stocked PX made the wait tolerable. Men rated most of the movies shown as "mediocre" or "lousy."

RELIGION The 494th tent chapel was struck and religious services were moved to Theater No. 1. Attendance at services, as always, was packed. Three men were baptized in the ocean by Chaplain Dowden.

IT'S NO DEATH RAY, BUT . . .

Imagine a world where you can see events miles away on a screen, knowing their size, direction, movement and precise location. You don't have to imagine that world, you live in it. But in the early 1940s, radar (**Ra**dio **D**etection **a**nd **R**anging) was still in its infancy.

It was known that when radio waves struck an object in their path, a tiny part of the wave's energy was reflected back in the direction of the transmitter, where it could be collected by an antenna. The time required for the trip, as well as the compass direction of the wave transmission/reception yielded location.

Defensive radar was first developed by the British in response to fears that Germany was developing an electromagnetic "death" ray. After a study revealed that a death ray was impractical but aircraft detection was possible with radar, Robert Watt developed what led to the Chain Home network of radars defending Great Britain, which in turn resulted in H2S, an airborne system first used in 1943 for precision bombing at night and in inclement weather over Germany.

UPPER RIGHT Building on H2S, Americans developed H2X, the first ground-mapping radar used in combat. Because it used a shorter wavelength than H2S, it yielded a sharper picture. But the equipment, called a "Mickey" set, was heavy and could only be used in large aircraft like bombers. The operator, stationed behind the co-pilot in a B-24, gave headings to the pilot and assisted the bombardier in guiding the aircraft on its bomb run. After the War H2X was converted into an efficient and accurate storm warning radar.

BABY, IT'S COLD INSIDE

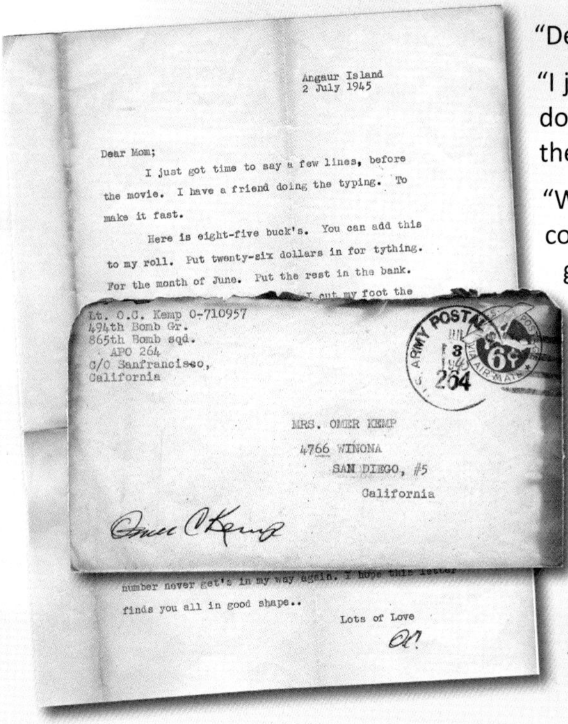

Angaur Island
2 July 1945

Dear Mom;

I just got time to say a few lines, before the movie. I have a friend doing the typing. To make it fast.

Here is eight-five buck's. You can add this to my roll. Put twenty-six dollars in for tything. For the month of June. Put the rest in the bank. ... I cut my foot the

Lt. O.C. Kemp 0-710957
494th Bomb Gr.
865th Bomb sqd.
APO 264
C/O Sanfrancisco,
California

ARMY POSTAL 3 264
VIA AIR MAIL 6¢

MRS. OMER KEMP
4766 WINONA
SAN DIEGO, #5
California

Omer O Kemp

number never get's in my way again. I hope this letter finds you all in good shape..

Lots of Love
O.C.

"Dear Mom:

"I just got time to say a few lines before the movie. I have a friend doing the typing to make it fast. I'm still feeling good. I cut my foot the other day but I'll live through it. At least I can still walk on it.

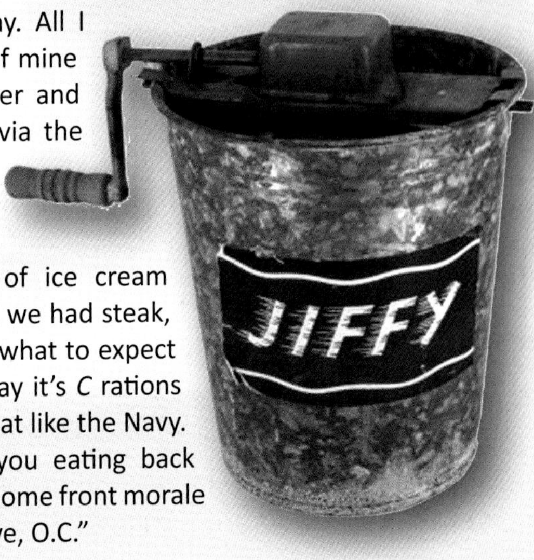

"We had ice cream today. All I could eat, too. A friend of mine got an ice cream freezer and we made ice cream via the arm method. We ended up with about five gallons. Everybody was full of ice cream for a change. Oh yes, we had steak, too. You never know what to expect next out here. One day it's *C* rations and the next day we eat like the Navy. Incidentally, how are you eating back there? I can't have the home front morale in the gutter. Lots of love, O.C."

DOGFIGHT OVER SAIPAN

The move was on and Crew 23A delivered men and supplies to Yontan Air Field on Okinawa. On one of his trips, O.C. stopped off on Saipan in the Marianas, 1,000 miles northeast of Angaur. While there, he tracked down his cousin Jay Kemp at an airstrip at Marpi Point on the north end of the island. Jay tells the story well:

After morning chow, we were standing around shooting the breeze. An Army officer pulled up in a jeep, but we didn't pay any attention to him until he said, "Hey, Jay!" I turned around. O.C. had tracked me down again. He hung around all day and we talked of home and family. He told me to get a day pass for tomorrow and he would be back bright and early in the morning to take me for a ride in his B-24.

The next morning, after a Jeep ride to Aslito Air Field at the south end of the island, O.C. told me to get in the right seat—I was to be his co-pilot. We went through the checklist, got clearance, and took off, heading south. In moments we were passing Tinian Island. After we got to altitude, he asked me if I'd like to fly for awhile. "Sure!" I made a few banks and turns and was able to maintain reasonably level flight—it was like driving a big truck.

In a few minutes Guam came into view. O.C. headed for Anderson Field on the north end of the island. I had been stationed there and wanted to see if I could see my squadron's old bivouac from the air. The tent city was still there. When we passed over the air field, we saw a lot of B-29s warming up for a flight to Japan. At least we hoped that was where they were going. We wanted this war to be over!

We did some sightseeing around Guam, then headed back to Saipan. Rota Island is about halfway between the two. As we flew over it, I told O.C. that I'd heard there were still a couple of Jap soldiers on Rota with a 20 mm anti-aircraft gun that they would move to different places on the island and take pot-shots at any planes they saw. O.C. gave me a dirty look and said, "Thanks a lot!" and shoved the throttles forward as far as they would go. We got out of there fast.

When we were about ten miles from Saipan, O.C. spotted a TBF (Torpedo Bomber Fighter) flying at our altitude on an intersecting course. He radioed the pilot to give him a head's up. The pilot made a smart-ass remark about getting that big hunk of junk out of his way. O.C.'s response was to put the B-24 into a tight turn and make a run at the TBF.

"Zo, you vant to play games!" said the TBF pilot in a bad German accent, arcing toward us. We had a real dog fight, going round and round. Of course a TBF can make much tighter turns than a bomber, so he was able to get inside our turns. Finally, he streaked past us with a parting remark: "Gotcha!"

Five minutes later we were off the north end of Marpi Point where I was stationed. O.C.'s plan was to land and let me off but the tower said the strip was too short for a bomber. O.C. ignored the guy and lined up on the runway anyway and the controller started going nuts, yelling, "Do not land! Do *not* land!"

O.C. went down that runway at full throttle about fifty feet off the deck, pulled sharply up, tipped his wings, then headed back to Aslito Field.

When I got back to base, the line shack guys were all excited. Some crazy B-24 had buzzed the field! I told them it was my cousin and me, but they didn't believe it. I didn't care. It was the best joy ride I ever had.

JUNE ON ANGAUR

LOSSES IN ACTION Two officers killed, three officers and seven enlisted men wounded.

MISSION On 2 June, the ground echelon embarked on the *USS Crockett* for movement to Okinawa, Ryukyu Islands, to begin transfer of operations there. The ship arrived at Ulithi on 4 June and joined a convoy on 21 June, arriving at Okinawa on 24 June. On 21 June the air echelon embarked on the *USS Alkaid* but was hung up at Ulithi the remainder of the month awaiting a convoy.

OPERATIONS During July eleven formation operations were flown against the northern Ryukyus and Japan and four missions were flown against Shanghai, China. Thirteen "snooper" missions involving individual aircraft were flown late in the month. On 7 June a strike was flown against a boat repair basin on Aurapushekaru Island of the northern Palaus, achieving excellent results with light and inaccurate flak being the only opposition.

ACCIDENT On 10 June, 865th Squadron plane #730 was taking off when about half-way down the runway the pilots discovered they had not turned on their superchargers and lacked lift-off power, so they cut the engines and hit the brakes. The aircraft careened off the runway and the #2 engine burst into flames. Fire quickly consumed the aircraft, killing the pilot and co-pilot. Two ramp mechanics working nearby ran and helped nine men escape. They were awarded the Soldier's Medal.

SUPPLY On 29 June, the *USS Jeremiah Daily,* carrying 494th personnel, arrived safely at Okinawa and began unloading. The trip was marred by the discovery that Navy personnel had pilfered personal property of Group crews.

MORALE With news that the transports had arrived safely at Okinawa, those who remained behind were eager to be on their way too. What they did not realize is that Okinawa was still very much on the front lines of the War. The second night after arrival, the Group was subjected to a four-hour air raid alert in which a *kamikaze* crashed into the water just short of the ship from which they had just disembarked. On the positive side, weather on Okinawa was vastly superior to Angaur. The climate was cooler and wetter, although the ever-present dust raised by construction projects was aggravating.

RIGHT In this poorly-focused photo, we see the challenging accommodations of the three-week boat trip to Okinawa.

R&R

13 - 27 July 1945
Hickam Army Air Field
Honolulu, O'ahu
Territory of Hawaii

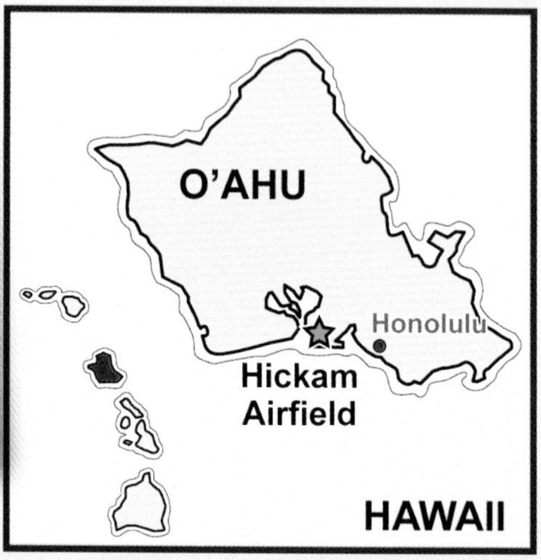

Notwithstanding the fact that they didn't have their required 20 missions, Crew 23A was given R&R anyway. "We came in a C-54 most of the way to Hawaii," O.C. wrote from O'ahu. "It was one of the most enjoyable airplane rides I have ever taken. It was fixed up just like United Airlines, with reclining seats and all. We flew from the Marianas with only two one-hour stops. It sure is marvelous what the airplane can do.

"I stayed at a serviceman's hostel called Malamakoa, which means 'Take care of the soldier' in Hawaiian. It was once the mansion of a wealthy family. It only costs a dollar a day to stay there."

It just so happened that O.C. showed up just as an LDS conference was convening in Honolulu. Hundreds of members came from all over the Islands to hear Harold Lee, a leader of the Church, speak. There were native choirs and meetings to benefit the church's welfare program.

There were also mixers, pot-luck dinners, traditional dance demonstrations, and a luau put on by native church members. There were scores of servicemen and, even more importantly, more than a few single young women. Needless to say, O.C. had a fine time.

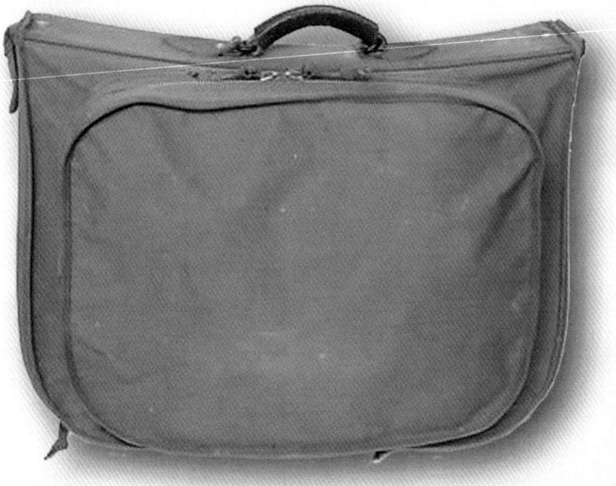

RIGHT The OD ("olive drab") B-4 bag, the staple of officers' luggage in WWII. O.C. used his for 20 years after the War. It was virtually indestructible.

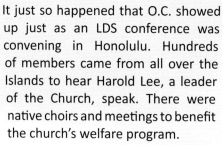

ALOHA!

Like anyone visiting Hawaii, as soon as he was checked in at Malamakoa, O.C. went exploring. Back then, as now, the biggest tourist attraction on O'ahu's southern shore was Waikiki Beach, where O.C. may have seen his first surfboard, even though he grew up in San Diego. Surfing had not yet hit the mainland and it must have stunned him to see men riding waves on giant mahogany planks—some of them weighing fifty pounds or more. Like all GIs, he saw the sights and bought black-and-white postcards, twelve for a dollar, as proof he'd been there, even if it was only for a few days.

In addition, he got this 6" tall ceramic hula girl with a magnet on the base and a spring for a midsection which made her shimmy and shake all across the Pacific, affixed atop the instrument panel of O.C.'s B-24.

A GIRL IN EVERY PORT? WELL, MAYBE ONE

By now, O.C. has written home threatening to give up women forever. The letters from Marian and Verna and others had slowed to a trickle or stopped altogether. He realized he'd simply been gone too long and there were boys who weren't 6,000 miles away who were interested in these girls.

But they say promises are made to be broken and on O'ahu O.C. met a pretty blonde gal named Maxine Christensen and he suddenly found himself back in the fray. After not seeing a woman for six months, lounging on Waikiki Beach with a beautiful girl and Diamond Head in the background must have satisfied any possible definition of "rest and recreation."

"I met a number of nice kids in Honolulu," he wrote home. "We decided to go out, so on Saturday night we all went to down to Waikiki. There was a big moon and you could see very well. We had a nice picnic and ate sandwiches and had a gay time.

"When we got back to our car there was a cop waiting for us. He took all our names and then arrested us. But it was a big mistake. He had mistaken our car for another that was involved in some shenanigans in Honolulu."

While on O'ahu, O.C. met a buddy from Pampa, Texas who was a B-25 pilot. He invited O.C. to go with him for a ride to another air field. While there, O.C. met a pal from Hoover High in San Diego and they had a great reunion.

For the first time in months O.C. felt like things might work out. He even began believing he'd get more missions to fly.

PACIFIC OPERATIONS AREA

6 August - 19 October, 1945
Yontan Army Air Field
Okinawa, Ryukyu Islands
865th Bombardment Squadron
494th Bombardment Group (H)
7th Army Air Force

Okinawa is the main island in the Ryukyu island chain curving south and west from Kyushu (southernmost of Japan's four main islands) toward Taiwan. Long a prefecture of Japan, Okinawa proved it was loyal as well, putting up a resistance to the Allied invasion that resulted in the death of over a quarter of its inhabitants and tens of thousands of American soldiers. When the island was declared secure on 20 June, the engineers had already been working for weeks to expand and repair the existing air fields on the island. With only 350 miles separating Okinawa from Kyushu, the plan was to take the War from his doorstep to the Emperor's living room.

Yontan Air Field was seized on the first day of the invasion. It was quickly repaired, allowing fighters and bombers to land. Yontan soon became headquarters for the 41st and the 494th bomb groups of the 7th AAF and the 35th fighter group and the 213th bomb group of the 5th AAF as well as the prime staging area for the attack on Japan scheduled to begin 1 November 1945.

Okinawa was unlike any other island we had encountered. It had a large civilian population to be concerned with and was reputed to be literally crawling with snakes and fleas. Few snakes were seen but the scuttlebutt on fleas was painfully accurate. The island was entirely developed, painstakingly cultivated, and honeycombed with rock tombs that were better built than most of the native homes. Though four times bigger than Guam at 65 miles in length, the Americans still felt like giants. Everything was tiny. Every road on the island had to be widened; the Okinawans got by with narrow rutted cart paths and there were few motor vehicles on the island before the Allies arrived.

Americans discovered the Okinawans, though ethnically related to Japanese, shared few of their negative traits. Expecting widespread sabotage and infiltration, Americans instead found the Okinawans to be humble, hungry and small—most weighing less than 100 pounds. GIs quickly discovered that Okinawans responded to kindness, bowed politely, loved to salute, and would talk and laugh with anyone who spoke Japanese.

OKINAWA - JUNE '45
SECOND DAY OF CAMP CONSTRUCTION

LIFE ON JAPAN'S DOORSTEP

Yontan Air Field on Okinawa came together like the typhoon that would take it apart three months later: quickly. No sooner had the engineers unloaded their equipment, dug slit trench bomb shelters, and set up their tents than they started working 12-hour shifts seven days a week. And when they were done—in just 17 days—they moved three miles south to Kadena Air Field to do it all over again.

TOP LEFT As the photo says, just two days after the engineers arrived, the land west of the airstrip is already dotted with the engineers' pyramid tents.

TOP RIGHT Then, just three weeks later, the same scene has changed dramatically. Soon the air echelon will arrive with even more tents.

MIDDLE RIGHT T.5 Albert Weisenbach, a steam-shovel operator, must have set a record when, on one long hot day in late June, he loaded six scoops of coral into a truck every 47 seconds—and did it all day long.

BOTTOM LEFT A weary but proud engineering crew poses for a photo on their bulldozer.

BOTTOM RIGHT In mere weeks, Yontan Air Field has been transformed. What looks like a residential subdivision is actually two directional runways (evidence of the unpredictable Okinanawan winds) and scores of hardstands with interconnecting taxiways.

YOKOSUKA MXY-7 "OHKA"

It was at Yontan that American forces found copies of the Yokosuka MXY-7 Ohka, a rocket-propelled, manned flying bomb that was carried under the belly of a Betty bomber. Upon release, the pilot would glide toward the target and when he was within range he would fire the Ohka's three solid-fuel rockets (yes, they had them back then; that's what a firecracker is) and steer towards the ship he intended to destroy. The Ohka was almost unstoppable because it reached speeds approaching 600 mph. Seven U.S. ships were damaged or sunk by Ohkas during the War. Americans called them Baka Bombs, which means "fool" or "idiot" in Japanese.

BELOW A captured Ohka at Yontan (left) and O.C. exploring the same aircraft (right) while it was stored under camouflage netting. This same Ohka is now on display at the Planes of Fame Museum in Chino, CA.

OPERATIONS ORDER)
NUMBER 138)

TACTICAL AIR FORCE, TENTH ARMY
APO #903, 3 July 1945

S E C R E T

MISSION: Strike Omura Airfield on 5 July 1945

RENDEZVOUS POINT AND ALTITUDE: Bombers and escorts: Kusagaki Shima 30-5- North; 29-25 East at 10,000 feet.

METHOD OF ATTACK: Rocket and strafing for Thunderbolts, medium altitude bombing for mediums and heavies.

INITIAL POINT: Ohiki Shima, 32-52 N. 129-45 East at 0900.

RALLY POINT: 15 miles due West from Point Omiki Saki on Amakusa Shirio Shima, 32-13 N, 129-45 East.

INSTRUCTIONS TO INDIVIDUAL UNITS:

A. 32 Thunderbolts to rocket and strafe AA installations, depart Initial Point at 0900.
B. 48 B-24s bomb dispersal areas depart Initial Point at 0905.
C. 24 B-25s bomb dispersal areas following the B-24s.
D. 32 Thunderbolts to cover B-24s.
E. 32 Thunderbolts to cover B-24s.
F. 32 Thunderbolts for roving top cover for all units between Initial Point and target.
G. Lightning photo plane to photograph target before and after strike.
H. 4 Thunderbolts to escort Lightning photo plane.
I. 8 Thunderbolts to cover Dumbo the entire mission.

SPECIAL INSTRUCTIONS:

(1) Loading: 48 Liberators each with 40 M1-A1 frag clusters. 24 Mitchells each with 24 M47-A2. 32 Thunderbolts with full ammo, 4 rockets. Strike escort Thunderbolts with full ammo.

(2) Alternate Objective: Iwakawa Airfield, Kyushu

(3) Other: Dumbo with 8 VF cover to orbit 15 miles due west from Point Oniki Saka on Amakusa, Shimo Shima. Window to be dropped by B-24s and B-25s in target area. Target time and escort to be coordinated with all units involved prior to take off for mission.

MISSION ORDER AND SUMMARY

ABOVE This order came just two days before a mission which involves over 200 aircraft. P-47 Thunderbolts escort the bombers and watch over the waiting Dumbo. Fragmentation bombs ensure maximum destruction.

There were over 1,000 Japanese planes at Omura, which is twelve miles from Nagasaki, including 600 fighters. Every ship outside a fifty mile radius from Okinawa was considered fair game. If shot down over enemy territory, pilots were instructed to head for the coast and get in the water for easier pick-up.

BELOW The Intelligence Summary following the mission. Photos taken by the P-38 Lightnings later revealed that only 46 of our aircraft were successful in dropping their bombs within the vicinity of the target.

A-2 BOMCOM SEVEN)
RE: ORDER NUMBER 138)

TACTICAL AIR FORCE, TENTH ARMY
APO #903, 5 July 1945

INTELLIGENCE SUMMARY

23 B-25s and 1 RCM Mitchell over Omura Airfield dispersal area at 0420Z dropped 290X 100-lb indenciary clusters from 7000 feet. 90% in target area. Starting many fires with smoke rising to 7000 feet. No interception. Minor damage to one B-25 from heavy AA which was moderate and inaccurate. No planes sighted on ground. Crews observed twenty small ships in harbor at 32-27N, 130-16E at 0520Z, and one probable DD with small landing craft nearby position 29-16N 129-27E off Kotakara Shima at 0630Z. Weather 4/10.

47 B-24s over eastern dispersal area same target dropped 1780x125 lb frag clusters at 0415Z from 9500 to 10500 feet. 50% in target area, remainder short of target and in adjoining airfield area. Some fires started. No interception. Minor damage to nine B-24s by heavy AA which was moderate to meager and accurate to inaccurate. Fire was predicted concentration and was most accurate for lead flight. Crews observed luggers and miscellaneous shipping at anchor in Nagusuku harbor and Sasebo harbor. Weather 3/10 visibility 12 miles.

All aircraft returned to base. One casualty, T.Sgt. Donald Leddy, 37553818, lacerations and contusions of left hand from flak.

MAKE YOURSELF A HOME

No sooner were they back from R&R than the officers of Crew 23A had to figure out their lodgings. While they were in Hawaii their belongings had been shipped to Okinawa and were now under a tarp somewhere. Okinawa was markedly different than Angaur: it had rolling hills, cultivated fields, natives eager to trade, and new roads. The first servicemen on the island pitched their pup tents on flat areas that turned out to be rice paddies and flooded in the first rains. Officers, learning a lesson, erected their frame tents on the hillsides overlooking Yontan Air Field. By the time the officers of Crew 23A got there, the best views were taken. But the best accommodations were not: they would be built by O.C. and Co. "We had to build our own shack," he wrote home. "We live on the side of a hill, which makes it rather nice."

RIGHT Bombardier Jack Berger and co-pilot "Oly" Olson relax in front of the "castle" the officers of Crew 23A built for themselves using the wood tent frame the Air Force Engineers provided and trading with the Navy for lumber for the floor and walls.

Though the roof was canvas, the structure was as solid as any living quarters around, which was fortunate because Okinawa was both cooler and wetter than Angaur had been.

How much cooler and wetter they would discover a couple of months down the road when a certain gal named "Louise" came calling.

"HOME COOKING OUR SPECIALTY"

Jack Berger—called "Angle" Berger by O.C.—lived up to his nickname, making friends with Chief Petty Officers on some of the hundreds of ships anchored in nearby Buckner Bay. The Navy had what the airmen needed: fresh food and building supplies. And Crew 23A had what the seamen craved: alcohol.

None of the officers of Crew 23A drank liquor. But every month the Army issued each of them a bottle of whiskey anyway, and on Okinawa that liquid gold was nearly as valuable as the solid kind. Jack requisitioned a Jeep and took their whiskey ration down to the dock, returning with canned tuna and chicken, crates of dozens of eggs, sheet cake, and even ice cream. The ice cream and cake went to the officer's mess, but the lumber built their 18x18-foot castle. The nonperishable food went into a cool, dry hole for later use.

Someone got a hold of a hot plate, which they hooked up to the electrical grid. They cooked for themselves and the officers of other crews. The 865th officers' mess was adequate, but O.C., Oly, Fred, and Jack preferred their own cooking. Each morning they had eggs, flapjacks, and fresh fruit and were often joined by other officers, who were happy to benefit from Jack's bargains. As he said later, "We lived great... like family."

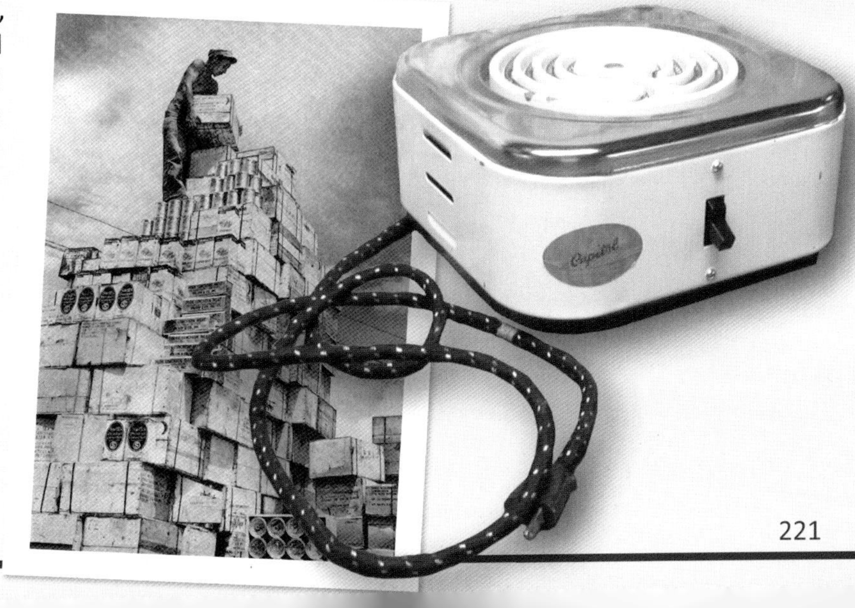

RIGHT A mountain of what everyone else on Okinawa was eating: Spam.

THE STARS AND STRIPES
Newspaper of U.S. Armed Forces
Two Cents U.S.

The 27th Infantry Division's Revenge

by Sgt. John W. Thorburn, Stars and Stripes Staff Writer

OKINAWA, 9 July 1945 — We bombed Japan today from an altitude of 10,000 feet. I should have stood in bed. Now that I'm safe on the ground I keep trying to find my heart. It's wandering around my body. Although it's rather warm on Okinawa, cold chills keep dancing up and down my spine.

It began before dawn when we assembled in the briefing room with a B-24 crew and heard the major say, "Gentlemen, here is today's target." We sat on long wooden benches watching the major's pointer move over a map on which the word *Kyushu* stared at me in red. It was not quite daylight and a light rain was falling. The major finished and a captain explained how many fighter planes would accompany the bombers and other tactical information. A third officer outlined the amount of flak likely to be encountered and the chances of enemy fighter interception. The crew took the information calmly. A weak grin spread over my face as I nonchalantly tried to light my cigarette with a pencil.

The briefing over, crewmen moved toward the rear platform. The chaplains were waiting for them. Full daylight had come. We trooped to breakfast. After a meal of coffee and buttered bread, we rode to the air strip in a truck. The driver told us our ship would be easy to find. "It's named *Innocence A-Broad* and has a nude painted on it," he explained. Pulling up in front of the nude, I walked over to the co-pilot, Darwin Dively. "Hello, Thorburn," he said. "It's been a long time." We went to high school together and played on the same teams.

The pilot, Lt. Eifler cut in, "That's fine, boys, but have your reunion over Japan. We've only got seven minutes."

We climbed inside, past the bombs. On one was written, "From the 27th Infantry Division, who died fighting you bastards." The bombardier promised me he'd drop the whole load smack on the target.

The bomb bay doors slammed shut. My heart slammed with them. Lt. Eifler wheeled the plane around and started down the runway. A rumble and we were off. One of the crew leaned out a window and yelled, "There's the chaplain!" I looked. The ball gunner, Sgt. Hughes, said, "He always stands on the same spot when we take off and waves us on. He's our good luck charm."

The bloody hills of Okinawa fell away beneath us. Sgt. Thackson, armorer gunner, pulled the pins from the bombs and began opening tin boxes of .50 caliber machine gun bullets. "I'm hoping to get 40 missions by Christmas," he said.

Nose gunner Sgt. Sellers stuck a fresh piece of gum in his mouth. He chewed several during each flight.

I looked out. We were flying through thick clouds at 12,000 feet. The sky seemed to be filled with B-24s roaring toward Japan. After a while we picked up our fighter escort and soon dozens of P-51 Mustangs surrounded us. The fighter on our right did a slow roll, twisting over on its belly. "Ain't it beautiful?" Dively said. "He's showing off, but it's beautiful."

Reaching our rendezvous, the crew began pulling on flak suits and helmets. We were starting the target run. The entire crew swept the sky for enemy planes.

We were now over an outlying Jap island. A dry voice cracked through the intercom. "Pretty country, isn't it?" I peered out. Red-roofed Jap homes swished by. I could see roads and neat rows of rice paddy fields.

"Can the small talk," said the pilot. "Target run in seven minutes. Over target in thirteen."

A large lump began rising and crowding up inside of me. The plane broke away from the formation and slid down across the sky. The crew was at ease, working with a cool business-like attitude.

We were almost over the target now. Puffs of ack-ack burst in front of us and thumps of 15 and 20 at a time rocked the plane. We rolled and bobbed. The pilot cut our speed and leveled over the target at 10,000 feet. Flak was all around us. We were helpless; there are no foxholes in the sky.

A sharp rap, and we were hit! The ship staggered, then recovered. Nothing serious. The bombardier shouted, "Bombs away!" The pilot calmly repeated the phrase as the clouds broke momentarily. I could see the target. There were troop barracks and about 35 Jap planes on the ground. Hell was dropping on those Nips as the sky filled with falling fragmentation cluster bombs and parachute explosives. The bomber heaved a sigh of relief as its bombs cascaded down, then straightened its shoulders like a soldier relieved of a heavy field pack.

The bombs hit. Heavy brown smoke rose 5,000 feet into the sky. A fuel dump went up with a roar. The entire area was ablaze with 100 separate fires. The bombardier said, "This is the 27th Division's revenge."

The fighters and bombers reassembled into formation. The flak continued to bob us about but we moved swiftly out of the target area. The tension broke. Crewmen began laughing and joking, breaking out coffee and K-rations.

Yes, we bombed Japan. I should have stood in bed.

The author, Sgt. John Thorburn, was scheduled to fly with his buddy Darwin Dively again on 17 July over Shanghai, China, in another nude lady, *Sittin' Pretty*. That day he apparently stood in bed, but his friend flew and did not come back.

THE ARTIST'S PALLET

The reader has certainly noted that black and white photos do not do the WWII experience justice. Fortunately, painters have been using color for thousands of years.

Gareth Williams was a good pilot in the 866th Squadron, and also adept at watercolor, one of the more difficult painting media to master. His watercolors recorded life on Okinawa and make it seem almost idyllic.

ABOVE 867th Squadron area 22 August 1945. The emergency trucks are a reminder that occasionally planes came back with injured crew members.

RIGHT Capt. Sansouci's "home," complete with veranda and a tanning bed out front.

BOTTOM LEFT Officer's huts of the 864th Squadron cover the hillsides above an anti-aircraft site and bomb shelter on Okinawa in October 1945.

BOTTOM RIGHT Tent in the 866th Squadron housing officers of a crew that weren't overly concerned with stability, just shade from the sun. They would later come to regret this house of straw.

HUNTING FOR BARGAINS

Souvenir hunting is traditional among serviceman. In the Pacific in WWII, everyone wanted a Jap pistol or, even better, a flag or Samurai sword. The Marines and Infantry located the items and covered the retail, and made—pardon the pun—a killing. Unfortunately, there were some friendly-fire casualties. One Navy officer, the skipper of an LST, blushed crimson about the clipping he got on Iwo Jima. He had a lot of loose cash in his pants and after things died down on Iwo, he went ashore to do a little souvenir shopping. He dickered with a gyrene for a genuine Japanese rifle, paying forty bucks. It wasn't until he got back to his ship that someone told him he had bought a rare old 1903 Springfield—a quintessentially American weapon.

CENTER RIGHT O.C. obtained a good luck pennant once carried by a Japanese soldier, inscribed with best wishes by friends and family.

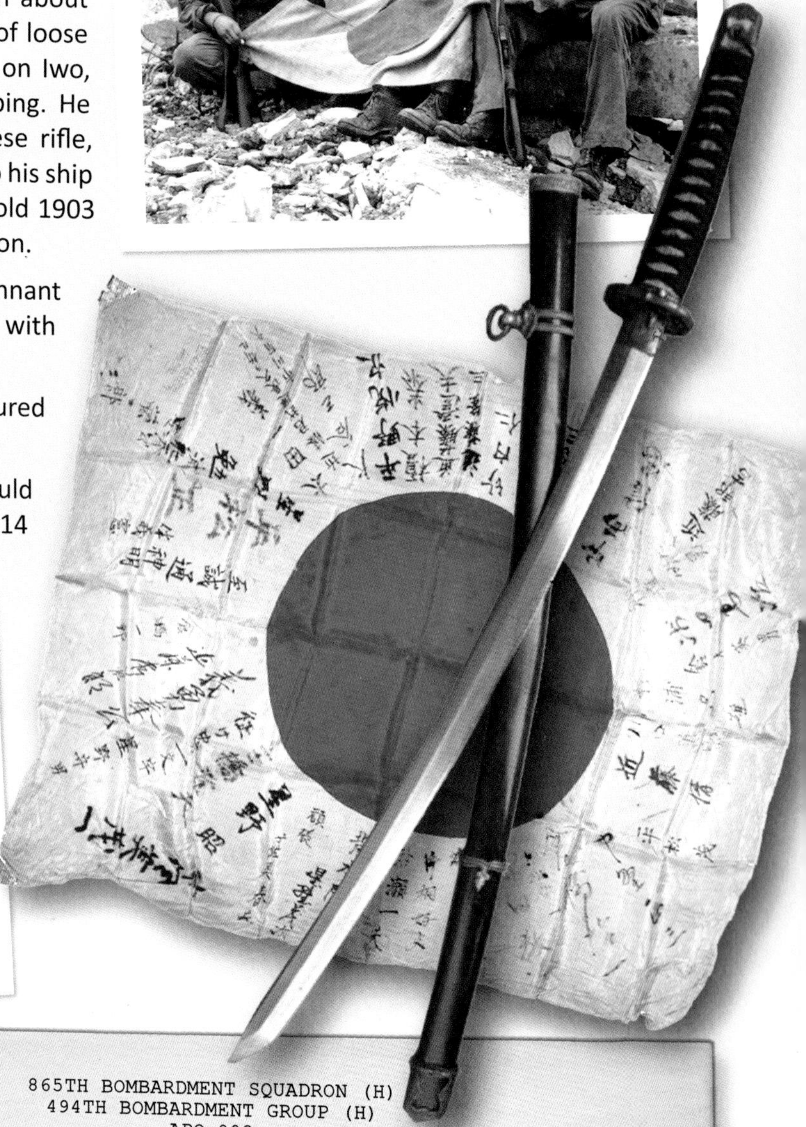

BELOW LEFT Servicemen examine two captured Japanese artillery pieces on Angaur.

BOTTOM Rich from his whiskey sales, O.C. could afford a Japanese .38 caliber Nambu Type 14 automatic pistol for his collection.

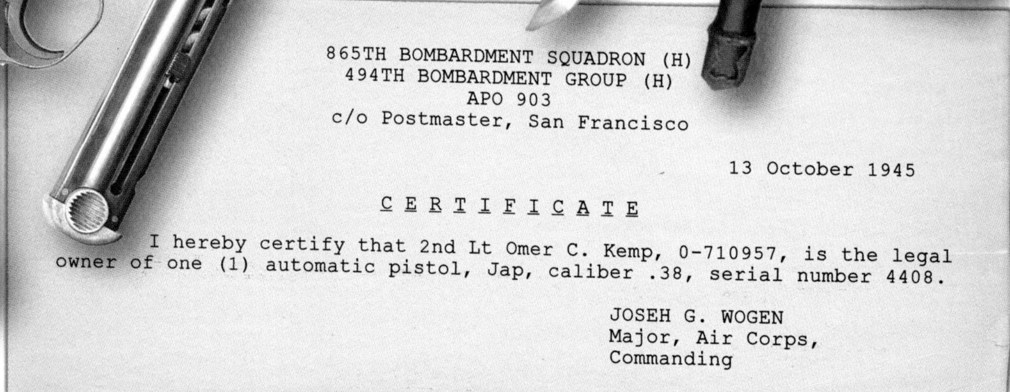

865TH BOMBARDMENT SQUADRON (H)
494TH BOMBARDMENT GROUP (H)
APO 903
c/o Postmaster, San Francisco

13 October 1945

CERTIFICATE

I hereby certify that 2nd Lt Omer C. Kemp, 0-710957, is the legal owner of one (1) automatic pistol, Jap, caliber .38, serial number 4408.

JOSEH G. WOGEN
Major, Air Corps,
Commanding

INTO THE DRINK WITH MISS GIBSON

It was the first mission over China. The objective was Chiangwan Airfield north of Shanghai. We knew little about the defenses and so we went in with hundreds of bombers, P-47 escorts, and Dumbo PBMs. Crews were briefed on escape and evasion and were given Chinese money and "blood chits," two flags that introduced them as American airmen who needed help. One was a Chinese flag with text ordering the citizen to help them escape Japanese capture. If that didn't work, they were to show the American chit, which contained the same information, but also offered a reward.

The ack-ack over the target downed two aircraft. Ill-fated *Sittin' Pretty* crashed and though all crewmen jumped safely, co-pilot Darwin Dively was killed resisting capture, three men were captured and held as POWs until the War's end, and six escaped with the help of Chinese guerillas.

#957, a brand new unnamed B-24M, went down over the East China Sea, all of the crew getting out in parachutes. Stanford and Cianfrini, two gunners, found each other in the rough water. Cianfrini was terrified as he could not swim and his Mae West life preserver would not inflate. Stanford gave him his and they floated alone in the warm water, not seeing anyone else. Then they saw the first shark fins circling, getting progressively closer. They slapped the water, yelled, and kicked their feet. Then, as quickly as they came, the sharks disappeared. As night fell, both men saw luminescent streaks in the water all around them. Both thought they were losing their minds until each confirmed that the other had seen it too.

When dawn came, the sky was clear but the sea was rough with immense swells. Spotting a distant plane, they opened their yellow dye packet. The plane continued on and both men despaired. Then a Martin PBM appeared, spotted them, and dropped a life raft which sunk before they could reach it. It dropped another and both men dragged themselves into it. They were so exhausted they collapsed into sleep, but were soon awakened when the PBM landed nearby and they were hauled onboard. Two other crewmen were also rescued, but five others were never found.

Back on Okinawa, Stanford was informed that a telegram had been sent to his mother telling her that he was MIA. He quickly sent another, letting her know he was okay. Fortunately, his telegram reached home first.

RIGHT The Gibson Girl radio, named after the Victorian era female ideal because of its hourglass shape (which allowed it to be held between the knees), generated a Morse code distress signal when the crank was turned. It came with a fold-up metal frame box kite that acted as an antenna. Its 500 kHz emergency frequency had a range of 200 miles and could be keyed to automatic SOS or manual sending. It was also water-tight and more than one downed airman survived by using it as a life preserver.

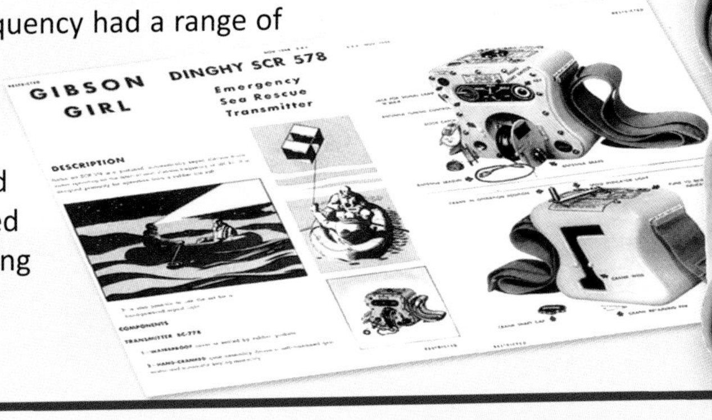

SHANGHAIED IN SHANGHAI

When *Sittin' Pretty* was hit by flak over China on 17 July, three men were captured by the Japanese: Pilot Hal Eifler, navigator Bill Martin, and nose gunner Clyde Sellers. Eifler pointed the aircraft toward the sea and the possibility of rescue. The bomb bays were afire, the flames fed by fuel from punctured tanks. The interphone was out. Word was passed to bail out. Eifler was the last to go; he got out at 2,000 feet and barely pulled his D-ring before hitting the muddy brown water of the Yangtze River—they hadn't reached the safety of the open sea.

Bill Martin was captured and taken to a Japanese major who had an English phrase book and continually referred to the navigator as a "knight in armor," which amused Martin. The smile left his face when the major said, "I'm sorry, but I'll have to shoot you." He was not shot but the mosquitoes in his cell that night did try to eat him alive.

Capt. Eifler found himself floating in the Yangtze River. A Chinese peasant on a passing junk told him in broken English to float downstream and he'd be found by guerillas. But he too was captured. The Japanese were curious about his Mae West flotation vest. One captor thought the dye marker was chocolate and got a surprise when he bit into it. Eifler had heard China was crowded but was astounded to see thousands of peasants curiously lining the banks of the river, watching him as the boat he was on passed by. The boat stopped regularly so Japanese soldiers on the riverbank could get snapshots of the American prisoner with their cameras.

At a prison Eifler was interrogated. He was delighted to find nose gunner Sellers there. Eifler was fed rice and fish and placed alone in a tiny cell with a flea-ridden blanket. The next morning Eifler and Sellers were taken to Shanghai by boat. As they traveled, Eifler saw B-24s pounding the city in the distance, which lifted his spirits.

Martin, held elsewhere, was nearly strafed by an attacking P-51 Mustang. He was not offended.

All three men ended up at Bridge House Prison in Shanghai. They were informed that their interrogators had lived in the U.S. and just "happened" to be in Japan when the War broke out and so were "forced" into the military as interpreters. Though they were asked many questions, the sessions always ended with: "When and where will the Americans invade Japan?" Of course none of them knew.

Eifler's thumbs were bound with twine about six inches apart and rope was looped through the twine and thrown over a tree branch. He was hoisted off the ground, suspended by his thumbs for thirty minutes as the same question was put to him over and over again. All he could answer was, "I don't *know*!"

Each man spent the next two weeks in solitary confinement. Finally on 5 August they were put together in a cell. All had beards and had lost so much weight they barely recognized each other. A few days later a Chinese prisoner made the "V" sign as he passed their cell. That evening all Chinese prisoners were released but the Americans were not, though their food did improve. On 17 August the prison C.O. told them they would be turned over to the Americans soon. They were transferred to the YMCA and constantly reminded that the prison C.O. was responsible for their improved treatment—as if that would make Eifler forget being tortured.

Guards tried to persuade them to shave their beards for photographs. The men refused, knowing they were going to be used as propaganda to defend their Japanese occupiers. Their picture was taken *with* beards.

They were finally turned over to the Chinese on 6 September and were wined and dined in Shanghai and generally treated like kings. Hitching a ride in a Navy vice-admiral's C-53 transport plane, they soon arrived back on Okinawa and were reunited with their buddies of the 865th Squadron.

JULY ON OKINAWA

LOSSES Five B-24s to operations, five to combat. Veteran crews had predicted this.

TRANSITION The water voyage detachment of the air echelon arrived uneventfully at Okinawa on 11 July. 48 aircraft arrived the same day. The remaining aircraft were flown to Okinawa throughout the month.

OPERATIONS Only eleven formation missions were flown against targets in the northern Ryukyu Islands and Japan during the month. Missions were also flown to mainland China near Shanghai. Thirteen solo aircraft "snooper" missions were flown during the last ten days of the month.

ENEMY RESISTANCE The level of enemy resistance on Japan's home soil was much greater than the 494th had encountered in the Philippines, resulting in unprecedented losses in both personnel and aircraft during the first month on Okinawa. As a result, fighter escorts were scheduled, though only two missions encountered enemy aircraft. But on 25 July on a mission over Tsuiki Airfield on Kyushu Island, thirty Japanese fighters attacked the formation. Even though the B-24 gunners were out of practice, they downed five Zeros and damaged four others. But it wasn't enough to prevent the downing of one bomber which crashed, killing all but two who parachuted to safety and were rescued by a U.S. Navy Dumbo amphibious aircraft.

Of greater concern was the increasing amount of flak, substantially more than the Group had seen thus far in the War. Planes also encountered strange air-borne objects, including silver objects resembling belly tanks falling past the formation although no one could determine from whence they came. They also saw helium balloons tethered at bombing altitude and forty foot-long strips of tin foil drifting through the formations, again from an unknown origin. These bizarre countermeasures were effective: two B-24s crashed as a result.

MISSION BRIEFS Preparatory for the Navy's return to operations targeting Tokyo, all effort was made to destroy the Japanese Air Force on Kyushu Island, southernmost of the Japanese home islands. On 5 July, the 494th put all 48 of its resident planes into the air in a record 48 minutes. The 5 July strike on Omura Airfield on Kyushu, with its 50% hit rate, made the 494th the first Bomb Group to hit a target on the enemy mainland from Okinawa. The feat was repeated four days later with an even better 85% hit rate.

Weather continued to be a factor over Japan, often diverting missions to secondary targets and targets of opportunity. On 17 July, Japanese installations in China were hit by 47 planes at Chiangwan Airfield near Shanghai. The next day, the nearby airdrome at Wusung was bombed with an 80% hit rate.

On 27 July, the 494th left the railway marshalling yards at Kagoshima, Kyushu ablaze with 85% of their bombs hitting target. They paid the price the next day when two B-24s failed to return from a bombing run against the battleship *Haruna* at Kure Harbor on Honshu Island.

RIGHT The 494th is briefed on upcoming missions over Japan.

Note O.C. standing on the far right with his navigator Fred Sperling to his right.

OFFICERS OF CREW 23A

Here we have the only (and admittedly casual) photo of all the officers of Crew 23A together (L to R): O.C. Kemp, Norman Olson, Fred Sperling, and Jack Berger.

They came from all over the country: from the beaches of San Diego to a sixth floor walk-up tenement in Brooklyn. They are of average weight, height, and education. They boasted no famous forebears or wealth. Their average age was 21.

They volunteered for the Air Force and flew sixteen nerve-wracking missions together. But each knew his job and did it well: O.C. was a natural pilot. Oly was the quiet second in command who, if not for wartime politics, would have commanded his own bomber. Fred could sight the stars or sun and place *Rover Boy's Baby* over an island one mile square after a flight of six hours across the emptiest stretch of water on earth. And Jack could sight through clouds, flak, or rain and place his bombs on target an astonishing 90% of the time.

They were not best friends who bummed, drank, gambled, or caroused together. They were co-workers, serious young men who risked their lives while taking many other lives so that millions more lives could be lived in freedom. And though they would no doubt disagree, to me these young men look like heroes.

BELOW O.C. recounts a harrowing experience in this audio recording made many years after the fact. Once again, he believed he had been lucky or blessed—it didn't matter which—and he was still alive. But shortly after he returned from R&R, he would get his chance to fly over Japan and meet the terrible defenses the Japanese were putting up to battle our bomber missions.

AUDIO TRANSCRIPT 14:05:10

After we got back from R&R, Crew 22A, which had taken our place on the flight rotation schedule, encountered the first enemy fighters the Group had seen since December. They were bombing Tsuiki Airdrome on Kyushu Island on 25 July.

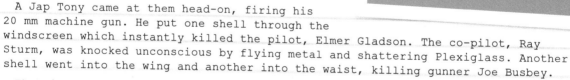

A Jap Tony came at them head-on, firing his 20 mm machine gun. He put one shell through the windscreen which instantly killed the pilot, Elmer Gladson. The co-pilot, Ray Sturm, was knocked unconscious by flying metal and shattering Plexiglass. Another shell went into the wing and another into the waist, killing gunner Joe Busbey.

The airplane didn't blow up, but the windscreen frame was bent down over the yoke, pulling it forward and putting the bomber into a steep dive. It was soon going over 300 miles an hour almost straight down.

Luckily, engineer Harry Fisler wasn't in his usual place standing between the pilots and wasn't hurt by the shell that killed Gladson. He crawled forward and pulled the steel away from the wheel with his bare hands and then managed to pull the plane back to level flight. Then he revived Sturm, who was all cut up, and together they turned the plane around. They were able to land safely.

If I hadn't gone on R&R when I did, I would have been flying Gladson's position on that run. I remember feeling uneasy about these first missions over Japan because I believed the Japanese would defend their home islands with maximum force.

A HIDE-BOUND MYSTERY

For years after the War—until he could no longer squeeze into it—O.C. proudly wore this leather flight jacket. But it has a mystery connected to it.

Though it bears the emblem of O.C.'s squadron on the left breast and the 7th Air Force emblem on the left sleeve, on the right sleeve is the emblem of the Burma-China-India Theater (left). The CBI was most famous for the "Flying Tigers," pilots recruited from American aviation who became the American Volunteer Group (AVG), part of the Chinese Air Force in 1941-1942 and commanded by Claire Lee Chennault prior to our entry in WWII.

The Tigers' mission was to defend China against Japanese forces. Their shark-nosed P-40 fighters remain the most iconic aircraft of the War. They destroyed 300 enemy planes while losing only fourteen pilots and their victories were welcome news at a time when the papers were filled with stories of defeat at the hands of the Japanese. In 1942, the Army's 23rd Fighter Group replaced them and they were later absorbed into the 14th Air Force (emblem at right).

For much of the War, the 7th AAF was shuttled between various commands, used by the Navy and then by the Army. For a period of time it was part of the Far East command and thus under the auspices of the BCI—thus the emblem on the right sleeve.

The graphic on the back is a "blood chit" and was seen primarily in the BCI Theater. It features the American and Chinese flags and Chinese characters that say: "The United States Army Air Force has come to China to help in the war effort. We rely on your military and people to aid and defend this man. (signed) The Aviation Committee of the National Government."

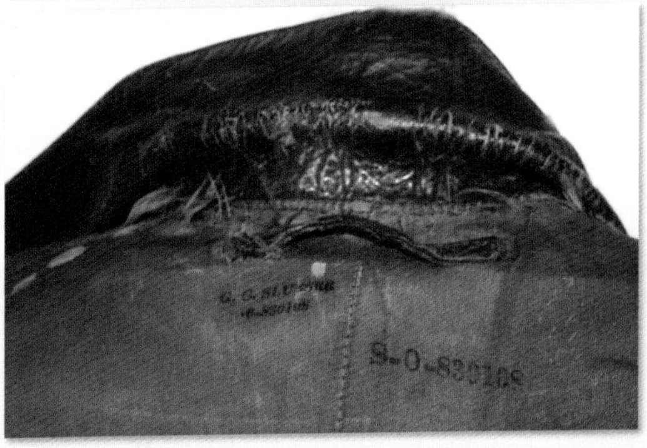

The jacket was likely first owned by a fellow who flew in the BCI theater and passed through Okinawa on his way home. We have a clue about him. The name "G.C. SLU _ _ER" and a serial number 0-839108 are stenciled on the lining in black ink. Unfortunately, an exhaustive search has failed to reveal the identity of the airman who sold O.C. his prized bomber jacket.

FAT MAN & LITTLE BOY: MEN AT WORK

The "Manhattan Project," so named because its first offices were located in New York, began with a letter signed by Albert Einstein to President Roosevelt warning him of the destructive potential of the "atom" bomb U.S. scientists feared Germany was developing. The resulting project was so secret that it was not until FDR died that Vice-President Truman was informed about it. Some more interesting facts:

- Over 130 factories and 130,000 people worked on the atomic bomb, through few knew its potential.
- The fissionable material was Uranium-235, which forms just .07% of natural uranium. For this reason uranium had to be "enriched" using gas, heat, or electromagnet energy. In addition, two other lines of enrichment research were pursued: heavy water and graphite uranium moderation.
- The program had already been underway for several years before uranium was discovered in 1941.
- The world's first nuclear reactor was located under the bleachers at the University of Chicago's football stadium. Enrico Fermi's self-sustaining nuclear chain reaction went critical on 2 December 1942.
- Robert Oppenheimer became the second head of "Project Y," which was tasked with building the bomb. His qualifying expertise involved critical mass and detonation calculations.
- The British preceded America in nuclear technology but would not share the data. But when the U.S. program outstripped Britain's, they relented and sent several scientists to Los Alamos, NM to help.
- Before the uranium bombs were tested, Edward Teller suggested an even more powerful bomb using a uranium bomb to ignite a fusion reaction in deuterium and tritium. This later became the hydrogen bomb.
- "Fat Man" was an implosion weapon in which explosives were used to crush a subcritical sphere of fissile material, causing an increased rate of neutron capture, leading to a critical mass. The "trinity" test at Alamogordo Army Air Field, NM expended over a billion dollars worth of plutonium in the Fat Man design.
- "Little Boy" was a gun-type bomb in which a uranium bullet was shot into a 110-pound sphere of uranium surrounded by dense material focusing neutrons inward to increase efficiency. Due to certainty that the design would detonate, it was never tested before it was used at Hiroshima.

EXTRA! **Pacific Post** EXTRA!

Section One THURSDAY, AUGUST 10, 1945 Ten Cents

"ATOM" BOMBS BLAST JAPAN

A SINGLE BOMB DETONATES EQUIVALENT OF 21 KILOTONS OF TNT

WASHINGTON, D.C., Aug. 6 — Operation Silverplate, the plan to deliver the nuclear bombs to target, was initiated just a few months after the Manhattan Project began.

Col. Paul Tibbets was selected as captain of a modified B-29 that would deliver the bomb "Little Boy" to an undisclosed target. By early 1945, Tinian Island in the Marianas became the point of origin.

The bomb components were delivered separately, arriving in late July. Still the targets had not been chosen. A committee had recommended Kokura, Hiroshima, Niigata and Kyoto. Secretary of War Stimson would not authorize Kyoto due to its historical and religious significance. One of Kyoto's substitutes was Nagasaki.

At the Potsdam Conference in Germany, Truman received word that the Trinity test was successful. He told Josef Stalin the U.S. had a new superweapon but Stalin appeared uninterested. (He had already learned about it from Soviet spies.)

Hiroshima Annihilated

TINIAN, MARIANA ISLANDS, Aug. 6 — Before dawn, the 393rd Bomb Squadron's *Enola Gay* lifted off with "Little Boy" in the bomb bay and Col. Tibbets at the wheel. Its target was Hiroshima, an important army depot and embarkation port, with Nagasaki as an alternative. The bombardier

completed the bomb assembly in the air to minimize risks on takeoff. The sky was clear over the target and the bomb was dropped, detonating at 1,800 feet, destroying 70% of the buildings in a five square mile area, killing 75,000 people and injuring another 70,000.

But the Japanese refused to surrender.

Nagasaki Next

NAGASAKI, JAPAN, Aug. 9 — Today, the B-29 *Bockscar* with 393rd Squadron commander Charles Sweeney at the helm lifted off with the "Fat Man" bomb on board. The bomb was already armed, but with electrical safety plugs engaged.

They were bound for Kokura, but clouds obscured the city and they were under orders for visual bombing only.

After three passes, they diverted to the alternate target: Nagasaki. It too was obscured, but a last-minute break in the clouds allowed visual targeting and the bomb was dropped over the industrial area.

The explosion was half again as big as Hiroshima, destroying almost half the city, killing more than 35,000 and injuring double that number.

And yet the Japanese have not surrendered.

Third Bomb Readied

LOS ALAMOS — There was no third bomb waiting on Tinian. General Leslie Groves, head of the Manhattan Project, would not have another bomb ready until 19 August. On Tinian, two more "Fat Man" assemblies were prepared and a third core was scheduled to leave the mainland for Tinian on 12 August.

And still the Japanese have not surrendered.

NAZIS UNSURPRISED

BERLIN, GERMANY — Nazi leaders interned at Mondorf Prison were not surprised at the effects of the atomic bomb and one declared the Nazis had feared its earlier development and use against Germany.

HIROSHIMA CASUALTIES MAY REACH 200,000

HIROSHIMA, JAPAN — Sixty percent of Hiroshima's built-up area was leveled Monday and as many as 200,000 of that city's 340,000 residents perished or were injured under the impact of history's greatest explosion.

There was little doubt that the second atomic bomb blast would prove as effective as the first.

The second bomb fell on Nagasaki, the great ship-building city, while Japan still sought to survey the seared and blistered corpses—"too numerous to count"—scattered among the wreckage of what once was Hiroshima.

Testifying to the magnitude of Hiroshima's disaster, the enemy reported that as late as Thursday evening—four days after the attack—they still were unable to ascertain the full extent of the damage inflicted by the parachute-borne bomb.

A special meeting of the Japanese Cabinet was called at the residence of Premier Baron Kantaro Suzuki to hear a preliminary report on the devastation, but there was no information about the decisions which were made at the meeting.

And still the Japanese have not surrendered.

RUSSIA DECLARES WAR

CHUNGKING, CHINA — Soviet Russia's Far Eastern Army of more than one million men early today launched a broad attack across the Manchurian border, gaining several miles in the first hours of the attack which began only a short time after the Russian declaration of war became effective.

The Russian operation was carried out in the strictest secrecy, though it was known that the attack concentrated on three main points.

MOLOTOV REVEALS JAPANESE PEACE BID AS HE DECLARES WAR

MOSCOW, RUSSIA — Foreign Commissar Molotov disclosed that Emperor Hirohito had asked "about mid-July" for the Soviets to mediate in the Pacific war, but added that Tokyo's rejection of the Potsdam unconditional surrender ultimatum caused the proposals to "lose all significance."

"THEY WERE SHOOTING AT ME"

When Harry Truman was told that the invasion of Japan could be averted by use of the atom bomb, he ordered it done and reputedly went to bed, his conscience clear.

Japan's defensive plan, "Operation Decision," called for 10,000 suicide planes, 53 infantry divisions and 25 brigades, 2.3 million troops who would fight on the beaches, 4 million civil employees, and a militia of 28 million. Therefore, according to historian Paul Johnson, assuming comparable ratios to those already experienced in Pacific battles, total casualties of an invasion of Japan would be in the range of 10 to 20 million.

Since the dropping of the atom bombs, many have gainsaid the decision. Some scientists at the time counseled a demonstration of the bombs' capability. Others believed the Soviet declaration of war was decisive in Japan's decision to surrender. Still others evoked the moral price the U.S. would pay for using such a weapon.

Johnson gives a compelling response to these arguments:

> The evidence does not suggest that the surrender could have been obtained without the A-bombs being used. Without them, there would have been heavy fighting in Manchuria, and a further intensification of the conventional bombardment (already nearing the nuclear threshold of about 10,000 tons of TNT a day), even if an invasion had not been required. The use of nuclear weapons thus saved Japanese as well as Allied lives. Those who died in Hiroshima and Nagasaki were the victims not so much of Anglo-American technology as of a paralyzed system of government made possible by an evil ideology which had expelled not only absolute moral values but reason itself.

When I was a callow, antagonistic teenager in the 1970s, I gave O.C. some simplistic guff about killing people in the War. His answer may have lacked Johnson's elegant language but not its logic:

"Well," he said, shrugging. "They were shooting at me."

General Orders No. 99 classified SECRET and distributed to those concerned.

GENERAL ORDERS)
:
NUMBER 100)

HEADQUARTERS SEVENTH AIR FORCE,
APO #903, 10 August 1945.

E X T R A C T

AWARD OF FIRST BRONZE OAK LEAF CLUSTER TO AIR MEDAL: - By direction of t President, under the provisions of Executive Order No. 9158, 11 May 1942 (Bull. 25, W.D., 1942), as amended by Executive Order No. 9242-A, 11 September 1942 (Bu No. 49, W.D., 1942), and pursuant to authority contained in paragraphs 17 and 18, AR 600-45, 22 September 1943 and Ltr Hq AAFPOA, 18 October 1944, in addition to th Air Medal previously awarded, the first Bronze Oak Leaf Custer is awarded by the Commanding General, Seventh Air Force, to the following named officers and enlisted men, Air Corps, United States Army, for meritorious achievement while participating in sustained aerial operations against the enemy from 21 October 1944 to 9 May 1945. During this period, each as a crew member of a heavy bombardment airplane, participated in numerous missions against heavily defended enemy held bases involving long over water flights to and from the target. Throughout these operations, which were accomplished with distinction above and beyond that normally expected, each displayed high skill and courage, inflicting severe damage to enemy air bases and shipping, reflecting great credit upon himself and the Army Air Forces:

2nd Lt (1092) OMER C KEMP 0710957
2nd Lt (1055) NORMAN J OLSON 0927583
2nd Lt (1036) FREDERICK C SPERLING JR 02060604
2nd Lt (1035) JACK A BERGER 0928139
Sgt (737) Juan F Gutierrez 39550289
Sgt (612) Joseph A Trasatti 13133599
Sgt (757) Calvin G Morrow 19130002
Sgt (611) Eugene W Vaughn 37616773
Sgt (611) Charles K Yetter 3758620
Sgt (612) Lloyd I Nygren 39280958

BY COMMAND OF BRIGADIER GENERAL WHITE:

D. G. GROTHAUS,
Colonel, G.S.C.,
Deputy Chief of Staff.

DISTRIBUTION: "B"

brief JAPAN'S INVISIBLE ALLY

by Cpl Richard Dugan and S.Sgt Bob Speer

The B-29 crew stuck to their fantastic story although the intelligence officer scoffed. "We couldn't get to the target," they insisted. "We came up to the coast of Japan. The closer we got, the less progress we made. Then we began flying backwards. Finally we lost sight of the coast altogether and never did see it again."

Another crew told a similar tale: "We were slugging our way along when we came to the coast. With all four engines roaring full blast, we couldn't gain an inch. We weren't flying backwards, but we weren't going forwards, either. We were just hovering like a giant seagull. Finally, we gave up and came back."

The G-2 boys shook their heads. We had met the biggest single obstacle to high-altitude precision bombing: the weather. For a few black weeks in late 1944 it threatened to change the strategy of the war. Winds over Honshu were incredible; crews had never seen anything like it. When planes *did* succeed in fighting their way to target, and then turned to slide downward over it, they clocked speeds in excess of 500 miles an hour with that wind on their tail. Before the bombardier could even begin his calculations, he was past the target and they had to go back and try it again, which made him unpopular with everybody in the crew who didn't happen to like flak in double doses.

Then there were the clouds, often several layers, each moving swiftly in different directions, which made bombing accuracy impossible. You might hit something as big as a city, but those bombs weren't made to miss their targets. Southeasterly trade winds, warm and moist as they follow the Japanese current northward, boil up against the opposing cold front from Asia along the Japanese coastline.

There were also the crosswinds. At 30,000 feet, you might drop your bombs into the teeth of a 250-knot westerly gale and calculate accordingly. But when the bomb reached 10,000 feet, it might meet a 60-knot easterly wind, and a deflection at that altitude might mean a whopping error of several hundred yards which in turn might mean the difference between pulverizing a factory or just helping to cultivate a rice paddy.

But the AAF had eight experts who, though unable to tame the weather, managed to work out ways to turn it to our advantage. They accompanied bombing and snooper missions for weeks, sweating out the ack-ack, searchlights, and fighters, getting the firsthand dope. Four of them experienced crack-ups and were forced to take to life rafts. But they learned a few things on the way: they learned of the importance of up-to-date maps of which there were none. There were few studies of Japanese climate. But after trial and error and observation, they discovered that Japanese weather was like the weather on the east coast of the U.S. though much more intense: Great masses of cold air sweep eastward out of Siberia. By analyzing the air mass velocity, density and moisture content—like they do stateside—they found they could predict almost exactly what kind of weather they were going to have over Japan the same way they do over New York City. But instead of a network of ground stations from Seattle to Maine, our boys did it aloft in snooper flights over Russia and China. Nevertheless, this greatly improved the scheduling of missions and thus accuracy.

Fortunately, winter is nearly past and the winds have died down. Forecasters predict quiet weather until autumn, when the typhoon season begins. Unfortunately, warmer weather builds more clouds, so it's six of one and half a dozen of another. Clear skies will be rare until the fall. Fortunately, radar doesn't mind clouds and the war will go on.

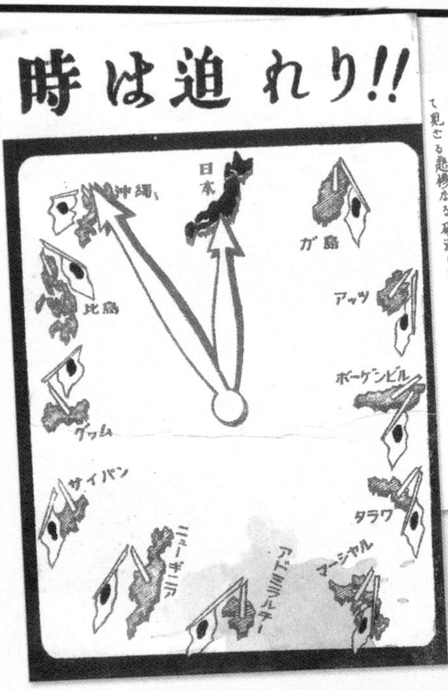

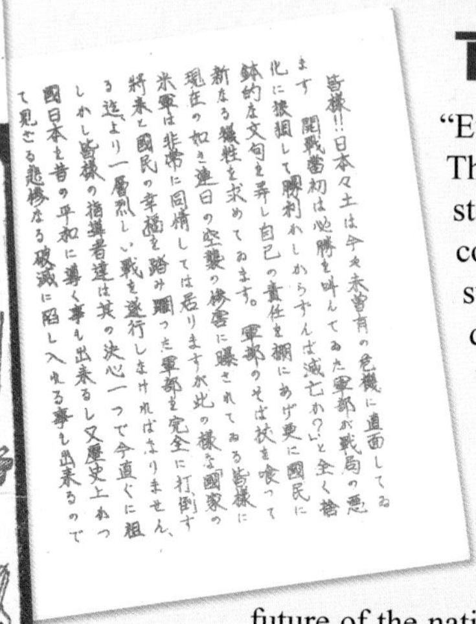
皆様!!日本々土は今や未曾有の危機に直面してゐます　開戦當初は必勝を叫んでゐた軍部が戦局の悪化に狼狽して勝利かしからずんば滅亡か?と全く捨鉢的な文句を弄し自己の責任を棚にあげ更に國民に新なる犠牲を求めてゐます。軍部のそば杖を食って現在の如き連日の空襲の惨害に曝されてゐる皆様に米軍は非常に同情しては居りますが此の様な「國家の将来と國民の幸福を踏み躙った軍部を完全に打倒するまでより一層烈しい戦を遂行しなければなりません、しかし皆様の指導者達は其の決心一つで今直ぐに祖國日本を昔の平和に導く事も出来るし又歴史上かつて見ざる悲惨なる破滅に陥し入れる事も出来るので

TIME IS DRAWING NIGH!

"Everyone! Japan is facing unprecedented danger. The military that boasted of certain victory at the start of the war is now panicking over the worsening course of the war. They bandy desperate phrases such as 'Shall it be victory or destruction?' and demand even more sacrifice from the citizens while ignoring their own responsibility. America greatly sympathizes with those who are suffering the horrors of daily air raids, who bear the brunt of attacks directed against your military. We must, however, engage in even more intense battles until a military that tramples underfoot the future of the nation and the happiness of its people is overthrown. Even so, with unified determination, your leaders could immediately guide your ancestral land to its former state of peace. They could also plunge you into a horrible destruction never before witnessed in your history.

"'Unconditional Surrender' is a military term that means nothing more than the demise of the military and the cessation of war. However, the military tries to convince you that this means the eradication of the Japanese people through enslavement. This is a lie by a military frantic to save its own prestige, meant to spur on a hopeless resistance of the nation's citizens at the eleventh hour. Because of the military's reluctance to accept responsibility for losing the war, it refuses the extended hand of peace. Will you do nothing as Japan plunges into destruction?

"Everyone! While you still can, wouldn't you rather save your nation and help rebuild a new Japan?"

ABOVE On missions over Japan late in the War, crews dropped flyers instead of bombs, encouraging the citizens to rise up against their military overlords who seemed intent upon the destruction of their own country.

RIGHT An ordnance man packs a wooden leaflet "bomb." Dozens will be loaded into the bomb bay for distribution over Japan.

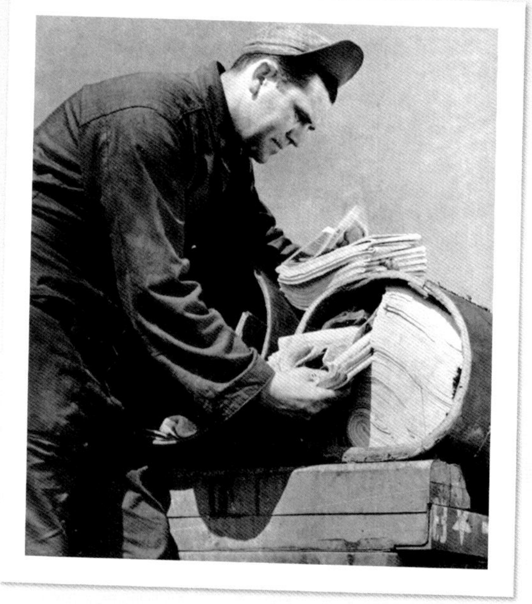

沖縄の幼ない可愛い子供が
兵隊さんとすっかり仲良しに
128-J-1

LEFT The Japanese military spewed horrific propaganda of American atrocities upon conquered peoples (including the eating of young children) in an attempt to prevent its soldiers and citizens from surrendering. We fought back with this flyer which was dropped over Japan as the land invasion neared:

"The adorable little children of Okinawa are becoming fast friends with the soldiers and are surprising their big American buddies with calls of 'Candy, please!' and 'Let's play!'

A scene of simple innocence, wouldn't you agree?"

Translations by Ronald Arthur

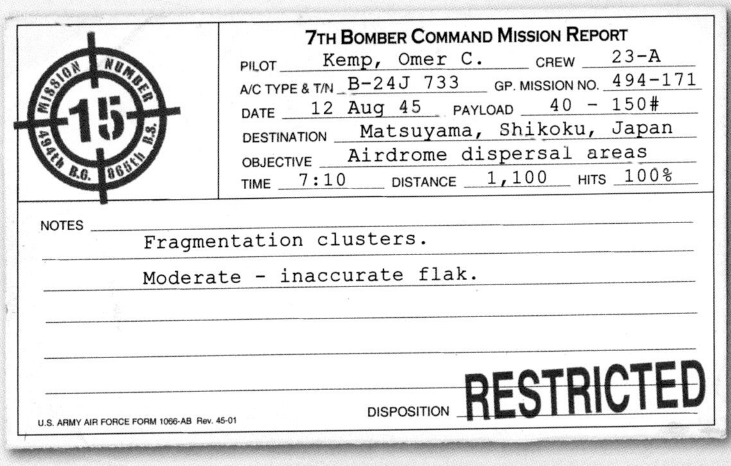
MISSION NUMBER 15 494th B.G. 866th B.S.

7TH BOMBER COMMAND MISSION REPORT

PILOT Kemp, Omer C. CREW 23-A

A/C TYPE & T/N B-24J 733 GP. MISSION NO. 494-171

DATE 12 Aug 45 PAYLOAD 40 - 150#

DESTINATION Matsuyama, Shikoku, Japan

OBJECTIVE Airdrome dispersal areas

TIME 7:10 DISTANCE 1,100 HITS 100%

NOTES

Fragmentation clusters.

Moderate - inaccurate flak.

DISPOSITION RESTRICTED

U.S. ARMY AIR FORCE FORM 1066-AB Rev. 45-01

. . . AND STILL THEY DID NOT SURRENDER

To us today, the use of the atom bomb was a game-changer; we've seen the photos of the devastation. But the men on the islands of the Pacific knew nothing about that. Besides, the fire-bombing of Tokyo and other Japanese cities had already neared the nuclear threshold in terms of damage. So to the bomber crews of the 494th, the atom bomb was a more powerful bomb, but still just a bomb.

So they were not surprised when Japan did not surrender after the first bomb fell on Hiroshima. They may not have even known about it. (Newspapers of the day typically reported the second bombing, not the first.) So when Crew 23A got their orders for their first bombing run over the Japanese mainland, they did not expect it to be their last. (In reality, the last bombing run the 494th flew was the very next day, 13 August.)

But even this mission was fraught with complexities. Al "Rusty" Restuccia, radio operator and prolific nose-art painter, reminded Jack Berger years later that this was the only mission in which Crew 23A did not fly their beloved *Rover Boy's Baby,* instead flying Rusty's plane *Innocence A-Broad.* Rusty said, "Your crew flew our plane over Matsuyama while our crew was in the lead ship because it had radar which we needed to penetrate a strong weather front containing two typhoons. Lt. Gregory, crew chief that day, assured us that you folks would not encounter any difficulty. We worried so much about *Innocence* that it became a fetish with us."

Superstition abides in airmen because the inexplicable is not susceptible to logic. And it was heightened on the Japan missions because of the terrible losses previous crews had encountered. Their objective this time was the dispersal areas at the airdrome. They encountered moderate and inaccurate flak, dropping fragmentation cluster bombs on the field. Jack Berger racked up an impressive 100% hit rate through clouds and gusty weather.

O.C. said they hit a number of aircraft, or at least cardboard cutouts of aircraft. The Japanese had taken to populating their airdromes with painted facsimiles in an attempt to convince us that they were withstanding our hundred-plane bombing runs. All they succeeded in doing was ensuring future visits.

RIGHT Aerial photo of the airdrome at Matsuyama, which was already heavily damaged by months of high-altitude bombing.

SOMEWHERE IN THE RYUKYUS

As part of replacement crew 43B, pilot Gareth Williams didn't fly as often as he wished either, so in his spare time he painted. Excerpts from a letter home: "We're now allowed to say we're 'somewhere in the Ryukyus.' [Williams, like O.C., was Censor Officer of his crew.]

"We may mention the tombs in our area, practically the only signs of civilization around here. Our tent is forty feet from the entrance of one, and a square 15 foot court (cut while quarrying) reaches out toward us. By military order, all tombs are sealed, so ours has stones blocking the door. Inside the tombs are urns in square glazed designs and vase-like plain pottery to hold the bones.

The tombs are built into the sides of hills and struck me at first as gun emplacements, being horseshoe-shaped, made out of porous volcanic rock covered with a thin layer of grey cement.

There is a slight oriental flavor about them. Some are large, some small, but all have the same design, a few mostly white, but most grey. Next door they use a court for a backyard, a corner of which contains broken urns and bones.

"I'm going to paint the one behind us; it has a mellowed look, crumbling, overgrown, and apparently damaged by AA fragments."

IMPRISONED AT GROUND ZERO

The remnant of the Imperial Navy was moored at Kure Harbor, near Hiroshima. Though there were dozens of warships at anchor, the primary target was the battleship *Haruna*, which had been involved in nearly every sea battle since the War began. In addition, Kure was the "Annapolis of Japan." The strike was for revenge, then, and the avengers were destined to suffer.

On 28 July, 24 bombers faced a near opaque curtain of flak over the harbor. Two planes went down, including 716 *Taloa* and 680 *Lonesome Lady*, both from the 866th Squadron.

Taloa's crew perished except for the two who parachuted to safety. After being hit by flak, Tom Cartwright, pilot of *Lonesome Lady*, headed toward the sea. Then fire broke out, the hydraulics failed, and Cartwright ordered his crew to bail out. By the time he himself got out, the plane was in a vertical dive.

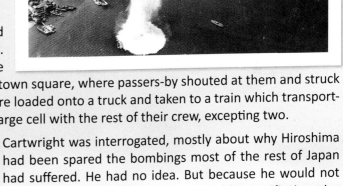

Cartwright landed in a pine forest and surrendered to a farmer, who took him to a local police station. There he saw co-pilot Durden Looper. They were bound and blindfolded and spent the night in the town square, where passers-by shouted at them and struck them. The next morning, still blindfolded, they were loaded onto a truck and taken to a train which transported them to a prison where they were placed in a large cell with the rest of their crew, excepting two.

Cartwright was interrogated, mostly about why Hiroshima had been spared the bombings most of the rest of Japan had suffered. He had no idea. But because he would not divulge his own movements across the Pacific in prior months, he was separated from his crew, bound and blindfolded again, and taken to a train station.

The trip took two days and Cartwright began to feel sorry for himself because he was separated from his comrades. When they arrived at a military base, he was put into solitary confinement. He later found out that the base was in the Tokyo area. There they interrogated him for three days, the questioning always starting out friendly and gradually turning angrier, with threats of punishment if he did not cooperate. They questioned him particularly closely about a new powerful bomb, of which he of course knew nothing.

Shortly after that interrogation, he was blindfolded, taken outside, and forced to kneel before some troops. His head was pressed against a hard wooden surface. There were shouts and angry voices. He could feel the sizzling hatred of those around him, coupled with an intense desire for vengeance against him personally. He believed he was about to be beheaded.

Then suddenly he was jerked to his feet and led back to his cell. A few days later, Cartwright was informed that the War was over. When he inquired about his crew, he was informed that the prison where they had been held was just a half-mile from the epicenter of the explosion of the atomic bomb over Hiroshima.

Cartwright, who became a college professor after the War, vowed he would never feel sorry for himself again.

EXTRA! **Pacific Post** **EXTRA!**

Section One | WEDNESDAY, AUGUST 15, 1945 | Ten Cents

PEACE!

JAPS ACCEPT TERMS UNRESERVEDLY

WASHINGTON, D.C., Aug. 14. – President Truman announced that the Japanese government has accepted the surrender terms without qualifications, reading a statement which said:

"I deem this reply a full acceptance of the Potsdam declaration which specified the unconditional surrender of Japan. In the reply there are no qualifications."

The President also revealed that he had named General Douglas MacArthur the supreme commander to receive the Japanese surrender.

Meanwhile, he said Allied armed forces have been ordered to suspend offensive operations.

V-J Day will not be proclaimed until after the formal signing of the surrender terms by Japan.

The three Allies in the Pacific war—Great Britain, Russia, and China—will be represented at the signing by high ranking officials.

The Japanese government's message accepting the Allied terms said that Emperor Hirohito is prepared "to authorize and insure the signature" by the Japanese government and the Imperial general headquarters of the necessary terms for carrying out provisions of the Potsdam declaration.

"His Majesty is also prepared to issue commands to all the military, naval and air authorities of Japan and all forces under their control wherever located to cease active operations and to surrender arms."

Air Onslaught on Japan Continues

GUAM, Aug. 15 – Allied aerial bombing of Japan continued in nonstop around-the-clock fury today with bombing, strafing and rocketing planes accentuating Allied demands for acceptance of surrender terms laid down for Nippon.

More than 800 Marianas-based Superfortress bombers have dropped 6,000 tons of demolition and fire bombs onto the home islands in the last 24 hours. The B-29 raids were underway even as Tokyo radio yesterday said an answer to the Allied note of Saturday was en route, and the raids continued into the early hours today. Two hundred Iwo-based P-51 Mustang fighters gave escort.

General Douglas MacArthur's communique from Manila today reported the strongest Japanese resistance in weeks was met over Korea by Pacific Air Forces pilots.

President Declares Two-Day Holiday

WASHINGTON, D.C., Aug. 14 – President Truman tonight declared a two-day holiday tomorrow and Thursday for all Federal employees in Washington and throughout the country.

He told a press conference that the reason for two days was that the employees had not had a chance to celebrate the last surrender on V-E Day.

Celebrations are now being planned all across the nation.

REVELING IN THE RYUKYUS

For those on the front lines of the War, the end was anticlimactic. Their circumstances prevented them from appreciating the significance of the event. O.C. was no exception:

"Well, the old war is over. I can't say I feel any different than before. I can hardly believe it really is over, though. I just can't get used to there not being a war on somewhere.

"About three nights ago we had a celebration out here with tracers and flares and everything imaginable. That was when Japan first made their peace offer. With the official announcement coming through today, so far there hasn't been any fireworks tonight. The results from the last one weren't so good."

He's referring to several deaths caused by falling bullets shot into the air in celebration and two munitions dumps accidentally ignited by small arms fire, killing several people.

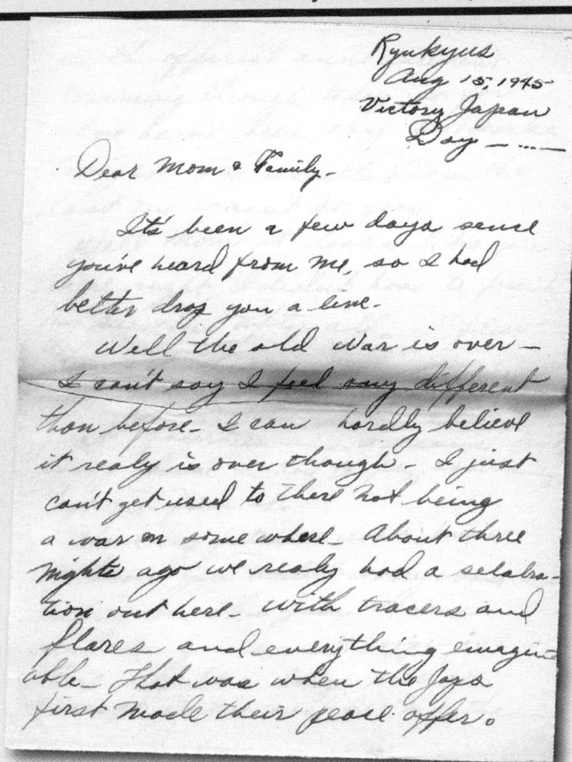

Ryukyus
Aug 15, 1945
Victory Japan
Day —

Dear Mom & Family—

It's been a few days since you've heard from me, so I had better drop you a line.

Well the old war is over— I can't say I feel any different than before— I can hardly believe it really is over though— I just can't get used to there not being a war on some where— About three nights ago we really had a celebration out here— with tracers and flares and everything imaginable— That was when the Japs first made their peace offer.

ONCE UPON A TIME . . .

The USSR was our ally against Japan, as seen by this leaflet dropped over occupied China. Note however the self-congratulatory tone of the flyer, which is obviously of Russian provenance:

A THRILLING HANDSHAKE

The Soviet Union's declaration of war against Japan means Japan is now in a hopeless conflict with the armies of the entire world. You are no doubt aware of the fate of Hitler, whose military was famed for its reckless attack strategies and who attempted to conquer Russia and western Asia in one fell swoop. What should be etched deeply in your mind is that those same German forces, when confronted with Soviet and Allied armies, suffered ultimate annihilation.

With the end of the war with Germany, the Soviet Union now turns its attention to the east and Japan. Its battle-tested and hardened military has been replenished and enhanced—both in quality and quantity—to levels far above its pre-war capabilities.

感激の握手
蘇聯の對日戰參加は日本國民にとつて日本が遂
に全世界の陸軍を相手に絶望的抗戰を餘儀な
く繼續しなければならぬ羽目に陷つたことを意味する。
露西亞を一擧に席巻せんとしたあの精鋭を誇

The imminent invasion of Japan by the allied countries will result in its inevitable, utter destruction. In order to save the beautiful land of your ancestors from the horrible ravages of war, the people of Japan know which path they should take!

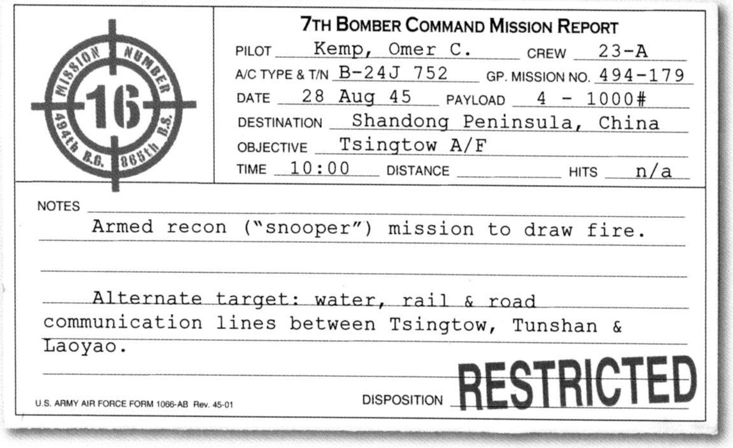

MISSION NUMBER 16 494th B.G. 865th B.S.

7TH BOMBER COMMAND MISSION REPORT

PILOT Kemp, Omer C. CREW 23-A
A/C TYPE & T/N B-24J 752 GP. MISSION NO. 494-179
DATE 28 Aug 45 PAYLOAD 4 - 1000#
DESTINATION Shandong Peninsula, China
OBJECTIVE Tsingtow A/F
TIME 10:00 DISTANCE HITS n/a

NOTES
Armed recon ("snooper") mission to draw fire.

~~Alternate target: water, rail & road~~ communication lines between Tsingtow, Tunshan & Laoyao.

DISPOSITION **RESTRICTED**

U.S. ARMY AIR FORCE FORM 1066-AB Rev. 45-01

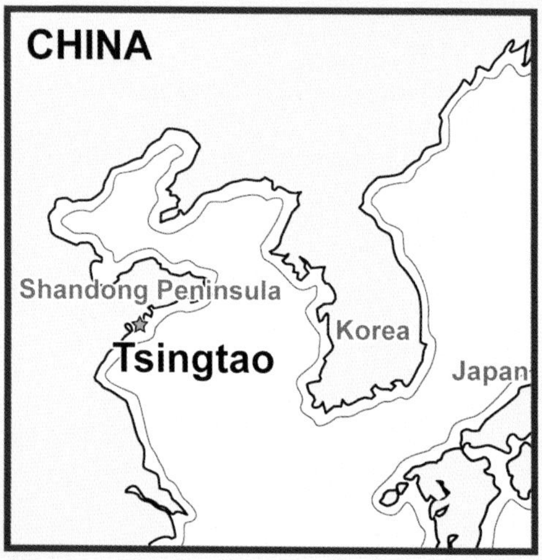

SNOOPING AROUND

Since it arrived on Okinawa, the 494th had been flying "snooper"—armed reconnaissance—missions over Japan and China to gauge weather patterns, scout out enemy positions, and choose bombing targets. Snooper missions were considered dangerous, lonely fights, often solo or in small formations and thus with little protection against attacking fighters. Now that the War was over, the snooper missions were re-purposed: they were to go out and see whether the Japanese had truly surrendered. In other words, they were bait.

In the final weeks of the War, Japan's communications systems had been destroyed, so it was supposed that there were still many enemy soldiers who did not know they had been beaten, or if they did, they did not care and would, like many of their comrades, fight to the death according to the principles of *bushidō*.

Part of O.C.'s mission on 28 August over the Shandong Peninsula in China, a camel-head shaped peninsula across the Yellow Sea from Korea, was to fly over an airdrome and see if his presence drew anti-aircraft fire or scrambled enemy fighters. If it did, he was to swing around, line up on the airdrome, and drop his four 1000 pound bombs on any "target of opportunity" that presented itself.

Specifically, the target was Tsingtow (now Qingdao) Airdrome, a coastal installation on the camel's "neck." If he drew no fire, alternate targets would be water, rail, and roadways in order to inhibit Japanese escape routes. Because of the atrocities committed by the Japanese against the Chinese, the Allies wanted to keep the invaders in the general area to face their accusers and receive justice. If they found no suitable targets, *Rover Boy's Baby* was to return to Okinawa with her bombs.

On this mission, there was no ground fire and no apparent enemy activity, so they turned back toward Okinawa. O.C. recounted his decision about what to do with his bomb load in an audio recording many years later:

AUDIO TRANSCRIPT 15:02:16

I knew when I left Okinawa with those bombs that I wasn't going to land with them because that is one of the most dangerous situations you can find yourself in. Here the War is over and we're gonna <u>save</u> the bombs? All the plane would have had to do is blow a tire, skid along on its belly, and collide with something... and we'd all be history.

So I just told Jack [Berger], "Let's get rid of 'em."

When we were out over the ocean, we dropped them with the safeties on, but they still all went off. They made quite a big splash, killing fish for the Chinese.

AUGUST ON OKINAWA

LOSSES IN ACTION Three men killed, two wounded. Three B-24s were lost to operational causes.

MISSION Continued destruction of military installations in Japan and, following the end of the War, operational readiness for troop transport and courier service.

ENEMY OPPOSITION Final contact with enemy fighters came on 1 August. The P-47 escorts were late in arriving at the rendezvous and 20-30 Zekes attacked. B-24 crews held their own, however, downing five enemy aircraft, though two bombers were damaged and two crewmen were killed.

FIRST FIRE BOMBING On 5 August, the 494th used napalm bombs for the first time, dropping them on Tarumizu, Kyushu Island. More were dropped over the next few days but smoke from previous bombings and heavy cloud cover made ascertaining the results difficult.

BOMBING MISSIONS The Group continued its Japan bombings, noting on 10 August that there was a "peculiar reddish dust with a burned smell rising to 14,000 feet" near Nagasaki. Two missions occurred after the Japanese manifested interest in surrendering on 10 August.

OOPS! When news came that the Japanese might surrender, men celebrated by firing their guns into the air. At least one bomb dump on Okinawa was destroyed this way, resulting in a shortage of bombs for the final missions on 11-12 August.

SNOOPERS Nightly flights were made to Japan and China for reconnaissance, snooper, and propaganda purposes.

OPERATIONS In the first two weeks in August over 700 sorties were flown with a 96% effective rate, for a total of 25,000 combat hours on Okinawa, dropping 1,800 tons of bombs with a 58% hit rate. Over two thirds of the bombs dropped were unobserved due to cloud obscuration.

OPERATIONS TOTAL Since beginning its operations against the enemy, the 494th few almost 50,000 hours, over half of which were combat hours. 95% of its 3,200 sorties were effective. Average time aloft was 8.4 hours. Twenty aircraft were lost to operational causes, killing six crews. Ten aircraft were lost in combat, with the loss of seven crews. 6,400 tons of bombs were dropped, 69% of observable hits were on target.

CHANGE IN MISSION Following the cessation in hostilities, the 494th began acting as a courier and troop carrier service. On 30 August, it ferried air traffic controllers to Manila and returned with Air Force replacement crews. Though the pilots on the Okinawa-Philippines route groused about being "bus drivers," there was still danger: on 31 August, two aircraft were lost in bad weather (*See* p.244).

MORALE Though high after the 10 August announcement of Japan's imminent capitulation, morale dropped when rumors circulated that the 494th might act as an occupation force in Japan. In addition, many Group members had earned up to seven bronze combat stars but had received only one as of 31 August.

ENTERTAINMENT Two new movie areas were constructed for use by all squadrons, as well as softball fields and a library. Two talent shows were held, and the USO came and entertained servicemen. However, by month's end the supply of movies had degraded and troops were seeing the same movies over and over.

IT ENDS WHERE IT STARTED

The "Trinity" nuclear test took place on 16 July. Ten days later, at the Allied conference at Potsdam, Germany (appropriately code named "Terminal"), President Truman boldly told Japan, "Surrender or suffer prompt and utter destruction." Three days later Japan gave its terse reply: the declaration was "beneath notice."

On 6 August, four days after the Potsdam conference ended, "Little Boy" was dropped on Hiroshima. Three days after that, the USSR declared war on Japan and began operation "August Storm," attacking the Japanese in Manchuria. That same day, 9 August, the "Fat Man" atomic bomb was dropped on Nagasaki. On 12 August, still without notice of surrender, O.C. Kemp and Crew 23A were sent to bomb Matsuyama Airdrome on Shikoku Island (#15). Finally, three days later on 15 August the Japanese government surrendered unconditionally.

LEFT On 2 September, on the *USS Missouri*, the Japanese delegation, including Foreign Minister Mamoru Shigemitsu, waits to be beckoned to the table where the surrender documents await his signature in this rare color photo.

At the conclusion of the ceremony, General MacArthur approached the microphones and said, "It is my earnest hope—indeed the hope of all mankind—that from this solemn occasion a better world shall emerge out of the blood and carnage of the past, a world founded upon faith and understanding, a world dedicated to the dignity of man and the fulfillment of his most cherished wish for freedom, tolerance, and justice."

At home, Americans celebrated as if "joy had been rationed and saved up for the three years, eight months and seven days since Sunday, December 7, 1941."

BELOW On 7 September, a Japanese military delegation that included two generals and an admiral came to Yontan Airfield on Okinawa to formally surrender the Ryukyu Islands to the Allied forces. Officers of the 494th attended the ceremony held on the airfield, and O.C. snapped photos of the event, including an artsy one with a tank barrel looming above the participants.

865TH BOMBARDMENT SQUADRON (H)
494TH BOMBARDMENT GROUP (H)

201 Kemp, Omer C. 7 September 1945

SUBJECT: Promotion of Officer.

TO : Commanding General, Far East Air Forces, APO 925.

1. Under the provisions of AR 605-12, 17 August 1944, and changes thereto, it is recommended that the following-named officer be promoted as indicated:

a. Name Kemp, Omer C. Serial No. 0-710957 (ASRS 75)
b. Permanent Grade None SVC. & Date None
c. Present AUS grade 2nd Lieut. SVC. & Date 34 Pampa Tex. 8 Feb 44
d. Recommended grade **1st Lieutenant**
e. Organization 865th Bomb Sq (H) 494 Bomb Gp (H) Age 22
f. Arm or Service AC Component: RA ___ ORC ___ NG ___ AUS X
g. Total active commissioned service 19 Months
h. Other Military Service 14 months as EM & Cadet Trng
i. Date of entry on ED 8 February 1944 Grade 2nd Lieutenant
j. Present duty Pilot B-24
k. Aeronautical rating Pilot Active Yes
l. Combat missions Cen Pac 13 Combat hours Cen Pac 111:35
m. Combat missions SOPAU 2 Combat hours SOPAU 17:40
n. Total combat missions 15 Total combat hours 129:15
o. Date entry on foreign duty, present tour 15 November 1944
p. Total cumulative position vacancies existing in this organization under: P/O 1-117 & GO 83 (DATE) 21 Jul 44 & 31 May 45
q. Combat missions ETO, MTO or other Theatre (Designate) None
r. Combat hours ETO, MTO or other Theatre (Designate) None

2. a. This officer has held his present grade for 23 26/30 months months, during which time he has demonstrated his fitness for the position and grade for which recommended. His service during this period is recorded as follows:

	Duty Assignment	Organization	From	To	Manner of Performance
(1)	Pilot B-24	865th Bomb Sq (H)	5 Jan 45	Date	3.7
(2)	Pilot B-24	91st Airdrome Sq	14 Nov 44	30 Dec 44	Unk.
(3)	Pilot B-24	421st AAFBU, Cal.	8 Jun 44	10 Oct 44	V.S.
(4)	B-24 Trans Tng	527 BHq&AB Sq Kans	19 Feb 44	18 May 44	---

b. A full statement of how, when and where he has demonstrated his fitness for the position and grade for which recommended: Subject officer has performed the duties of Pilot B-24 fr 6 Jan 45 to date in an excellent manner. This duty was performed at APO 264 and APO 903 with this organization.

3. The relative rank of this officer has been considered; and, to the best of my knowledge and belief, he is the best fitted officer available in this command for the grade and position for which promotion is recommended.

4. This officer has demonstrated clearly his qualifications for promotion by actual occupation of a position and performance of duties appropriate to the next higher grade, for over 3 months prior to this recommendation.

5. The officer is not now under orders for reassignment nor is his reassignment contemplated in the immediate future.

6. A position vacancy does exist in accordance with approved Tables of Organization or Allotment for this unit and the filling of such vacancy by the promotion of this officer, together with all previous recommendations not acted upon, will not operate to exceed the number of position vacancies that are authorized under Tables of Organization on 1-117 & GO 83 dd 21 Jul 44 & 31 May 45.

a. Subject Officer is not scheduled for return to the United States under Readjustment Regulations during the next two and one half months.

JOSEPH G. WOGEN,
Major, Air Corps, Commanding.

ABOVE On the same day the Japanese delegation surrendered on Okinawa, O.C. was recommended for promotion. However, this is the only record we have of it; as far as is known, the Army never followed through and formalized the advancement. He was mustered out two months later as a second lieutenant.

EX-P.O.W. AIRLINES

Unlike POWs held by Germany, 99% of which came back alive, a third of those held by Japan died in captivity. It was for this reason that Admiral Halsey did not wait for the formal surrender ceremony to secure the release of the dozens of Americans held on Omori Island, a POW prison in Tokyo Bay. He feared the fanatical Japanese military, known to oppose the surrender (and which indeed had just staged a coup attempt) would murder all the Americans in their custody.

Once the POWs were released, they were to be transported home quickly, a task that was given to the 494th Bomb Group. By mid-September, 12,000 American ex-POWs had been evacuated from Japan, Manchuria, and Korea. Most would be flown to the Philippines and go the rest of the way home by ship. But to get them there required flights from Okinawa. Most arrived safely, but one flight on 9 September reminds us that the rain falls on the just as well as the unjust.

Monsoon season had arrived. A typhoon was brewing south of Okinawa, directly in the path of flights to Luzon Island. Pilots were advised to take a dog-leg detour around the western side of Formosa (Taiwan) and then south to Luzon. Before leaving, the Liberator crews instructed the ex-POWs on safety and escape procedures.

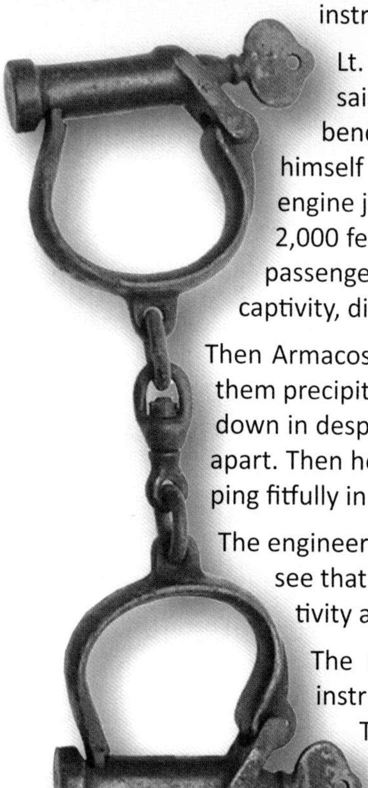

Lt. Bob Armacost, piloting 666 *Les Miserables*, had fifteen British soldiers, a Dutch sailor, and four U.S. soldiers, all en route to freedom, sitting on makeshift plywood benches in his bomb bay. But no sooner were they off the ground than he found himself in instrument conditions—the soup was so thick Armacost couldn't see the #2 engine just outside his left window. The air was too rough for the autopilot, hurling them 2,000 feet up one minute, plunging them down the same distance the next. But his stoic passengers, shivering, suffering from beri-beri and scurvy, emaciated and weak from their captivity, did not complain. They were going home.

Then Armacost lost the #1 engine, which would not feather but simply windmilled, dropping them precipitously to just a couple thousand feet above the turbulent ocean. Armacost looked down in despair at the twenty foot swells. If he ditched, the rough seas would tear his aircraft apart. Then he saw something. A tiny ship was cresting a huge wave, the Union Jack flag snapping fitfully in the wind. He thanked God and rang the bail-out bell.

The engineer led his charges to the rear hatch, helping each one through, but was horrified to see that some failed to open their chutes once they were out of the aircraft. Years of captivity and illness had reduced their thinking to a nullity.

The next three popped their chutes *inside* the plane. These he bundled up and instructed the men to hold tightly to their chests. Once outside they all blossomed. Then the crew bailed out. Soon they were bobbing in the ocean, awaiting pick-up from the ship, a British destroyer escort. In the end, thirteen of their flight were saved but twelve men died, including nine British and three American POWs.

ABOVE Scores of POWs at Omori POW camp in Tokyo Bay cheer as a Higgins boat approaches the island to take them home in this iconic photo.

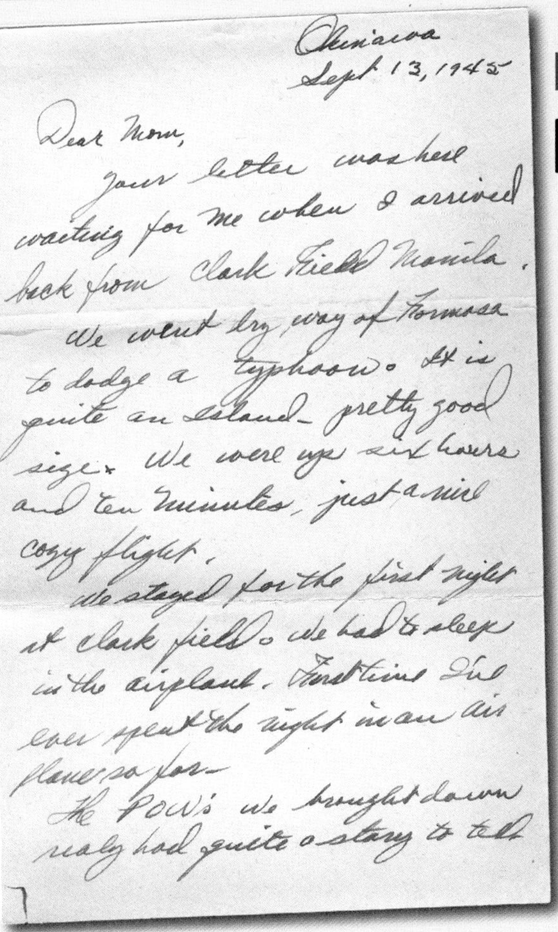

Okinawa
Sept 13, 1945

Dear Mom,

Your letter was here waiting for me when I arrived back from Clark Field Manila.

We went by way of Formosa to dodge a typhoon. It is quite an island- pretty good size. We were up six hours and ten minutes, just a nice cozy flight.

We stayed for the first night at Clark field. We had to sleep in the airplane. First time I'll ever spent the night in an air plane so far.

The POW's we brought down realy had quite a story to tell

MEANWHILE, ON O.C.'S PLANE . . .

He flew that same mission, following the same detour around Formosa to avoid the typhoon that Lt. Armacost did, but O.C. was somehow able to get through the storm that downed the two other planes from the 494th. He landed without incident on Clark Field on Luzon Island.

"The POWs we brought down had quite a story to tell. One of the boys was from Kansas. He told me some of his experiences while he worked for the Nips near Tokyo. He said they gave him tennis shoes to wear to work in six feet of snow. He had been in the Bataan Death March.

"You should have seen some of those boys' faces when we flew up Cagayan Valley and they saw their former base and also the Jap prison they were in before they were sent to Tokyo.

"One of the boys said he was working at Clark Field when the Japs invaded Luzon and captured him. Looking down on the field he said it had changed a lot. I'll say."

The prison O.C. refers to was Cabanatuan Penal Colony, which O.C.'s first mission narrowly avoided bombing. It must have been the height of inconceivable irony to fly with a man he might have killed had not late-arriving intelligence re-routed his first mission.

AUDIO TRANSCRIPT 12:01:08

I flew over Cabanatuan Town at treetop level to see what we'd done to it. There were some pretty big holes in the ground. People were hanging out of the windows, though, waving at us.

We let the POWs off at Nichols Field near Manila and refueled. When we got airborne again, I wanted to look at Corregidor Island down in Manila Bay. That was the mission I missed because I had an engine go out [#3]. It had been quite the fortress. The Japs couldn't get it from us and when they had it, we couldn't get it back. It was like a giant concrete pillbox. Our Group had bombed it for weeks with 24 airplanes a day, each carrying five 1,000 pound bombs. I wanted to see the effects of all that bombing.

So we came down right on the deck across Manila Bay and passed Corregidor, and practically looked right in the door of the fortress. The Bay was as smooth as glass. I decided I wanted to fly <u>really</u> low, so I dropped it down and down and down to about twenty feet off the deck, roaring along at about 190 mph across the Bay, which was so smooth it was just like a mirror.

Suddenly there was an old Chinese-type junk right in front of us. If I dipped the wing to avoid him I'd go right in the water. I was so low, even his sail was higher than we were, so I side-slipped right past him and this old guy was standing out there on his boat waving his hat at us as we went by.

Oly said, "Let me take it," and he took us down to about five feet off the water. These RAF guys practiced low level flying all the time. I knew then how the rest of the crew felt when I buzzed things: excited but just a little scared.

EDITORIAL . . .

Campaign Stars

There are almost as many guardhouse
lawyers on this subject of campaign
stars as there are on the subject of
the reassignment policy. Everybody has
his version of the straight dope, and will
tell you that you are authorized any
number of stars from one to eight (to be
worn on the special six-inch ribbon).
They will tell you that if you have flown
over the Bonins you are authorized a
special campaign star, and that you can
get still another for flying over the
Philippines.

Don't believe it. Here are the facts.

It is impossible for a man who has
served exclusively in the Central Pacific
to have more than two stars to his Asia-
tic-Pacific Theater ribbon. The only two
that have been authorized are: ... Campaign

or were in the Gilbert Islands or over
Nauru in that time, or, 3) Were on Midway Island from June 3-6, 1942.

You might, by hurrying, have managed to get in on more than one of these
places at the right—or wrong—times.
But you still get only one star.

You are allowed to wear the Mandated Islands Campaign Star if you
served west of the 180th meridian, ex-
clusive of the Gilbert Islands. The open
season on this star began on Dec. 7, 1943,
for air combat, and Jan. 31, 1944, for
ground forces. The closing date has not
yet been announced. The Mandated Islands include the Marshalls, Marianas
and Carolines, but each island conquest
or group conquest counts only as an
engagement and doesn't qualify you for
any extra stars.

And one more thing. The award of ... automatic. We un-

THAT AND A NICKEL . . .

Every branch of the military gave medals out differently. Some doled out Purple Hearts for paper cuts. In others you had to die in action to get one. The 7th AAF fell somewhere between generous and stingy. But in any case they were *slow*.

The *brief* editorial at right reminds us that severe consequences would befall those who wore medals they had not earned.

In mid-September, the brass finally got around to awarding the medals for participation in various Pacific campaigns, as noted in the Order below. O.C.'s Asia-Pacific campaign medal, received in May, had four stars for his missions over the Philippines, the Carolines, and Japan. Because he was on R&R in Hawaii during the 494th's move to Okinawa, he missed out on a fifth star for the Ryukyu campaign.

General Orders No. 109 classified SECRET and distributed to those concerned.

GENERAL ORDERS)
:
NUMBER 109)

HEADQUARTERS SEVENTH AIR FORCE,
APO #903, 15 September 1945.

E X T R A C T

AWARD OF BRONZE SERVICE STARS TO ASIA-PACIFIC MEDAL: - By direction of the President, under the provisions of Executive Order No. 9158, 11 May 1942 (Bull. No. 25, W.D., 1942), as amended by Executive Order No. 9242-A, 11 September 1942 (Bull. No. 49, W.D., 1942), and pursuant to authority contained in paragraphs 17 and 18, AR 600-45, 22 September 1943 and Ltr Hq AAFPOA, 18 October 1944, in addition to the Asia-Pacific Medal previously awarded, Bronze Service Stars are awarded by the Commanding General, S Air Force, to the following named officers and enlisted men, Air Corps, United St Army, for meritorious achievement while participating in sustained aerial operatio against the enemy from 21 October 1944 to 15 August 1945. During this period, eac crew member of a heavy bombardment airplane, flew missions in the following campa

1. Ryukyu Islands (arrival on Okinawa prior to 2 July 1945 only)
2. Luzon Island, Philippines
3. Southern Philippine Islands
4. Eastern Mandates (Gilberts, Marshalls, Carolines)
5. Japan

against heavily defended enemy held bases involving long over water flights to and fr the target. Throughout these operations, which were accomplished with distinction a and beyond that normally expected, each displayed high skill and courage, inflictin severe damage to enemy air bases and shipping, reflecting great credit upon himsel the Army Air Forces:

2nd Lt (1092) OMER C KEMP 0710957
2nd Lt (1055) NORMAN J OLSON 0927583
2nd Lt (1036) FREDERICK C SPERLING JR 02060604
2nd Lt (1035) JACK A BERGER 0928139
Sgt (737) Juan F Gutierrez 39550289
Sgt (612) Joseph A Trasatti 13133599
Sgt (757) Calvin G Morrow 19130002
Sgt (611) Eugene W Vaughn 37616773
Sgt (611) Charles K Yetter 3758620
Sgt (612) Lloyd I Nygren 39280958

BY COMMAND OF BRIGADIER GENERAL WHITE:

D. G. GROTHAUS,
Colonel, G.S.C.,
Deputy Chief of Staff.

DISTRIBUTION: "B"

AFTERMATH

While O.C. was flying ex-POWs to Nichols Field just south of Manila, he dropped low over the countryside to gauge for himself the effects of the bombing runs in which he had participated. He did a wingstand over Cabanatuan Penal Colony, again grateful for the eleventh hour intelligence that prevented the bombing of American POWs held there back in late January.

All down the central Luzon plain, not much was left of the unfortunate country except bomb craters, burned-out buildings, and blasted trees. With Manila behind him, he dropped to fishing boat level and roared across Manila Bay for his first look at Corregidor Island, the one mission he had missed because of a malfunctioning engine.

Overnighting in Manila, he walked the city streets and must have wondered at the strange nature of war. No one on the morning's busy street knew he was a pilot who had rained death from the now unthreatening skies, perhaps killing relatives or neighbors of the very people who greeted him with smiles and respectful salutes.

The Filipinos had been occupied by the Japanese for three long years and had suffered untold atrocities. They understood, through their costly suffering, the price of peace. One can't help but believe that even had the people he met on those Manila streets known his part in the waging of the War, they would nevertheless have shaken his hand and thanked him for the incomparable gift of freedom.

THE SHORT SNORTER

Every era has its own friendship-building traditions. World War II had the "short snorter," slang for a small mixed drink which the holder had to buy if he couldn't produce the banknote his buddy had signed when they were crew mates.

Believed to have started with Alaskan bush pilots in the 1920s, the tradition soon spread throughout the aviation world. A snorter was believed to bring good luck, both to the holder and the signer. In addition, it was a keepsake of friends' signatures, and as such was not used as legal tender, which is why most short snorters are made from small denominations. They were often taped together end to end, rolled up, and secured with a rubber band. There have been many famous short snorters. FDR signed one at the 1942 Casablanca Conference and another at Yalta. Several snorters signed by General Patton exist.

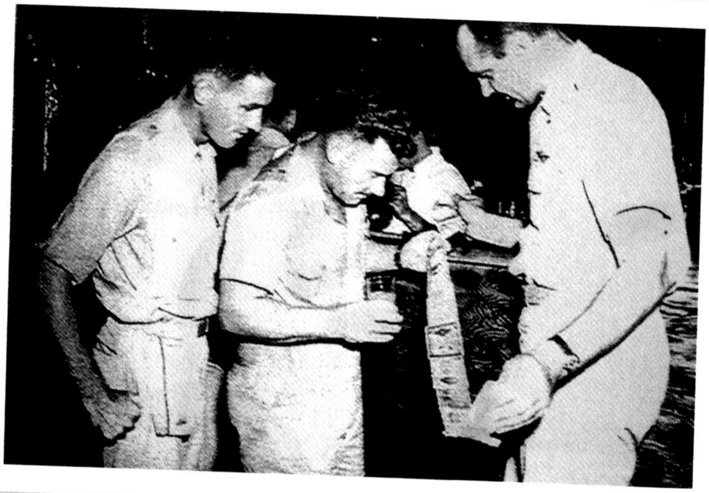

RIGHT O.C.'s snorter is made up mostly of Filipino and Japanese currency. Few of the signatures are legible, the roll going through the washer one too many times.

LEFT 494th C.O. Colonel Laurence Kelley shows his snorter to two officers.

BELOW During September, O.C. flew a number of ex-POW and transport missions to Manila, as his 18 landings assert.

<u>INDIVIDUAL FLIGHT RECORD</u>	O.C. KEMP
STATION	APO 903 (Yontan Army Air Field)
FLYING CLASSIFICATION	Plt. 2-9-44
ORGANIZATION ASSIGNED	7th AAF, 494th BG, 865th BS
MONTH	**September 1945**
AIRCRAFT TYPE	B-24J, B-24L, B-24M
LANDINGS	18
COMMAND PILOT	
CO-PILOT	21:55
QUALIFIED PILOT (DUAL)	
FIRST PILOT (DAY)	20:55
FIRST PILOT (NIGHT)	
NON-PILOT DUTY	1:00 (PAI)
INSTRUMENT (DAY)	1:50
INSTRUMENT (NIGHT)	
INSTRUMENT TRAINER	
TOTAL TIME THIS MONTH	20:55
TOTAL PILOT TIME TO DATE	851:00

SEPTEMBER ON OKINAWA

LOSSES Two aircraft to operational causes, resulting in the death of five crew members and 32 ex-POW passengers on 9 September.

STRENGTH, PERSONNEL 801 officers, 3,387 enlisted men as of 30 September.

STRENGTH, AIRPLANES 25 B-24J, 7 B-24L, 23 B-24M as of 30 September. Here we see the weeding-out of older J models, many of which have already gone home with crews who had their 40 missions in on V-J Day.

ADMINISTRATION On 15 September, the Group was notified that it had been designated a Class IV unit for return to the mainland for demobilization. The anxiety about being posted to Japan as an occupation force was groundless after all. Nothing motivates men like getting ready to go home. Meticulously built houses were struck and paper backlogs were soon cleared, but still no transport ships anchored in Buckner Bay.

S-2 SECTION The intelligence section prepared to leave by destroying or giving away its files as souvenirs. Many of the aerial photos in this book were obtained by O.C. from the Group S-2 section, each one with a hand-written explanation on the back that the photo had been "declassified pursuant to AR 380-5."

S-3 SECTION The training and operations section initiated over a hundred flights between Okinawa and the Philippines, carrying passengers, ex-POWs, and cargo. When the Class IV order came through, the ferrying operations were suspended.

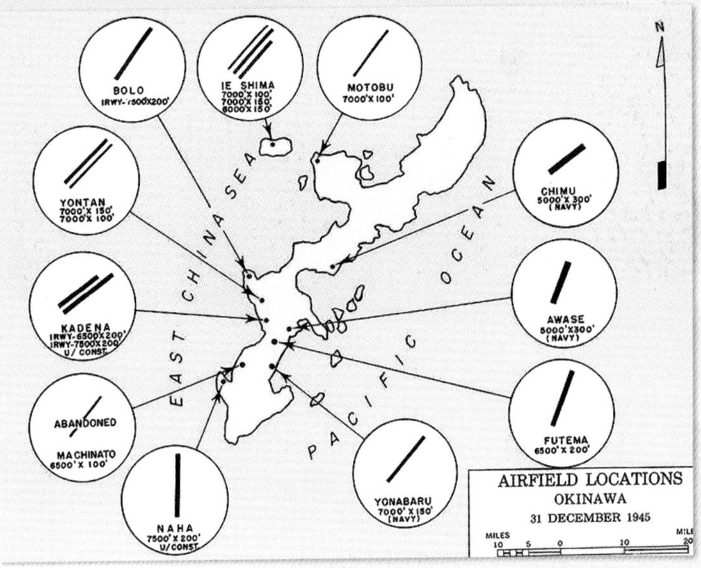

S-4 SECTION The supply section transferred several bombers to other groups and arranged crews to fly the remaining ships to the States.

MORALE Since few servicemen lacked sufficient points for transfer home, morale remained high. (Excepting Crew 23A, which was one of the last crews to leave Okinawa due to the replacement curse.) Special Services equipment was collected and disposed of, so entertainment was limited. Religious services were conducted as usual.

RE-PURPOSING OKINAWA Though soldiers were leaving Okinawa, the U.S. was not. It would serve as an area military base for decades to come. The only difference is that now permanent structures and paved air fields were being constructed. As of 31 December 1945, ten airfields were open or under construction on the island.

CIVIL ADMINISTRATION On 7 September, when the Japanese formally surrendered Okinawa to the Allies, the first order of business was rebuilding the decimated Okinawan economy. To supplement existing Japanese coins, the U.S. military issued military scrip as interim currency.

GENTLEMEN, MEET LOUISE

Cyclone, typhoon, hurricane—what's the difference? Apart from the names, very little except where the storm originates. In the Atlantic it's called a hurricane. In the western Pacific, a typhoon. The South Pacific's version is called a cyclone. But all three originate in tropical oceans and result in violent winds, mountainous waves, torrential rains, and devastating destruction.

Typhoon Louise developed in early October in the Carolines and headed straight for Okinawa, which she blasted with 90 mph winds starting on 8 October.

36 people died, 47 went missing, and 100 were injured. 35 foot waves swept across Buckner Bay, destroying 80% of the buildings on shore. 12 ships were sunk, over 200 were grounded, and 32 more were severely damaged. Over 100 amphibious landing craft were grounded or damaged.

When the wind kicked up, Crew 23A ran to Yontan Air Field to ensure that *Rover Boy's Baby* would not be toppled. They turned the plane into the wind and attached a cable from a fuel truck winch to the landing gear. Then they raced back to their "castle" as warm, nearly horizontal rain began to fall.

Jack Berger remembers Fred, O.C., and Oly climbing on the roof, splaying themselves across the whipping canvas, pelted by rain, hoping they wouldn't suffer Dorothy's fate. "I stayed on the ground because I only weighed 134 pounds and didn't want to be blown away," says Berger. "I took pictures instead."

The storm eventually blew the canvas roof off anyway, but the structure survived. "Other tents in the area took a beating and were blown away," says Berger. "But not ours."

Sixty aircraft on the Yontan ramp were damaged, hurled into each other and into airport structures. The control tower was toppled and light vehicles overturned. But *Rover Boy's Baby* got through Louise's visit unscathed.

By the time Louise reached Kyushu Island on 12 October, she had weakened to a tropical storm.

BOTTOM LEFT The 10th Army HQ flagpole was bent sideways by Louse's gale-force winds.

BOTTOM RIGHT After the typhoon passes, a disgusted airman stands outside his collapsed tent.

SOME ENEMIES CAN'T BE BEATEN, JUST ENDURED

Louise was one of the most violent typhoons ever to hit Okinawa, the center passing just 15 miles south of the island. The damage out in Buckner Bay on the east coast of the island was terrific, easterly winds first grounding ships on the lee shore, then shifting to the northwest and dislodging the vessels, pushing them again across the bay, where they collided with other ships and grounded again on the southern shore.

On land, men huddled in caves or tombs as sheets of corrugated metal torn from Quonset huts knifed through the air like giant scythes. Pyramid tent canvas wafted away and frames were shredded, the 2x4s becoming giant winging arrows. When it was over, four fifths of the housing on Okinawa had been leveled.

Though they had warning of the typhoon and had secured their belongings in duffle bags inserted in plastic envelopes, everything that didn't blow away was soaked. When the storm hit, the airfield generator was shut down to avoid accidents, so men huddled in the dark inside tents threatened to be ripped skyward any moment, sharing cans of peaches and shivering as unnerving shrieks pierced the darkness.

When the storm passed, everyone was rousted out of their wet cots to police the area. Debris was everywhere, half buried in mud. The mess hall was completely gone. Days later, when bread was finally available, the men noticed what looked like caraway seeds in the loaves. They were weevils. They ate the bread anyway.

Out on the flight line, the air field weather station had recorded 115 mph winds. Much of the fabric control surfaces (ailerons, flaps, stabilizers) on the B-24s were shredded. Fighters on the strip had been tossed about like so many toys. But most of the Liberators had been tended by ground crews and turned into the wind. They survived.

BELOW O.C.'s final flight record primarily records his trip back home to the states.

INDIVIDUAL FLIGHT RECORD	O.C. KEMP
STATION	Mather Field, Calif.
FLYING CLASSIFICATION	Plt. 2-9-44
ORGANIZATION ASSIGNED	ATC, PD, WCW 1505th AAFBU
MONTH	**October 1945**
AIRCRAFT TYPE	B-24M
LANDINGS	11
COMMAND PILOT	
CO-PILOT	27:55
QUALIFIED PILOT (DUAL)	
FIRST PILOT (DAY)	16:40
FIRST PILOT (NIGHT)	15:25
NON-PILOT DUTY	
INSTRUMENT (DAY)	9:35
INSTRUMENT (NIGHT)	22:30
INSTRUMENT TRAINER	
TOTAL TIME THIS MONTH	60:00
TOTAL PILOT TIME TO DATE	911:00

R E S T R I C T E D

HEADQUARTERS
22ND REPLACEMENT DEPOT
FAR EAST AIR FORCES

SUBJECT: Air Travel Orders.
TO : Personnel Concerned.

APO 351, APO 714
18 Oct 45

1. Pursuant to auth contained in WD Rad WX 65170, 18 Sept 45, and in accordance with prov of RR 1-2, 11 Apr 45, ea of the fol named O and EM are reld fr pres asgmt and fur dy in this theatre and WP o/a 19 Oct 45, via mil acft, by and under the control of the CGATC as surplus readjustment pers to the US airport of debarkation at Mather Field, Calif for fur disposition. EDCMR 31 Oct 45. Acft #0946.

RANK	NAME	ASN	MOS	ASRS	ADDRESS
2nd Lt	KEMP, OMER C.	0710957	1092	75	4768 Winona Ave., San Diego, Calif.
2nd Lt	OLSON, NORMAN J.	0927583	1092	99	Rt #1, Dallas, Wisc.
2nd Lt	SPERLING, FREDERICK C.	02060604	1034	91	334 3rd Ave., Joliet, Ill.
2nd Lt	BERGER,JACK A.	0-928139	1035	79	86 E. 94th St., Brooklyn, N.Y.
S/Sgt	GUTIERREZ, JUAN F.	39550289	748	77	632 1/2 Clover St., Los Angeles, Cal.
S/Sgt	MORROW, CALVIN G.	19130002	757	82	1126 S. Grevilea St., Inglewood, Cal.
S/Sgt	VAUGHN, EUGENE W.	37616773	612	76	1923 Marcus Ave., St. Louis, Mo.
S/Sgt	YETTER, CHARLES K.	37558620	612	79	Box 66, Plainview, Minn.

2. Per diem autho ea O while traveling by air in accordance with AR 35-4820, 19 Apr 45, and ea EM in accordance with AR 35-4810, 19 Apr 45.

3. Baggage to accompany the above named O by air will be limited to 80 lbs and EM to 50 lbs. All other baggage wil be packed and marked with the name, rank, and ASN of the indiv and will be turned over to proper auth for shpmt to US.

4. TDN 212/60425 FSA 1945-46 65-000 P431-02 (Auth: WD Rad 79420, 19 May 45, AFWESPAC Rad FX 40145, GSTEM, 7 June 45; Ltr, Hq FEAF, File 370.5, 8 June 45, Subj: "Movement Orders for return of Per to the US."

BY ORDER OF COLONEL BRUNS:

FRANCIS J. JENKINS,
Captain, Air Corps,
Actg Asst Adj Gen.

PACK YOUR BAGS

ABOVE After sitting around on Okinawa for weeks, the order finally came: they were going home. Two names are missing from the list: Gunners Lloyd Nygren and Joseph Trasatti had already gone home because their "ASRS" (Army Service Rotation System) score exceeded 85. The others, with scores ranging from O.C.'s low of 75, to Cal Morrow's heartbreaking 82, had to wait their turn. While they waited, rumors that the 494th would get occupation duty on Japan persisted, so when these orders finally arrived, they heaved a sigh of relief. The replacement curse that had hung over them for so long was finally lifted.

RIGHT In addition to his footlocker, O.C. had obtained some civilian luggage, upon which he stenciled a record of his missions. You'll note only 15 bombs are painted on the suitcase. This is because he had to turn back from the 12 February mission (#3) to Corregidor Island due to engine problems. If you did not complete a mission—for whatever reason—you didn't get credit. Each mission was worth one point under ASRS, which is why crews fought over them, even the dangerous ones, as each mission brought a crew one step closer to going home.

THE SUNSET PROJECT

1 November 1945 never came, at least not in the dreaded form of Operation Downfall, the invasion of Japan. But now, at bases on Guam, Saipan, Luzon, and Okinawa there were hundreds of bombers that would likely never be needed again. What to do with them?

"Operation Sunset" was designed to transport B-24 and B-29 bombers back to the States. Initiated on 27 September 1945, it was overseen by the Air Transport Command, the same outfit that sent Crew 23A to the Pacific a little less than a year ago. Here we're lucky to have a college English paper O.C. wrote after the War:

Weeks before, we said goodbye to two crew members who rotated home under the Army's point system. The rest of us would fly home in a new B-24M that had arrived on Okinawa in July and hadn't been there long enough to even have a name. We just called her by her serial number: 946. She passed the pre-flight inspection with flying colors.

Early one cool morning in late October, we were driven to the Yontan Air Field ramp on Okinawa, carrying our B-4 bags, footlockers, and duffles. We were part of a flight of ten aircraft that would take off that day for Guam. Air Transport Command (ATC) would have sent more but there was limited housing for overnight stays on Guam.

After eight uneventful hours, we landed at Harmon Field, named after Lt. Gen. Millard Harmon, whose plane went down in March over the Marshall Islands. Despite a search that lasted weeks, the aircraft was never found. At the time of our flight, they were still searching for him, though with little hope.

At Harmon, our M was given another thorough inspection, which I oversaw. We'd heard the best mechanics had already rotated home and the boys taking their place didn't care as much about planes flying back to the States. But the Harmon mechanics did a good job inspecting our plane and so we hit the sack.

The next morning, the fuel truck pumped 2,800 gallons of fuel into our plane for the next hop to Kwajalein atoll, another eight-hour flight. Once again, we encountered no mechanical difficulties or bad weather—it was beautiful the whole way—and we landed on Kwajalein without incident.

Take-off the next morning was exciting. Our Liberator was loaded to the gills with 3,100 gallons of gas, which makes it about 65,000 pounds, the very definition of a "heavy" bomber. With that much weight, takeoffs are more dangerous than landings. And with that much fuel on board, it wasn't much different than having a loaded bomb bay.

Our destination that day was O'ahu, Hawaii, a twelve-hour stretch of water and more water. Johnston Island, at about 1,600 miles, was there if we needed it. Some gas-worrying crews put in there just in case.

We landed at John Rogers Naval Air Field on O'ahu, where the plane was given a real going over, getting a 100-hour inspection in record time—the same inspection that on Okinawa would have taken a week. The mechanical crews' expertise gave us much-needed confidence: the final leg of our trip was over the longest uninterrupted stretch of water in the world.

ABOVE RIGHT O.C. photographed the inspection of his aircraft at Harmon Field, Guam.

ABOVE LEFT Crews gather at the "Kwajal Inn" on Kwajalein to await the call for the next leg of their trip.

SURPLUS PERSONNEL

19 - 24 October 1945
Mather Army Air Field
Sacramento, California
Air Transport Command
4th Army Air Force

"SURPLUS PERSONNEL"?

Yep, overnight, bomber crews went from being indispensable to surplus. But the boys didn't mind. If being labeled "surplus" meant they got to go home, no problem. We continue with O.C.'s college English essay:

Though we landed at 0230, John Rogers Naval Air Field in Hawaii was going full blast. It seemed like every ten minutes a Superfortress or a Liberator was landing and the ground crews were leading them to revetments to begin their inspections. Those same planes would be taking off within hours, stateside bound. Not wasting a minute, we hit the sack.

We were awakened at noon to attend a briefing at 1430 hours. I took my place in a chair labeled "PILOT." We received instructions on weather, local anti-aircraft firing areas, and local mountain elevations. There was also an extensive lecture about rescue procedures and emergency landing fields in California. Just hearing the word "California" sent a thrill up my spine. It had finally sunk in: the War was over.

At 1700 hours the "Follow Me" Jeep screeched to a stop in front of our planes and the line officer circled his forefinger. Oly cranked the engines and we followed him out onto the ramp. After our run-up, we taxied out to make our last takeoff in a B-24. Even though it wasn't *Rover Boy's Baby*, it was still an emotional moment for me. I took a deep breath and shoved the balls to the wall (the engine power levers pressed toward the instrument panel) and in seconds we were aloft. It was twilight as we began *our* sunset flight.

In the long darkness that followed, we listened to the radio and were delighted to hear good old stateside big bands and commercials. The weather was clear and the stars were out. Fred, our navigator, said that his sense of destination was so strong, he didn't really need his sextant—he felt like a homing pigeon and could practically *smell* his way back.

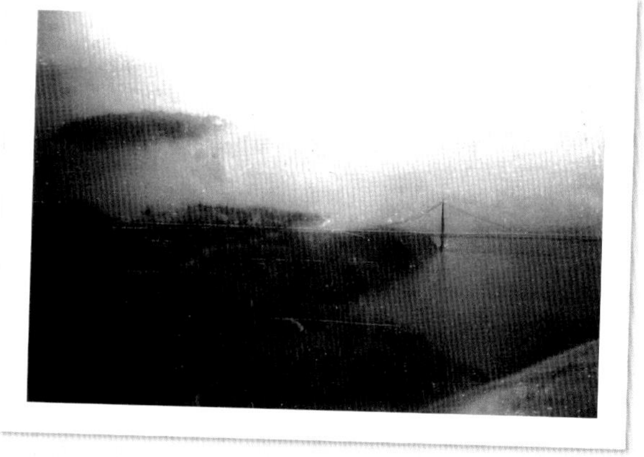

Hours later, when we saw the sun coming up over the horizon and felt its welcome warmth on faces that had so long been turned westward, I secretly wiped a tear away.

The biggest thrill was when the Golden Gate Bridge came into sight. Jack and Fred were crowded in between Oly's and my seats, admiring the view. I said, "What do you say, fellas? Shall we?" and put the plane into a dive. Jack laughed and pounded my shoulder but Fred shook his head in dismay. He never did like my "buzz jobs."

We roared under the bridge with room to spare, but still breaking about a dozen Air Force regulations and just as many civilian laws. Let them court martial us. We didn't care.

We were home.

By the end of 1945, over 1,200 B-29s and B-24s had made the homeward journey. Many were sent to training airfields but most ended up in scrapyards, including the famous aircraft "Boneyard" in Tucson, Arizona.

R E S T R I C T E D

AIR TRANSPORT COMMAND
PACIFIC DIVISION, WEST COAST WING
1505TH AAF BASE UNIT
MATHER FIELD, SACRAMENTO, CALIFORNIA

SPECIAL ORDERS) 24 October 1945
:
NUMBER 261)

E X T R A C T

23. The following named O and EM, ACU, W having rptd fr overseas this date reld asgmt & duty this Hq o/a dates indicated and WP home as indicated, via AAF Sep as indicated below, reporting 0800 on date indicated, for TDY as required for proce and separation from the service under the provisions of RR 1-5 for officers and RR for enlisted men. CO Sep Base will issue necessary orders specifying amount of term lv, date of release fr sep base and date O reverts to inactive status. Terminal lv WD AGO Form 53-98 auth ea O. Mail received after dep fr this sta will be fwd to O or home address as indicated and not to AAF Sep Bases. EM to be given WE AGO Form 53-55 (Hon Disch. AUS) and is to be disch under the prov of AR 615-365. O and EM have ASRS as indicated. All personnel under "Sunset Project." In accordance with AR 35-4810 FD will pay in advance to ea EM prescribed mon alws in lieu of rats A/R $1.00 per meal for no o meals indicated.

TDN. PCS. 601-31 P 431-02-03-07 A 212/60425 S 99-999. Auth: WD RR 1-5, TWX Hq, 16 Aug 45 and Sec V WD Cir 269, 1945 applies to EM disch because of over-age.

SAN BERNARDINO AAF, SAN BERNARDINO, CALIF

RANK	NAME	ASN	MOS	ASRS	ADDRESS
2nd Lt	KEMP, OMER C.	0710957	1092	75	4768 Winona Ave, San Diego, Cal.
S/Sgt	Gutierrez, Juan F.	39550289	748	77	632 1/2 Clover St, Los Angeles, Cal.
S/Sgt	Morrow, Calvin G.	19130002	757	82	1126 S Grevillea St, Inglewood, Cal.

BY ORDER OF LIEUTENANT COLONEL PETERSEN:

RUPERT E. FERGUSON,
Capt, AC
Adj

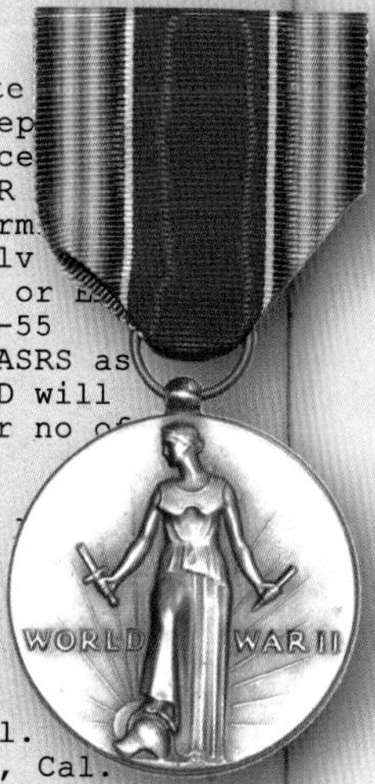

CARRY ON

When he got up the next morning, O.C. found the above order pinned to his duffel. He was to take a civilian bus (the Air Force had again commandeered his B-24) 400 miles down the Central Valley to San Bernardino, along with his gunners Juan Gutierrez and Cal Morrow, both of whom were from Los Angeles.

After breakfast, O.C. bid goodbye to the men who had become his best friends: Oly Olson, who had helped him nurse *Rover Boy's Baby* back to Saipan at stalling speed, flying on fumes the whole way; Fred Sperling, who had guided them through storms to find targets and then home safely; and Jack Berger, who dropped bombs and quips with equal aplomb. Hand shakes were exchanged. They promised to keep in touch. They knew the War was over because they were being separated. It was a bittersweet moment.

Left to right: Norman Olson, Jack Berger, Omer Kemp, and Fred Sperling.

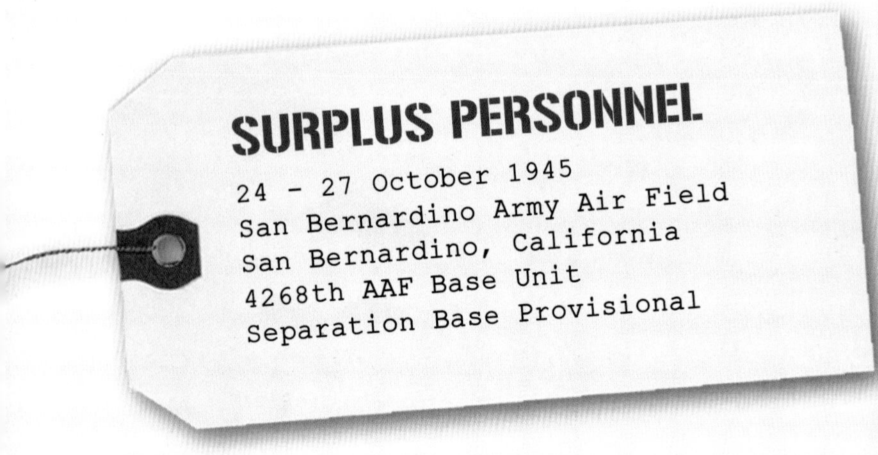

HURRY UP AND WAIT

It must have been torture to spend three days just a hundred and fifty miles from home, standing in line, filling out paperwork, attending lectures, and being weighed down with pamphlets, explanations, and reintroductions to civilian life. As if he had forgotten how to be a free young American man.

O.C. was assigned to group 39-F, told to report for processing and not to forget his "201" personnel file as well as six copies of his orders. He should be on time, remain with his group, follow the guides, and cooperate with all instructions. He was reminded that his failure to be at a scheduled place at the proper time might mean reprocessing and a delay of several days in his separation.

There was an Officers' Club in Area 1 but he was not allowed to leave Area 2 during processing hours. The Finance Section was available to answer questions about the GI Bill. His $10,000.00 life insurance policy could continue in force so long as he paid the monthly $6.50 premium. V.A. loans were available for homes, farms, and businesses. And he would get $300.00 in mustering-out pay.

Federal law ensured that a man could get his old job back if he applied for it within ninety days of discharge. If there was as problem, the local Selective Service Board could help. If necessary, the federal District Attorney would handle your employment lawsuit without charge. If you had a service-related disability, the Veterans' Administration would help you train for a job.

But you rode the bus home, like any civilian.

. . . OFF LIKE A RUPTURED DUCK

Upon discharge, O.C. was entitled to wear the Honorable Service lapel button. In 1939, sculptor Anthony de Francisci copied the design of Roman legion standards, placing a spread-winged eagle within a ring of thirteen vertical stripes. The U.S. Army allowed veterans to wear their uniform for up to a month after discharge, after which the uniform went into the closet and the button was pinned to a civvie suit lapel.

Veterans called the award the "Ruptured Duck" because the eagle faced left, which was the direction doctors instructed inductees to turn to cough during hernia examinations. The term was an in-joke among veterans since civilians did not undergo an induction examination.

The term soon became slang for anyone in a great hurry, like discharged veterans, as in, "He took off like a ruptured duck."

RESTRICTED

HEADQUARTERS
4268TH AAF BASE UNIT (SEPARATION BASE PROVISIONAL)
SAN BERNARDINO ARMY AIR FIELD, CALIFORNIA

SPECIAL ORDERS)
:
NO. 38)

27 October 1945

EXTRACT

7. DP fol named Offs (W) are granted terminal lv of absence and tvl time as indicated eff o/a 28 October 45 and WP to home address to arrive thereat not later than EDCMR on which date OFFs are reld fr AD not by reason of physical disability. Temp apmt in AUS will continue in force during present emerg and six MO thereafter unless sooner terminated DP. Off will be given WD AGO Form 53-98.

NAME-RANK-ASN-ARM OR SERVICE-HOME ADDRESS	LV & TVL TIME AUTH	EDCMR
2nd Lt KEMP, OMER C. 0710957 AC (AUS) 4766 Winona Ave., San Diego, Calif.	1 MO 13 days lv 1 day tvl	12 Dec 45

PCS. TDN. TPA. (601-31 P 431-02-03-07 S 99-999 A 212/60425. Auth: RRL-5, 30 Apr 45 Supplemented by TWX AFPMP 1098 Hq AAF 8 Sep 45.

BY ORDER OF COLONEL MARK:

HARRY A SMITH
Capt. AC
Adj

TERMINAL LEAVE OF ABSENCE

Doesn't sound like something a serviceman would want, but they all did. It was the Army's way of saying, "You still belong to us." O.C. was ordered to report to his parents' home (they included the address in case he had forgotten it) within a day of his release. Upon arrival, he was released from active duty, and "not by reason of physical disability," lest anyone think he had any physical or mental handicaps as a result of his service.

Notwithstanding what the Army cryptically called the War (a "present emergency"), it was expected that by 12 December 1945 O.C. Kemp would receive his final release from the Army Air Forces of the United States.

O.C. said, "See you around" to his engineer Juan Gutierrez and his radioman Cal Morrow and jumped on the Greyhound bus. He sat anxiously through the three-hour ride to San Diego, where his parents, sisters, and little brother were waiting for him.

Back in San Diego for the first time in twenty months, he posed for a photo on his parent's front porch, masking his delight to be home with a soldier's practiced "I-don't-give-a-damn" glare.

No one bought it for a second.

THE

PRESIDENT

OF

THE UNITED STATES OF AMERICA

To all who shall see these presents, greeting:

Know Ye, that reposing special trust and confidence in the patriotism, valor, fidelity and abilities of OMER CARROLL KEMP, *I do appoint him* SECOND LIEUTENANT, AIR CORPS *in the*

Army of the United States

such appointment to date from the TWENTY-EIGHTH *day of* OCTOBER, *nineteen hundred and* FORTY-FIVE. *He is therefore carefully and diligently to discharge the duty of the office to which he is appointed by doing and performing all manner of things thereunto belonging.*

He will enter upon active duty under this commission only when specifically ordered to such active duty by competent authority.

And I do strictly charge and require all Officers and Soldiers under his command when he shall be employed on active duty, to be obedient to his orders as an officer of his grade and position. And he is to observe and follow such orders and directions, from time to time, as he shall receive from me, or the future President of the United States of America, or the General or other Superior Officers set over him, according to the rules and discipline of War.

This Commission evidences an appointment in the Army of the United States, under the provisions of section 37, National Defense Act, as amended, and is to continue in force for a period of five years from the date above specified, and during the pleasure of the President of the United States, for the time being.

Done at the City of Washington, this FOURTEENTH *day of* MAY, *in the year of our Lord one thousand nine hundred and* FORTY-SIX, *and of the Independence of the United States of America the one hundred and* SEVENTIETH.

By the President:

F. R. Golembieski

Adjutant General.

W. D., A. G. O. FORM No. 0650 C.
AUGUST 1, 1938

THE COST OF VICTORY

Though it was called the Second World War, in almost every imaginable way it ranked first: first in the number of nations at war (60), first in the number of battlefields (over 1,000), first in the number of military dead (25 million), first in the number of civilian dead (55 million), bringing the total death tally to almost 80 million. And first in the minds and hearts of hundreds of millions of people in terms of heartache and tragedy.

It was also first in a terrible legacy: American and Britain, eager to believe their job was done, paid scant attention to erstwhile allies now loosed across the globe, their armies turned against their own people. Over the next few years, tens of millions would die under Stalin's brutal Soviet regime. Europe would be sundered by an iron curtain, half of its citizens imprisoned. China would descend into communism, oppressing hundreds of millions of its own citizens. Korea would be partitioned by a DMZ.

Even the United States, which had largely escaped the War's devastation, was scarred, yet its suffering in terms of overseas deaths and privation at home united the country in a way only war seems to do. The U.S. had 16 million men under arms, losing 400,000 to the conflict. Every single American knew someone who had died defending democracy. That generation would never forget the terrible cost of the War.

The U.S. lost 170 planes a day, over 43,000 total. 8 million bombs were dropped during 2 million sorties. 15,000 pilots died. In a single raid over Germany in August 1943, 60 B-17s were shot down and 600 bunks were empty in England that night.

Every month between December 1942 and August 1945, 6,600 Americans died—over 200 a day. 41,000 were captured. One third of those held by the Japanese died in captivity, while only 1% of those held by Germany died. Nazi Germany killed 6 million Jews, including 1.5 million children. The Japanese Empire murdered 15 million people from Manchuria to Guadalcanal.

The 494th Bomb Group flew 3,000 sorties over the Philippines, the Mandates, Japan, and China, dropping 6,000 tons of bombs with 70% accuracy. It lost 30 aircraft, including 20 to "operational" causes (mechanical failure and pilot error). 150 crewmen died. The Distinguished Flying Cross ("for extraordinary achievement in flight") was given to hundreds of worthy men.

The 494th Bomb Group flew the final mission of the War over Shikoku Island, Japan, on 12 August 1945, a smoke cloud rising 3,000 feet into the air as they turned for home.

On 4 January 1946, the Group was inactivated, along with its four bomb squadrons. Col. Kelley was transferred to the War Department in Washington. He eventually became a general.

The vast majority of the 3,000 men who had served under Kelley returned to civilian life. Most spoke rarely about the War. Instead they were busy reclaiming jobs, going to college, getting married, and supporting their young families. They had no time to look back: the uncertain future loomed too large on their horizon. They knew they had been lucky to survive a war that had taken so many of their friends. They quietly thanked God and tried to forget what they had seen, though few would ever be able to do so.

The War would always have a place in their lives; their challenge was to not let it burn a hole in their hearts.

A MAN OF HIS WORD

You'll recall that when O.C. was in basic training at Camp Swift, Texas, he went onto the parade ground one night and made a pact with God. And he was more than a little surprised when God answered. Soon after, he was in the Army Air Force learning to fly. In short order he was a bomber skipper.

Yet his fortune had a dark aspect. He saw men die in freak accidents when a tire blew on take-off and the plane crashed, exploding into a ball of fire. He saw bodies of Japanese snipers who would have killed him if they had lined him up in their sights. He saw belongings of crews who never came back from a mission packed to ship home to grieving parents and sweethearts. He saw close calls of his own: flak exploding in his windscreen; instrument flying conditions for hours on end; limping home from Marcus Island at stalling speed, expecting at any moment for the engines to cough to a fuel-starved stop. He saw the shocking devastation of Nagasaki.

Some men believe in chance. Others, in luck. O.C. believed in God, drawing a straight line from that cool spring evening at Camp Swift to the moment he got off the Greyhound bus in San Diego thirty months later, alive and unscathed, enveloped in the tearful hugs of his parents.

He took a job doing what he always figured he'd end up doing: working as an airplane mechanic on North Island in San Diego making 58 cents an hour. His friends were getting married, going to college... in short, moving on with their lives. But O.C. felt his life was not yet his own—there was something yet to be done.

His church is a proselyting church. Its young men traditionally donate two years after high school to serve as missionaries all over the world. Most of O.C.'s veteran friends believed they'd served enough already, but he felt he should do more. So he exchanged his denim work overalls for a wool suit and soon found himself walking the streets of Eau Claire, Wisconsin. For the next two years he would knock doors, button-hole people on the street, and produce a radio program featuring scripture readings, inspirational messages, and music from the Tabernacle Choir.

He shared his belief in a God who answers prayers. He walked the soles off his shoes and relied on the kindness of Church members in Wisconsin, Michigan, and Illinois for an occasional Sunday dinner.

In Illinois, he met a female missionary named Virginia Tensmeyer, of Pocatello, ID, who had blue eyes and a sassy manner. O.C. fell for Virginia immediately; she was not as impressed with him. To her, he was just another marriage-hungry veteran who expected to corral a gal and then have her put him through college. Nothing doing.

Besides, she was going home. O.C. was devastated; it would be ten months before he completed his missionary service.

"But," she said, noting his deep disappointment, "if you write me, I *might* write back."

THE JOYFUL WORK

Never bet against O.C. He wrote Virginia regularly over the next ten months. She soon discovered there was more to him than she first supposed. Soon her answers grew warmer. They fell in love the old fashioned way: through letters.

The very day he returned to San Diego, O.C. borrowed his folks' car and aimed it at Utah, where Ginny now lived with her parents in Salt Lake City. Her father was a timekeeper for the Union Pacific railroad and O.C. wanted to impress him (and Ginny) with how quickly he could make it from San Diego to Salt Lake.

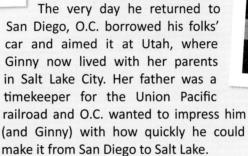

Within six weeks, O.C. and Ginny were married. She then broke her own rule and put him through pharmacy school at the University of Utah.

The *C* high school student still had more work ahead of him. But Ginny had always been a good student and she corrected O.C.'s English papers and helped him with his chemistry. She was impressed with his mechanical ability (apparently, he could fix *anything*) and his simple way of seeing a complicated world: "Do what is right, let the consequences follow."

By the time O.C. graduated from college, they had three children. Weary of cold climes, they moved to San Diego, where O.C. got a job in a small corner pharmacy.

When color film became affordable in the 1950s, O.C. upgraded his camera and took thousands of photos. In many of them there is an airplane in the background. Indeed, every Sunday drive inevitably wound up at the airport to watch the planes take off and land.

ALL GOOD THINGS . . .

Time flies, even when you're not aloft. O.C. and Virginia built a life around family and faith. He became Chief Pharmacist at a major San Diego hospital and a pioneer in medication dosing procedures. For thirty years the fellow who got *Cs* in college chemistry was consulted by physicians, fellow pharmacists, and administrators. He had learned how to learn and then he learned how to teach with the best of 'em.

He and Ginny prayed for strong children, hoping for healthy kids, but God smiled and sent them strong-willed progeny. No matter; they burst onto the world, winning recitals, art contests, sports letters, and valedictories.

When he retired in the mid-1980s, eager to park his trailer in varied desert and mountain campgrounds and relax under the shade of a yucca or pine tree, O.C. noticed a faint quivering in his forearm muscles. Tests revealed a devastating diagnosis: Amyotrophic Lateral Sclerosis (ALS), commonly called "Lou Gehrig's Disease."

Undaunted, O.C. knew this was merely flak over the target. He studied his illness with scientific detachment. Was it multiple sclerosis or perhaps even cancer? Symptoms/Solutions: Reduced muscular control/Exercise more. Elevated white cell count/Undergo chemotherapy. Vocal cords failing/Learn sign language.

But on 17 August 1990, God called in the marker and O.C. Kemp passed away at home with his family. He was 66 years old.

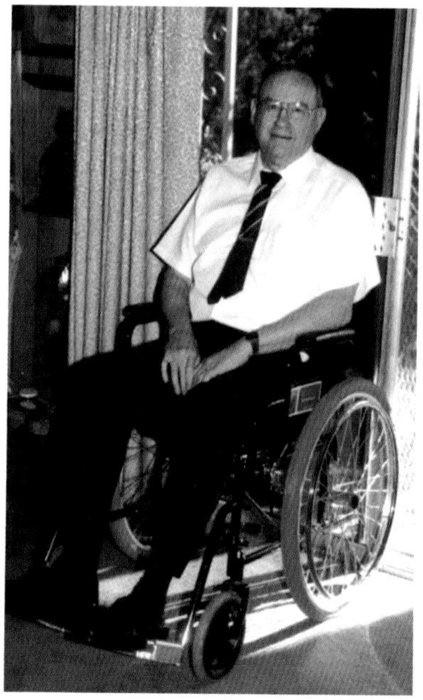

Then, three years later, in the July issue of *Kelley's Kobras,* the biannual 494th Bomb Group newsletter, the following short entry appeared:

> Some 494th crews served on Guam for three weeks in 1945. If you were in that group, the VA would like your help. There is a high incidence of Parkinson's and Lou Gehrig's Disease among the native population of Guam. The causative agent is still uncertain and may lie dormant in many individuals for years.

Only an optimist understands irony. To the pessimist it's just more tragedy. But consider the possibility that on a cool spring night in March 1943 on a deserted parade ground under a bright Texas moon, God watched a young man pour his heart out and whispered, "I *will* save you from the Normandy beaches. I *will* preserve your life during this War. And I will go further: after the War, I will grant you health, love, children, and a life longer than many of the boys you'll serve with in this War. But when you have fulfilled *your* part of our agreement, I will bring you home."

On that day, O.C. stode to the flight line with a happy heart. After all, in heaven they fly without wings.

TRANSITION

17 August 1990 -
The Wild Blue Yonder

OMER CARROLL KEMP

29 February 1924 - 17 August 1990

ULTIMUM FIT PRIMUM

The motto of the 494th Bombardment Group was "The Last Shall Be First" because they were the last major bomb group to enter the War (and engaged in its last bombing missions as well), but their accuracy statistics were the best and their loss rate the lowest of any of the entire 7th Army Air Force. And yet they, along with the rest of the 7th, went largely unsung—the B-17s of the 8th and the 15th AAFs over Europe grabbed most of the headlines—deservedly, because they also suffered the most casualties. But no matter, the young flyers of the 7th took incredible chances, faced daunting odds, and uniformly distinguished themselves against the most rabid, single-minded enemy the world has ever seen.

O.C. called them "Japs" until his dying day, but there was little hatred in the term. They were "Japs" to him the way he was a "Yankee" to them. Though for many years after the War, when Japan produced only cheap tin toys and transistor radios and he would disparage a bent nail as a "Jap" nail, in time he purchased Japanese cars when they matched—and eventually surpassed—the quality of American vehicles. He harbored no ill will toward a nation that had literally gone berserk and murdered millions of people, including vast numbers of its own citizens. O.C. and his generation had a lot of forgiveness in their hearts, I think. More than we have today.

After the War, General MacArthur was put in charge of the occupying and rebuilding of Japan. He instituted sweeping political, social, and cultural reforms that today would be decried as unacceptably imperialist—and in so doing transformed Japan from an irrational medieval monarchy into a bastion of individual liberty, innovation, and peace. He required the Emperor to admit his mortality. The practice of Shinto was sharply curtailed. *Bushidō* was discredited and marginalized. And when his work was done, like the army he led, MacArthur handed the vanquished nation the keys to their future and went home.

And once home, our soldiers returned to their lives. For the most part, they left the ugliness of the War buried in their footlockers with their uniforms and medals and embarked on a new adventure of being husbands and fathers and bread-winners.

Every day, over 1,000 WWII veterans die. The average age of the survivors is now past 90. In a very few, short years, there will be no survivors of World War II.

Take a moment today and ask a vet about his War experience. Whether he was a cook or a mechanic, held a rifle or brandished a typewriter, flew a desk or a B-29, he will have an amazing story to tell, one that he has not been asked about in a very long time and one he may not even realize needs desperately to be told. Listen carefully and ask questions. Find out why he went to war, what he believed they were fighting for, and ask about his friends who gave an eye, a limb, or a life.

And when his tongue is tired and a faraway look fills his eyes, take his hand and thank him. You will see surprise on his face. No one has thanked him for what he did in many years and that is simply *wrong*.

I can't thank O.C. now. He has been gone for almost twenty five years. I owe him a debt of gratitude, not only for being my mother's loving husband and my stern but fair father, but for what he did as a young man, before he ever imagined he would have a wife and a family. What he did—what they *all* did—I can never repay . . . they literally gave us our world.

"Ultimum Fit Primum." The last shall be first. Just so.

— Kenny Kemp

SPECIAL THANKS TO

Bonnie & Jeff Sheets · Stuart & Marbe Campbell · Larry King
Gail & Rick Arthur · Ronald Arthur · Cheryl Dearing · Jay Kemp
Mavis & Evan Cramer · Douglas Page · Cheri Gittins · Lee & Dottie Machado
David & Kendra Burton · Bill & Lisa Hansen · Kirsten Noyes
Jack Berger & family · Kay Morris & family · Robert C. Kemp

SELECTED BIBLIOGRAPHY

Ambrose, Hugh. *The Pacific*. New York: Penguin Books, 2010.

Birdsall, Steve. *Log of the Liberators: An Illustrated History of the B-24*. New York: Doubleday & Company, 1973.

____________. *The B-24 Liberator.* New York: Arco Publishing, 1968.

Blue, Allan G. *The B-24 Liberator: A Pictorial History*. New York: Charles Scribner's Sons, 1976.

Bradley, James. *Flags of Our Fathers.* New York, Random House, 2000.

Ferrario, Brian., et al. *Liberator.* San Diego: General Dynamics, 1989.

Gels, Darlene ed. *Front Page: A Collection of Historical Headlines from the Los Angeles Times 1881-1987*. New York: Harry N. Abrams, 1981.

Howard, Clive, and Joe Whitley. *One Damned Island After Another.* New York: Can Rees Press, 1946.

Jablonski, Edward. *Airwar: Volume II: Tragic Victories.* New York: Doubleday & Company, 1971.

________. *Airwar: Volume III: Outraged Skies.* New York: Doubleday & Company, 1971.

________. *Airwar: Volume IV: Wings of Fire.* New York: Doubleday & Company, 1972.

Johnson, Paul. *Modern Times: The World from the Twenties to the Eighties*. New York: Harper & Row, 1983.

Kinzey, Bert. *B-24 Liberator: In Detail*. Carrollton, Texas: Squadron/Signal Publications, 2000.

Mann, Chris, ed. *Great Battles of World War II*. London: Parragon, 2008.

Overy, Richard. *War in the Pacific.* Long Island City, New York: Osprey Publishing, 2010.

Rogers, David, et al. *494th Bombardment Group (H) WWII History.* Annandale, Minnesota: 494th Bombardment Group (H) Association, 1996.

Sledge, E.B. *With the Old Breed: at Peleliu and Okinawa*. New York: Random House, 1981.

Tourtellot, Arthur. *Life's Picture History of World War II*. New York: Time Incorporated, 1950.

Wels, Susan. *Pearl Harbor: America's Darkest Day*. New York: Time-Life Books, 2001.

ALSO BY KENNY KEMP

I Hated Heaven

Dad Was a Carpenter

The Welcoming Door

The Carpenter of Galilee

City on a Hill

Oki's Island

Lightland

The Wise Man Returns

Dad, Are You There?

Parables for Today (Editor)

MORE INFORMATION

kenny@kennykemp.com

www.kennykemp.com

www.flyingwiththeflakpak.com